Vol. 80

J.C. Calhoun

FAMOUS AMERICANS

OF

RECENT TIMES

BY

JAMES PARTON

AUTHOR OF "LIFE OF ANDREW JACKSON," "LIFE AND TIMES OF AARON BURR,"
"LIFE AND TIMES OF BENJAMIN FRANKLIN," ETC.

BOSTON AND NEW YORK
HOUGHTON, MIFFLIN AND COMPANY
The Riverside Press, Cambridge
1895

NOTE.

THE papers contained in this volume were originally published in the *North American Review,* with four exceptions. Those upon THEODOSIA BURR and JOHN JACOB ASTOR first appeared in *Harper's Magazine ;* that upon COMMODORE VANDERBILT, in the *New York Ledger ;* and that upon HENRY WARD BEECHER AND HIS CHURCH, in the *Atlantic Monthly.*

CONTENTS.

HENRY CLAY.

HENRY CLAY.

THE close of the war removes the period preceding it to a great distance from us, so that we can judge its public men as though we were the "posterity" to whom they sometimes appealed.   James Buchanan still haunts the neighborhood of Lancaster, a living man, giving and receiving dinners, paying his taxes, and taking his accustomed exercise; but as an historical figure he is as complete as Bolingbroke or Walpole. It is not merely that his work is done, nor that the results of his work are apparent; but the thing upon which he wrought, by their relation to which he and his contemporaries are to be estimated, has perished.   The statesmen of his day, we can all now plainly see, inherited from the founders of the Republic a problem impossible of solution, with which some of them wrestled manfully others meanly, some wisely, others foolishly. If the workmen have not all passed away, the work is at once finished and destroyed, like the Russian ice-palace, laboriously built, then melted in the sun.   We can now have the requisite sympathy with those late doctors of the body politic, who came to the consultation pledged not to attempt to *remove* the thorn from its flesh, and trained to regard it as the spear-head in the side of Epaminondas, — extract it, and the patient dies.   In the writhings of the sufferer the barb has fallen out, and lo! he lives and is getting well.   We can now forgive most of those blind healers, and even admire such of them as were honest and not cowards; for, in truth, it *was* an impossibility with which they had to grapple, and it was not one of their creating.

Of our public men of the sixty years preceding the war, Henry Clay was certainly the most shining figure.   Was there ever a public man, not at the head of a state, so beloved as he? Who ever heard such cheers, so hearty, distinct, and ringing, as those which his name evoked? Men shed tears at his defeat, and women went to bed sick from pure sympathy with his disappointment. He could not travel during the last thirty years of his life, but only make progresses. When he left his home the public seized him and bore him along over the land, the committee of one State passing him on to the committee of another, and the hurrahs of one town dying away as those of the next caught his ear. The country seemed to place all its resources at his disposal; all commodities sought his acceptance. Passing through Newark once, he thoughtlessly ordered a carriage of a certain pattern: the same evening the carriage was at the door of his hotel in New York, the gift of a few Newark friends. It was so everywhere and with everything. His house became at last a museum of curious gifts. There was the counterpane made for him by a lady ninety-three years of age, and Washington's camp-goblet given him by a lady of eighty; there were pistols, rifles, and fowling-pieces enough to defend a citadel; and, among a bundle of walking-sticks, was one cut for him from a tree that shaded Cicero's grave. There were gorgeous prayer-books, and Bibles of exceeding magnitude and splendor, and silver-ware in great profusion. On one occasion there arrived at Ashland the substantial present of twenty-three barrels of salt. In his old age, when his fine estate, through the misfortunes of his sons, was burdened with mortgages to the amount of thirty thousand dollars, and other large debts weighed heavily upon his soul, and he feared to be compelled to sell the home of fifty years and seek a strange abode, a few old friends secretly raised the needful sum, secretly paid the mortgages and discharged the debts, and then caused the aged orator to be informed of what had been done, but not of the names of the donors. " Could my life insure the success of Henry Clay, I would freely lay it down this day," exclaimed an old Rhode Island sea-captain on the morning of the Presidential election of 1844. Who has forgotten the passion of disappointment, the amazement and despair, at the result of that day's fatal work? Fatal we thought it then, little dreaming that, while it precipitated evil, it brought nearer the day of deliverance.

Our readers do not need to be reminded that popularity the most intense is not a proof of merit. The two most mischievous men this country has ever produced were extremely popular, — one in a State, the other in every State, — and both for long periods of time. There are certain men and women and children who are natural heart-winners, and their gift of winning hearts seems something apart from their general character. We have known this sweet power over the affections of others to be possessed by very worthy and by very barren natures. There are good men who repel, and bad men who attract. We cannot, therefore, assent to the opinion held by many, that popularity is an evidence of shallowness or ill-desert. As there are pictures expressly designed to be looked at from a distance by great numbers of people at once, — the scenery of a theatre, for example, — so there are men who appear formed by Nature to stand forth before multitudes, captivating every eye, and gathering in great harvests of love with little effort. If, upon looking closely at these pictures and these men, we find them less admirable than they seemed at a distance, it is but fair to remember that they were not meant to be looked at closely, and that "scenery" has as much right to exist as a Dutch painting which bears the test of the microscope.

It must be confessed, however, that Henry Clay, who was for twenty-eight years a candidate for the Presidency, cultivated his popularity. Without ever being a hypocrite, he was habitually an actor; but the part which he enacted was Henry Clay exaggerated. He was naturally a most courteous man; but the consciousness of his position made him more elaborately and universally courteous than any man ever was from mere good-nature. A man on the stage must overdo his part, in order not to seem to underdo it. There was a time when almost every visitor to the city of Washington desired, above all things, to be presented to three men there, Clay, Webster, and Calhoun, whom to have seen was a distinction. When the country member brought forward his agitated constituent on the floor of the Senate-chamber

and introduced him to Daniel Webster, the Expounder was likely
enough to thrust a hand at him without so much as turning his
head or discontinuing his occupation, and the stranger shrunk
away painfully conscious of his insignificance.   Calhoun, on the
contrary, besides receiving him with civility, would converse with
him, if opportunity favored, and treat him to a disquisition on
the nature of government and the "beauty" of nullification, striving to make a lasting impression on his intellect.   Clay would
rise, extend his hand with that winning grace of his, and instantly captivate him by his all-conquering courtesy.   He would
call him by name, inquire respecting his health, the town whence
he came, how long he had been in Washington, and send him
away pleased with himself and enchanted with Henry Clay.
And what was his delight to receive a few weeks after, in his
distant village, a copy of the Kentuckian's last speech, bearing
on the cover the frank of "H. Clay"!   It was almost enough to
make a man think of "running for Congress"!   And, what was
still more intoxicating, Mr. Clay, who had a surprising memory,
would be likely, on meeting this individual two years after the
introduction, to address him by name.

There was a gamy flavor, in those days, about Southern men,
which*was very pleasing to the people of the North.   Reason
teaches us that the barn-yard fowl is a more meritorious bird
than the game-cock; but the imagination does not assent to the
proposition.   Clay was at once game-cock and domestic fowl.
His gestures called to mind the magnificently branching trees of
his Kentucky forests, and his handwriting had the neatness and
delicacy of a female copyist.   There was a careless, graceful ease
in his movements and attitudes, like those of an Indian chief;
but he was an exact man of business, who docketed his letters,
and could send from Washington to Ashland for a document, telling in what pigeon-hole it could be found.   Naturally impetuous,
he acquired early in life an habitual moderation of statement, an
habitual consideration for other men's self-love, which made him
the pacificator of his time.   The great compromiser was himself
a compromise.   The ideal of education is to tame men without
lessening their vivacity, — to unite in them the freedom, the dig-

nity, the prowess of a Tecumseh, with the serviceable qualities of the civilized man. This happy union is said to be sometimes produced in the pupils of the great public schools of England, who are savages on the play-ground and gentlemen in the school-room. In no man of our knowledge has there been combined so much of the best of the forest chief with so much of the good of the trained man of business as in Henry Clay. This was one secret of his power over classes of men so diverse as the hunters of Kentucky and the manufacturers of New England.

It used to be accounted a merit in a man to rise to high station from humble beginnings; but we now perceive that humble beginnings are favorable to the development of that force of character which wins the world's great prizes. Let us never again commend any one for "rising" from obscurity to eminence, but reserve our special homage for those who have become respectable human beings in spite of having had every advantage procured for them by rich fathers. Henry Clay found an Eton and an Oxford in Old Virginia that were better for *him* than those of Old England. Few men have been more truly fortu-nate in their education than he. It was said of a certain lady, that to know her was a liberal education; and there really have been, and are, women of whom that could be truly averred. But perhaps the greatest good fortune that can befall an intelligent and noble-minded youth is to come into intimate, confidential relations with a wise, learned, and good old man, one who has been greatly trusted and found worthy of trust, who knows the world by having long taken a leading part in its affairs, and has outlived illusions only to get a firmer footing in realities. This, indeed, is a liberal education; and this was the happiness of Henry Clay. Nothing in biography is so strange as the cer-tainty with which a superior youth, in the most improbable cir-cumstances, finds the mental nourishment he needs. Here, in the swampy region of Hanover County, Virginia, was a bare-footed, ungainly urchin, a poor widow's son, without one influ-ential relative on earth; and there, in Richmond, sat on the chancellor's bench George Wythe, venerable with years and honors, one of the grand old men of Old Virginia, the preceptor

of Jefferson, signer of the Declaration of Independence, the most
learned man in his profession, and one of the best men of any
profession.   Who could have foreseen that this friendless orphan,
a Baptist preacher's son, in a State where to be a "dissenter"
was social inferiority, should have found in this eminent judge a
friend, a mentor, a patron, a father?

Yet it came about in the most natural way.   We catch our
first glimpse of the boy when he sat in a little log school-house,
without windows or floor, one of a humming score of shoeless
boys, where a good-natured, irritable, drinking English schoolmaster taught him to read, write, and cipher as far as Practice.
This was the only school he ever attended, and that was all he
learned at it.   His widowed mother, with her seven young children, her little farm, and two or three slaves, could do no more
for him.   Next, we see him a tall, awkward, slender stripling of
thirteen, still barefoot, clad in homespun butternut of his mother's
making, tilling her fields, and going to mill with his bag of corn
strapped upon the family pony.   At fourteen, in the year 1791,
a place was found for him in a Richmond drug-store, where he
served as errand-boy and youngest clerk for one year.

Then occurred the event which decided his career.   His
mother having married again, her husband had influence enough
to procure for the lad the place of copying clerk in the office of
the Court of Chancery.   The young gentlemen then employed in
the office of that court long remembered the entrance among
them of their new comrade.   He was fifteen at the time, but very
tall for his age, very slender, very awkward, and far from handsome.   His good mother had arrayed him in a full suit of pepper-
and-salt "figginy," an old Virginia fabric of silk and cotton.   His
shirt and shirt-collar were stiffly starched, and his coat-tail stood
ut boldly behind him.   The dandy law clerks of metropolitan
Richmond exchanged glances as this gawky figure entered, and
took his place at a desk to begin his work.   There was some-
hing in his manner which prevented their indulgence in the jests
that usually greet the arrival of a country youth among city
blades; and they afterwards congratulated one another that they
had waited a little before beginning to tease him, for they soon

found that he had brought with him from the country an exceedingly sharp tongue. Of his first service little is known except the immense fact that he was a most diligent reader. It rests on better authority than "Campaign Lives," that, while his fellow-clerks went abroad in the evening in search of pleasure, this lad stayed at home with his books. It is a pleasure also to know that he had not a taste for the low vices. He came of sound English stock, of a family who would not have regarded drunkenness and debauchery as "sowing wild oats," but recoiled from the thought of them with horror. Clay was far from being a saint; but it is our privilege to believe of him that he was a clean, temperate, and studious young man.

Richmond, the town of the young Republic that had most in it of the metropolitan, proved to this aspiring youth as true a University as the printing-office in old Boston was to Benjamin Franklin; for he found in it the culture best suited to him and his circumstances. Chancellor Wythe, then sixty-seven years of age, overflowing with knowledge and good nature, was the president of that university. Its professors were the cluster of able men who had gone along with Washington and Jefferson in the measures which resulted in the independence of the country. Patrick Henry was there to teach him the arts of oratory. There was a flourishing and famous debating society, the pride of the young men of Richmond, in which to try his half-fledged powers. The impulse given to thought by the American Revolution was quickened and prolonged by the thrilling news which every vessel brought from France of the revolution there. There was an atmosphere in Virginia favorable to the growth of a sympathetic mind. Young Clay's excellent handwriting brought nim gradually into the most affectionate relations with Chancellor Wythe, whose aged hand trembled to such a degree that he was glad to borrow a copyist from the clerk's office. For nearly four years it was the young man's principal duty to copy the decisions of the venerable Chancellor, which were curiously learned and elaborate; for it was the bent of the Chancellor's mind to trace the law to its sources in the ancient world, and fortify his positions by citations from Greek and Latin authors. The Greek

1 *

passages were a plague to the copyist, who knew not the alphabet of that language, but copied it, so to speak, by rote.

Here we have another proof that, no matter what a man's opportunities are, he only learns what is congenial with his nature and circumstances. Living under the influence of this learned judge, Henry Clay might have become a man of learning. George Wythe was a "scholar" in the ancient acceptation of the word. The whole education of his youth consisted in his acquiring the Latin language, which his mother taught him. Early inheriting a considerable fortune, he squandered it in dissipation, and sat down at thirty, a reformed man, to the study of the law To his youthful Latin he now added Greek, which he studied assiduously for many years, becoming, probably, the best Greek scholar in Virginia. His mind would have wholly lived in the ancient world, and been exclusively nourished from the ancient literatures, but for the necessities of his profession and the stirring political events of his later life. The Stamp Act and the Revolution varied and completed his education. His young copyist was not attracted by him to the study of Greek and Latin, nor did he catch from him the habit of probing a subject to the bottom, and ascending from the questions of the moment to universal principles. Henry Clay probed nothing to the bottom, except, perhaps, the game of whist; and though his instincts and tendencies were high and noble, he had no grasp of general truths. Under Wythe, he became a stanch Republican of the Jeffersonian school. Under Wythe, who emancipated his slaves before his death, and set apart a portion of his estate for their maintenance, he acquired a repugnance to slavery which he never lost. The Chancellor's learning and philosophy were not for him, and so he passed them by.

The tranquil wisdom of the judge was counteracted, in some degree, by the excitements of the debating society. As he grew older, the raw and awkward stripling became a young man whose every movement had a winning or a commanding grace. Handsome he never was; but his ruddy face and abundant light hair the grandeur of his forehead and the speaking intelligence of his countenance, more than atoned for the irregularity of his features

His face, too, was a compromise. With all its vivacity of expression, there was always something that spoke of the Baptist preacher's son, — just as Andrew Jackson's face had the set expression of a Presbyterian elder. But of all the bodily gifts bestowed by Nature upon this favored child, the most unique and admirable was his voice. Who ever heard one more melodious? There was a depth of tone in it, a volume, a compass, a rich and tender harmony, which invested all he said with majesty. We heard it last when he was an old man past seventy; and all he said was a few words of acknowledgment to a group of ladies in the largest hall in Philadelphia. He spoke only in the ordinary tone of conversation; but his voice filled the room as the organ fills a great cathedral, and the ladies stood spellbound as the swelling cadences rolled about the vast apartment. We have heard much of Whitefield's piercing voice and Patrick Henry's silvery tones, but we cannot believe that either of those natural orators possessed an organ superior to Clay's majestic bass. No one who ever heard him speak will find it difficult to believe what tradition reports, that he was the peerless star of the Richmond Debating Society in 1795.

Oratory was then in the highest vogue. Young Virginians did not need to look beyond the sea in order to learn that the orator was the man most in request in the dawn of freedom. Chatham, Burke, Fox, Sheridan, and Pitt were inconceivably imposing names at that day; but was not Patrick Henry the foremost man in Virginia, only because he could speak and entertain an audience? And what made John Adams President but his fiery utterances in favor of the Declaration of Independence? There were other speakers then in Virginia who would have had to this day a world-wide fame if they had spoken where the world could hear them. The tendency now is to undervalue oratory, and we regret it. We believe that, in a free country, every citizen should be able to stand undaunted before his fellow-citizens, and give an account of the faith that is in him. It is no argument against oratory to point to the Disraelis of both countries, and say that a gift possessed by such men cannot be a valuable one. It is the unmanly timidity and shamefacedness of

the rest of us that give to such men their preposterous importance. It were a calamity to America if, in the present rage for
ball-playing and boat-rowing, which we heartily rejoice in, the
debating society should be forgotten. Let us rather end the
sway of oratory by all becoming orators. Most men who can
talk well seated in a chair can *learn* to talk well standing on
their legs; and a man who can move or instruct five persons in a
small room can learn to move or instruct two thousand in a large
one.

That Henry Clay cultivated his oratorical talent in Richmond, we have his own explicit testimony. He told a class of
law students once that he owed his success in life to a habit early
formed, and for some years continued, of reading daily in a book
of history or science, and declaiming the substance of what he
had read in some solitary place, — a cornfield, the forest, a barn,
with only oxen and horses for auditors. "It is," said he, "to
this early practice of the art of all arts that I am indebted for the
primary and leading impulses that stimulated my progress, and
have shaped and moulded my entire destiny." We should be
glad to know more of this self-training; but Mr. Clay's "campaign" biographers have stuffed their volumes too full of eulogy
to leave room for such instructive details. We do not even know
the books from which he declaimed. Plutarch's Lives were favorite reading with him, we accidentally learn; and his speeches
contain evidence that he was powerfully influenced by the writings of Dr. Franklin. We believe it was from Franklin that he
learned very much of the art of managing men. Franklin, we
think, aided this impetuous and exaggerating spirit to acquire
his habitual moderation of statement, and that sleepless courtesy
which, in his keenest encounters, generally kept him within parliamentary bounds, and enabled him to live pleasantly with men
from whom he differed in opinion. Obsolete as many of his
speeches are, from the transient nature of the topics of which
they treat, they may still be studied with profit by young orators
and old politicians as examples of parliamentary politeness. I
was the good-natured and wise Franklin that helped him to this.
It is certain, too, that at some part of his earlier life he rea-

translations of Demosthenes; for of all modern orators Henry Clay was the most Demosthenian. Calhoun purposely and consciously imitated the Athenian orator; but Clay was a kindred spirit with Demosthenes. We could select passages from both these orators, and no man could tell which was American and which was Greek, unless he chanced to remember the passage. Tell us, gentle reader, were the sentences following spoken by Henry Clay after the war of 1812 *at* the Federalists who had opposed that war, or by Demosthenes against the degenerate Greeks who favored the designs of Philip?

"From first to last I have uniformly pursued the just and virtuous course, — asserter of the honors, of the prerogatives, of the glory of my country. Studious to support them, zealous to advance them, my whole being is devoted to this glorious cause. I was never known to walk abroad with a face of joy and exultation at the success of the enemy, embracing and announcing the joyous tidings to those who I supposed would transmit it to the proper place. I was never known to receive the successes of my own country with trembling, with sighs, with my eyes bent to the earth, like those impious men who are the defamers of their country, as if by such conduct they were not defamers of themselves."

Is it Clay, or is it Demosthenes? Or have we made a mistake, and copied a passage from the speech of a Unionist of 1865?

After serving four years as clerk and amanuensis, barely earning a subsistence, Clay was advised by his venerable friend, the Chancellor, to study law; and a place was procured for him in the office of the Attorney-General of the State. In less than a year after formally beginning his studies he was admitted to the bar. This seems a short preparation; but the whole period of his connection with Chancellor Wythe was a study of the law. The Chancellor was what a certain other chancellor styles "a full man," and Henry Clay was a receptive youth.

When he had obtained his license to practise he was twenty years of age. Debating-society fame and drawing-room popularity do not, in an old commonwealth like Virginia, bring practice

to a lawyer of twenty. But, as a distinguished French author
has recently remarked of Julius Cæsar, " In him was united the
elegance of manner which wins, to the energy of character which
commands." He sought, therefore, a new sphere of exertion far
from the refinements of Richmond. Kentucky, which Boone
explored in 1770, was a part of Virginia when Clay was a child,
and only became a State in 1792, when first he began to copy
Chancellor Wythe's decisions. The first white family settled in
it in 1775; but when our young barrister obtained his license,
twenty-two years after, it contained a white population of nearly
two hundred thousand. His mother, with five of her children
and a second husband, had gone thither five years before. In
1797 Henry Clay removed to Lexington, the new State's oldest
town and capital, though then containing, it is said, but fifty
houses. He was a stranger there, and almost penniless. He
took board, not knowing where the money was to come from to
pay for it. There were already several lawyers of repute in the
place. "I remember," said Mr. Clay, forty-five years after,
" how comfortable I thought I should be if I could make one
hundred pounds a year, Virginia money; and with what delight
I received my first fifteen-shilling fee. My hopes were more
than realized. I immediately rushed into a successful and lucrative practice." In a year and a half he was in a position to
marry the daughter of one of the first men of the State, Colonel
Thomas Hart, a man exceedingly beloved in Lexington.

It is surprising how addicted to litigation were the early settlers of the Western States. The imperfect surveys of land,
the universal habit of getting goods on credit at the store, and
" difficulties " between individuals ending in bloodshed, filled the
court calendars with land disputes, suits for debt, and exciting
murder cases, which gave to lawyers more importance and better
chances of advancement than they possessed in the older States.
Mr. Clay had two strings to his bow. Besides being a man of
red tape and pigeon-holes, exact, methodical, and strictly attentive
to business, he had a power over a Kentucky jury such as no
other man has ever wielded. To this day nothing pleases aged
Kentuckians better than to tell stories which they heard their

fathers tell, of Clay's happy repartees to opposing counsel, his ingenious cross-questioning of witnesses, his sweeping torrents of invective, his captivating courtesy, his melting pathos. Single gestures, attitudes, tones, have come down to us through two or three memories, and still please the curious guest at Kentucky firesides. But when we turn to the cold records of this part of his life, we find little to justify his traditional celebrity. It appears that the principal use to which his talents were applied during the first years of his practice at the bar was in defending murderers. He seems to have shared the feeling which then prevailed in the Western country, that to defend a prisoner at the bar is a nobler thing than to assist in defending the public against his further depredations; and he threw all his force into the defence of some men who would have been "none the worse for a hanging." One day, in the streets of Lexington, a drunken fellow whom he had rescued from the murderer's doom cried out, "Here comes Mr. Clay, who saved my life." "Ah! my poor fellow," replied the advocate, "I fear I have saved too many like you, who ought to be hanged." The anecdotes printed of his exploits in cheating the gallows of its due are of a quality which shows that the power of this man over a jury lay much in his manner. His delivery, which "bears absolute sway in oratory," was bewitching and irresistible, and gave to quite commonplace wit and very questionable sentiment an amazing power to please and subdue.

We are far from thinking that he was not a very able lawyer. Judge Story, we remember, before whom he argued a cause later in life, was of opinion that he would have won a high position at the bar of the Supreme Court, if he had not been early drawn away to public life. In Kentucky he was a brilliant, successful practitioner, such as Kentucky wanted and could appreciate. In a very few years he was the possessor of a fine estate near Lexington, and to the single slave who came to him as his share of his father's property were added several others. His wife being a skilful and vigorous manager, he was in independent circumstances, and ready to serve the public, if the public wished him, when he had been but ten years in his Western home. Thus he

had a basis for a public career, without which few men can long
serve the public with honor and success. And this was a principal reason of the former supremacy of Southern men in Washington; nearly all of them being men who owned land, which
slaves tilled for them, whether they were present or absent.

The young lawyer took to politics very naturally. Posterity,
which will judge the public men of that period chiefly by their
course with regard to slavery, will note with pleasure that Clay's
first public act was an attempt to deliver the infant State of
Kentucky from that curse. The State Constitution was to be
remodelled in 1799. Fresh from the society of Chancellor
Wythe, an abolitionist who had set free his own slaves, — fresh
from Richmond, where every man of note, from Jefferson and
Patrick Henry downwards, was an abolitionist, — Henry Clay
began in 1798, being then twenty-one years of age, to write a
series of articles for a newspaper, advocating the gradual abolition of slavery in Kentucky. He afterwards spoke on that side
at public meetings. Young as he was, he took the lead of the
public-spirited young men who strove to purge the State from
this iniquity; but in the Convention the proposition was voted
down by a majority so decisive as to banish the subject from politics for fifty years. Still more honorable was it in Mr. Clay,
that, in 1829, when Calhoun was maturing nullification, he could
publicly say that among the acts of his life which he reflected
upon with most satisfaction was his youthful effort to secure
emancipation in Kentucky.

The chapter of our history most abounding in all the elements
of interest will be that one which will relate the rise and first
national triumph of the Democratic party. Young Clay came to
the Kentucky stump just when the country was at the crisis of
the struggle between the Old and the New. But in Kentucky
it was not a struggle; for the people there, mostly of Virginian
birth, had been personally benefited by Jefferson's equalizing
measures, and were in the fullest sympathy with his political
doctrines. When, therefore, this brilliant and commanding youth,
with that magnificent voice of his, and large gesticulation, mounted the wagon that usually served as platform in the open-ai.

meetings of Kentucky, and gave forth, in fervid oratory, the republican principles he had imbibed in Richmond, he won that immediate and intense popularity which an orator always wins who gives powerful expression to the sentiments of his hearers. We cannot wonder that, at the close of an impassioned address upon the Alien and Sedition Laws, the multitude should have pressed about him, and borne him aloft in triumph upon their shoulders; nor that Kentucky should have hastened to employ him in her public business as soon as he was of the requisite age. At thirty he was, to use the language of the stump, "Kentucky's favorite son," and incomparably the finest orator in the Western country. Kentucky had tried him, and found him perfectly to her mind. He was an easy, comfortable man to associate with, wholly in the Jeffersonian taste. His wit was not of the highest quality, but he had plenty of it; and if he said a good thing, he had such a way of saying it as gave it ten times its natural force. He chewed tobacco and took snuff, — practices which lowered the tone of his health all his life. In familiar conversation he used language of the most Western description; and he had a singularly careless, graceful way with him, that was in strong contrast with the vigor and dignity of his public efforts. He was an honest and brave young man, altogether above lying, hypocrisy, and meanness, — full of the idea of Republican America and her great destiny. The splendor of his talents concealed his defects and glorified his foibles; and Kentucky rejoiced in him, loved him, trusted him, and sent him forth to represent her in the national council.

During the first thirteen years of Henry Clay's active life as a politician, — from his twenty-first to his thirty-fourth year, — he appears in politics only as the eloquent champion of the policy of Mr. Jefferson, whom he esteemed the first and best of living men. After defending him on the stump and aiding him in the Kentucky Legislature, he was sent in 1806, when he was scarcely thirty, to fill for one term a seat in the Senate of the United States, made vacant by the resignation of one of the Kentucky Senators. Mr Jefferson received his affectionate young disciple with cordiality, and admitted him to his confi-

B

dence.   Clay had been recently defending Burr before a Kentucky court, entirely believing that his designs were lawful and sanctioned.   Mr. Jefferson showed him the cipher letters of that mysterious and ill-starred adventurer, which convinced Mr. Clay that Burr was certainly a liar, if he was not a traitor.   Mr. Jefferson's perplexity in 1806 was similar to that of Jackson in 1833, — too much money in the treasury.   The revenue then was fifteen millions; and, after paying all the expenses of the government and the stipulated portion of the national debt, there was an obstinate and most embarrassing surplus.   What to do with this irrepressible surplus was the question then discussed in Mr. Jefferson's Cabinet.   The President, being a free-trader, would naturally have said, Reduce the duties.   But the younger men of the party, who had no pet theories, and particularly our young Senator, who had just come in from a six weeks' horseback flounder over bridgeless roads, urged another solution of the difficulty, — Internal Improvements.   But the President was a strict-constructionist, denied the authority of Congress to vote money for public works, and was fully committed to that opinion.

Mr. Jefferson yielded.   The most beautiful theories will not always endure the wear and tear of practice.   The President, it is true, still maintained that an amendment to the Constitution ought to precede appropriations for public works; but he said this very briefly and without emphasis, while he stated at some length, and with force, the desirableness of expending the surplus revenue in improving the country.   As time wore on, less and less was said about the amendment, more and more about the importance of internal improvements; until, at last, the Republican party, under Clay, Adams, Calhoun, and Rush, went as far in this business of road-making and canal-digging as Hamilton him self could have desired.   Thus it was that Jefferson rendered true his own saying, " We are all Federalists, we are all Republicans."   Jefferson yielded, also, on the question of free-trade. There is a passage of a few lines in Mr. Jefferson's Message of 1806, the year of Henry Clay's first appearance in Washington, which may be regarded as the text of half the Kentuckian's speeches, and the inspiration of his public life. The President is discussing the question, What shall we do with the surplus?

"Shall we suppress the impost, and give that advantage to foreign over domestic manufactures? On a few articles of more general and necessary use, the suppression, in due season, will doubtless be right; but the great mass of the articles upon which impost is paid are foreign luxuries, purchased by those only who are rich enough to afford themselves the use of them. Their patriotism would certainly prefer its continuance, and application to the great purposes of the public education, roads, rivers, canals, and such other objects of public improvement as it may be thought proper to add to the constitutional enumeration of Federal powers. By these operations, new channels of communication will be opened between the States, the lines of separation will disappear, their interests will be identified, and their union cemented by new and indissoluble bonds."

Upon these hints, the young Senator delayed not to speak and act; nor did he wait for an amendment to the Constitution. His first speech in the Senate was in favor of building a bridge over the Potomac; one of his first acts, to propose an appropriation of lands for a canal round the Falls of the Ohio at Louisville; and soon he brought forward a resolution directing the Secretary of the Treasury to report a system of roads and canals for the consideration of Congress. The seed of the President's Message had fallen into good ground.

Returning home at the end of the session, and re-entering the Kentucky Legislature, we still find him a strict follower of Mr Tefferson. In support of the President's non-intercourse policy (which was Franklin's policy of 1775 applied to the circumstances of 1808), Mr. Clay proposed that the members of the Legislature should bind themselves to wear nothing that was not of American manufacture. A Federalist, ignorant of the illustrious origin of this idea, ignorant that the homespun system had caused the repeal of the Stamp Act, and *would* have postponed the Revolution but for the accident of Lexington, denounced Mr. Clay's proposition as the act of a shameless demagogue. Clay challenged this ill-informed gentleman, and a duel resulted, in which two shots were exchanged, and both antagonists were slightly wounded. Elected again to the Senate for an unexpired term, he reappeared in that body in 1809, and sat during two sessions. Homespun was again the theme of his speeches. His ideas on the subject of protecting and encouraging American manufactures were not derived from books, nor expressed in the language of political economy. At his own Kentucky home, Mrs. Clay, assisted by her servants, was spinning and weaving, knitting and sewing, most of the garments required in her little kingdom of six hundred acres, while her husband was away over the mountains serving his country. "Let the nation do what we Kentucky farmers are doing," said Mr. Clay to the Senate. "Let us manufacture enough to be independent of foreign nations in things essential, — no more." He discoursed on this subject in a very pleasant, humorous manner, without referring to the abstract principle involved, or employing any of the technical language of economists.

His service in the Senate during these two sessions enhanced his reputation greatly, and the galleries were filled when he was expected to speak, little known as he was to the nation at large. We have a glimpse of him in one of Washington Irving's letters of February, 1811 : "Clay, from Kentucky, spoke against the Bank. He is one of the finest fellows I have seen here, and one of the finest orators in the Senate, though I believe the youngest man in it. The galleries, however, were so much crowded with ladies and gentlemen, and such expectations had been expressed concerning his speech, that he was completely frightened, and acquitted himself very little to his own satisfaction. He is a man I have great personal regard for." This was the anti-bank speech which General Jackson used to say had convinced him of the impolicy of a national bank, and which, with ingenious malice, he covertly quoted in making up his Bank Veto Message of 1832

Mr. Clay's public life proper began in November, 1811, when he appeared in Washington as a member of the House of Representatives, and was immediately elected Speaker by the war party, by the decisive majority of thirty-one. He was then thirty-four years of age. His election to the Speakership on his

first appearance in the House gave him, at once, national stand
ing. His master in political doctrine and his partisan chief,
Thomas Jefferson, was gone from the scene; and Clay could now
be a planet instead of a satellite. Restive as he had been under
the arrogant aggressions of England, he had schooled himself to
patient waiting, aided by Jefferson's benign sentiments and great
example. But his voice was now for war; and such was the
temper of the public in those months, that the eloquence of
Henry Clay, seconded by the power of the Speaker, rendered the
war unavoidable.

It is agreed that to Henry Clay, Speaker of the House of
Representatives, more than to any other individual, we owe the
war of 1812. When the House hesitated, it was he who,
descending from the chair, spoke so as to reassure it. When
President Madison faltered, it was the stimulus of Clay's
resistless presence that put heart into him again. If the
people seemed reluctant, it was Clay's trumpet harangues
that fired their minds. And when the war was declared,
it was he, more than President or Cabinet or War Committee, that carried it along upon his shoulders. All our wars
begin in disaster; it was Clay who restored the country to confidence when it was disheartened by the loss of Detroit and its
betrayed garrison. It was Clay alone who could encounter without flinching the acrid sarcasm of John Randolph, and exhibit
the nothingness of his telling arguments. It was he alone who
could adequately deal with Quincy of Massachusetts, who alluded to the Speaker and his friends as " young politicians, with their
pin-feathers yet unshed, the shell still sticking upon them, — perfectly unfledged, though they fluttered and cackled on the floor."
Clay it was whose clarion notes rang out over departing regi-
ments, and kindled within them the martial fire; and it was
Clay's speeches which the soldiers loved to read by the camp-fire.
Fiery Jackson read them, and found them perfectly to his taste.
Gentle Harrison read them to his Tippecanoe heroes. When the
war was going all wrong in the first year, President Madison
wished to appoint Clay Commander-in-Chief of the land forces;
but, said Gallatin, " What shall we do without him in the House
of Representatives?"

Henry Clay was not a man of blood.   On the contrary, he was
eminently pacific, both in his disposition and in his politics.   Yet
he believed in the war of 1812, and his whole heart was in it.
The question occurs, then, Was it right and best for the United
States to declare war against Great Britain in 1812?   The
proper answer to this question depends upon another: What
ought we to think of Napoleon Bonaparte?   If Napoleon *was*,
what English Tories and American Federalists said he was, the
enemy of mankind, — and if England, in warring upon him, *was*
fighting the battle of mankind, — then the injuries received by
neutral nations might have been borne without dishonor.   When
those giant belligerents were hurling continents at one another,
the damage done to bystanders from the flying off of fragments
was a thing to be expected, and submitted to as their share of the
general ruin, — to be compensated by the final suppression of the
common foe.   To have endured this, and even to have submitted,
for a time, to the searching of ships, so that not one Englishman
should be allowed to skulk from such a fight, had not been pusil-
lanimity, but magnanimity.   But if, as English Whigs and American Democrats contended, Napoleon Bonaparte was the armed
soldier of democracy, the rightful heir of the Revolution, the sole
alternative to anarchy, the *legitimate* ruler of France; if the
responsibility of those enormous desolating wars does not lie at
his door, but belongs to George III. and the Tory party of England; if it is a fact that Napoleon always stood ready to make a
just peace, which George III. and William Pitt refused, *not* in
the interest of mankind and civilization, but in that of the Tory
party and the allied dynasties, — then America was right in
resenting the searching and seizure of her ships, and right, after
exhausting every peaceful expedient, in declaring war.

That this was really the point in dispute between our two
parties is shown in the debates, newspapers, and pamphlets of the
time.   The Federalists, as Mr. Clay observed in one of his
speeches, compared Napoleon to " every monster and beast, from
that mentioned in the Revelation down to the most insignifican
quadruped."   The Republicans, on the contrary, spoke of him
always with moderation and decency, sometimes with commenda

ion, and occasionally he was toasted at their public dinners with enthusiasm. Mr. Clay himself, while lamenting his enormous power and the suspension of ancient nationalities, always had a lurking sympathy with him. " Bonaparte," said he in his great war speech of 1813, "has been called the scourge of mankind, the destroyer of Europe, the great robber, the infidel, the modern Attila, and Heaven knows by what other names. Really, gentle-men remind me of an obscure lady, in a city not very far off, who also took it into her head, in conversation with an accomplished French gentleman, to talk of the affairs of Europe. She, too, spoke of the destruction of the balance of power; stormed and raged about the insatiable ambition of the Emperor; called him the curse of mankind, the destroyer of Europe. The French-man listened to her with perfect patience, and when she had ceased said to her, with ineffable politeness, ' Madam, it would give my master, the Emperor, infinite pain if he knew how hard-ly you thought of him.' " This brief passage suffices to show the prevailing tone of the two parties when Napoleon was the theme of discourse.

It is, of course, impossible for us to enter into this question of Napoleon's moral position. Intelligent opinion, ever since the means of forming an opinion were accessible, has been constantly judging Napoleon more leniently, and the Tory party more severely. We can only say, that, in our opinion, the war of 1812 was just and necessary ; and that Henry Clay, both in supporting Mr. Jefferson's policy of non-intercourse and in supporting Pres-ident Madison's policy of war, deserved well of his country. Postponed that war might have been. But, human nature being what it .is, and the English government being what it was, we do not believe that the United States could ever have been distinctly recognized as one of the powers of the earth without another fight for it.

The war being ended and the Federal party extinct, upon the young Republicans, who had carried on the war, devolved the task of " reconstruction." Before they had made much pro-gress in it, they came within an ace of being consigned to pri-vate life, — Clay himself having as narrow an escape as any of them.

And here we may note one point of superiority of the Ameri
can government over others. In other countries it can sometimes be the interest of politicians to foment and declare war
A war strengthens a tottering dynasty, an imperial *parvenu*, an
odious tyrant, a feeble ministry; and the glory won in battle on
land and sea redounds to the credit of government, without
raising up competitors for its high places. But let American
politicians take note. It is never *their* interest to bring on a
war; because a war is certain to generate a host of popular
heroes to outshine them and push them from their places. It
may sometimes be their duty to advocate war, but it is never
their interest. At this moment we see both parties striving
which shall present to the people the most attractive list of military candidates; and when a busy ward politician seeks his
reward in custom-house or department, he finds a dozen lame
soldiers competing for the place; one of whom gets it, — as he
ought. What city has presented Mr. Stanton with a house, or
Mr. Welles with fifty thousand dollars' worth of government
bonds? Calhoun precipitated the country into a war with Mexico; but what did he gain by it but new bitterness of disappointment, while the winner of three little battles was elected
President? Henry Clay was the animating soul of the war
of 1812, and we honor him for it; but while Jackson, Brown,
Scott, Perry, and Decatur came out of that war the idols of the
nation, Clay was promptly notified that *his* footing in the public
councils, *his* hold of the public favor, was by no means stable.

His offence was that he voted for the compensation bill of 1816,
which merely changed the pay of members of Congress from
the pittance of six dollars a day to the pittance of fifteen hundred dollars a year. He who before was lord paramount
in Kentucky saved his seat only by prodigious efforts on the
stump, and by exerting all the magic of his presence in the
canvass.

No one ever bore cutting disappointment with an airier grace
than this high-spirited thorough-bred; but he evidently felt this
apparent injustice. Some years later, when it was proposed
in Congress to pension Commodore Perry's mother, Mr. Clay

in a speech of five minutes, totally extinguished the proposition. Pointing to the vast rewards bestowed upon such successful soldiers as Marlborough, Napoleon, and Wellington, he said, with thrilling effect : " How different is the fate of the statesman ! In his quiet and less brilliant career, after having advanced, by the wisdom of his measures, the national prosperity to the highest point of elevation, and after having sacrificed his fortune, his time, and perhaps his health, in the public service, what, too often, are the rewards that await him ? Who thinks of *his* family, impoverished by the devotion of his attention to his country, instead of their advancement ? Who proposes to pension him, — much less his *mother ?* " He spoke the more feelingly, because he, who could have earned more than the President's income by the practice of his profession, was often pinched for money, and was once obliged to leave Congress for the sole purpose of taking care of his shattered fortune. He felt the importance of this subject in a national point of view. He wrote in 1817 to a friend : " Short as has been my service in the public councils, I have seen some of the most valuable members quitting the body from their inability to sustain the weight of these sacrifices. And in process of time, I apprehend, this mischief will be more and more felt. Even now there are few, if any, instances of members dedicating their lives to the duties of legislation. Members stay a year or two ; curiosity is satisfied; the novelty wears off ; expensive habits are brought or acquired ; their affairs at home are neglected ; their fortunes are wasting away ; and they are compelled to retire."

The eight years of Mr. Monroe's administration — from 1817 to 1825 — were the most brilliant period of Henry Clay's career. His position as Speaker of the House of Representatives would naturally have excluded him from leadership ; but the House was as fond of hearing him speak as he could be of speaking, and opportunities were continually furnished him by going into Committee of the Whole. In a certain sense he was in opposition to the administration. When one party has so frequently and decidedly beaten the party opposed to it, that the defeated

2

party goes out of existence, the conquering party soon divides. The triumphant Republicans of 1816 obeyed this law of their position ; — one wing of the party, under Mr. Monroe, being reluctant to depart from the old Jeffersonian policy; the other wing, under Henry Clay, being inclined to go very far in internal improvements and a protective tariff. Mr. Clay now appears as the great champion of what he proudly styled the American System. He departed farther and farther from the simple doctrines of the earlier Democrats. Before the war, he had opposed a national bank; now he advocated the establishment of one, and handsomely acknowledged the change of opinion. Before the war, he proposed only such a tariff as would render America independent of foreign nations in articles of the first necessity ; now he contemplated the establishment of a great manufacturing system, which should attract from Europe skilful workmen, and supply the people with everything they consumed, even to jewelry and silver-ware. Such success had he with his American System, that, before many years rolled away, we see the rival wings of the Republican party striving which could concede most to the manufacturers in the way of an increased tariff. Every four years, when a President was to be elected, there was an inevitable revision of the tariff, each faction outbidding the other in conciliating the manufacturing interest ; until at length the near discharge of the national debt suddenly threw into politics a prospective surplus, — one of twelve millions a year, — which came near crushing the American System, and gave Mr. Calhoun his pretext for nullification.

At present, with such a debt as we have, the tariff is no longer a question with us. The government must have its million a day ; and as no tax is less offensive to the people than a duty on imported commodities, we seem compelled to a practically protective system for many years to come. But, of all men, a citizen of the United States should be the very last to accept the protective system as final; for when he looks abroad over the great assemblage of sovereignties which he calls the United States, and asks himself the reason of their rapid and uniform prosperity for the last eighty years, what answer can he give but this ? — *There is free trade among them.* And if he extends his survey over the whole earth, he can scarcely avoid the conclusion that free trade among all nations would be as advantageous to all nations as it is to the thirty-seven States of the American Union. But nations are not governed by theories and theorists, but by circumstances and politicians. The most perfect theory must sometimes give way to exceptional fact. We find, accordingly, Mr. Mill, the great English champion of free trade, fully sustaining Henry Clay's moderate tariff of 1816, but sustaining it only as a temporary measure. The paragraph of Mr. Mill's Political Economy which touches this subject seems to us to express so exactly the true policy of the United States with regard to the tariff, that we will take the liberty of quoting it.

" The only case in which, on mere principles of political economy, protecting duties can be defensible, is when they are imposed temporarily, (especially in a young and rising nation,) in hopes of naturalizing a foreign industry, in itself perfectly suitable to the circumstances of the country. The superiority of one country over another in a branch of production often arises only from having begun it sooner. There may be no inherent advantage on one part, or disadvantage on the other, but only a present superiority of acquired skill and experience. A country which has this skill and experience yet to acquire may, in other respects, be better adapted to the production than those which were earlier in the field ; and, besides, it is a just remark of Mr. Rae, that nothing has a greater tendency to promote improvement in any branch of production, than its trial under a new set of conditions. But it cannot be expected that individuals should, at their own risk, or rather to their certain loss, introduce a new manufacture, and bear the burden of carrying it on, until the producers have been educated up to the level of those with whom the processes are traditional. A protecting duty, continued for a reasonable time, will sometimes be the least inconvenient mode in which the nation can tax itself for the support of such an experiment. But the protection should be confined to cases in which there is good ground of assurance that the industry which it fosters will after a time be able to dispense with it ; nor should the domestic producers ever be allowed to expect that it will be continued to them beyond the time necessary for a fair trial of what they are capable of accomplishing." *

* Mill's Principles of Political Economy, Book V. Ch. X. § 1.

In the quiet of his library at Ashland, Mr. Clay, we believe, would, at any period of his public life, have assented to the doctrines of this passage. But at Washington he was a party leader and an orator. Having set the ball in motion, he could not stop it; nor does he appear to have felt the necessity of stopping it, until, in 1831, he was suddenly confronted by three Gorgons at once, — a coming Surplus, a President that vetoed internal improvements, and an ambitious Calhoun, resolved on using the surplus either as a stepping-stone to the Presidency or a wedge with which to split the Union. The time to have put down the brakes was in 1828, when the national debt was within seven years of being paid off; but precisely *then* it was that both divisions of the Democratic party — one under Mr. Van Buren, the other under Mr. Clay — were running a kind of tariff race, neck and neck, in which Van Buren won. Mr. Clay, it is true, was not in Congress then, — he was Secretary of State; but he was the soul of his party, and his voice was the voice of a master. In all his letters and speeches there is not a word to show that he then anticipated the surplus, or the embarrassments to which it gave rise; though he could not have forgotten that a very trifling surplus was one of the chief anxieties of Mr. Jefferson's administration. Mr. Clay's error, we think, arose from his not perceiving clearly that a protective tariff, though justifiable sometimes, is always in itself an evil, and is never to be accepted as the permanent policy of any country; and that, being an evil, it must be reduced to the minimum that will answer the temporary purpose.

In estimating Henry Clay, we are always to remember that he was an orator. He had a genius for oratory. There is, we believe, no example of a man endowed with a genius for oratory who also possessed an understanding of the first order. Mr. Clay's oratory was vivified by a good heart and a genuine love of country; and on occasions which required only a good heart, patriotic feeling, and an eloquent tongue, he served his country well. But as a party leader he had sometimes to deal with matters which demanded a radical and far-seeing intellect; and then, perhaps he failed to guide his followers aright. At Washington, during the thirteen years of his Speakership, he led the gay life of a popular hero and drawing-room favorite; and his position was supposed to compel him to entertain much company. As a young lawyer in Kentucky, he was addicted to playing those games of mere chance which alone at that day were styled gambling. He played high and often, as was the custom then all over the world. It was his boast, even in those wild days, that he never played at home, and never had a pack of cards in his house; but when the lawyers and judges were assembled during court sessions, there was much high play among them at the tavern after the day's work was done. In 1806, when Mr. Clay was elected to the Senate, he resolved to gamble no more, — that is, to play at hazard and "brag" no more, — and he kept his resolution. Whist, being a game depending partly on skill, was not included in this resolution; and whist was thenceforth a very favorite game with him, and he greatly excelled in it. It was said of him, as it was of Charles James Fox, that, at any moment of a hand, he could name all the cards that remained to be played. He discountenanced high stakes; and we believe he never, after 1806, played for more than five dollars "a corner." These, we know, were the stakes at Ghent, where he played whist for many months with the British Commissioners during the negotiations for peace in 1815. We mention his whist-playing only as part of the evidence that he was a gay, pleasant, easy man of the world, — not a student, not a thinker, not a philosopher. Often, in reading over his speeches of this period, we are ready to exclaim, " Ah ! Mr. Clay, if you had played whist a little less, and studied history and statesmanship a great deal more, you would have avoided some errors! " A trifling anecdote related by Mr. Colton lets us into the Speaker's way of life. "How can you preside over that House to-day?" asked a friend, as he set Mr. Clay down at his own door, *after sunrise*, from a party. "Come up, and you shall see how I will throw the reins over their necks," replied the Speaker, as he stepped from the carriage.*

* Daniel Webster once said of him in conversation . " Mr. Clay is a great man ; beyond all question a true patriot. He has done much for his country. He ought long ago to have been elected President. I think, however, he was

But when noble feeling and a gifted tongue sufficed for the occasion, how grandly sometimes he acquitted himself in those brilliant years, when, descending from the Speaker's lofty seat, he held the House and the crowded galleries spellbound by his magnificent oratory ! His speech of 1818, for example, favoring the recognition of the South American republics, was almost as wise as it was eloquent; for, although the provinces of South America are still far from being what we could wish them to be, yet it is certain that no single step of progress was possible for them until their connection with Spain was severed. Cuba, to-day, proves Mr. Clay's position. The amiable and intelligent Creoles of that beautiful island are nearly ready for the abolition of slavery and for regulated freedom; but they lie languishing under the hated incubus of Spanish rule, and dare not risk a war of independence, outnumbered as they are by untamed or half-tamed Africans. Mr. Clay's speeches in behalf of the young republics of South America were read by Bolivar at the head of his troops, and justly rendered his name dear to the struggling patriots. He had a clear conviction, like his master, Thomas Jefferson, that the interests of the United States lie chiefly *in America*, not Europe ; and it was a favorite dream of his to see the Western Continent occupied by flourishing republics independent, but closely allied, — a genuine Holy Alliance.

The supreme effort of Mr. Clay's Congressional life was in connection with the Missouri Compromise of 1821. He did not originate the plan of compromise, but it was certainly his influence and tact which caused the plan to prevail. Fortunately, he had been absent from Congress during some of the earlier

never a man of books, a hard student; but he has displayed remarkable genius. I never could imagine him sitting comfortably in his library, and reading quietly out of the great books of the past. He has been too fond of the world to enjoy anything like that. He has been too fond of excitement, — he has lived upon it; he has been too fond of company, not enough alone; and has had few resources within himself. Now a man who cannot, to some extent. depend upon himself for happiness, is to my mind one of the unfortunate. Bu Clay is a great man; and if he ever had animosities against me, I forgive him and forget them."

These words were uttered at Marshfield when the news reached there that Mr Clay was dying.

attempts to admit Missouri; and thus he arrived in Washington in January, 1821, calm, uncommitted, and welcome to both parties. Fierce debate had wrought up the minds of members to that point where useful discussion ceases to be possible. Almost every man had given personal offence and taken personal offence; the two sides seemed reduced to the most hopeless incompatibility; and the affair was at a dead lock. No matter what the subject of debate, Missouri was sure, in some way, to get involved in it; and the mere mention of the name was like a spark upon loose gunpowder. In February, for example, the House had to go through the ceremony of counting the votes for President of the United States, — a mere ceremony, since Mr. Monroe had been re-elected almost unanimously, and the votes of Missouri were of no importance. The tellers, to avoid giving cause of contention, announced that Mr. Monroe had received two hundred and thirty-one votes, including those of Missouri, and two hundred and twenty-eight if they were excluded. At this announcement members sprang to their feet, and such a scene of confusion arose that no man could make himself heard. After a long struggle with the riot, the Speaker declared the House adjourned.

For six weeks Mr. Clay exerted his eloquence, his arts of pacification, and all the might of his personality, to bring members to their senses. He even had a long conference with his ancient foe, John Randolph. He threw himself into this work with such ardor, and labored at it so continuously, day and night, that, when the final triumph was won, he declared that, if Missouri had been kept out of the Union two weeks longer, he should have been a dead man. Thirty-four years after these events Mr. S. G. Goodrich wrote: "I was in the House of Representatives but a single hour. While I was present there was no direct discussion of the agitating subject which already filled everybody's mind, but still the excitement flared out occasionally in incidental allusions to it, like puffs of smoke and jets of flame which issue from a house that is on fire within. I recollect that Clay made a brief speech, thrilling the House by a single passage, in which he spoke of '*poor, unheard Missouri,*' she being then without a representative in Congress. His tall, tossing form, his long, sweeping gestures, and, above all, his musical yet thrilling tones, made an impression upon me which I can never forget."

Mr. Clay, at length, had completed his preparations. He moved for a committee of the House to confer with a committee of the Senate. He himself wrote out the list of members whom he desired should be elected, and they were elected. At the last conference of the joint committees, which was held on a Sunday, Mr. Clay insisted that their report, to have the requisite effect upon Congress and the country, must be unanimous; and unanimous it was. Both Houses, with a surprising approach to unanimity, adopted the compromise proposed; and thus was again postponed the bloody arbitrament to which the irrepressible controversy has since been submitted.

Clay's masterly conduct on this occasion added his name to the long list of gentlemen who were mentioned for the succession to Mr. Monroe in 1825. If the city of Washington had been the United States, if the House of Representatives had possessed the right to elect a President, Henry Clay might have been its choice. During the thirteen years of his Speakership not one of his decisions had been reversed; and he had presided over the turbulent and restive House with that perfect blending of courtesy and firmness which at once restrains and charms. The debates just before the war, during the war, and after the war, had been violent and acrimonious; but he had kept his own temper, and compelled the House to observe an approach to decorum. On one occasion he came into such sharp collision with the excitable Randolph, that the dispute was transferred to the newspapers, and narrowly escaped degenerating from a war of "cards" to a conflict with pistols. But the Speaker triumphed; the House and the country sustained him. On occasions of ceremony the Speaker enchanted every beholder by the superb dignity of his bearing, the fitness of his words, and the tranquil depth of his tones. What could be more eloquent, more appropriate, than the Speaker's address of welcome to Lafayette, when the guest of the nation was conducted to the floor of the House of Representatives? The House and the galleries were proud of the Speaker that day. No one who never heard this captiva tor of hearts can form the slightest conception of the penetrating effect of the closing sentences, though they were spoken only in the tone of conversation.

" The vain wish has been sometimes indulged, that Providence would allow the patriot, after death, to return to his country, and to contemplate the intermediate changes which had taken place; to view the forests felled, the cities built, the mountains levelled, the canals cut, the highways constructed, the progress of the arts, the advance- ment of learning, and the increase of population. General, your pres- ent visit to the United States is a realization of the consoling object of that wish. You are in the midst of posterity. Everywhere you must have been struck with the great changes, physical and moral, which have occurred since you left us. Even this very city, bearing a vener- ated name, alike endeared to you and to us, has since emerged from the forest which then covered its site. In one respect you behold us unaltered, and this is in the sentiment of continued devotion to liberty, and of ardent affection and profound gratitude to your departed friend, the father of his country, and to you, and to your illustrious associates in the field and in the cabinet, for the multiplied blessings which sur- round us, and for the very privilege of addressing you which I now exercise. This sentiment, now fondly cherished by more than ten millions of people, will be transmitted with unabated vigor down the tide of time, through the countless millions who are destined to inhabit this continent, to the latest posterity."

The appropriateness of these sentiments to the occasion and to the man is evident to every one who remembers that Lafay- ette's love of George Washington was a Frenchman's romantic passion. Nor, indeed, did he need to have a sensitive French heart to be moved to tears by such words and such a welcome.

From 1822 to 1848, a period of twenty-six years, Henry Clay lived the strange life of a candidate for the Presidency. It was enough to ruin any man, body and soul. To live always in the gaze of millions; to be the object of eulogy the most extrava- gant and incessant from one half of the newspapers, and of vitu- peration still more preposterous from the other half; to be sur rounded by flatterers interested and disinterested, and to be

2 *   c

confronted by another body intent on misrepresenting every
act and word ; to have to stop and consider the effect of every
utterance, public and private, upon the next " campaign " ; not
to be able to stir abroad without having to harangue a depu-
tation of political friends, and stand to be kissed by ladies and
pump-handled by men, and hide the enormous bore of it beneath
a fixed smile till the very muscles of the face are rigid ; to receive
by every mail letters enough for a large town ; to have your life
written several times a year ; to be obliged continually to refute
calumnies and " define your position " ; to live under a horrid
necessity to be pointedly civil to all the world ; to find your most
casual remarks and most private conversations getting distorted
in print, — this, and more than this, it was to be a candidate for
the Presidency.   The most wonderful thing that we have to say
of Henry Clay is, that, such were his native sincerity and health-
fulness of mind, he came out of this fiery trial still a patriot and
a man of honor.   We believe it was a weakness in him, as it is in
any man, to set his heart upon living four years in the White
House ; but we can most confidently say, that, having entered the
game, he played it fairly, and bore his repeated disappointments
with genuine, high-bred composure.   The closest scrutiny into the
life of this man still permits us to believe that, when he said, " I
would rather be right than be President," he spoke the real sentiments of his heart ; and that, when he said to one of his political
opponents, " Tell General Jackson that, if he will sign my Land
Bill, I will pledge myself to retire from public life and never to
re-enter it," he meant what he said, and would have stood to it.
It is our privilege to believe this of Henry Clay ; nor do we
think that there was ever anything morbidly excessive in his
desire for the Presidency.   He was the head and choice of a
great political party ; in the principles of that party he fully
believed ; and we think he did truly desire an election to the
Presidency more from conviction than ambition.   This may not
have been the case in 1824, but we believe it was in 1832 and
in 1844.

The history of Henry Clay's Presidential aspirations and de-
feats is little more than the history of a personal feud.   In the

year 1819, it was his fortune to incur the hatred of the best hater then living, — Andrew Jackson. They met for the first time in November, 1815, when the hero of New Orleans came to Washington to consult with the administration respecting the Indian and military affairs of his department. Each of these eminent men truly admired the other. Jackson saw in Clay the civil hero of the war, whose fiery eloquence had powerfully seconded its military heroes. Clay beheld in Jackson the man whose gallantry and skill had done most to justify the war in the sight of the people. They became immediately and cordially intimate. Jackson engaged to visit Ashland in the course of the next summer, and spend a week there. On every occasion when Mr. Clay spoke of the heroes of the war, he bestowed on Jackson the warmest praise.

In 1818 General Jackson invaded Florida, put to death two Indian chiefs in cold blood, and executed two British subjects, Arbuthnot and Armbrister.* During the twenty-seven days' debate upon these proceedings, in 1819, the Speaker sided with those who disapproved them, and he delivered a set speech against Jackson. This speech, though it did full justice to General Jackson's motives, and contained a fine eulogium upon his previous services, gave the General deadly offence. Such was Jackson's self-love that he could not believe in the honesty of any opposition to him, but invariably attributed such opposition to low personal motives. Now it was a fact well known to Jackson, that Henry Clay had expected the appointment of Secretary of State under Mr. Monroe; and it was part of the gossip of the time that Mr. Monroe's preference of Mr. Adams was the reason of Clay's occasional opposition to measures favored by the administration. We do not believe this, because the measures which Mr. Clay opposed were such as he *must* have disapproved, and which well-informed posterity will forever disapprove. After much debate in the Cabinet, Mr. Monroe, who was peculiarly bound to Jackson, and who had reasons of his own for not offending him, determined to sustain him *in toto* both at home and in

* This is the correct spelling of the name, as we learn from a living relative of the unfortunate man. It has been hitherto spelled Ambrister.

the courts of Spain and England.   Hence, in condemning General Jackson, Mr. Clay was again in opposition to the administration; and the General of course concluded, that the Speaker designed, in ruining him, merely to further his own political schemes.   How he boiled with fury against Mr. Clay, his published letters amusingly attest.   " The hypocrisy and baseness of Clay," wrote the General, " in pretending friendship to me, and endeavoring to crush the Executive through me, makes me despise the villain."

Jackson, as we all know, was triumphantly sustained by the House.   In fact, Mr. Clay's speech was totally unworthy of the occasion.   Instead of argument and fact, he gave the House and the galleries beautiful declamation.   The evidence was before him; he had it in his hands; but, instead of getting up his case with patient assiduity, and exhibiting the damning proofs of Jackson's misconduct, he merely glanced over the mass of papers, fell into some enormous blunders, passed over some most material points, and then endeavored to supply all deficiencies by an imposing eloquence.   He even acknowledges that he had not examined the testimony.   " It is *possible*," said he, " that a critical examination of the evidence *would* show" that Arbuthnot was an innocent trader.   We have had occasion to examine that evidence since, and we can testify that this conjecture was correct.   But why was it a *conjecture?*   Why did Mr. Clay neglect to convert the conjecture into certainty?   It fell to him, as representing the civilization and humanity of the United States, to vindicate the memory of an honorable old man, who had done all that was possible to prevent the war, and who had been ruthlessly murdered by men wearing the uniform of American soldiers.   It fell to him to bar the further advancement of a man most unfit for civil rule.   To this duty he was imperatively called, but he only half did it, and thus exasperated the tiger without disabling him.

Four years passed.   In December, 1823, General Jackson reappeared in Washington to take his seat in the Senate, to which he had been elected by his wire-pullers for the purpose of promoting his interests as a candidate for the Presidency.   Before

he left home two or three of his friends had besought him to
assume a mild and conciliatory demeanor at the capitol. It would
never do, they told him, for a candidate for the Presidency to
threaten to cut off the ears of gentlemen who disapproved his
public conduct; he must restrain himself and make friends.
This advice he followed. He was reconciled with General Winfield Scott, whom, in 1817, he had styled an " assassin," a " hector-
ing bully," and an " intermeddling pimp and spy of the War Office." He made friends with Colonel Thomas H. Benton, with
whom he had fought in the streets of Nashville, while he still
carried in his body a bullet received in that bloody affray. With
Henry Clay, too, he resumed friendly intercourse, met him twice
at dinner-parties, rode and exchanged visits with him, and attended one of the Speaker's Congressional dinners.

When next these party chieftains met, in the spring of 1825, it
was about to devolve upon the House of Representatives to decide which of three men should be the next President, — Jackson, Adams, or Crawford. They exchanged visits as before ; Mr.
Clay being desirous, as he said, to show General Jackson that, in
the vote which he had determined to give, he was influenced only
by public considerations. No reader needs to be informed that
Mr. Clay and his friends were able to decide the election, and
that they decided it in favor of Mr. Adams. We believe that
Mr. Clay was wrong in so doing. As a Democrat he ought, we
think, to have been willing to gratify the plurality of his fellow-
citizens, who had voted for General Jackson. His motives we
fully believe to have been disinterested. Indeed, it was plainly
intimated to him that, if he gave the Presidency to General
Jackson, General Jackson would make him his heir apparent, or,
in other words, his Secretary of State.

The anger of General Jackson at his disappointment was not
the blind and wild fury of his earlier days ; it was a deeper, a
deadlier wrath, which he governed and concealed in order to
wreak a feller vengeance. On the evening of the day on which
the election in the House occurred there was a levee at the
Presidential mansion, which General Jackson attended. Who,
that saw him dart forward and grasp Mr. Adams cordially by the

hand, could have supposed that he then entirely believed that Mr. Adams had stolen the Presidency from him by a corrupt bargain with Mr. Clay? Who could have supposed that he and his friends had been, for fourteen days, hatching a plot to blast the good name of Mr. Adams and Mr. Clay, by spreading abroad the base insinuation that Clay had been bought over to the support of Adams by the promise of the first place in the Cabinet? Who could have supposed that, on his way home to Tennessee, while the newspapers were paragraphing his magnanimity in defeat, as shown by his behavior at the levee, he would denounce Adams and Clay, in bar-rooms and public places, as guilty of a foul compact to frustrate the wishes of the people?

It was calumny's masterpiece. It was a rare stroke of art to get an old dotard of a member of Congress to publish, twelve days *before* the election, that Mr. Clay had agreed to vote for Mr. Adams, and that Mr. Adams had agreed to reward him by the office of Secretary of State. When the vote had been given and the office conferred, how plausible, how convincing, the charge of bargain!

It is common to censure Mr. Clay for accepting office under Mr. Adams. We honor him for his courage in doing so. Having made Mr. Adams President, it had been unlike the gallant Kentuckian to shrink from the possible odium of the act by refusing his proper place in the administration. The calumny which anticipated his acceptance of office was a defiance: *Take office if you dare!* It was simply worthy of Henry Clay to accept the challenge, and brave all the consequences of what he had deliberately and conscientiously done.

In the office of Secretary of State Mr. Clay exhibited an admirable talent for the despatch of business. He negotiated an unusual number of useful treaties. He exerted himself to secure a recognition of the principles, that, in time of war, private property should enjoy on the ocean the same protection as on land, and that paper blockades are not to be regarded. He econded Mr. Adams in his determination not to remove from office any man on account of his previous or present opposition to the administration; and he carried this policy so far, that, in selecting the newspapers for the publication of the laws, he refused to consider their political character. This was in strict accordance with the practice of all previous administrations; but it is so pleasant to recur to the times when that honorable policy prevailed, that we cannot help alluding to it. In his intercourse with foreign ministers, Mr. Clay had an opportunity to display all the charms of an unequalled courtesy: they remained his friends long after he had retired. His Wednesday dinners and his pleasant evening receptions were remembered for many years. How far he sympathized with Mr. Adams's extravagant dreams of a system of national works that should rival the magnificent structures of ancient Rome, or with the extreme opinions of his colleague, Mr. Rush, as to the power and importance of government, we do not know. He worked twelve hours a day in his office, he tells us, and was content therewith. He was the last high officer of the government to fight a duel. That bloodless contest between the Secretary of State and John Randolph was as romantic and absurd as a duel could well be. Colonel Benton's narrative of it is at once the most amusing and the most affecting piece of gossip which our political annals contain. Randolph, as the most unmanageable of members of Congress, had been for fifteen years a thorn in Mr. Clay's side, and Clay's later politics had been most exasperating to Mr. Randolph; but the two men loved one another in their hearts, after all. Nothing has ever exceeded the thorough-bred courtesy and tender consideration with which they set about the work of putting one another to death; and their joy was unbounded when, after the second fire, each discovered that the other was unharmed. If all duels could have such a result, duelling would be the prettiest thing in the world.

The election of 1828 swept the administration from power. No man has ever bowed more gracefully to the decision of the people than Henry Clay. His remarks at the public dinner given him in Washington, on his leaving for home, were entirely admirable. Andrew Jackson, he said, had wronged him, but he was now the Chief Magistrate of his country, and, as such, he should be treated with decorum, and his public acts judged with candor.   His journey to Ashland was more like the progress of a victor than the return homeward of a rejected statesman.

He now entered largely into his favorite branch of rural business, the raising of superior animals.   Fifty merino sheep were driven over the mountains from Pennsylvania to his farm, and he imported from England some Durham and Hertford cattle. He had an Arabian horse in his stable.   For the improvement of the breed of mules, he imported an ass from Malta, and another from Spain.   Pigs, goats, and dogs he also raised, and endeavored to improve.   His slaves being about fifty in number, he was able to carry on the raising of hemp and corn, as well as the breeding of stock, and both on a considerable scale.   Mrs. Clay sent every morning to the principal hotel of Lexington thirty gallons of milk, and her husband had large consignments to make to his factor in New Orleans.   His letters of this period show how he delighted in his animals and his growing crops, and how thoughtfully he considered the most trifling details of management.   His health improved.   He told his old friend, Washington Irving, that he found it was as good for men as for beasts to be turned out to grass occasionally.   Though not without domestic afflictions, he was very happy in his home.   One of his sons graduated second at West Point, and two of his daughters were happily married.   He was, perhaps, a too indulgent father; but his children loved him most tenderly, and were guided by his opinion.   It is pleasing to read in the letters of his sons to him such passages as this: "You tell me that you wish me to receive your opinions, not as commands, but as advice.   Yet I must consider them as commands, doubly binding; for they proceed from one so vastly my superior in all respects, and to whom I am under such great obligations, that the mere intimation of an opinion will be sufficient to govern my conduct."

The President, meanwhile, was paying such homage to the farmer of Ashland as no President of the United States had ever paid to a private individual.   General Jackson's principal object — the object nearest his heart — appears to have been to wound and injure Henry Clay.   His appointments, his measures, and his vetoes seem to have been chiefly inspired by resentment against him. Ingham of Pennsylvania, who had taken the lead in that State in giving currency to the " bargain " calumny, was appointed Secretary of the Treasury. Eaton, who had aided in the original concoction of that foul slander, was appointed Secretary of War. Branch, who received the appointment of Secretary of the Navy, was one of the few Senators who had voted and spoken against the confirmation of Henry Clay to the office of Secretary of State in 1825 ; and Berrien, Attorney-General, was another. Barry, appointed Postmaster-General, was the Kentuckian who had done most to inflict upon Mr. Clay the mortification of seeing his own Kentucky siding against him. John Randolph, Clay's recent antagonist in a duel, and the most unfit man in the world for a diplomatic mission, was sent Minister to Russia. Pope, an old Kentucky Federalist, Clay's opponent and competitor for half a lifetime, received the appointment of Governor of the Territory of Arkansas. General Harrison, who had generously defended Clay against the charge of bargain and corruption, was recalled from a foreign mission on the fourth day after General Jackson's accession to power, though he had scarcely reached the country to which he was accredited. In the place of General Harrison was sent a Kentuckian peculiarly obnoxious to Mr. Clay. In Kentucky itself there was a clean sweep from office of Mr. Clay's friends ; not one man of them was left. His brother-in-law, James Brown, was instantly recalled from a diplomatic post in Europe. Kendall, the chief of the Kitchen Cabinet, had once been tutor to Mr. Clay's children, and had won the favor of Jackson by lending a dexterous hand in carrying Kentucky against his benefactor. Francis Blair, editor of the Globe, had also been the particular friend and correspondent of Mr. Clay, but had turned against him. From the Departments in Washington, all of Mr. Clay's known friends were immediately removed, except a few who had made themselves indispensable, and a few others whom Mr. Van Buren contrived to spare. In nearly every instance, the men who succeeded to the best places had made themselves conspicuous by their vituperation of Mr. Clay. He was strictly correct when he said, " Every movement of the President is dictated by personal hostility toward me "; but he was deceived when he added that it all conduced to his benefit. Every mind that was both just and well-informed warmed toward the object of such pitiless and demoniac wrath but in what land are minds just and well-informed a majority .

It was not only the appointments and removals that were aimed at Mr. Clay. The sudden expulsion of gray hairs from the offices they had honored, the precipitation of hundreds of families into poverty, — this did not satisfy the President's vengeance. He assailed Henry Clay in his first Message. In recommending a change in the mode of electing the President, he said that, when the election devolves upon the House of Representatives, circumstances may give the power of deciding the election to one man. "May he not be tempted," added the President, " to name his reward?" He vetoed appropriations for the Cumberland Road, because the name and the honor of Henry Clay were peculiarly identified with that work. He destroyed the Bank of the United States, because he believed its power and influence were to be used in favor of Mr. Clay's elevation to the Presidency. He took care, in his Message vetoing the recharter of the Bank, to employ some of the arguments which Clay had used in opposing the recharter of the United States Bank in 1811. Miserably sick and infirm as he was, he consented to stand for re-election, because there was no other candidate strong enough to defeat Henry Clay ; and he employed all his art, and the whole power of the administration, during his second term, to smooth Mr. Van Buren's path to the Presidency, to the exclusion of Henry Clay. Plans were formed, too, and engagements made, the grand object of which was to keep Clay from the Presidency, even after Mr. Van Buren should have served his anticipated eight years. General Jackson left Washington in 1837, expecting that Martin Van Buren would be President until 1845, and that he would then be succeeded by Thomas H. Benton. Nothing prevented the fulfilment of this programme but the financial collapse of 1837, the effects of which continued during the whole of Mr. Van Buren's term, and caused his defeat in 1840.

Mr. Clay accepted the defiance implied in General Jackson

conduct. He reappeared in Washington in 1831, in the character of Senator and candidate for the Presidency. His journey to Washington was again a triumphal progress, and again the galleries were crowded to hear him speak. A great and brilliant party gathered round him, strong in talents, character, property, and supposed to be strong in numbers. He at once proved himself to be a most unskilful party leader. Every movement of his in *that* character was a mistake. He was precipitate when he ought to have been cautious, and cautious when nothing but audacity could have availed. The first subject upon which he was called upon to act was the tariff. The national debt being within two or three years of liquidation, Calhoun threatening nullification, and Jackson vetoing all internal improvement bills, it was necessary to provide against an enormous surplus. Clay maintained that the *protective* duties should remain intact, and that only those duties should be reduced which protected no American interest. This was done ; the revenue was reduced three millions ; and the surplus was as threatening as before. It was *impossible* to save the protective duties entire without raising too much revenue. Mr. Clay, as it seems to us, should have plainly said this to the manufacturers, and compelled his party in Congress to warn and save them by making a judicious cut at the protective duties in 1832. This would have deprived Calhoun of his pretext, and prepared the way for a safe and gradual reduction of duties in the years following. Such was the prosperity of the country in 1832, that the three millions lost to the revenue by Mr. Clay's bill were likely to be made up to it in three years by the mere increase in the imports and land sales.

Mr. Clay's next misstep was one of precipitation. General Jackson, after a three years' war upon the Bank, was alarmed at the outcry of its friends, and sincerely desired to make peace with it. We know, from the avowals of the men who stood nearest his person at the time, that he not only wished to keep the Bank question out of the Presidential campaign of 1832, but that he was willing to consent, on very easy conditions, to a recharter. It was Mr. Clay's commanding influence that induced the directors of the Bank to press for a recharter in 1832, and force the

President to retraction or a veto. So ignorant was this able and high-minded man of human nature and of the American people, that he supposed a popular enthusiasm could be kindled in behalf of a *bank!* Such was the infatuation of some of his friends, that they went to the expense of circulating copies of the veto message gratis, for the purpose of lessening the vote for its author! Mr. Clay was ludicrously deceived as to his strength with the masses of the people, — the *dumb* masses, — those who have no eloquent orators, no leading newspapers, no brilliant pamphleteers, to speak for them, but who assert themselves with decisive effect on election day.

It was another capital error in Mr. Clay, as the leader of a party, to run at all against General Jackson. He should have hoarded his prestige for 1836, when the magical name of Jackson would no longer captivate the ignorant voter. Mr. Clay's defeat in 1832, so unexpected, so overwhelming, lamed him for life as a candidate for the Presidency. He lost faith in his star. In 1836, when there *was* a chance of success, — just a chance, — he would not suffer his name to appear in the canvass. The vote of the opposition was divided among three candidates, — General Harrison, Hugh L. White, and Daniel Webster; and Mr. Van Buren, of course, had an easy victory. Fortunately for his own happiness, Mr. Clay's desire for the Presidency diminished as his chances of reaching it diminished. That desire had never been morbid, it now became exceedingly moderate; nor do we believe that, after his crushing defeat of 1832, he ever had much expectation of winning the prize. He knew too well the arts by which success is assured, to believe that an honorable man could be elected to the Presidency by honorable means only.

Three other attempts were made to raise him to the highest office, and it was always Andrew Jackson who struck him down. In 1840, he was set aside by his party, and General Harrison nominated in his stead. This was Jackson's doing; for it was the great defeat of 1832 which had robbed Clay of prestige, and it was General Jackson's uniform success that suggested the selection of a military candidate. Again, in 1844, when the Texas issue was presented to the people, it was by the adroit use of

General Jackson's name that the question of annexation was precipitated upon the country. In 1848, a military man was again nominated, to the exclusion of Henry Clay.

Mr. Clay used to boast of his consistency, averring that he h; l never changed his opinion upon a public question but once. W think he was much too consistent. A notable example of an ex cessive consistency was his adhering to the project of a United States Bank, when there was scarcely a possibility of establishing one, and his too steadfast opposition to the harmless expedient of the Sub-treasury. The Sub-treasury system has now been in operation for a quarter of a century. Call it a bungling and antiquated system, if you will; it has nevertheless answered its purpose. The public money is taken out of politics. If the few millions lying idle in the "Strong Box" do no good, they at least do no harm; and we have no overshadowing national bank to compete with private capital, and to furnish, every few years, a theme for demagogues. Mr. Clay saw in the Sub-treasury the ruin of the Republic. In his great speech of 1838, in opposition to it, he uttered, in his most solemn and impressive manner, the following words: —

"Mr. President, a great, novel, and untried measure is perseveringly urged upon the acceptance of Congress. That it is pregnant with tremendous consequences, for good or evil, is undeniable, and admitted by all. We firmly believe that it will be *fatal to the best interests of this country, and ultimately subversive of its liberties.*"

No one acquainted with Mr. Clay, and no man, himself sincere, who reads this eloquent and most labored speech, can doubt Mr. Clay's sincerity. Observe the awful solemnity of his first sentences: —

"I have seen some public service, passed through many troubled times, and often addressed public assemblies, in this Capitol and elsewhere but never before have I risen in a deliberative body under more c\ pressed feelings, or with a deeper sense of awful responsibility. Never before have I risen to express my opinions upon any public measure fraught with such tremendous consequences to the welfare and prosperity of the country, and so perilous to the liberties of the people, as I solemnly believe the bill under consideration will be. If you knew, sir, what sleepless hours reflection upon it has cost me, if you knew with what fervor and sincerity I have implored Divine assistance to strengthen and sustain me in my opposition to it, I should have credit with you, at least, for the sincerity of my convictions, if I shall be so unfortunate as not to have your concurrence as to the dangerous character of the measure. And I have thanked my God that he has prolonged my life until the present time, to enable me to exert myself, in the service of my country, against a project far transcending in pernicious tendency any that I have ever had occasion to consider. I thank him for the health I am permitted to enjoy; I thank him for the soft and sweet repose which I experienced last night; I thank him for the bright and glorious sun which shines upon us this day."

And what *was* the question at issue? It was whether Nicholas Biddle should have the custody of the public money at Philadelphia, and use the average balance in discounting notes; or whether Mr. Cisco should keep it at New York in an exceedingly strong vault, and not use any of it in discounting notes.

As the leader of a national party Mr. Clay failed utterly; for he was neither bad enough to succeed by foul means, nor skilful enough to succeed by fair means. But in his character of patriot, orator, or statesman, he had some brilliant successes in his later years. When Jackson was ready to concede *all* to the Nullifiers, and that suddenly, to the total ruin of the protected manufacturers, it was Clay's tact, parliamentary experience, and personal power that interposed the compromise tariff, which reduced duties gradually instead of suddenly. The Compromise of 1850, also, which postponed the Rebellion ten years, was chiefly his work. That Compromise was the best then attainable; and we think that the country owes gratitude to the man who deferred the Rebellion to a time when the United States was strong enough to subdue it.

Posterity, however, will read the speeches of Mr. Clay upon the various slavery questions agitated from 1835 to 1850 with mingled feelings of admiration and regret. A man compelled to live in the midst of slavery must hate it and actively oppose it, or else be, in some degree, corrupted by it. As Thomas Jefferson came at length to acquiesce in slavery, and live contentedly with it, so did Henry Clay lose some of his early horror of the system, and accept it as a necessity. True, he never lapsed into the imbecility of pretending to think slavery right or best, but he saw no way of escaping from it; and when asked his opinion as to the final solution of the problem, he could only throw it upon Providence. Providence, he said, would remove the evil in its own good time, and nothing remained for men but to cease the agitation of the subject. His first efforts, as his last, were directed to the silencing of both parties, but most especially the Abolitionists, whose character and aims he misconceived. With John C. Calhoun sitting near him in the Senate-chamber, and with fire-eaters swarming at the other end of the Capitol, he could, as late as 1843, cast the whole blame of the slavery excitement upon the few individuals at the North who were beginning to discern the ulterior designs of the Nullifiers. Among his letters of 1843 there is one addressed to a friend who was about to write a pamphlet against the Abolitionists. Mr. Clay gave him an outline of what he thought the pamphlet ought to be.

" The great aim and object of your tract should be to arouse the laboring classes in the Free States against abolition. Depict the consequences to them of immediate abolition. The slaves, being free, would be dispersed throughout the Union; they would enter into competition with the free laborer, with the American, the Irish, the German; reduce his wages; be confounded with him, and affect his moral and social standing. And as the ultras go for both abolition and amalgamation, show that their object is to unite in marriage the laboring white man and the laboring black man, and to reduce the white laboring man to the despised and degraded condition of the black man.

" I would show their opposition to colonization. Show its humane, religious, and patriotic aims; that they are to separate those whom God has separated. Why do the Abolitionists oppose colonization? To keep and amalgamate together the two races, in violation of God's will, and to keep the blacks here, that they may interfere with, degrade, and debase the laboring whites. Show that the British nation is co-operating with the Abolitionists, for the purpose of dissolving the Union, etc."

This is so very absurd, that, if we did not know it to express Mr. Clay's habitual feeling at that time, we should be compelled to see in it, not Henry Clay, but the candidate for the Presi

dency. He really thought so in 1843. He was perfectly convinced that the white race and the black could not exist together
on equal terms. One of his last acts was to propose emancipation in Kentucky; but it was an essential feature of his plan to
transport the emancipated blacks to Africa. When we look over
Mr. Clay's letters and speeches of those years, we meet with so
much that is short-sighted and grossly erroneous, that we are
obliged to confess that this man, gifted as he was, and dear as
his memory is to us, shared the judicial blindness of his order
Its baseness and arrogance he did not share. His head was often
wrong, but his heart was generally right. It atones for all his
mere errors of abstract opinion, that he was never admitted to
the confidence of the Nullifiers, and that he uniformly voted
against the measures inspired by them. He was against the un-
timely annexation of Texas; he opposed the rejection of the
anti-slavery petitions; and he declared that no earthly power
should ever induce him to consent to the addition of one acre of
slave territory to the possessions of the United States.

It is proof positive of a man's essential soundness, if he im-
proves as he grows old. Henry Clay's last years were his best;
he ripened to the very end. His friends remarked the moderation of his later opinions, and his charity for those who had
injured him most. During the last ten years of his life no one
ever heard him utter a harsh judgment of an opponent. Domestic afflictions, frequent and severe, had chastened his heart; his
six affectionate and happy daughters were dead; one son was a
hopeless lunatic in an asylum; another was not what such a
father had a right to expect; and, at length, his favorite and
most promising son, Henry, in the year 1847, fell at the battle
of Buena Vista. It was just after this last crushing loss, and
probably in consequence of it, that he was baptized and confirmed
a member of the Episcopal Church.

When, in 1849, he reappeared in the Senate, to assist, if possible, in removing the slavery question from politics, he was an in
firm and serious, but not sad, old man of seventy-two. He never
lost his cheerfulness or his faith, but he felt deeply for his dis
tracted country. During that memorable session of Congress he

spoke seventy times. Often extremely sick and feeble, scarcely able, with the assistance of a friend's arm, to climb the steps of the Capitol, he was never absent on the days when the Compromise was to be debated. It appears to be well attested, that his last great speech on the Compromise was the immediate cause of his death. On the morning on which he began his speech, he was accompanied by a clerical friend, to whom he said, on reaching the long flight of steps leading to the Capitol, "Will you lend me your arm, my friend? for I find myself quite weak and exhausted this morning." Every few steps he was obliged to stop and take breath. "Had you not better defer your speech?" asked the clergyman. "My dear friend," said the dying orator, "I consider our country in danger; and if I can be the means, in any measure, of averting that danger, my health or life is of little consequence." When he rose to speak, it was but too evident that he was unfit for the task he had undertaken. But, as he kindled with his subject, his cough left him, and his bent form resumed all its wonted erectness and majesty. He may, in the prime of his strength, have spoken with more energy, but never with so much pathos and grandeur. His speech lasted two days, and, though he lived two years longer, he never recovered from the effects of the effort. Toward the close of the second day, his friends repeatedly proposed an adjournment; but he would not desist until he had given complete utterance to his feelings. He said afterwards that he was not sure, if he gave way to an adjournment, that he should ever be able to resume.

In the course of this long debate, Mr. Clay said some things to which the late war has given a new interest. He knew, at last, what the fire-eaters meant. He perceived now that it was not the few abhorred Abolitionists of the Northern States from whom danger to the Union was to be apprehended. On one occasion allusion was made to a South Carolina hot-head, who had publicly proposed to raise the flag of disunion. Thunders of applause broke from the galleries when Mr. Clay retorted by saying, that, if Mr. Rhett had really made that proposition, and should follow it up by corresponding acts, he would be a TRAITOR; "and,

3   D

added Mr. Clay, "I hope he will meet a traitor's fate." When
the chairman had succeeded in restoring silence, Mr. Clay made
that celebrated declaration which was so frequently quoted in
1861: "If Kentucky to-morrow should unfurl the banner of resistance unjustly, I will never fight under that banner. I owe a
paramount allegiance to the whole Union, — a subordinate one to
my own State." He said also: "If any one State, or a portion
of the people of any State, choose to place themselves in military
array against the government of the Union, I am for trying the
strength of the government. I am for ascertaining whether we
have a government or not." Again: "The Senator speaks of
Virginia being my country. This UNION, sir, is my country;
the thirty States are my country; Kentucky is my country, and
Virginia no more than any State in the Union." And yet again:
"There are those who think that the Union must be preserved
by an exclusive reliance upon love and reason. That is not my
opinion. I have some confidence in this instrumentality; but,
depend upon it that no human government can exist without the
power of applying force, and the actual application of it in extreme cases."

Who can estimate the influence of these clear and emphatic
utterances ten years after? The crowded galleries, the numberless newspaper reports, the quickly succeeding death of the great
orator, — all aided to give them currency and effect. We shall
never know how many wavering minds they aided to decide in
1861. Not that Mr. Clay really believed the conflict would
occur: he was mercifully permitted to die in the conviction that
the Compromise of 1850 had removed all immediate danger, and
greatly lessened that of the future. Far indeed was he from
foreseeing that the ambition of a man born in New England,
calling himself a disciple of Andrew Jackson, would, within five
years, destroy all compromises, and render all future compromise
impossible, by procuring the repeal of the first, — the Missouri
Compromise of 1821.

Henry Clay was formed by nature to please, to move, and to
impress his countrymen. Never was there a more captivating
presence   We remember hearing Horace Greeley say that, if a

man only saw Henry Clay's back, he would know that it was the back of a distinguished man. How his presence filled a drawing-room! With what an easy sway he held captive ten acres of mass-meeting! And, in the Senate, how skilfully he showed himself respectfully conscious of the galleries, without appearing to address them! Take him for all in all, we must regard him as the first of American orators; but posterity will not assign him that rank, because posterity will not hear that matchless voice, will not see those large gestures, those striking attitudes, that grand manner, which gave to second-rate composition first-rate effect. He could not have been a great statesman, if he had been ever so greatly endowed. While slavery existed no states-manship was possible, except that which was temporary and tem-porizing. The thorn, we repeat, was in the flesh; and the doctors were all pledged to try and cure the patient without extracting it. They could do nothing but dress the wound, put on this salve and that, give the sufferer a little respite from anguish, and, after a brief interval, repeat the operation. Of all these physicians Henry Clay was the most skilful and effective. He both handled the sore place with consummate dexterity, and kept up the con-stitution of the patient by stimulants, which enabled him, at last, to live through the appalling operation which removed the cause of his agony.

Henry Clay was a man of honor and a gentleman. He kept his word. He was true to his friends, his party, and his convic-tions. He paid his debts and his son's debts. The instinct of solvency was very strong in him. He had a religion, of which the main component parts were self-respect and love of country. These were supremely authoritative with him; he would not do anything which he felt to be beneath Henry Clay, or which he thought would be injurious to the United States. Five times a candidate for the Presidency, no man can say that he ever pur-chased support by the promise of an office, or by any other en-gagement savoring of dishonor. Great talents and a great under-standing are seldom bestowed on the same individual. Mr. Clay's usefulness as a statesman was limited by his talent as an orator. He relied too much on his oratory; he was never such a student as a man intrusted with public business ought to be. Hence he originated nothing and established nothing. His speeches will long be interesting as the relics of a magnificent and dazzling personality, and for the light they cast upon the history of parties; but they add scarcely anything to the intellectual property of the nation. Of American orators he was the first whose speeches were ever collected in a volume. Millions read them with admiration in his lifetime; but already they have sunk to the level of the works "without which no gentleman's library is complete," — works which every one possesses and no one reads.

Henry Clay, regarded as a subject for biography, is still untouched. Campaign Lives of him can be collected by the score; and the Rev. Calvin Colton wrote three volumes purporting to be the Life of Henry Clay. Mr. Colton was a very honest gentleman, and not wanting in ability; but writing, as he did, in Mr. Clay's own house, he became, as it were, enchanted by his subject. He was enamored of Mr. Clay to such a degree that his pen ran into eulogy by an impulse which was irresistible, and which he never attempted to resist. In point of arrangement, too, his work is chaos come again. A proper biography of Mr. Clay would be one of the most entertaining and instructive of works. It would embrace the ever-memorable rise and first triumphs of the Democratic party; the wild and picturesque life of the early settlers of Kentucky; the war of 1812; Congress from 1806 to 1852; the fury and corruption of Jackson's reign; and the three great compromises which postponed the Rebellion. Al! the leading men and all the striking events of our history would contribute something to the interest and value of the work. Why go to antiquity or to the Old World for subjects, when such a subject as this remains unwritten?

DANIEL WEBSTER.

DANIEL WEBSTER.

OF words spoken in recent times, few have touched so many hearts as those uttered by Sir Walter Scott on his death-bed. There has seldom been so much of mere enjoyment crowded into the compass of one lifetime as there was into his. Even his work — all of his best work — was only more elaborate and keenly relished play; for story-telling, the occupation of his maturity, had first been the delight of his childhood, and remained always his favorite recreation. Triumph rewarded his early efforts, and admiration followed him to the grave. Into no human face could this man look, nor into any crowd of faces which did not return his glance with a gaze of admiring love. He lived precisely where and how it was happiest for him to live; and he had above most men of his time that disposition of mind which makes the best of bad fortune and the most of good. But when his work and his play were all done, and he came calmly to review his life, and the life of man on earth, this was the sum of his reflections, this was what he had to say to the man to whom he had confided his daughter's happiness: "Lockhart, I may have but a minute to speak to you. My dear, be a good man, — be virtuous, — be religious, — be a good man. Nothing else will give you any comfort when you come to lie here."

So do we all feel in view of the open coffin, much as we may differ as to what it *is* to be good, virtuous, and religious. Was this man, who lies dead here before us, faithful to his trust? Was he sincere, pure, just, and benevolent? Did he help civilization, or was he an obstacle in its way? Did he ripen and improve to the end, or did he degenerate and go astray? These are the questions which are silently considered when we look upon the still countenance of death, and especially when the departed was a person who influenced his generation long and powerfully. Usually it is only the last of these questions which mortals can answer with any certainty; but from the answer to that one we infer the answers to all the others. As it is only the wise who learn, so it is only the good who improve. When we see a man gaining upon his faults as he advances in life, when we find him more self-contained and cheerful, more learned and inquisitive, more just and considerate, more single-eyed and noble in his aims, at fifty than he was at forty, and at seventy than he was at fifty, we have the best reason perceptible by human eyes for concluding that he has been governed by right principles and good feelings. We have a right to pronounce such a person *good*, and he is justified in believing us.

The three men most distinguished in public life during the last forty years in the United States were Henry Clay, John C. Calhoun, and Daniel Webster. Henry Clay improved as he grew old. He was a venerable, serene, and virtuous old man. The impetuosity, restlessness, ambition, and love of display, and the detrimental habits of his earlier years, gave place to tranquillity, temperance, moderation, and a patriotism without the alloy of personal objects. Disappointment had chastened, not soured him. Public life enlarged, not narrowed him. The city of Washington purified, not corrupted him. He came there a gambler, a drinker, a profuse consumer of tobacco, and a turner of night into day. He overcame the worst of those habits very early in his residence at the capital. He came to Washington to exhibit his talents, he remained there to serve his country; nor of his country did he ever think the less, or serve her less zealously, because she denied him the honor he coveted for thirty years. We cannot say this of Calhoun. He degenerated frightfully during the last twenty years of his life. His energy degenerated into intensity, and his patriotism narrowed into sectionalism. He became unteachable, incapable of considering an opinion opposite to his own, or even a fact that did not favor it. Exempt by his bodily constitution from all temptation to physical

excesses, his body was worn out by the intense, unhealthy working of his mind. False opinions falsely held and intolerantly
maintained were the debauchery that sharpened the lines of his
face, and converted his voice into a bark. Peace, health, and
growth early became impossible to him, for there was a canker
in the heart of the man. His once not dishonorable desire of the
Presidency became at last an infuriate lust after it, which his
natural sincerity compelled him to reveal even while wrathfully
denying it. He considered that he had been defrauded of the
prize, and he had some reason for thinking so. Some men
avenge their wrongs by the pistol, others by invective; but the
only weapons which this man could wield were abstract propositions. From the hills of South Carolina he hurled paradoxes at
General Jackson, and appealed from the dicta of Mrs. Eaton's
drawing-room to a hair-splitting theory of States' Rights. Fifteen hundred thousand armed men have since sprung up from
those harmless-looking dragon's teeth, so recklessly sown in the
hot Southern soil.

Of the three men whom we have named, Daniel Webster was
incomparably the most richly endowed by nature. In his lifetime it was impossible to judge him aright. His presence usually overwhelmed criticism; his intimacy always fascinated it.
It so happened, that he grew to his full stature and attained his
utmost development in a community where human nature appears to be undergoing a process of diminution, — where people
are smaller-boned, less muscular, more nervous, and more susceptible than their ancestors. He possessed, in consequence, an
enormous physical magnetism, as we term it, over his fellow-
citizens, apart from the natural influence of his talents and understanding. Fidgety men were quieted in his presence, women
were spellbound by it, and the busy, anxious public contemplated
his majestic calm with a feeling of relief, as well as admiration.
Large numbers of people in New England, for many years, re-
posed upon Daniel Webster. He represented to them the majesty and the strength of the government of the United States.
He gave them a sense of safety. Amid the flighty politics of the
time and the loud insincerities of Washington, there seemed one

3 *

solid thing in America, so long as he sat in an arm-chair of the Senate-chamber.   When he appeared in State Street, slowly pacing, with an arm behind him, business was brought to an absolute stand-still.   As the whisper passed along, the windows filled with clerks, pen in mouth, peering out to catch a glimpse of the man whom they had seen fifty times before; while the bankers and merchants hastened forth to give him salutation, or exchange a passing word, happy if they could but catch his eye.   At home, and in a good mood, he was reputed to be as entertaining a man as New England ever held, — a gambolling, jocund leviathan out on the sea-shore, and in the library overflowing with every kind of knowledge that can be acquired without fatigue, and received without preparation.   Mere celebrity, too, is dazzling to some minds.   While, therefore, this imposing person lived among us, he was blindly worshipped by many, blindly hated by some, calmly considered by very few.   To this hour he is a great influence in the United States.   Perhaps, with the abundant material now accessible, it is not too soon to attempt to ascertain how far he was worthy of the estimation in which his fellow-citizens held him, and what place he ought to hold in the esteem of posterity.   At least, it can never be unpleasing to Americans to recur to the most interesting specimen of our kind that has lived in America since Franklin.

He could not have been born in a better place, nor of better stock, nor at a better time, nor reared in circumstances more favorable to harmonious development.   He grew up in the Switzerland of America.   From a hill on his father's New Hampshire farm, he could see most of the noted summits of New England. Granite-topped Kearsarge stood out in bold relief near by, Mount Washington and its attendant peaks, not yet named, bounded the northern horizon like a low, silvery cloud; and the principal heights of the Green Mountains, rising near the Connecticut River, were clearly visible.   The Merrimack, most serviceable of rivers, begins its course a mile or two off, formed by the union of two mountain torrents.   Among those hills, high up, sometimes near the summits, lakes are found, broad, deep, and still; and down the sides run innumerable rills, which form those noisy brooks that rush along the bottom of the hills, where now the roads wind along, shaded by the mountain, and enlivened by the music of the waters. Among these hills there are, here and there, expanses of level country large enough for a farm, with the addition of some fields upon the easier acclivities and woodlands higher up. There was one field of a hundred acres upon Captain Webster's mountain farm so level that a lamb could be seen on any part of it from the windows of the house. Every tourist knows that region now, — that wide, billowy expanse of dark mountains and vivid green fields, dotted with white farm-houses, and streaked with silvery streams. It was rougher, seventy years ago, secluded, hardly accessible, the streams unbridged, the roads of primitive formation; but the worst of the rough work had been done there, and the production of superior human beings had become possible, before the Webster boys were born.

Daniel Webster's father was the strong man of his neighborhood; the very model of a republican citizen and hero, — stalwart, handsome, brave, and gentle. Ebenezer Webster inherited no worldly advantages. Sprung from a line of New Hampshire farmers, he was apprenticed, in his thirteenth year, to another New Hampshire farmer; and when he had served his time, he enlisted as a private soldier in the old French war, and came back from the campaigns about Lake George a captain. He never went to school. Like so many other New England boys, he learned what is essential for the carrying on of business in the chimney-corner, by the light of the fire. He possessed one beautiful accomplishment: he was a grand reader. Unlettered as he was, he greatly enjoyed the more lofty compositions of poets and orators; and his large, sonorous voice enabled him to read them with fine effect. His sons read in his manner, even to his rustic pronunciation of some words. Daniel's calm, clear-cut rendering of certain noted passages — favorites in his early home — was all his father's. There is a pleasing tradition in the neighborhood, of the teamsters who came to Ebenezer Webster's mill saying to one another, when they had discharged their load and tied their horses, "Come, let us go in, and hear little Dan read a psalm." The French war ended, Captain Webster, in compensation for his services, received a grant of land in the mountain wilderness at the head of the Merrimack, where, as miller and farmer, he lived and reared his family. The Revolutionary War summoned this noble yeoman to arms once more. He led forth his neighbors to the strife, and fought at their head, with his old rank of captain, at White Plains and at Bennington, and served valiantly through the war. From that time to the end of his life, though much trusted and employed by his fellow-citizens as legislator, magistrate, and judge, he lived but for one object, — the education and advancement of his children. All men were poor then in New Hampshire, compared with the condition of their descendants. Judge Webster was a poor, and even embarrassed man, to the day of his death. The hardships he had endured as soldier and pioneer made him, as he said, an old man before his time. Rheumatism bent his form, once so erect and vigorous. Black care subdued his spirits, once so joyous and elastic. Such were the fathers of fair New England.

This strong-minded, uncultured man was a Puritan and a Federalist, — a catholic, tolerant, and genial Puritan, an intolerant and almost bigoted Federalist. Washington, Adams, and Hamilton were the civilians highest in his esteem; the good Jefferson he dreaded and abhorred. The French Revolution was mere blackness and horror to him; and when it assumed the form of Napoleon Bonaparte, his heart sided passionately with England in her struggle to extirpate it. His boys were in the fullest sympathy with him in all his opinions and feelings. They, too, were tolerant and untheological Puritans; they, too, were most strenuous Federalists; and neither of them ever recovered from their father's influence, nor advanced much beyond him in their fundamental beliefs. Readers have, doubtless, remarked, in Mr. Webster's oration upon Adams and Jefferson, how the stress of the eulogy falls upon Adams, while cold and scant justice is meted out to the greatest and wisest of our statesmen. It was Ebenezer Webster who spoke that day, with the more melodious voice of his son. There is a tradition in New Hampshire that Judge Webster fell sick on a journey in a town of Republiran politics, and besought the doctor to help him speedily on his way home, saying that he was born a Federalist, had lived a Federalist, and could not die in peace in any but a Federalist town.

Among the ten children of this sturdy patriot and partisan, eight were ordinary mortals, and two most extraordinary, — Ezekiel, born in 1780, and Daniel, born in 1782, — the youngest of his boys. Some of the elder children were even less than ordinary. Elderly residents of the neighborhood speak of one half-brother of Daniel and Ezekiel as penurious and narrow; and the letters of others of the family indicate very plain, good, commonplace people. But these two, the sons of their father's prime, inherited all his grandeur of form and beauty of countenance, his taste for high literature, along with a certain energy of mind that came to them, by some unknown law of nature, from their father's mother. From her Daniel derived his jet-black hair and eyes, and his complexion of burnt gunpowder; though all the rest of the children except one were remarkable for fairness of complexion, and had sandy hair. Ezekiel, who was considered the handsomest man in the United States, had a skin of singular fairness, and light hair. He is vividly remembered in New Hampshire for his marvellous beauty of form and face, his courtly and winning manners, the weight and majesty of his presence. He was a signal refutation of Dr. Holmes's theory, that grand manners and high breeding are the result of several generations of culture. Until he was nineteen, this peerless gentleman worked on a rough mountain farm on the outskirts of civilization, as his ancestors had for a hundred and fifty years before him; but he was refined to the tips of his finger-nails and to the buttons of his coat. Like his more famous brother, he had an artist's eye for the becoming in costume, and a keen sense for all the proprieties and decorums both of public and private life. Limited in his view by the narrowness of his provincial sphere, as well as by inherited prejudices, he was a better man and citizen than his brother, without a touch of his genius. Nor was that half-brother of Daniel, who had the black hair and eyes and gunpowder skin, at all like Daniel, or equal to him in mental power.

There is nothing in our literature more pleasing than the glimpses it affords of the early life of these two brothers ; — Ezekiel, robust, steady-going, persevering, self-denying ; Daniel, careless of work, eager for play, often sick, always slender and weakly, and regarded rather as a burden upon the family than a help to it. His feebleness early habituated him to being a recipient of aid and favor, and it decided his destiny. It has been the custom in New England, from the earliest time, to bring up one son of a prosperous family to a profession, and the one selected was usually the boy who seemed least capable of earning a livelihood by manual labor. Ebenezer Webster, heavily burdened with responsibility all his life long, had most ardently desired to give his elder sons a better education that he had himself enjoyed, but could not. When Daniel was a boy, his large family was beginning to lift his load a little ; the country was filling up ; his farm was more productive, and he felt somewhat more at his ease. His sickly youngest son, because he was sickly, and only for that reason, he chose from his numerous brood to send to an academy, designing to make a schoolmaster of him. We have no reason to believe that any of the family saw anything extraordinary in the boy. Except that he read aloud unusually well, he had given no sign of particular talent, unless it might be that he excelled in catching trout, shooting squirrels, and fighting cocks. His mother, observing his love of play and his equal love of books, said he " would come to something or nothing, she could not tell which " ; but his father, noticing his power over the sympathies of others, and comparing him with his bashful brother, used to remark, that he had fears for Ezekiel, but that Daniel would assuredly make his way in the world. It is certain that the lad himself was totally unconscious of possessing extraordinary talents, and indulged no early dream of greatness. He tells us himself, that he loved but two things in his youth, — play and reading. The rude schools which he trudged two or three miles in the winter every day to attend, taught him scarcely anything. His father's saw-mill, he used to say, was the real school of his youth. When he had set the saw and turned on the water, there would be fifteen minutes of tranquillity before the log again required his attention, during which he sat and absorbed knowledge. "We had so few books," he records in the exquisite fragment of autobiography he has left us, "that to read them once or twice was nothing. We thought they were all to be got by heart."

How touching the story, so well known, of the mighty struggle and long self-sacrifice it cost this family to get the youth through college! The whole expense did not average one hundred and fifty dollars a year; but it seemed to the boy so vast and unattainable a good, that, when his father announced his purpose to attempt it, he was completely overcome; his head was dizzy; his tongue was paralyzed; he could only press his father's hands and shed tears. Slender indeed was his preparation for Dartmouth. From the day when he took his first Latin lesson to that on which he entered college was thirteen months. He could translate Cicero's orations with some ease, and make out with difficulty and labor the easiest sentences of the Greek Reader, and that was the whole of what was called his "preparation" for college. In June, 1797, he did not know the Greek alphabet; in August of the same year he was admitted to the Freshman Class of Dartmouth on engaging to supply his deficiencies by extra study.

Neither at college nor at any time could Daniel Webster be properly called a student, and well he knew it. Many a time he has laughed, in his jovial, rollicking manner, at the preposterous reputation for learning a man can get by bringing out a fragment of curious knowledge at the right moment at college. He was an absorbent of knowledge, never a student. The Latin of Cicero and Virgil was congenial and easy to him, and he learned more of it than the required portion. But even in Latin, he tells us, he was excelled by some of his own class; and "his attainments were not such," he adds, "as told for much in the recitation-room." Greek he never enjoyed: his curiosity was never awakened on the edge of that boundless contiguity of interesting knowledge, and he only learned enough Greek to escape censure. He said, forty years after, in an after-dinner speech: "When I was at school I felt exceedingly obliged to

Homer's messengers for the exact literal fidelity with which they delivered their messages. The seven or eight lines of good Homeric Greek in which they had received the commands of Agamemnon or Achilles they recited to whomsoever the message was to be carried; and as they repeated them verbatim, sometimes twice or thrice, it saved me the trouble of learning so much Greek." It was not at 'school" that he had this experience, but at Dartmouth College. For mathematics, too, he had not the slightest taste. He humorously wrote to a fellow-student, soon after leaving college, that "all that he knew about conterminous arches or evanescent subtenses might be collected on the pupil of a gnat's eye without making him wink." At college, in fact, he was simply an omnivorous reader, studying only so much as to pass muster in the recitation-room. Every indication we possess of his college life, as well as his own repeated assertions, confirms the conclusion that Nature had formed him to use the products of other men's toil, not to add to the common fund. Those who are conversant with college life know very well what it means when a youth does not take to Greek, and has an aversion to mathematics. Such a youth may have immense talent, and give splendid expression to the sentiments of his countrymen, but he is not likely to be one of the priceless few of the human race who dicover truth or advance opinion. It is the energetic, the originating minds that are susceptible to the allurements of difficulty.

On the other hand, Daniel Webster had such qualities as made every one feel that he was the first man in the College. Tall, gaunt, and sallow, with an incomparable forehead, and those cavernous and brilliant eyes of his, he had much of the large and tranquil presence which was so important an element of his power over others at all periods of his life. His letters of this time, as well as the recollections of his fellow-students, show him the easy, humorous, rather indolent and strictly correct "good-fellow," whom professors and companions equally relished. He browsed much in the College library, and had the habit of bringing to bear upon the lesson of the hour the information gathered in his miscellaneous reading, — a practice that much enlivens the monotony of recitation. The half-dozen youths of his particular se it appears, plumed themselves upon resembling the early Christians in having all things in common. The first to rise in the morning — and he must have been an early riser indeed who was up before Daniel Webster — "dressed himself in the best which the united apartments afforded"; the next made the best selection from what remained; and the last was happy if he found rags enough to justify his appearance in the chapel. The relator of this pleasant reminiscence adds, that he was once the possessor of an eminently respectable beaver hat, a costly article of resplendent lustre. It was missing one day, could not be found, and was given up for lost. Several weeks after "friend Dan" returned from a distant town, where he had been teaching school, wearing the lost beaver, and relieving its proprietor from the necessity of covering his head with a battered and long-discarded hat of felt. How like the Daniel Webster of later years, who never could acquire the sense of *meum* and *tuum*, supposed to be the basis of civilization!

Mr. Webster always spoke slightingly of his early oratorical efforts, and requested Mr. Everett, the editor of his works, not to search them out. He was not just to the productions of his youth, if we may judge from the Fourth-of-July oration which he delivered in 1800, when he was a Junior at Dartmouth, eighteen years of age. This glowing psalm of the republican David is perfectly characteristic, and entirely worthy of him. The times that tried men's souls, — how recent and vivid they were to the sons of Ebenezer Webster, who had led forth from the New Hampshire hills the neighbors at whose firesides Ezekiel and Daniel had listened, open-mouthed, to the thousand forgotten incidents of the war. Their professors of history were old John Bowen, who had once been a prisoner with the Indians; Robert Wise, who had sailed round the world and fought in the Revolution on *both* sides; George Bayly, a pioneer, who saw the first tree felled in Northern New Hampshire; women of the neighborhood, who had heard the midnight yell of savages; and, above all, their own lion-hearted father, who had warred with Frenchmen, Indians, wild nature, British troops, and French ideas. "O," wrote Daniel once, "I shall never hear such story telling

E

again!" It was not in the cold pages of Hildreth, nor in the brief summaries of school-books, that this imaginative, sympathetic youth had learned that part of the political history of the United States — from 1787 to 1800 — which will ever be its most interesting portion. He learned it at town-meetings, in the newspapers, at his father's house, among his neighbors, on election days; he learned it as an intelligent youth, with a passionately loyal father and mother, learned the history of the late war, and is now learning the agonizing history of "reconstruction." This oration is the warm and modest expression of all that the receptive and unsceptical student had imbibed and felt during the years of his formation, who saw before him a large company of Revolutionary soldiers and a great multitude of Federalist partisans. He saluted the audience as "Countrymen, brethren, and fathers." The oration was chiefly a rapid, exulting review of the history of the young Republic, with an occasional pomposity, and a few expressions caught from the party discussions of the day. It is amusing to hear this young Federalist of 1800 speak of Napoleon Bonaparte as "the gasconading pilgrim of Egypt," and the government of France as the "supercilious, five-headed Directory," and the President of the United States as "the firm, the wise, the inflexible Adams, who with steady hand draws the disguising veil from the intrigues of foreign enemies and the plots of domestic foes." It is amusing to read, as the utterance of Daniel Webster, that "Columbia is now seated in the forum of nations, and the empires of the world are amazed at the bright effulgence of her glory." But it is interesting to observe, also, that at eighteen, not less fervently than at forty-eight, he felt the importance of the message with which he was charged to the American people, — the necessity of the Union, and the value of the Constitution as the uniting bond. The following passage has, perhaps, more in it of the Webster of 1830 than any other in the oration. The reader will notice the similarity between one part of it and the famous passage in the Bunker Hill oration, beginning "Venerable men," addressed to the survivors of the Revolution.

"Thus, friends and citizens, did the kind hand of overruling Provi dence conduct us, through toils, fatigues, and dangers, to independence and peace. If piety be the rational exercise of the human soul, if religion be not a chimera, and if the vestiges of heavenly assistance are clearly traced in those events which mark the annals of our nation, it becomes us on this day, in consideration of the great things which have been done for us, to render the tribute of unfeigned thanks to that God who superintends the universe, and holds aloft the scale that weighs the destinies of nations.

" The conclusion of the Revolutionary War did not accomplish the entire achievements of our countrymen. Their military character was then, indeed, sufficiently established; but the time was coming which should prove their political sagacity, their ability to govern themselves.

" No sooner was peace restored with England, (the first grand article of which was the acknowledgment of our independence,) than the old system of Confederation, dictated at first by necessity, and adopted for the purposes of the moment, was found inadequate to the government of an extensive empire. Under a full conviction of this, we then saw the people of these States engaged in a transaction which is undoubtedly the greatest approximation towards human perfection the political world ever yet witnessed, and which, perhaps, will forever stand in the history of mankind without a parallel. A great republic, composed of different States, whose interest in all respects could not be perfectly compatible, then came deliberately forward, discarded one system of government, and adopted another, without the loss of one man's blood.

" There is not a single government now existing in Europe which is not based in usurpation, and established, if established at all, by the sacrifice of thousands. But in the adoption of our present system of jurisprudence, we see the powers necessary for government voluntarily flowing from the people, their only proper origin, and directed to the public good, their only proper object.

" With peculiar propriety, we may now felicitate ourselves on that happy form of mixed government under which we live. The advantages resulting to the citizens of the Union are utterly incalculable, and the day when it was received by a majority of the States shall stand on the catalogue of American anniversaries second to none but the birthday of independence.

" In consequence of the adoption of our present system of government, and the virtuous manner in which it has been administered by a Washington and an Adams, we are this day in the enjoyment of peace.

while war devastates Europe ! We can now sit down beneath the shadow of the olive, while her cities blaze, her streams run purple with blood, and her fields glitter with a forest of bayonets ! The citizens of America can this day throng the temples of freedom, and renew their oaths of fealty to independence ; while Holland, our once sister republic, is erased from the catalogue of nations ; while Venice is destroyed, Italy ravaged, and Switzerland — the once happy, the once united, the once flourishing Switzerland — lies bleeding at every pore ! "

He need not have been ashamed of this speech, despite the lumbering bombast of some of its sentences. All that made him estimable as a public man is contained in it, — the sentiment of nationality, and a clear sense of the only means by which the United States can remain a nation ; namely, strict fidelity to the Constitution as interpreted by the authority itself creates, and modified in the way itself appoints. We have never read the production of a youth which was more prophetic of the man than this. It was young New England that spoke through him on that occasion ; and in all the best part of his life he never touched a strain which New England had not inspired, or could not reach.

His success at college giving him ascendency at home, he employed it for the benefit of his brother in a manner which few sons would have dared, and no son ought to attempt. His father, now advanced in years, infirm, " an old man before his time " through hardship and toil, much in debt, depending chiefly upon his salary of four hundred dollars a year as Judge of the Court of Common Pleas, and heavily taxed to maintain Daniel in college, had seen all his other sons married and settled except Ezekiel, upon whom he leaned as the staff of his declining years, and the main dependence of his wife and two maiden daughters. Nevertheless, Daniel, after a whole night of consultation with his brother, urged the old man to send Ezekiel to college also. The fond and generous father replied, that he had but little property, and it would take all that little to carry another son through college to a profession ; but he lived only for his children, and, for his own part, he was willing to run the risk ; but there was the mother and two unmarried sisters, to whom the risk was far more serious. If they consented, he was willing. The mother said: "I have lived long in the world, and have been happy in my children. If Daniel and Ezekiel will promise to take care of me in my old age, I will consent to the sale of all our property at once, and they may enjoy the benefit of that which remains after our debts are paid." Upon hearing this, all the family, we are told, were dissolved in tears, and the old man gave his assent. This seems hard, — two stout and vigorous young men willing to risk their aged parents' home and dignity for such a purpose, or for any purpose! In the early days, however, there was a singular unity of feeling and interest in a good New England family, and there were opportunities for professional men which rendered the success of two such lads as these nearly certain, if they lived to establish themselves. Nevertheless, it was too much to ask, and more than Daniel Webster would have asked if he had been properly alive to the rights of others. Ezekiel shouldered his bundle, trudged off to school, where he lived and studied at the cost of one dollar a week, worked his way to the position of the second lawyer in New Hampshire, and would early have gone to Congress but for his stanch, inflexible Federalism.

Daniel Webster, schoolmaster and law-student, was assuredly one of the most interesting of characters. Pinched by poverty, as he tells us, till his very bones ached, eking out his income by a kind of labor that he always loathed (copying deeds), his shoes letting in, not water merely, but " pebbles and stones," — father, brother, and himself sometimes all moneyless together, all dunned the same time, and writing to one another for aid, — he was nevertheless as jovial a young fellow as any in New England. How merry and affectionate his letters to his young friends! He writes to one, soon after leaving college: " You will natu rally inquire how I prosper in the article of cash; finely, finely! I came here in January with a horse, watch, etc., and a few rascally counters in my pocket. Was soon obliged to sell my horse, and live on the proceeds. Still straitened for cash, I sold my watch, and made a shift to get home, where my friends supplied me with another horse and another watch. My horse is sold again, and my watch goes, I expect, this week; thus you see how I lay up cash." How like him! To another college friend, James Hervey Bingham, whom he calls, by turns, "brother Jemmy," "Jemmy Hervey," and "Bingham," he discourses thus "Perhaps you thought, as I did, that a dozen dollars would slide out of the pocket in a Commencement jaunt much easier than 'hey would slide in again after you got home. That was the exact reason why I was not there. . . . . I flatter myself that none of my friends ever thought me greatly absorbed in the sin of avarice, yet I assure you, Jem, that in these days of poverty I look upon a round dollar with a great deal of complacency. These rascal dollars are so necessary to the comfort of life, that next to a fine wife they are most essential, and their acquisition an object of prime importance. O Bingham, how blessed it would be to retire with a decent, clever bag of Rixes to a pleasant country town, and follow one's own inclination without being shackled by the duties of a profession!" To the same friend, whom he now addresses as "dear Squire," he announces joyfully a wondrous piece of luck: "My expenses [to Albany] were all amply paid, and on my return I put my hand in my pocket and found one hundred and twenty dear delightfuls! Is not that good luck? And these dear delightfuls were, 'pon honor, all my own; yes, every dog of them!" To which we may add from another source, that they were straightway transferred to his father, to whom they were dear delightfuls indeed, for he was really getting to the end of his tether.

The schoolmaster lived, it appears, on the easiest terms with his pupils, some of whom were older than himself. He tells a story of falling in with one of them on his journey to school, who was mounted "on the ugliest horse I ever saw or heard of, except Sancho Panza's pacer." The schoolmaster having two good horses, the pupil mounted one of them, strapped his bag to his own forlorn animal and drove him before, where his odd gait and frequent stumblings kept them amused. At length, arriving at a deep and rapid river, "this satire on the animal creation, as if to revenge herself on us for our sarcasms, plunged into the river, then very high by the freshet, and was wafted down the current like a bag of oats! I could hardly sit on my horse for laughter. I am apt to laugh at the vexations of my friends. The fellow, who was of my own age, and my room-mate, half checked the current by oaths as big as lobsters, and the old Rosinante, who was all the while much at her ease, floated up among the willows far below on the opposite side of the river."

At the same time he was an innocent young man. If he had any wild oats in his composition, they were not sown in the days of his youth. Expecting to pass his life as a country lawyer, having scarcely a premonition of his coming renown, we find him enjoying the simple country sports and indulging in the simple village ambitions. He tried once for the captaincy of a company of militia, and was not elected; he canvassed a whole regiment to get his brother the post of adjutant, and failed. At one time he came near abandoning the law, as too high and perilous for him, and settling down as schoolmaster and clerk of a court. The assurance of a certain six hundred dollars a year, a house, and a piece of land, with the prospect of the clerkship by and by, was so alluring to him that it required all the influence of his family and friends to make him reject the offer. Even then, in the flush and vigor of his youth, he was *led*. So was it always. He was never a leader, but always a follower. Nature made him very large, but so stinted him in propelling force, that it is doubtful if he had ever emerged from obscurity if his friends had not urged him on. His modesty in these innocent days is most touching to witness. After a long internal conflict, he resolved, in his twentieth year, to "make one more trial" at mastering the law. "If I prosecute the profession, I pray God to fortify me against its temptations. To the wind I dismiss those light hopes of eminence which ambition inspired and vanity fostered. To be honest, to be capable, to be faithful' to my client and my conscience, I earnestly hope will be my first endeavor." How exceedingly astonished would these affectionate young friends have been, if they could have looked forward forty years, and seen the timid law-student Secretary of State, and his ardent young comrade a clerk in his department. They seemed equals in 1802; in 1845, they had grown so far apart, that the excellent Bingham writes to Webster as to a demigod.

In these pleasant early letters of Daniel Webster there are a thousand evidences of a good heart and of virtuous habits, but not one of a superior understanding. The total absence of the sceptical spirit marks the secondary mind. For a hundred and fifty years, *no* young man of a truly eminent intellect has accepted his father's creeds without having first called them into question; and this must be so in periods of transition. The glorious light which has been coming upon Christendom for the last two hundred years, and which is now beginning to pervade the remotest provinces of it, never illumined the mind of Daniel Webster. Upon coming of age, he joined the Congregational Church, and was accustomed to open his school with an extempore prayer. He used the word " Deist " as a term of reproach; he deemed it " criminal " in Gibbon to write his fifteenth and sixteenth chapters, and spoke of that author as a " learned, proud, ingenious, foppish, vain, self-deceived man," who " from Protestant connections deserted to the Church of Rome, and thence to the faith of Tom Paine." And he never delivered himself from this narrowness and ignorance. In the time of his celebrity, he preferred what Sir Walter Scott called " the genteeler religion of the two," the Episcopal. In his old age, his idea of a proper sermon was incredibly narrow and provincial. He is reported to have said, late in life: —

" Many of the ministers of the present day take their text from St. Paul, and preach from the newspapers. When they do so, I prefer to enjoy my own thoughts rather than to listen. I want my pastor to come to me in the spirit of the Gospel, saying, ' You are mortal! your probation is brief; your work must be done speedily; you are immortal too. You are hastening to the bar of God; the Judge standeth before the door.' When I am thus admonished, I have no disposition to muse or to sleep."

This does not accord with what is usually observed in our churches, where sermons of the kind which Mr. Webster extolled dispose many persons to sleep, though not to muse.

In the same unquestioning manner, he imbibed his father's political prejudices. We hear this young Federalist call the Republican party " the Jacobins," just as the reactionists and tories of the present day speak of the present Republican party as "the radicals." It is amusing to hear him, in 1802, predict the speedy restoration to power of a party that was never again to taste its sweets. "Jacobinism and iniquity," he wrote in his twentieth year, "are so allied in signification, that the latter always follows the former, just as in grammar 'the accusative case follows the transitive verb.'" He speaks of a young friend as "too honest for a Democrat." As late as his twenty-second year, he was wholly unreconciled to Napoleon, and still wrote with truly English scorn of "Gallic tastes and Gallic principles." There is a fine burst in one of his letters of 1804, when he had been propelled by his brother to Boston to finish his law studies:—

"Jerome, the brother of the Emperor of the Gauls, is here; every day you may see him whisking along Cornhill, with the true French air, with his wife by his side. The lads say that they intend to prevail on American misses to receive company in future after the manner of Jerome's wife, that is, in bed. The gentlemen of Boston (i. e. we Feds) treat Monsieur with cold and distant respect. They feel, and every honest man feels, indignant at seeing this lordly grasshopper, this puppet in prince's clothes, dashing through the American cities, luxuriously rioting on the property of Dutch mechanics or Swiss peasants."

This last sentence, written when he was twenty-two years old, is the first to be found in his published letters which tells anything of the fire that was latent in him. He was of slow growth; he was forty-eight years of age before his powers had reached their full development.

When he had nearly completed his studies for the bar, he was again upon the point of abandoning the laborious career of a lawyer for a life of obscurity and ease. On this occasion, it was the clerkship of his father's court, salary fifteen hundred dollars a year, that tempted him. He jumped at the offer, which promised an immediate competency for the whole family, pinched and anxious for so many years. He had no thought but to accept it. With the letter in his hand, and triumphant joy in his face, he communicated the news to Mr. Gore, his instructor in the law; thinking of nothing, he tells us, but of "rushing to the immediate enjoyment of the proffered office." Mr. Gore, however, exhibited

4

a provoking coolness on the subject. He said it was very civil in the judges to offer such a compliment to a brother on the bench, and, of course, a respectful letter of acknowledgment must be sent. The glowing countenance of the young man fell at these most unexpected and unwelcome words. They were, to use his own language, " a shower-bath of ice-water." The old lawyer, observing his crestfallen condition, reasoned seriously with him, and persuaded him, against his will, to continue his preparation for the bar. At every turning-point of his life, whenever he came to a parting of the ways, one of which must be chosen and the other forsaken, he required an impulse from without to push him into the path he was to go. Except once ! Once in his long public life, he seemed to venture out alone on an unfamiliar road, and lost himself. Usually, when great powers are conferred on a man, there is also given him a strong propensity to exercise them, sufficient to carry him through all difficulties to the suitable sphere. Here, on the contrary, there was a Great Eastern with only a Cunarder's engine, and it required a tug to get the great ship round to her course.

Admitted to the bar in his twenty-third year, he dutifully went home to his father, and opened an office in a New Hampshire village near by, resolved never again to leave the generous old man while he lived. Before leaving Boston, he wrote to his friend Bingham, " If I am not earning my bread and cheese in exactly nine days after my admission, I shall certainly be a bankrupt " ; — and so, indeed, it proved. With great difficulty, he " hired " eighty-five dollars as a capital to begin business with, and this great sum was immediately lost in its transit by stage. To any other young man in his situation, such a calamity would have been, for the moment, crushing ; but this young man, indifferent to *meum* as to *tuum*, informs his brother that he can in no conceivable way replace the money, cannot therefore pay for the books he had bought, believes he is earning his daily bread, and as to the loss, he has " *no uneasy sensations on that account.*" He concludes his letter with an old song, beginning,

" Fol de dol, dol de dol, di dol,
I'll never make money my idol."

In the New Hampshire of 1805 there was no such thing possible as leaping at once into a lucrative practice, nor even of slowly acquiring it. A country lawyer who gained a thousand dollars a year was among the most successful, and the leader of the bar in New Hampshire could not earn two thousand. The chief employment of Daniel Webster, during the first year or two of his practice, was collecting debts due in New Hampshire to merchants in Boston. His first tin sign has been preserved to the present day, to attest by its minuteness and brevity the humble expectations of its proprietor. " D. Webster, Attorney," is the inscription it bears. The old Court-House still stands in which he conducted his first suit, before his own father as presiding judge. Old men in that part of New Hampshire were living until within these few years, who remembered well seeing this tall, gaunt, and large-eyed young lawyer rise slowly, as though scarcely able to get upon his feet, and giving to every one the impression that he would soon be obliged to sit down from mere physical weakness, and saying to his father, for the first and last time, " May it please your Honor." The sheriff of the county, who was also a Webster, used to say that he felt ashamed to see the family represented at the bar by so lean and feeble a young man. The tradition is, that he acquitted himself so well on this occasion that the sheriff was satisfied, and clients came, with their little suits and smaller fees, in considerable numbers, to the office of D. Webster, Attorney, who thenceforth in the country round went by the name of " All-eyes." His father never heard him speak again. He lived to see Daniel in successful practice, and Ezekiel a student of law, and died in 1806, prematurely old. Daniel Webster practised three years in the country, and then, resigning his business to his brother, established himself at Portsmouth, the seaport of New Hampshire, then a place of much foreign commerce. Ezekiel had had a most desperate struggle with poverty. At one time, when the family, as Daniel observed, was " heinously unprovided," we see the much-enduring " Zeke " teaching an Academy by day, an evening school for sailors, and keeping well up with his class in college besides. But these preliminary troubles were now at an end, and both the brothers took the places won by so much toil and self sacrifice.

Those are noble old towns on the New England coast, the commerce of which Boston swallowed up forty years ago, while it left behind many a large and liberally provided old mansion, with a family in it enriched by ventures to India and China. Strangers in Portsmouth are still struck by the largeness and elegance of the residences there, and wonder how such establishments can be maintained in a place that has little " visible means of support." It was while Portsmouth was an important seaport that Daniel Webster learned and practised law there, and acquired some note as a Federalist politician.

The once celebrated Dr. Buckminster was the minister of the Congregational church at Portsmouth then. One Sunday morning in 1808, his eldest daughter sitting alone in the minister's pew, a strange gentleman was shown into it, whose appearance and demeanor strongly arrested her attention. The slenderness of his frame, the pale yellow of his complexion, and the raven blackness of his hair, seemed only to bring out into grander relief his ample forehead, and to heighten the effect of his deepset, brilliant eyes. At this period of his life there was an air of delicacy and refinement about his face, joined to a kind of strength that women can admire, without fearing. Miss Buckminster told the family, when she went home from church, that there had been a remarkable person with her in the pew, — one that she was sure had " a marked character for good or evil." A few days after, the remarkable person came to live in the neighborhood, and was soon introduced to the minister's family as Mr. Daniel Webster, from Franklin, New Hampshire, who was about to open a law office in Portsmouth. He soon endeared himself to every person in the minister's circle, and to no one more than to the minister himself, who, among other services, taught him the art of preserving his health. The young man, like the old clergyman, was an early riser, up with the dawn in summer, and long before the dawn in winter; and both were out of doors with the sun, each at one end of a long saw, cutting wood for an appetite. The joyous, uncouth singing and shouting of the new

comer aroused the late sleepers.   Then in to breakfast, where
the homely, captivating humor of the young lawyer kept the
table in a roar, and detained every inmate.   " Never was there
such an actor lost to the stage," Jeremiah Mason, his only
rival at the New Hampshire bar, used to say, " as he would have
made."   Returning in the afternoon from court, fatigued and
anguid, his spirits rose again with food and rest, and the evening
was another festival of conversation and reading.   A few months
after his settlement at Portsmouth he visited his native hills,
saying nothing respecting the object of his journey; and returned with a wife, — that gentle and high-bred lady, a clergyman's daughter, who was the chief source of the happiness of
his happiest years, and the mother of all his children.   He improved in health, his form expanded, his mind grew, his talents
ripened, his fame spread, during the nine years of his residence
at this thriving and pleasant town.

    At Portsmouth, too, he had precisely that external stimulus to
exertion which his large and pleasure-loving nature needed.
Jeremiah Mason was, literally speaking, the giant of the American bar, for he stood six feet seven inches in his stockings.   Like
Webster, he was the son of a valiant Revolutionary officer; like
Webster, he was an hereditary Federalist; like Webster, he had
a great mass of brain: but his mind was more active and acquis-
itive than Webster's, and his nineteen years of arduous practice
at the bar had stored his memory with knowledge and given him
dexterity in the use of it.   Nothing shows the eminence of Webster's talents more than this, that, very early in his Portsmouth
career, he should have been regarded at the bar of New Hampshire as the man to be employed against Jeremiah Mason, and
his only fit antagonist.   Mason was a vigilant, vigorous opponent,
— sure to be well up in the law and the facts of a cause, sure to
detect a flaw in the argument of opposing counsel.   It was in
keen encounters with this wary and learned man that Daniel
Webster learned his profession; and this he always acknowledged.   "If," he said once in conversation, — "if anybody thinks
I am somewhat familiar with the law on some points, and should
be curious to know how it happened, tell him that Jeremiah

Mason compelled me to study it. *He* was my master." It is
honorable, too, to both of them, that, rivals as they were, they
were fast and affectionate friends, each valuing in the other the
qualities in which he was surpassed by him, and each sincerely
believing that the other was the first man of his time and country. "They say," in Portsmouth, that Mason did not shrink
from remonstrating with his friend upon his carelessness with
regard to money; but, finding the habit inveterate and the man
irresistible, desisted.   Webster himself says that two thousand
dollars a year was all that the best practice in New Hampshire
could be made to yield; and that that was inadequate to the sup
port of his family of a wife and three little children.   Two
thousand dollars in Portsmouth, in 1812, was certainly equal, in
purchasing power, to six thousand of the ineffectual things that
now pass by the name of dollars; and upon such an income large
families in a country town contrive to live, ride, and save.

He was a strenuous Federalist at Portsmouth, took a leading
part in the public meetings of the party, and won great distinction as its frequent Fourth-of-July orator.   All those mild and
economical measures by which Mr. Jefferson sought to keep
the United States from being drawn into the roaring vortex of
the great wars in Europe, he opposed, and favored the policy of
preparing the country for defence, not by gunboats and embar-
goes, but by a powerful navy of frigates and ships of the line.
His Fourth-of-July orations, if we may judge of them by the
fragments that have been found, show that his mind had strengthened more than it had advanced.   His style wonderfully improved
from eighteen to twenty-five; and he tells us himself why it did.
He discovered, he says, that the value, as well as the force, of a
sentence, depends chiefly upon its meaning, not its language;
and that great writing is that in which much is said in few words,
and those words the simplest that will answer the purpose.
Having made this notable discovery, he became a great eraser of
adjectives, and toiled after simplicity and directness.   Mr Everett
quotes a few sentences from his Fourth-of-July oration of 1806,
when he was twenty-four, which shows an amazing advance upon
the effort of his eighteenth year, quoted above : —

"Nothing is plainer than this: if we will have commerce, we must protect it. This country is commercial as well as agricultural. *Indissoluble bonds connect him who ploughs the land with him who ploughs the sea.* Nature has placed us in a situation favorable to commercial pursuits, and no government can alter the destination. Habits confirmed by two centuries are not to be changed. An immense portion of our property is on the waves. Sixty or eighty thousand of our most useful citizens are there, and are entitled to such protection from the government as their case requires."

How different this compact directness from the tremendous fulmination of the Dartmouth junior, who said: —

"Columbia stoops not to tyrants; her spirit will never cringe to France; neither a supercilious, five-headed Directory nor the gasconading pilgrim of Egypt will ever dictate terms to sovereign America. The thunder of our cannon shall insure the performance of our treaties, and fulminate destruction on Frenchmen, till the ocean is *crimsoned with blood and gorged with pirates!*"

The Fourth-of-July oration, which afterwards fell into some disrepute, had great importance in the earlier years of the Republic, when Revolutionary times and perils were fresh in the recollection of the people. The custom arose of assigning this duty to young men covetous of distinction, and this led in time to the flighty rhetoric which made sounding emptiness and a Fourth-of-July oration synonymous terms. The feeling that was real and spontaneous in the sons of Revolutionary soldiers was sometimes feigned or exaggerated in the young law students of the next generation, who had merely read the history of the Revolution. But with all the faults of those compositions, they were eminently serviceable to the country. We believe that to them is to be attributed a considerable part of that patriotic feeling which, after a suspended animation of several years, awoke in the spring of 1861 and asserted itself with such unexpected power, and which sustained the country during four years of a peculiarly disheartening war. How pleasant and spirit-stirring was a celebration of the Fourth of July as it was conducted in Webster's early day! We trust the old customs will be revived and improved upon, and become universal. Nor is it any objec tion to the practice of having an oration, that the population is too large to be reached in that way; for if only a thousand hear, a million may read. Nor ought we to object if the orator *is* a little more flowery and boastful than becomes an ordinary occasion. There is a time to exult; there is a time to abandon our selves to pleasant recollections and joyous hopes. Therefore, we say, let the young men reappear upon the platform, and show what metal they are made of by giving the best utterance they can to the patriotic feelings of the people on the national anniversary. The Republic is safe so long as we celebrate that day in the spirit of 1776 and 1861.

At least we may assert that it was Mr. Webster's Fourth-of-July orations, of which he delivered five in eleven years, that first made him known to the people of New Hampshire. At that period the two political parties could not unite in the celebration of the day, and accordingly the orations of Mr. Webster had much in them that could be agreeable only to Federalists. He was an occasional speaker, too, in those years, at meetings of Federalists, where his power as an orator was sometimes exerted most effectively. No speaker could be better adapted to a New England audience, accustomed from of old to weighty, argumentative sermons, delivered with deliberate, unimpassioned earnestness. There are many indications that a speech by Daniel Webster in Portsmouth in 1810 excited as much expectation and comment as a speech by the same person in the Senate twenty years after. But he was a mere Federalist partisan, — no more. It does not appear that he had anything to offer to his countrymen beyond the stately expression of party issues; and it was as a Federalist, pure and simple, that he was elected, in 1812, a member of the House of Representatives, after a keenly contested party conflict. His majority over the Republican candidate was 2,546, — the whole number of voters being 34,648.

The Federalists, from 1801 to 1825, were useful to the country only as an Opposition, — just as the present Tory party in England can be only serviceable in its capacity of critic and holdback. The Federalists under John Adams had sinned past forgiveness; while the Republican party, strong in being right, in the ability of its chiefs, in its alliance with Southern aristocrats, and in having possession of the government, was strong also in the odium and inconsistencies of its opponents. Nothing could shake the confidence of the people in the administration of Thomas Jefferson. But the stronger a party is, the more it needs an Opposition, — as we saw last winter in Washington, when the minority was too insignificant in numbers and ability to keep the too powerful majority from doing itself such harm as might have been fatal to it but for the President's well-timed antics. Next to a sound and able majority, the great need of a free country is a vigorous, vigilant, audacious, numerous minority. Better a factious and unscrupulous minority than none at all. The Federalists, who could justly claim to have among them a very large proportion of the rich men and the educated men of the country, performed the humble but useful service of keeping an eye upon the measures of the administration, and finding fault with every one of them. Daniel Webster, however, was wont to handle only the large topics. While Mr. Jefferson was struggling to keep the peace with Great Britain, he censured the policy as timorous, costly, and ineffectual; but when Mr. Madison declared war against that power, he deemed the act unnecessary and rash. His opposition to the war was never carried to the point of giving aid and comfort to the enemy; it was such an opposition as patriotic "War Democrats" exhibited during the late Rebellion, who thought the war might have been avoided, and ought to be conducted more vigorously, but nevertheless stood by their country without a shadow of swerving.

He could boast, too, that from his boyhood to the outbreak of the war he had advocated the building of the very ships which gave the infant nation its first taste of warlike glory. The Republicans of that time, forgetful of what Paul Jones and others of Dr. Franklin's captains had done in the war of the Revolution, supposed that, because England had a thousand ships in commission, and America only seventeen, therefore an American ship could not venture out of a harbor without being taken. We have often laughed at Colonel Benton s ludicrous confession of his own terrors on this subject.

" Political men," he says, " believed nothing could be done at sea but to lose the few vessels which we had; that even cruising was out of the question. Of our seventeen vessels, the whole were in port but one; and it was determined to keep them there, and the one at sea with them, if it had the luck to get in. I am under no obligation to make the admission, but I am free to acknowledge that I was one of those who supposed that there was no salvation for our seventeen men-of-war but to run them as far up the creek as possible, place them under the guns of batteries, and collect camps of militia about them to keep off the British. This was the policy at the day of the declaration of the war; and I have the less concern to admit myself to have been participator in the delusion, because I claim the merit of having profited from experience, — happy if I could transmit the lesson to posterity. Two officers came to Washington, — Bainbridge and Stewart. They spoke with Mr. Madison, and urged the feasibility of cruising. One half of the whole number of the British men-of-war were under the class of frigates, consequently no more than matches for some of our seventeen; the whole of her merchant marine (many thousands) were subject to capture. Here was a rich field for cruising; and the two officers, for themselves and brothers, boldly proposed to enter it.

" Mr. Madison had seen the efficiency of cruising and privateering, even against Great Britain, and in our then infantile condition, during the war of the Revolution; and besides was a man of sense, and amenable to judgment and reason. He listened to the two experienced and valiant officers; and without consulting Congress, which perhaps would have been a fatal consultation (for multitude of counsellors is not the counsel for *bold* decision), reversed the policy which had been resolved upon; and, in his supreme character of constitutional commander of the army and navy, ordered every ship that could cruise to get to sea as soon as possible. This I had from Mr. Monroe."

This is a curious example of the blinding effect of partisan strife, and of the absolute need of an Opposition. It was the hereditary prejudice of the Republicans against the navy, as an " aristocratic" institution, and the hereditary love of the navy cherished by the Federalists as being something stable and British, that enlivened the debates of the war. The Federalists had their way, but failed to win a partisan advantage from the fact. through their factious opposition to the military measures of the administration. Because the first attempt at the seizure of Can ada had failed through the incompetency of General Hull, which no wisdom of man could have foreseen, Daniel Webster called upon the government to discontinue all further attempts on the land, and fight the war out on the sea. " Give up your futile projects of invasion," said he in 1814. " Extinguish the fires that blaze on your inland borders." " Unclench the iron grasp of your embargo." " With all the war of the enemy on your commerce, if you would cease to make war upon it yourselves, you would still have some commerce. That commerce would give you some revenue. Apply that revenue to the augmentation of your navy. That navy, in turn, will protect your commerce." In war time, however, there are *two* powers that have to do with the course of events ; and very soon the enemy, by his own great scheme of invasion, decided the policy of the United States. Every port was blockaded so effectively that a pilot-boat could not safely go out of sight of land, and a frigate was captured within sight of it. These vigilant blockaders, together with the threatening armament which finally attacked New Orleans, compelled every harbor to prepare for defence, and most effectually refuted Mr. Webster's speech. The " blaze of glory" with which the war ended at New Orleans consumed all the remaining prestige of the Federalist party, once so powerful, so respectable, and so arrogant.

A member of the anti-war party during the existence of a war occupies a position which can only cease to be insignificant by the misfortunes of his country. But when we turn from the partisan to the man, we perceive that Daniel Webster was a great presence in the House, and took rank immediately with the half-dozen ablest debaters. His self-possession was perfect at all times, and at thirty-three he was still in the spring and first lustre of his powers. His weighty and deliberate manner, the brevity, force, and point of his sentences, and the moderation of his gestures, were all in strong contrast to the flowing, loose, impassioned manner of the Southern orators, who ruled the House. It was something like coming upon a stray number of the old Edinburgh Review in a heap of novels and Ladies' Magazines. Chief-Justice Marshall, who heard his first speech, being himself a Feder alist, was so much delighted to hear his own opinions expressed with such power and dignity, that he left the House, believing that this stranger from far-off New Hampshire was destined to become, as he said, " one of the very first statesmen of America, and perhaps the very first." His Washington fame gave him new *éclat* at home. He was re-elected, and came back to Congress in 1815, to aid the Federalists in preventing the young Republicans from being too Federal.

This last sentence slipped from the pen unawares ; but, ridiculous as it looks, it does actually express the position and vocation of the Federalists after the peace of 1815. Clay, Calhoun, Story, Adams, and the Republican majority in Congress, taught by the disasters of the war, as they supposed, had embraced the ideas of the old Federalist party, and were preparing to carry some of them to an extreme. The navy had no longer an enemy. The strict constructionists had dwindled to a few impracticables, headed by John Randolph. The younger Republicans were disposed to a liberal, if not to a latitudinarian construction of the Constitution. In short, they were Federalists and Hamiltonians, bank men, tariff men, internal-improvement men. Then was afforded to the country the curious spectacle of Federalists opposing the measures which had been among the rallying-cries of their party for twenty years. It was not in Daniel Webster's nature to be a leader; it was morally impossible for him to disengage himself from party ties. This exquisite and consummate artist in oratory, who could give such weighty and brilliant expression to the feelings of his hearers and the doctrines of his party, had less originating power, whether of intellect or of will, than any other man of equal eminence that ever lived. He adhered to the fag end of the old party, until it was absorbed, unavoidably, with scarcely an effort of its own, in Adams and Clay. From 1815 to 1825 he was in opposition, and in opposition to old Federalism revived ; and, consequently, we believe that posterity will decide that his speeches of this period are the only ones relating to details of policy which have the slightest permanent value. In fact, his position in Congress, as a member of a very small band of Federalists who had no hope of regain

ing power, was the next thing to being independent, and he made
an excellent use of his advantage.

That Bank of the United States, for example, of which, in
1832, he was the ablest defender, and for a renewal of which he
strove for ten years, he voted *against* in 1816; and for reasons
which neither he nor any other man ever refuted. His speeches
criticising the various bank schemes of 1815 and 1816 were
serviceable to the public, and made the bank, as finally established, less harmful than it might have been.

So of the tariff. On this subject, too, he always followed, —
never led. So long as there was a Federal party, he, as a member of it, opposed Mr. Clay's protective, or (as Mr. Clay delighted to term it) "American system." When, in 1825, the few
Federalists in the House voted for Mr. Adams, and were merged
in the "conservative wing" of the Republican party, which
became, in time, the Whig party, then, and from that time forward to the end of his life, he was a protectionist. His anti-pro-
tection speech of 1824 is wholly in the modern spirit, and takes
precisely the ground since taken by Ricardo, John Stuart Mill,
and others of the new school. It is so excellent a statement of
the true policy of the United States with regard to protection,
that we have often wondered it has been allowed to sleep so
long in the tomb of his works. And, oh! from what evils might
we have been spared, — nullification, surplus-revenue embarrassments, hot-bed manufactures, clothing three times its natural
price, — if the protective legislation of Congress had been
inspired by the Webster of 1824, instead of the Clay! Unim-
portant as this great speech may now seem, as it lies uncut in
the third volume of its author's speeches, its unturned leaves
sticking together, yet we can say of it, that the whole course of
American history had been different if its counsels had been
followed. The essence of the speech is contained in two of its
phrases: " Freedom of trade, the general principle ; restriction,
the exception." Free trade, the object to be aimed at; protection, a temporary expedient. Free trade, the interest of all
nations; protection, the occasional necessity of one. Free trade,
the final and universal good; protection, the sometimes necessary

evil. Free trade, as soon as possible and as complete as possible; protection, as little as possible and as short as possible.

The speech was delivered in reply to Mr. Clay; and, viewed merely *as* a reply, it is difficult to conceive of one more triumphant. Mr. Webster was particularly happy in turning Mr. Clay's historical illustrations against him, especially those drawn from the history of the English silk manufacture, and the Spanish system of restriction and prohibition. Admitting fully that manufactures the most unsuited to the climate, soil, and genius of a country *could* be created by protection, he showed that such manufactures were not, upon the whole, and in the long run, a benefit to a country; and adduced, for an illustration, the very instance cited by Mr. Clay, — the silk manufacture of England, — which kept fifty thousand persons in misery, and necessitated the continuance of a kind of legislation which the intelligence of Great Britain had outgrown. Is not the following brief passage an almost exhaustive statement of the true American policy?

"I know it would be very easy to promote manufactures, at least for a time, but probably for a short time only, if we might act in disregard of other interests. We *could* cause a sudden transfer of capital and a violent change in the pursuits of men. We *could* exceedingly benefit some classes by these means. But what then becomes of the interests of others? The power of collecting revenue by duties on imports, and the habit of the government of collecting almost its whole revenue in that mode, will enable us, without exceeding the bounds of moderation, to give great advantages to those classes of manufactures which we may think most useful to promote at home."

One of his happy retorts upon Mr. Clay was the following: —

"I will be so presumptuous as to take up a challenge which Mr. Speaker has thrown down. He has asked us, in a tone of interrogatory indicative of the feeling of anticipated triumph, to mention any country in which manufactures have flourished without the aid of prohibitory laws. . . . . Sir, I am ready to answer this inquiry.

"There is a country, not undistinguished among the nations, in which the progress of manufactures has been more rapid than in any other, and yet unaided by prohibitions or unnatural restrictions. That country, the happiest which the sun shines on, is our own."

Again, Mr. Clay had made the rash remark that it would cost

the nation, *as* a nation, nothing to convert our ore into iron. Mr. Webster's reply to this seems to us eminently worthy of consideration at the present moment, and at every moment when the tariff is a topic of debate.

"I think," said he, " it would cost us precisely what we can least afford, that is, *great labor*. . . . . Of manual labor no nation has more than a certain quantity; nor can it be increased at will. . . . . A most important question for every nation, as well as for every individual, to propose to itself, is, how it can best apply that quantity of labor which it is able to perform. . . . . Now, with respect to the quantity of labor, as we all know, different nations are differently circumstanced. Some need, more than anything, work for hands; *others require hands for work;* and if we ourselves are not absolutely in the latter class, we are still, most fortunately, very near it."

The applicability of these observations to the present condition of affairs in the United States — labor very scarce, and protectionists clamoring to make it scarcer — must be apparent to every reader.

But this was the last of Mr. Webster's efforts in behalf of the freedom of trade. In the spring of 1825, when it devolved upon the House of Representatives to elect a President, the few Federalists remaining in the House became, for a few days, an important body. Mr. Webster had an hereditary love for the house of Adams; and the aged Jefferson himself had personally warned him against Andrew Jackson. Webster it was who, in an interview with Mr. Adams, obtained such assurances as determined the Federalists to give their vote for the New England candidate; and thus terminated the existence of the great party which Hamilton had founded, with which Washington had sympathized, which had ruled the country for twelve years, and maintained a vigorous and useful opposition for a quarter of a century. Daniel Webster was in opposition no longer. He was a defender of the administration of Adams and Clay, supported all their important measures, and voted for, nay, advocated, the Tariff Bill of 1828, which went far beyond that of 1824 in its protective provisions. Taunted with such a remarkable and sudden change of opinion, he said that, New England having been compelled by the act of

1824 to transfer a large part of her capital from commerce to manufactures, he was bound, as her representative, to demand the continuance of the system. Few persons, probably, who heard him give this reason for his conversion, believed it was the true one; and few will ever believe it who shall intimately know the transactions of that winter in Washington. But if it *was* the true reason, Mr. Webster, in giving it, ruled himself out of the rank of the Great, — who, in every age and land, lead, not follow, their generation. In his speech of 1824 he objects to the protective system on *general* principles, applicable to every case not clearly exceptional; and the further Congress was disposed to carry an erroneous system, the more was he bound to lift up his voice against it. It seems to us that, when he abandoned the convictions of his own mind and took service under Mr. Clay, he descended (to use the fine simile of the author of " Felix Holt ") from the rank of heroes to that of the multitude for whom heroes fight. He was a protectionist, thenceforth, as long as he lived. If he was right in 1824, how wrong he was in 1846! In 1824 he pointed to the high wages of American mechanics as a proof that the protective system was unnecessary; and he might have quoted Adam Smith to show that, in 1770, wages in the Colonies were just as high, compared with wages in Europe, as in 1824. In 1846 he attributed high wages in America to the operation of the protective system. In 1824 free trade was the good, and restriction the evil; in 1846 restriction was the good, and free trade the evil.

Practical wisdom, indeed, was not in this man. He was not formed to guide, but to charm, impress, and rouse mankind. His advocacy of the Greek cause, in 1824, events have shown to be unwise; but his speech on this subject contains some passages so exceedingly fine, noble, and harmonious, that we do not believe they have ever been surpassed in extempore speech by any man but himself. The passage upon Public Opinion, for example, is always read with delight, even by those who can call to mind the greatest number of instances of its apparent untruth.

" The time has been, indeed, when fleets, and armies, and subsidies were the principal reliances, even in the best cause. But, happily for mankind, a great change has taken place in this respect. Moral causes come into consideration in proportion as the progress of knowledge is advanced; and the public opinion of the civilized world is rapidly gaining an ascendency over mere brutal force. . . . . It may be silenced by military power, but it cannot be conquered. It is elastic, irrepressible, and invulnerable to the weapons of ordinary warfare. It is that impassible, unextinguishable enemy of mere violence and arbitrary rule, which, like Milton's angels,

> ' Vital in every part, ...
> Cannot, but by annihilating, die.'

Until this be propitiated or satisfied, it is vain for power to talk either of triumphs or of repose. No matter what fields are desolated, what fortresses surrendered, what armies subdued, or what provinces overrun. . . . . There is an enemy that still exists to check the glory of these triumphs. It follows the conqueror back to the very scene of his ovations; it calls upon him to take notice that Europe, though silent, is yet indignant; it shows him that the sceptre of his victory is a barren sceptre ; that it shall confer neither joy nor honor ; but shall moulder to dry ashes in his grasp. In the midst of his exultation, it pierces his ear with the cry of injured justice ; it denounces against him the indignation of an enlightened and civilized age; it turns to bitterness the cup of his rejoicing, and wounds him with the sting which belongs to the consciousness of having outraged the opinion of mankind." — *Works*, Vol. III. pp. 77, 78.

Yes: if the conqueror had the moral feeling which inspired this passage, and if the cry of injured justice could pierce the flattering din of office-seekers surrounding him. But, reading the paragraph as the expression of a *hope* of what may one day be, how grand and consoling it is ! The information given in this fine oration respecting the condition of Greece and the history of her struggle for independence was provided for him by the industry of his friend, Edward Everett.

One of the minor triumphs of Mr Webster's early Congressional life was his conquest of the heart of John Randolph. In the course of a debate on the sugar tax, in 1816, Mr. Webster had the very common fortune of offending the irascible member from Virginia, and Mr. Randolph, as his custom was, demanded an explanation of the offensive words. Explanation was refused by the member from Massachusetts ; whereupon Mr. Ran-

dolph demanded "the satisfaction which his insulted feelings required." Mr. Webster's reply to this preposterous demand was
everything that it ought to have been. He told Mr. Randolph
that he had no right to an explanation, and that the temper and
style of the demand were such as to forbid its being conceded as
a matter of courtesy. He denied, too, the right of any man to
call him to the field for what he might please to consider an insult to his feelings, although he should be "always prepared to
repel in a suitable manner the aggression of any man who may
presume upon such a refusal." The eccentric Virginian was so
much pleased with Mr. Webster's bearing upon this occasion, that
he manifested a particular regard for him, and pronounced him a
very able man for a Yankee.

It was during these years that Daniel Webster became dear,
beyond all other men of his time, to the people of New England.
Removing to Boston in 1816, and remaining out of Congress for
some years, he won the first place at the New England bar, and
a place equal to the foremost at the bar of the Supreme Court
of the United States. Not one of his legal arguments has been
exactly reported, and some of the most important of them we
possess merely in outline; but in such reports as we have, the
weight and clearness of his mind are abundantly apparent. In
almost every argument of his, there can be found digressions
which relieve the strained attention of the bench, and please the
unlearned hearer; and he had a happy way of suddenly crys-
tallizing his argument into one luminous phrase, which often
seemed to prove his case by merely stating it. Thus, in the
Dartmouth College case, he made a rare display of learning (furnished him by associate counsel, he tells us); but his argument
is concentrated in two of his simplest sentences: — 1. The endowment of a college is private property; 2. The charter of a
college is that which constitutes its endowment private property.
The Supreme Court accepted these two propositions, and thus
secured to every college in the country its right to its endowment.
This seems too simple for argument, but it cost a prodigious and
powerfully contested lawsuit to reduce the question to this simplicity; and it was Webster's large, calm, and discriminating

glance which detected these two fundamental truths in the mountain mass of testimony, argument, and judicial decision. In arguing the great steamboat case, too, he displayed the same qualities of mind. New York having granted to Livingston and Fulton the exclusive right to navigate her waters by steamboats, certain citizens of New Jersey objected, and, after a fierce struggle upon the waters themselves, transferred the contest to the Supreme Court. Mr. Webster said: "The commerce of the United States, under the Constitution of 1787, is a unit," and "what we call the waters of the State of New York are, for the purposes of navigation and commerce, the waters of the United States"; therefore no State can grant exclusive privileges. The Supreme Court affirmed this to be the true doctrine, and thenceforth Captain Cornelius Vanderbilt ran his steamboat without feeling it necessary, on approaching New York, to station a lady at the helm and to hide himself in the hold. Along with this concentrating power, Mr. Webster possessed, as every school-boy knows, a fine talent for amplification and narrative. His narration of the murder of Captain White was almost enough of itself to hang a man.

But it was not his substantial services to his country which drew upon him the eyes of all New England, and made him dear to every son of the Pilgrims. In 1820, the Pilgrim Society of Plymouth celebrated the anniversary of the landing of their forefathers in America. At the dinner of the Society, that day, every man found beside his plate five kernels of corn, to remind him of the time when that was the daily allowance of the settlers, and it devolved upon Daniel Webster to show how worthy they were of better fare. His address on this anniversary is but an amplification of his Junior Fourth-of-July oration of 1800; but what an amplification! It differed from that youthful essay as the first flights of a young eagle, from branch to branch upon its native tree, differ from the sweep of his wings when he takes a continent in his flight, and swings from mountain range to mountain range. We are aware that eulogy is, of all the kinds of composition, the easiest to execute in a tolerable manner. What Mr. Everett calls "patriotic eloquence" should usually be left to persons who are in the gushing time of life for when men address men, they should say something, clear up something, help forward something, accomplish something. It is not becoming in a full-grown man to utter melodious wind. Nevertheless, it can be truly said of this splendid and irresistible oration, that it carries that kind of composition as far as we can ever expect to see it carried, even in this its native land. What a triumphant joy it must have been to an audience, accustomed for three or four generations to regard preaching as the noblest work of man, keenly susceptible to all the excellences of uttered speech, and who now heard their plain old fathers and grand-fathers praised in such massive and magnificent English! Nor can it be said that this speech says nothing. In 1820 it was still part of the industry of New England to fabricate certain articles required by slave-traders in their hellish business; and there were still descendants of the Pilgrims who were actually en-gaged in the traffic.

" If there be," exclaimed the orator, " within the extent of our knowl-edge or influence any participation in this traffic, let us pledge our-selves here, upon the rock of Plymouth, to extirpate and destroy it. It is not fit that the land of the Pilgrims should bear the shame longer. I hear the sound of the hammer, I see the smoke of the furnaces where manacles and fetters are still forged for human limbs. I see the visa-ges of those who by stealth and at midnight labor in this work of hell, foul and dark, as may become the artificers of such instruments of misery and torture. Let that spot be purified, or let it cease to be of New England." — *Works*, Vol. I. pp. 45, 46.

And he proceeds, in language still more energetic, to call upon his countrymen to purge their land of this iniquity. This ora-tion, widely circulated through the press, gave the orator uni-versal celebrity in the Northern States, and was one of the many causes which secured his continuance in the national councils.

Such was his popularity in Boston, that, in 1824, he was re-elected to Congress by 4,990 votes out of 5,000; and such was his celebrity in his profession, that his annual retainers from banks, insurance companies, and mercantile firms yielded an in-come that would have satisfied most lawyers even of great emi-

nence. Those were not the times of five-thousand-dollar fees.
As late as 1819, as we see in Mr. Webster's books, he gave "advice" in important cases for twenty dollars; his regular retaining
fee was fifty dollars; his "annual retainer," one hundred dollars,
his whole charge for conducting a cause rarely exceeded five hundred dollars; and the income of a whole year averaged about
twenty thousand dollars. Twenty years later, he has gained a
larger sum than that by the trial of a single cause; but in 1820
such an income was immense, and probably not exceeded by that
of any other American lawyer. Most lawyers in the United
States, he once said, "live well, work hard, and die poor"; and
this is particularly likely to be the case with lawyers who spend
six months of the year in Congress.

Northern members of Congress, from the foundation of the
government, have usually gratified their ambition only by the
sacrifice of their interests. The Congress of the United States,
modelled upon the Parliament of Great Britain, finds in the
North no suitable class of men who can afford to be absent from
their affairs half the year. We should naturally choose to be
represented in Washington by men distinguished in their several
spheres; but in the North, almost all such persons are so involved
in business that they cannot accept a seat in Congress, except at
the peril of their fortune; and this inconvenience is aggravated
by the habits that prevail at the seat of government. In the case
of a lawyer like Daniel Webster, who has a large practice in the
Supreme Court, the difficulty is diminished, because he can usually attend the court without seriously neglecting his duties in
Congress, — usually, but not always. There was one year in the
Congressional life of Mr. Webster when he was kept out of the
Supreme Court for four months by the high duty that devolved
upon him of refuting Calhoun's nullification subtilties; but even
in that year, his professional income was more than seven thousand dollars; and he ought by that time, after thirty years of
most successful practice, to have been independent of his profession. He was not, however; and never would have been, if he
had practised a century. Those habits of profusion, that reckless disregard of pecuniary considerations, of which we noticed

indications in his early days, seemed to be part of his moral constitution.   He never appeared to know how much money he had,
nor how much he owed; and, what was worse, he never appeared
to care.   He was a profuse giver and a careless payer.   It was
far easier for him to send a hundred-dollar note in reply to a begging letter, than it was to discharge a long-standing account; and
when he had wasted his resources in extravagant and demoralizing gifts, he deemed it a sufficient answer to a presented bill to ask
his creditor how a man could pay money who had none.

It is not true, therefore, that the frequent embarrassments of
his later years were due to the loss of practice by his attendance
in Congress; because, in the years when his professional gains
were smallest, his income was large enough for the wants of any
reasonable man.   Nevertheless, we cannot deny that when, in
1827, by his acceptance of a seat in the Senate, he gave himself
permanently to public life, he made a sacrifice of his pecuniary
interests which, for a man of such vast requirements and uncalcu-
lating habits, was very great.

But his reward was also very great.   On that elevated theatre he soon found an opportunity for the display of his talents,
which, while it honored and served his country, rendered him the
foremost man in that part of it where such talents as his could
be appreciated.

All wars of which we have any knowledge have consisted of
two parts: first, a war of words; secondly, the conflict of arms.
The war of words which issued in the late Rebellion began, in
1828, by the publication of Mr. Calhoun's first paper upon Nullification, called the South Carolina Exposition; and it ended in
April, 1861, when President Lincoln issued his call for seventy-
five thousand troops, which excited so much merriment at Mont-
gomery.   This was a period of thirty-three years, during which
every person in the United States who could use either tongue
or pen joined in the strife of words, and contributed his share
either toward hastening or postponing the final appeal to the
sword.   Men fight with one another, says Dr. Franklin, because
they have not sense enough to settle their disputes in any other
way; and when once they have begun, never stop killing one

another as long as they have money enough "to pay the butchers." So it appeared in our case. Of all the men who took part in this preliminary war of words, Daniel Webster was incomparably the ablest. He seemed charged with a message and a mission to the people of the United States; and almost everything that he said in his whole life of real value has reference to that message and that mission. The necessity of the Union of these States, the nature of the tie that binds them together, the means by which alone that tie can be kept strong, — this was what he came charged to impart to us; and when he had fully delivered this message, he had done his work. His numberless speeches upon the passing questions of the day, — tariff, Bank, currency, Sub-treasury, and the rest, — in which the partisan spoke rather than the man, may have had their value at the time, but there is little in them of durable worth. Those of them which events have not refuted, time has rendered obsolete. No general principles are established in them which can be applied to new cases. Indeed, he used often to assert that there *were* no general principles in practical statesmanship, but that the government of nations is, and must be, a series of expedients. Several times, in his published works, can be found the assertion, that there is no such thing as a science of political economy, though he says he had "turned over" all the authors on that subject from Adam Smith to his own time. It is when he speaks of the Union and the Constitution, and when he is rousing the sentiment of nationality, that he utters, not, indeed, eternal truths, but truths necessary to the existence of the United States, and which can only become obsolete when the nation is no more.

The whole of his previous life had been an unconscious preparation for these great debates. It was one of the recollections of his childhood, that, in his eighth year, he had bought a handkerchief upon which was printed the Constitution of 1787, which he then read through; and while he was a farmer's boy at home, the great question of its acceptance or rejection had been decided. His father's party was the party for the Constitution, whose only regret concerning it was, that it was not so much of a constitution as they wished it to be. The Republicans dwelt upon its defects and dangers; the Federalists, upon its advantages and beauties so that all that this receptive lad heard of it at his father's fireside was of its value and necessity. We see in his youthful orations that nothing in the history of the continent struck his imagination so powerfully as the spectacle of thirty-eight gentlemen meeting in a quiet city, and peacefully settling the terms of a national union between thirteen sovereign States, most of which gave up, voluntarily, what the sword alone was once supposed capable of extorting. In all his orations on days of national festivity or mourning, we observe that his weightiest eulogy falls upon those who were conspicuous in this great business. Because Hamilton aided in it, he revered his memory; because Madison was its best interpreter, he venerated his name and deferred absolutely to his judgment. It was clear to his mind that the President can only dismiss an officer of the government as he appoints him, by and with the advice and consent of the Senate; but he would not permit himself to think so against Mr. Madison's decision. His own triumphs at the bar — those upon which he plumed himself — were all such as resulted from his lonely broodings over, and patient study of, the Constitution of his country. A native of one of the smallest of the States, to which the Union was an unmixed benefit and called for no sacrifice of pride, he grew up into nationality without having to pass through any probation of States' rights scruples. Indeed, it was as natural for a man of his calibre to be a national man as it is for his own Monadnock to be three thousand feet above the level of the sea.

The South Carolina Exposition of 1828 appeared to fall stillborn from the press. Neither General Jackson nor any of his nearest friends seem to have been so much as aware of its existence; certainly they attached no importance to it. Colonel Benton assures us, that to him the Hayne debate, so far as it related to constitutional questions, seemed a mere oratorical display without adequate cause or object; and we know that General Jackson, intimately allied with the Hayne family and strongly attached to Colonel Hayne himself, wished him success in the debate, and heard with regret that Mr. Webster was " demolishing " him.   Far, indeed, was any one from supposing that a movement had been set on foot which was to end only with the total destruction of the " interest " sought to be protected by it.   Far was any one from foreseeing that so poor and slight a thing as the Exposition was the beginning of forty years of strife.   It is evident from the Banquo passage of Mr. Webster's principal speech, when, looking at Vice-President Calhoun, he reminded that ambitious man that, in joining the coalition which made Jackson President, he had only given Van Buren a push toward the Presidency, — " No son of *theirs* succeeding," — it is evident, we say, from this passage, and from other covert allusions, that he understood the game of Nullification from the beginning, so far as its objects were personal.   But there is no reason for supposing that he attached importance to it before that memorable afternoon in December, 1830, when he strolled from the Supreme Court into the Senate-chamber, and chanced to hear Colonel Hayne reviling New England, and repeating the doctrines of the South Carolina Exposition.

Every one knows the story of this first triumph of the United States over its enemies.   Daniel Webster, as Mr. Everett records, appeared to be the only person in Washington who was entirely at his ease ; and he was so remarkably unconcerned, that Mr. Everett feared he was not aware of the expectations of the public, and the urgent necessity of his exerting all his powers. Another friend mentions, that on the day before the delivery of the principal speech the orator lay down as usual, after dinner, upon a sofa, and soon was heard laughing to himself.   Being asked what he was laughing at, he said he had just thought of a way to turn Colonel Hayne's quotation about Banquo's ghost against himself, and he was going to get up and make a note of it.   This he did, and then resumed his nap.

Notwithstanding these appearances of indifference, he was fully roused to the importance of the occasion ; and, indeed, we have the impression that only on this occasion, in his whole life, were all his powers in full activity and his entire mass of being in full glow.   But even then the artist was apparent in all that he did.

5   G

and particularly in the dress which he wore. At that time, in his forty-eighth year, his hair was still as black as an Indian's, and it lay in considerable masses about the spacious dome of his fore head. His form had neither the slenderness of his youth nor the elephantine magnitude of his later years; it was fully, but finely developed, imposing and stately, yet not wanting in alertness and grace. No costume could have been better suited to it than his blue coat and glittering gilt buttons, his ample yellow waistcoat, his black trousers, and snowy cravat. It was in some degree, perhaps, owing to the elegance and daintiness of his dress that, while the New England men among his hearers were moved to tears, many Southern members, like Colonel Benton, regarded the speech merely as a Fourth-of-July oration delivered on the 6th of January. Benton assures us, however, that he soon discovered his error, for the Nullifiers were not to be put down by a speech, and soon revealed themselves in their true character, as " irreconcilable " foes of the Union. This was Daniel Webster's own word in speaking of that faction in 1830, — " irreconcilable."

After this transcendent effort, — perhaps the greatest of its kind ever made by man, — Daniel Webster had nothing to gain in the esteem of the Northern States. He was indisputably our foremost man, and in Massachusetts there was no one who could be said to be second to him in the regard of the people: he was a whole species in himself. In the subsequent winter of debate with Calhoun upon the same subject, he added many details to his argument, developed it in many directions, and accumulated a great body of constitutional reasoning; but so far as the people were concerned, the reply to Hayne sufficed. In all those debates we are struck with his colossal, his superfluous superiority to his opponents; and we wonder how it could have been that such a man should have thought it worth while to refute such puerilities. It was, however, abundantly worth while. The assailed Constitution needed such a defender. It was necessary that the patriotic feeling of the American people, which was destined to a trial so severe, should have an unshakable basis of intelligent conviction. It was necessary that all men should be made distinctly to see that the Constitution was not a "compact" to which the States "acceded," and from which they could secede, but the fundamental law, which the people had established and ordained, from which there could be no secession but by revolution. It was necessary that the country should be made to understand that Nullification and Secession were one and the same; and that to admit the first, promising to stop short at the second, was as though a man "should take the plunge of Niagara and cry out that he would stop half-way down." Mr. Webster's principal speech on this subject, delivered in 1832, has, and will ever have, with the people and the Courts of the United States, the authority of a judicial decision; and it might very properly be added to popular editions of the Constitution as an appendix. Into the creation of the feeling and opinion which fought out the late war for the Union a thousand and ten thousand causes entered; every man who had ever performed a patriotic action, and every man who ever from his heart had spoken a patriotic word, contributed to its production; but to no man, perhaps, were we more indebted for it than to the Daniel Webster of 1830 and 1832.

We cannot so highly commend his votes in 1832 as his speeches. General Jackson's mode of dealing with nullification seems to us the model for every government to follow which has to deal with discontented subjects:—1. To take care that the laws are obeyed; 2. To remove the real grounds of discontent. This was General Jackson's plan. This, also, was the aim of Mr. Clay's compromise. Mr. Webster objected to both, on the ground that nullification was rebellion, and that no legislation respecting the pretext for rebellion should be entertained until the rebellion was quelled. Thus he came out of the battle, dear to the thinking people of the country, but estranged from the three political powers,—Henry Clay and his friends, General Jackson and his friends, Calhoun and his friends; and though he soon lapsed again under the leadership of Mr. Clay, there was never again a cordial union between him and any interior circle of politicians who could have gratified his ambition. Deceived by the thunders of applause which greeted him wherever he went, and the intense adulation of his own immediate circle, he thought that he too could be an independent power in politics. Two wild vagaries seemed to have haunted him ever after : first, that a man could merit the Presidency ; secondly, that a man could get the Presidency by meriting it.

From 1832 to the end of his life it appears to us that Daniel Webster was undergoing a process of deterioration, moral and mental. His material part gained upon his spiritual. Naturally inclined to indolence, and having an enormous capacity for physical enjoyment, a great hunter, fisherman, and farmer, a lover of good wine and good dinners, a most jovial companion, his physical desires and tastes were constantly strengthened by being keenly gratified, while his mind was fed chiefly upon past acquisitions. There is nothing in his later efforts which shows any intellectual advance, nothing from which we can infer that he had been browsing in forests before untrodden, or feeding in pastures new. He once said, at Marshfield, that, if he could live three lives in one, he would like to devote them all to study, — one to geology, one to astronomy, and one to classical literature. But it does not appear that he invigorated and refreshed the old age of his mind, by doing more than glance over the great works which treat of these subjects. A new language every ten years, or a new science vigorously pursued, seems necessary to preserve the freshness of the understanding, especially when the physical tastes are superabundantly nourished. He could praise Rufus Choate for reading a little Latin and Greek every day, — and this was better than nothing, — but he did not follow his example. There is an aged merchant in New York, who has kept his mind from growing old by devoting exactly twenty minutes every day to the reading of some abstruse book, as far removed from his necessary routine of thought as he could find. Goethe's advice to every one to read every day a short poem, recognizes the danger we all incur in taking systematic care of the body and letting the soul take care of itself. During the last ten years of Daniel Webster's life, he spent many a thousand dollars upon his library, and almost ceased to be an intellectual being.

His pecuniary habits demoralized him. It was wrong and

mean in him to accept gifts of money from the people of Boston
it was wrong in them to submit to his merciless exactions. What
need was there that their Senator should sometimes be a mendi-
cant and sometimes a pauper? If he chose to maintain baronial
state without a baron's income; if he chose to have two fancy
farms of more than a thousand acres each; if he chose to keep
two hundred prize cattle and seven hundred choice sheep for his
pleasure; if he must have about his house lamas, deer, and all
rare fowls; if his flower-garden must be one acre in extent, and
his books worth thirty thousand dollars; if he found it pleasant
to keep two or three yachts and a little fleet of smaller craft; if
he could not refrain from sending money in answer to begging
letters, and pleased himself by giving away to his black man
money enough to buy a very good house; and if he could not
avoid adding wings and rooms to his spacious mansion at Marshfield, and must needs keep open house there and have a dozen
guests at a time, — why should the solvent and careful business
men of Boston have been taxed, or have taxed themselves, to
pay any part of the expense?

Mr. Lanman, his secretary, gives us this curious and contradictory account of his pecuniary habits: —

"He made money with ease, and spent it without reflection. He
had accounts with various banks, and men of all parties were always
glad to accommodate him with loans, if he wanted them. He kept no
record of his deposits, unless it were on slips of paper hidden in his
pockets; these matters were generally left with his secretary. His
notes were seldom or never regularly protested, and when they were,
they caused him an immense deal of mental anxiety. When the
writer has sometimes drawn a check for a couple of thousand dollars,
he has not even looked at it, but packed it away in his pockets, like so
much waste paper. During his long professional career, he earned
money enough to make a dozen fortunes, but he spent it liberally, and
gave it away to the poor by hundreds and thousands. Begging letters
from women and unfortunate men were received by him almost daily,
at certain periods; and one instance is remembered where, on six successive days, he sent remittances of fifty and one hundred dollars to
people with whom he was entirely unacquainted. He was indeed careless, but strictly and religiously honest, in all his money matters. He

knew not how to be otherwise. The last fee which he ever received for a single legal argument was $11,000. . . . .

" A sanctimonious lady once called upon Mr. Webster, in Washington, with a long and pitiful story about her misfortunes and poverty, and asked him for a donation of money to defray her expenses to her home in a Western city. He listened with all the patience he could manage, expressed his surprise that she should have called upon him for money, simply because he was an officer of the government, and that, too, when she was a total stranger to him, reprimanded her in very plain language for her improper conduct, and *handed her a note of fifty dollars.*

.   .   .   .   .

" He had called upon the cashier of the bank where he kept an account, for the purpose of getting a draft discounted, when that gentleman expressed some surprise, and casually inquired why he wanted so much money ? ' To spend ; to buy bread and meat,' replied Mr. Webster, a little annoyed at this speech.

" ' But,' returned the cashier, ' you already have upon deposit in the bank no less than three thousand dollars, and I was only wondering why you wanted so much money.'

" This was indeed the truth, but Mr. Webster had forgotten it."

Mr. Lanman's assertion that Mr. Webster, with all this recklessness, was religiously honest, must have excited a grim smile upon the countenances of such of his Boston readers as had had his name upon their books. No man can be honest long who is careless in his expenditures.

It is evident from his letters, if we did not know it from other sources of information, that his carelessness with regard to the balancing of his books grew upon him as he advanced in life, and kept pace with the general deterioration of his character. In 1824, before he had been degraded by the acceptance of pecuniary aid, and when he was still a solvent person, one of his nephews asked him for a loan. He replied : "If you think you can do anything useful with a thousand dollars, you may have that sum in the spring, or sooner, if need be, on the following conditions : — 1. You must give a note for it with reasonable security. 2. The interest must be payable annually, and must be paid at the day without fail. And so long as this continues to be done, the money not to be called for — the principal — under six months' notice

I am thus explicit with you, because you wish me to be so; and because also, having a little money, and but a little, I am resolved on keeping it." This is sufficiently business-like. He *had* a little money then, — enough, as he intimates, for the economical maintenance of his family. During the land fever of 1835 and 1836, he lost so seriously by speculations in Western land, that he was saved from bankruptcy only by the aid of that mystical but efficient body whom he styled his "friends"; and from that time to the end of his life he was seldom at his ease. He earned immense occasional fees, — two of twenty-five thousand dollars each; he received frequent gifts of money, as well as a regular stipend from an invested capital; but he expended so profusely, that he was sometimes at a loss for a hundred dollars to pay his hay-makers; and he died forty thousand dollars in debt.

The adulation of which he was the victim at almost every hour of his existence injured and deceived him. He was continually informed that he was the greatest of living men, — the "godlike Daniel"; and when he escaped even into the interior of his home, he found there persons who sincerely believed that making such speeches as his was the greatest of all possible human achievements. All men whose talents are of the kind which enable their possessor to give intense pleasure to great multitudes are liable to this misfortune; and especially in a new and busy country, little removed from the colonial state, where intellectual eminence is rare, and the number of persons who can enjoy it is exceedingly great. We are growing out of this provincial propensity to abandon ourselves to admiration of the pleasure-giving talents. The time is at hand, we trust, when we shall not be struck with wonder because a man can make a vigorous speech, or write a good novel, or play Hamlet decently, and when we shall be able to enjoy the talent without adoring the man. The talent is one thing, and the man another; the talent may be immense, and the man little; the speech powerful and wise, the speaker weak and foolish. Daniel Webster came at last to loathe this ceaseless incense, but it was when his heart was set upon homage of another kind, which he was destined never to enjoy.

Another powerful cause of his deterioration was the strange, strong, always increasing desire he had to be President. Any intelligent politician, outside of the circle of his own "friends," could have told him, and proved to him, that he had little more chance of being elected President than the most insignificant man in the Whig party. And the marvel is, that he himself should not have known it, — he who knew why, precisely why, every candidate had been nominated, from Madison to General Taylor. In the teeth of all the facts, he still cherished the amazing delusion that the Presidency of the United States, like the Premiership of England, is the natural and just reward of long and able public service. The Presidency, on the contrary, is not merely an accident, but it is an accident of the last moment. It is a game too difficult for mortal faculties to play, because some of the conditions of success are as uncertain as the winds, and as ungovernable. If dexterous playing could have availed, Douglas would have carried off the stakes, for he had an audacious and a mathematical mind; while the winning man in 1856 was a heavy player, devoid of skill, whose decisive advantage was that he had been out of the game for four years. Mr. Seward, too, was within an ace of winning, when an old quarrel between two New York editors swept his cards from the table.

No: the President of the United States is not prime minister, but chief magistrate, and he is subject to that law of nature which places at the head of regular governments more or less respectable Nobodies. In Europe this law of nature works through the hereditary principle, and in America through universal suffrage. In all probability, we shall usually elect a person of the non-committal species, — one who will have lived fifty or sixty years in the world without having formed an offensive conviction or uttered a striking word, — one who will have conducted his life as those popular periodicals are conducted, in which there are "no allusions to politics or religion." And may not this be part of the exquisite economy of nature, which ever strives to get into each place the smallest man that can fill it? How miserably out of place would be a man of active, originating, disinterested spirit, at the head of a strictly limited, constitutional government, such as ours is in time of peace, in which the best President is he who does the least? Imagine a live man thrust out over the bows of a ship, and compelled to stand as figure-head, lashed by the waves and winds during a four years' voyage, and expected to be pleased with his situation because he is gilt!

Daniel Webster so passionately desired the place, that he could never see how far he was from the possibility of getting it. He was not such timber as either Southern fire-eaters or Northern wire-pullers had any use for; and a melancholy sight it was, this man, once so stately, paying court to every passing Southerner, and personally begging delegates to vote for him. He was not made for that. An elephant does sometimes stand upon his head and play a barrel-organ, but every one who sees the sorry sight sees also that it was not the design of Nature that elephants should do such things.

A Marshfield elm may be for half a century in decay without exhibiting much outward change; and when, in some tempestuous night, half its bulk is torn away, the neighborhood notes with surprise that what seemed solid wood is dry and crumbling pith. During the last fifteen years of Daniel Webster's life, his wonderfully imposing form and his immense reputation concealed from the public the decay of his powers and the degeneration of his morals. At least, few said what perhaps many felt, that " he was not the man he had been." People went away from one of his ponderous and empty speeches disappointed, but not ill pleased to boast that they too had " heard Daniel Webster speak," and feeling very sure that he could be eloquent, though he had not been. We heard one of the last of his out-of-door speeches. It was near Philadelphia, in 1844, when he was " stumping the State" for Henry Clay, and when our youthful feelings were warmly with the object of his speech. What a disappointment! How poor and pompous and pointless it seemed! Nor could we resist the impression that he was playing a part, nor help saying to ourselves, as we turned to leave the scene, " This man is not sincere in this: he is a humbug." And when, some years later, we saw him present himself before a large audience in a state not far removed from intoxication, and mumble incoherence for ten minutes, and when, in the course of the evening, we saw him

5 *

make a great show of approval whenever the clergy were complimented, the impression was renewed that the man had expended his sincerity, and that nothing was real to him any more except wine and office. And even then such were the might and majesty of his presence, that he seemed to fill and satisfy the people by merely sitting there in an arm-chair, like Jupiter, in a spacious yellow waistcoat with two bottles of Madeira under it.

All this gradual, unseen deterioration of mind and character was revealed to the country on the 7th of March, 1850. What a downfall was there! That shameful speech reads worse in 1867 than it did in 1850, and still exerts perverting power over timid and unformed minds. It was the very time for him to have broken finally with the " irreconcilable " faction, who, after having made President Tyler *snub* Daniel Webster from his dearly loved office of Secretary of State, had consummated the scheme which gave us Texas at the cost of war with Mexico, and California as one of the incidents of peace. California was not down in their programme ; and now, while claiming the right to make four slave States out of Texas, they refused to admit California to freedom. *Then* was it that Daniel Webster of Massachusetts rose in the Senate of the United States and said in substance this : These fine Southern brethren of ours have now stolen all the land there is to steal. Let us, therefore, put no obstacle in the way of their peaceable enjoyment of the plunder.

And the spirit of the speech was worse even than its doctrine. He went down upon the knees of his soul, and paid base homage to his own and his country's irreconcilable foes. Who knew better than Daniel Webster that John C. Calhoun and his followers had first created and then systematically fomented the hostile feeling which then existed between the North and the South? How those men must have chuckled among themselves when they witnessed the willing degradation of the man who should have arraigned them before the country as the conscious enemies of its peace! How was it that no one laughed outright at such billing and cooing as this?

Mr. Webster. — " An honorable member [Calhoun], whose health does not allow him to be here to-day — "

A Senator. — " He is here."

Mr. Webster. — " I am very happy to hear that he is; may he long be here, and in the enjoyment of health to serve his country ! "

And this : —

Mr. Webster. — " The honorable member did not disguise his conduct or his motives."

Mr. Calhoun. — " Never, never."

Mr. Webster. — " What he means he is very apt to say."

Mr. Calhoun. — " Always, always."

Mr. Webster. — "And I honor him for it."

And this : —

Mr. Webster. — " I see an honorable member of this body [Mason of Virginia] paying me the honor of listening to my remarks; he brings to my mind, Sir, freshly and vividly, what I learned of his great ancestor, so much distinguished in his day and generation, so worthy to be succeeded by so worthy a grandson."

And this : —

Mr. Webster. — " An honorable member from Louisiana addressed us the other day on this subject. I suppose there is not a more amiable and worthy gentleman in this chamber, nor a gentleman who would be more slow to give offence to anybody, and he did not mean in his remarks to give offence. But what did he say ? Why, Sir, he took pains to run a contrast between the slaves of the South and the laboring people of the North, giving the preference in all points of condition and comfort and happiness to the slaves."

In the course of this speech there is one most palpable contradiction. In the beginning of it, the orator mentioned the change of feeling and opinion that had occurred as to the institution of slavery, — " the North growing much more warm and strong against slavery, and the South growing much more warm and strong in its support." "Once," he said, "the most eminent men, and nearly all the conspicuous politicians of the South, held the same sentiments, — that slavery was an evil, a blight, a scourge, and a curse "; but now it is " a cherished institution in that quarter ; no evil, no scourge, but a great religious, social, and moral blessing." He then asked how this change of opinion had been brought about, and thus answered the question : " I suppose, sir, this is owing to the rapid growth and sudden extensi-n cf the COTTON plantations in the South." And to make the statement more emphatic, he caused the word *cotton* to be printed in capitals in the authorized edition of his works. But later in the speech, when he came to add his ponderous condemnation to the odium in which the handful of Abolitionists were held, — the *élite* of the nation from Franklin's day to this, — then he attributed this remarkable change to *their* zealous efforts to awaken the nobler conscience of the country. After giving his own version of their proceedings, he said : " Well, what was the result ? The bonds of the slaves were bound more firmly than before, their rivets were more strongly fastened. Public opinion, which in Virginia had begun to be exhibited against slavery, and was opening out for the discussion of the question, drew back and shut itself up in its castle."

But all would not do. He bent the knee in vain. Vain too were his personal efforts, his Southern tour, his Astor House wooings, — the politicians would have none of him ; and he had the cutting mortification of seeing himself set aside for a Winfield Scott.

Let us not, however, forget that on this occasion, though Daniel Webster appeared for the first time in his life as a leader, he was in reality still only a follower, — a follower, not of the public opinion of the North, but of the wishes of its capitalists. And probably many thousands of well-meaning men, not versed in the mysteries of politics, were secretly pleased to find themselves provided with an excuse for yielding once more to a faction, who had over us the immense advantage of having made up their minds to carry their point or fight. If his was the shame of this speech, ours was the guilt. He faithfully represented the portion of his constituents whose wine he drank, who helped him out with his notes, and who kept his atmosphere hazy with incense ; and he faithfully represented, also, that larger number who wait till the wolf is at their door before arming against him, instead of meeting him afar off in the outskirts of the wood. Let us own it the North yearned for peace in 1850, — peace at almost any price.

One of the most intimate of Mr. Webster's friends said, in a public address : " It is true that he desired the highest politica.

position in the country, — that he thought he had fairly earned a claim to that position. And I solemnly believe that because that claim was denied his days were shortened." No enemy of the great orator ever uttered anything so severe against him as this, and we are inclined to think it an error. It was probably the strength of his desire for the Presidency that shortened his life, not the mere disappointment. When President Fillmore offered him the post of Secretary of State, in 1850, it appears to have been his preference, much as he loved office, to decline it. He longed for his beautiful Marshfield, on the shore of the ocean, his herds of noble cattle, his broad, productive fields, his yachts, his fishing, his rambles in the forests planted by his own hand, his homely chats with neighbors and beloved dependents. "Oh!" said he, "if I could have my own will, never, never would I leave Marshfield again!" But his "friends," interested and disinterested, told him it was a shorter step from the office of Secretary of State to that of President than from the Senate-chamber. He yielded, as he always did, and spent a long, hot summer in Washington, to the sore detriment of his health. And again, in 1852, after he had failed to receive the nomination for the Presidency, he was offered the place of Minister to England. His "friends" again advised against his acceptance. His letter to the President, declining the offer, presents him in a sorry light indeed. "I have made up my mind to think no more about the English mission. My principal reason is, that I think it would be regarded as a descent. . . . . I have been accustomed to give instructions to ministers abroad, and not to receive them." Accustomed! Yes: for two years! It is probable enough that his acceptance of office, and his adherence to it, hastened his death. Four months after the words were written which we have just quoted, he was no more.

His last days were such as his best friends could have wished them to be, — calm, dignified, affectionate. worthy of his lineage. His burial, too, was singularly becoming, impressive, and touching. We have been exceedingly struck with the account of it given by Mr. George S. Hillard, in his truly elegant and eloquent eulogy upon Mr. Webster, delivered in Faneuil Hall. In his last will, executed a few days before his death, Mr. Webster requested that he might be buried "without the least show or ostentation, but in a manner respectful to my neighbors, whose kindness has contributed so much to the happiness of me and mine." His wishes were obeyed; and he was buried more as the son of plain, brave Captain Ebenezer Webster, than as Secretary of State. "No coffin," said Mr. Hillard, "concealed that majestic frame. In the open air, clad as when alive, he lay extended in seeming sleep, with no touch of disfeature upon his brow, — as noble an image of reposing strength as ever was seen upon earth. Around him was the landscape that he had loved, and above him was nothing but the dome of the covering heavens. The sunshine fell upon the dead man's face, and the breeze blew over it. A lover of Nature, he seemed to be gathered into her maternal arms, and to lie like a child upon a mother's lap. We felt, as we looked upon him, that death had never stricken down, at one blow, a greater sum of life. And whose heart did not swell when, from the honored and distinguished men there gathered together, six plain Marshfield farmers were called forth to carry the head of their neighbor to the grave. Slowly and sadly the vast multitude followed, in mourning silence, and he was laid down to rest among dear and kindred dust."

In surveying the life and works of this eminent and gifted man, we are continually struck with the evidences of his magnitude. He was, as we have said, a very large person. His brain was within a little of being one third larger than the average, and it was one of the largest three on record. His bodily frame, in all its parts, was on a majestic scale, and his presence was immense. He liked large things, — mountains, elms, great oaks, mighty bulls and oxen, wide fields, the ocean, the Union, and all things of magnitude. He liked great Rome far better than refined Greece, and revelled in the immense things of literature, such as Paradise Lost, and the Book of Job, Burke, Dr. Johnson, and the Sixth Book of the Æneid. Homer he never cared much for, — nor, indeed, anything Greek. He hated, he loathed, the act of writing. Billiards, ten-pins, chess, draughts, whist, he never relished, though fond to excess of out-door pleasures, like hum ing, fishing, yachting. He liked to be alone with great Nature, — alone in the giant woods or on the shores of the resounding sea, — alone all day with his gun, his dog, and his thoughts, — alone in the morning, before any one was astir but himself, looking out upon the sea and the glorious sunrise. What a delicious picture of this large, healthy Son of Earth Mr. Lanman gives us, where he describes him coming into his bedroom, at sunrise, and startling him out of a deep sleep by shouting, " Awake, sluggard ! and look upon this glorious scene, for the sky and the ocean are enveloped in flames ! " He was akin to all large, slow things in nature. A herd of fine cattle gave him a keen, an inexhaustible enjoyment ; but he never "tasted" a horse : he had no horse enthusiasm. In England he chiefly enjoyed these five things, the Tower of London, Westminster Abbey, Smithfield Cattle Market, English farming, and Sir Robert Peel. Sir Robert Peel he thought was "head and shoulders above any other man" he had ever met. He greatly excelled, too, in describing immense things. In speaking of the Pyramids, once, he asked, " Who can inform us by what now unknown machines mass was thus aggregated to mass, and quarry piled on quarry, till solid granite seemed to cover the earth and reach the skies." His peculiar love of the Union of these States was partly due, perhaps, to this habit of his mind of dwelling with complacency on vastness. He felt that he wanted and required a continent to live in : his mind would have gasped for breath in New Hampshire.

But this enormous creature was not an exception to the law which renders giants harmless by seaming them with weakness, but for which the giants would possess the earth. If he had been completed throughout on the plan on which he was sketched, if he had been as able to originate as he was powerful to state, if he had possessed will proportioned to his strength, moral power equal to his moral feeling, intellect on a par with his genius, and principle worthy of his intellect, he would have subjugated mankind, and raised his country to a point from which it would have dropped when the tyrannizing influence was withdrawn. Every sphere of life has its peculiar temptations, which there is only one thing that can enable a man to resist, —

a religious, i. e. a disinterested devotion to its duties. Daniel Webster was one of those who fell before the seductions of his place. He was not one of those who find in the happiness and prosperity of their country, and in the esteem of their fellow-citizens, their own sufficient and abundant reward for serving her. He pined for something lower, smaller, — something personal and vulgar. He had no religion, — not the least tincture of it; and he seemed at last, in his dealings with individuals, to have no conscience. What he called his religion had no effect whatever upon the conduct of his life; it made him go to church, talk piously, puff the clergy, and " patronize Providence," — no more. He would accept retaining fees, and never look into the bundles of papers which accompanied them, in which were enclosed the hopes and the fortune of anxious households. He would receive gifts of money, and toss into his waste-paper basket the list of the givers, without having glanced at its contents; thus defrauding them of the only recompense in his power to grant, and the only one they wished. It shocked him if his secretary came to the dinner-table in a frock-coat, and he would himself appear drunk before three thousand people. And yet, such was the power of his genius, such was the charm of his manner, such the affectionateness of his nature, such the robust heartiness of his enjoyment of life, that honorable men who knew his faults best loved him to the last, — not in spite of them, but partly in consequence of them. What in another man they would have pronounced atrocious, appeared in him a kind of graceful rollicking helplessness to resist.

Such, as it seems to our very imperfect judgment, was Daniel Webster, one of the largest and one of the weakest of men, of admirable genius and deplorable character; who began life well and served his country well and often, but held not out faithful to the end. American statesmen are called to a higher vocation than those of other countries, and there is nothing in the politics of America which *can* reward a man of eminent ability for public service. If such a person feels that his country's happiness and greatness will not be a satisfying recompense for anything he can do for her, let him, as he values his peace and soul's health, cling to the safe obscurity of private life.

JOHN C. CALHOUN.

JOHN C. CALHOUN.

THERE were two ways of getting to South Carolina in Colonial
times. The first immigrants, many of whom were men of
capital, landed at Charleston, and, settling in the fertile low country along the coast, became prosperous planters of rice, indigo, and
corn, before a single white inhabitant had found his way to the
more salubrious upper country in the western part of the Province. The settlers of the upper country were plain, poorer people, who landed at Philadelphia or Baltimore, and travelled
southward along the base of the Alleghanies to the inviting table-
lands of the Carolinas. In the lower country, the estates were
large, the slaves numerous, the white inhabitants few, idle, and
profuse. The upper country was peopled by a sturdier race,
who possessed farms of moderate extent, hewn out of the wilderness by their own strong arms, and tilled by themselves with the
aid of few slaves. Between the upper and the lower country
there was a waste region of sandy hills and rocky acclivities, un-
inhabited, almost uninhabitable, which rendered the two sections
of one Province separate communities scarcely known to one
another. Down almost to the beginning of the Revolutionary
War, the farmers of the upper country were not represented in
the Legislature of South Carolina, though they were then as numerous as the planters of the lower country. Between the people of the two sections there was little unity of feeling. The
lordly planters of the lower country regarded their Western fellow-citizens as provincial or plebeian; the farmers of the upper
country had some contempt for the planters as effeminate, aristocratic, and Tory. The Revolution abased the pride, lessened the
wealth, and improved the politics of the planters; a revised Con-

stitution, in 1790, gave preponderance to the up-country farmers in the popular branch of the Legislature; and thenceforth South Carolina was a sufficiently homogeneous commonwealth.

Looking merely to the public career of Calhoun, the special pleader of the Southern aristocracy, we should expect to find him born and reared among the planters of the low country. The Calhouns, on the contrary, were up-country people, — farmers, Whigs, Presbyterians, men of moderate means, who wielded the axe and held the plough with their own hands, until enabled to buy a few "new negroes," cheap and savage; called new, because fresh from Africa. A family party of them (parents, four sons, and a daughter) emigrated from the North of Ireland early in the last century, and settled first in Pennsylvania; then removed to Western Virginia; whence the defeat of Braddock, in 1755, drove them southward, and they found a permanent abode in the extreme west of South Carolina, then an unbroken wilderness. Of those four sons, Patrick Calhoun, the father of the Nullifier, was the youngest. He was six years old when the family left Ireland; twenty-nine, when they planted the "Calhoun Settlement" in Abbeville District, South Carolina.

Patrick Calhoun was a strong-headed, wrong-headed, very brave, honest, ignorant man. His whole life, almost, was a battle. When the Calhouns had been but five years in their forest home, the Cherokees attacked the settlement, destroyed it utterly, killed one half the men, and drove the rest to the lower country; whence they dared not return till the peace of 1763. Patrick Calhoun was elected to command the mounted rangers raised to protect the frontiers, a duty heroically performed by him. After the peace, the settlement enjoyed several years of tranquillity, during which Patrick Calhoun was married to Martha Caldwell, a native of Virginia, but the daughter of an Irish Presbyterian emigrant. During this peaceful interval, all the family prospered with the settlement which bore its name; and Patrick, who in his childhood had only learned to read and write, availed himself of such leisure as he had to increase his knowledge. Besides reading the books within his reach, which were few, he learned to survey land, and practised that vocation to advantage

He was especially fond of reading history to gather new proofs of the soundness of his political opinions, which were Whig to the uttermost. The war of the Revolution broke in upon the settlement, at length, and made deadly havoc there; for it was warred upon by three foes at once, — the British, the Tories, and the Cherokees. The Tories murdered in cold blood a brother of Patrick Calhoun's wife. Another of her brothers fell at Cowpens under thirty sabre-wounds. Another was taken prisoner, and remained for nine months in close confinement at one of the British Andersonvilles of that day. Patrick Calhoun, in many a desperate encounter with the Indians, displayed singular coolness, courage, adroitness, and tenacity. On one memorable occasion, thirteen of his neighbors and himself maintained a forest fight for several hours with a force of Cherokees ten times their number. When seven of the white men had fallen, the rest made their escape. Returning three days after to bury their dead, they found upon the field the bodies of twenty-three Indian warriors. At another time, as his son used to relate, he had a very long combat with a chief noted for the certainty of his aim, — the Indian behind a tree, the white man behind a fallen log. Four times the wily Calhoun drew the Indian's fire by elevating his hat upon his ramrod. The chief, at last, could not refrain from looking to see the effect of his shot; when one of his shoulders was slightly exposed. On the instant, the white man's rifle sent a ball through it; the chief fled into the forest, and Patrick Calhoun bore off as a trophy of the fight his own hat pierced with four bullets.

This Patrick Calhoun illustrates well the North-of-Ireland character; one peculiarity of which is the possession of *will* disproportioned to intellect. Hence a man of this race frequently appears to striking advantage in scenes which demand chiefly an exercise of will; while in other spheres, which make larger demands upon the understanding, the same man may be simply mischievous. We see this in the case of Andrew Jackson, who at New Orleans was glorious; at Washington almost wholly pernicious; and in the case of Andrew Johnson, who was eminently useful to his country in 1861, but obstructive and perilous to it in

1866. For these Scotch-Irishmen, though they are usually very honest men, and often right in their opinions, are an uninstructable race, who stick to a prejudice as tenaciously as to a principle, and really suppose they are battling for right and truth, when they are only wreaking a private vengeance or aiming at a personal advantage. Patrick Calhoun was the most radical of Democrats; one of your despisers of conventionality; an enemy of lawyers, thinking the common sense of mankind competent to decide what is right without their aid; a particular opponent of the arrogant pretensions of the low-country aristocrats. When the up-country people began to claim a voice in the government, long since due to their numbers, the planters, of course, opposed their demand. To establish their right to vote, Patrick Calhoun and a party of his neighbors, armed with rifles, marched across the State to within twenty-three miles of Charleston, and there voted in defiance of the plantation lords. Events like this led to the admission of members from the up-country; and Patrick Calhoun was the first to represent that section in the Legislature. It was entirely characteristic of him to vote against the adoption of the Federal Constitution, on the ground that it authorized other people to tax Carolinians; which he said was taxation without representation. That was just like a narrow, cranky, opinionative, unmanageable Calhoun.

Devoid of imagination and of humor, a hard-headed, eager politician, he brought up his boy upon politics. This was sorry nourishment for a child's mind, but he had little else to give him. Gambling, hunting, whiskey, and politics were all there was to relieve the monotony of life in a Southern back settlement; and the best men naturally threw themselves upon politics. Calhoun told Miss Martineau that he could remember standing between his father's knees, when he was only five years old, and listening to political conversation. He told Duff Green that he had a distinct recollection of hearing his father say, when he was only nine, that that government is best which allows to each individual the largest liberty compatible with order and tranquillity, and that improvements in political science consist in throwing off needless restraints. It was a strange child that could remember such a remark. As Patrick Calhoun died in 1795, when his son was thirteen years old, the boy must have been very young when he heard it, even if he were mistaken as to the time. Whether Patrick Calhoun ever touched upon the subject of slavery in his conversations with his children, is not reported. We only know that, late in the career of Mr. Calhoun, he used to be taunted by his opponents in South Carolina with having once held that slavery was good and justifiable only so far as it was preparatory to freedom. He was accused of having committed the crime of saying, in a public speech, that slavery was like the " scaffolding " of an edifice, which, after having served its temporary purpose, would be taken down, of course. We presume he said this ; because *everything* in his later speeches is flatly contradicted in those of his earlier public life. Patrick Calhoun was a man to give a reason for everything. He was an habitual theorizer and generalizer, without possessing the knowledge requisite for safe generalization. It is very probable that this apology for slavery was part of his son's slender inheritance.

John Caldwell Calhoun — born in 1782, the youngest but one in a family of five children — was eighteen years old before he had a thought of being anything but a farmer. His father had been dead five years. His only sister was married to that famous Mr. Waddell, clergyman and schoolmaster, whose academy in North Carolina was for so many years a great light in a dark place. One of his brothers was a clerk in a mercantile house at Charleston ; another was settled on a farm near by ; another was still a boy. His mother lived upon the paternal farm ; and with her lived her son John, who ploughed, hunted, fished, and rode, in the manner of the farmers' sons in that country. At eighteen he could read, write, and cipher ; he had read Rollin, Robertson, Voltaire's Charles XII., Brown's Essays, Captain Cook, and parts of Locke. This, according to his own account, was the sum of his knowledge, except that he had fully imbibed his father's decided republican opinions. He shared to some degree his father's prejudice, and the general prejudice of the upper country against lawyers ; although a cousin, John Ewing Calhoun, had risen high in that profession, had long served in the Legislature of South Carolina and was about to be elected United States Senator on the Jeffersonian side. As late as May 1800, when he was past eighteen, preference and necessity appeared to fix him in the vocation of farmer. The family had never been rich. Indeed, the great Nullifier himself was a comparatively poor man all his life, the number of his slaves never much exceeding thirty; which is equivalent to a working force of fifteen hands or less.

In May, 1800, Calhoun's elder brother came home from Charleston to spend the summer, bringing with him his city notions. He awoke the dormant ambition of the youth, urged him to go to school and become a professional man. But how could he leave his mother alone on the farm? and how could the money be raised to pay for a seven years' education? His mother and his brother conferred upon these points, and satisfied him upon both; and in June, 1800, he made his way to the academy of his brother-in-law, Waddell, which was then in Columbia County, Georgia, fifty miles from the home of the Calhouns. In two years and a quarter from the day he first opened a Latin grammar, he entered the Junior Class of Yale College. This was quick work. Teachers, however, are aware that late beginners, who have spent their boyhood in *growing*, often stride past students who have passed theirs in stunting the growth of mind and body at school. Calhoun, late in life, often spoke of the immense advantage which Southern boys had over Northern in not going so early to school, and being so much on horseback and out of doors. He said one day, about the year 1845: "At the North you overvalue intellect; at the South we rely upon character; and if ever there should be a collision that shall test the strength of the two sections, you will find that character is stronger than intellect, and will carry the day." The prophecy has been fulfilled.

Timothy Dwight, Calvinist and Federalist, was President of Yale College during Calhoun's residence there, and Thomas Jefferson, Democrat and freethinker, was President of the United States. Yale was a stronghold of Federalism. A brother of the President of the College, in his Fourth-of-July oration delivered at New Haven four months after the inauguration of Jefferson and Burr, announced to the students and citizens, that " the great object " of those gentlemen and their adherents was " to destroy every trace of civilization in the world, and to force mankind back into a savage state." He also used the following language: " We have now reached the consummation of democratic blessedness. We have a country governed by blockheads and knaves; the ties of marriage, with all its felicities, are severed and destroyed; our wives and daughters are thrown into the stews; our children are cast into the world from the breast forgotten; filial piety is extinguished; and our surnames, the only mark of distinction among families, are abolished. Can the imagination paint anything more dreadful this side hell?" These remarkable statements, so far from surprising the virtuous people of New Haven, were accepted by them, it appears, as facts, and published with general approval. From what we know of President Dwight, we may conclude that he would regard his brother's oration as a pardonable flight of hyperbole, based on truth. He was a Federalist of the deepest dye.

Transferred to a scene where such opinions prevailed, it cost the young republican no great exertion either of his intellect or his firmness or his family pride to hold his ground. Of all known men, he had the most complete confidence in the infallibility of his own mind. He used to relate, that in the Senior year, when he was one of very few in a class of seventy who maintained republican opinions, President Dwight asked him, " What is the legitimate source of power?" " The people," answered the student. Dr. Dwight combated this opinion; Calhoun replied; and the whole hour of recitation was consumed in the debate. Dr. Dwight was so much struck with the ability displayed by the student, that he remarked to a friend that Calhoun had talent enough to be President of the United States, and that we should see him President in due time. In those innocent days, an observation of that nature was made of every young fellow who showed a little spirit and a turn for debate. Fathers did not *then* say to their promising offspring, Beware, my son, of self-seeking and shallow speaking, lest you should be con

6

signed to the White House, and be devoured by office-seekers. People then regarded the Presidency as a kind of reward of merit, the first step toward which was to get "up head" in the spelling-class. There is reason to believe that young Calhoun took the prediction of the Doctor very seriously. He took everything seriously. He never made a joke in his life, and was totally destitute of the sense of humor. It is doubtful if he was ever capable of unbending so far as to play a game of football.

The ardent political discussions then in vogue had one effect which the late Mr. Buckle would have pronounced most salutary; they prevented Dr. Dwight's severe theology from taking hold of the minds of many students. Calhoun wholly escaped it. In his speeches we find, of course, the stock allusions of a religious nature with which all politicians essay to flatter their constituents; but he was never interested in matters theological. A century earlier, he might have been the Jonathan Edwards of the South, if there had been a South then. His was just the mind to have revelled in theological subtilties, and to have calmly, closely, unrelentingly argued nearly the whole human race into endless and hopeless perdition. His was just the nature to have contemplated his argument with complacency, and its consequences without emotion.

Graduating with credit in 1804, he repaired to the famous Law School at Litchfield in Connecticut, where he remained a year and a half, and won general esteem. Tradition reports him a diligent student and an admirable debater there. As to his moral conduct, that was always irreproachable. That is to say, he was at every period of his life continent, temperate, orderly, and out of debt. In 1806, being then twenty-four years of age, he returned to South Carolina, and, after studying a short time in a law office at Charleston, he went at last to his native Abbeville to complete his preparation for the bar. He was still a law student at that place when the event occurred which called him into public life.

June 22d, 1807, at noon, the United States frigate Chesapeake, thirty-eight guns, left her anchorage at Hampton Roads, and put to sea, bound for the Mediterranean. The United States being at peace with all the world, the Chesapeake was very far from being in proper man-of-war trim. Her decks were littered with furniture, baggage, stores, cables, and animals. The guns were loaded, but rammers, matches, wadding, cannon-balls, were all out of place, and not immediately accessible. The crew were merchant sailors and landsmen, all undrilled in the duties peculiar to an armed ship. There had been lying for some time at the same anchorage the British frigate Leopard, fifty guns; and this ship also put to sea at noon of the same day. The Leopard being in perfect order, and manned by a veteran crew, took the lead of the Chesapeake, and kept it until three in the afternoon, when she was a mile in advance. Then she wore round, came within speaking distance, lowered a boat, and sent a lieutenant on board the American ship. This officer bore a despatch from the admiral of the station, ordering any captain who should fall in with the Chesapeake to search her for deserters. The American commander replied that he knew of no deserters on board his ship, and could not permit a search to be made, his orders not authorizing the same. The lieutenant returned. As soon as he had got on board, and his boat was stowed away, the Leopard fired a full broadside into the American frigate. The American commodore, being totally unprepared for such an event, could not return the fire; and therefore, when his ship had received twenty-one shot in her hull, when her rigging was much cut up, when three of her crew were killed and eighteen wounded, the commodore himself among the latter, he had no choice but to lower his flag. Then the search was made, and four men, claimed as deserters, were taken; after which the Leopard continued her course, and the crippled Chesapeake returned to Hampton Roads. The American commander was sentenced by a court-martial to five years' suspension for going to sea in such a condition. The English government recalled the admiral who ordered, and deprived of his ship the captain who committed, this unparalleled outrage, but made no other reparation.

No words of ours could convey any adequate idea of the rage which this event excited in the people of the United States. For a time, the Federalists themselves were ready for war. There were meetings everywhere to denounce it, and especially in the Southern States, always more disposed than the Northern to begin the shedding of blood, and already the main reliance of the Republican party.   Remote and rustic Abbeville, a very Republican district, was not silent on this occasion ; and who so proper to draw and support the denunciatory resolutions as young Calhoun, the son of valiant Patrick, fresh from college, though now in his twenty-sixth year? The student performed this duty, as requested, and spoke so well that his neighbors at once concluded that he was the very man, lawyer as he was, to represent them in the Legislature, where for nearly thirty years his father had served them. At the next election, in a district noted for its aversion to lawyers, wherein no lawyer had ever been chosen to the Legislature, though many had been candidates, he was elected at the head of his ticket.   His triumph was doubtless owing in a great degree to the paramount influence of his family. Still, even we, who knew him only in his gaunt and sad decline, can easily imagine that at twenty-six he must have been an engaging, attractive man.   Like most of his race, he was rather slender, but very erect, with a good deal of dignity and some grace in his carriage and demeanor. His eyes were always remarkably fine and brilliant. He had a well-developed and strongly set nose, cheek-bones high, and cheeks rather sunken. His mouth was large, and could never have been a comely feature. His early portraits show his hair erect on his forehead, as we all remember it, unlike Jackson, whose hair at forty still fell low over his forehead. His voice could never have been melodious, but it was always powerful. At every period of his life, his manners, when in company with his inferiors in age or standing, were extremely agreeable, even fascinating. We have heard a well-known editor, who began life as a "page" in the Senate-chamber, say that there was no Senator whom the pages took such delight in serving as Mr. Calhoun. "Why?" — "Because he was so democratic." — "How democratic?" — "He was as polite to a page as to the President of the Senate, and as considerate of his feelings." We have heard another member of the press, whose first employment was to report the speeches of Clay, Webster, and Calhoun.

beai similar testimony to the frank, engaging courtesy of his intercourse with the corps of reporters. It is fair, therefore, to conclude that his early popularity at home was due as much to his character and manners as to his father's name and the influence of his relatives.

He served two years in the Legislature, and in the intervals between the sessions practised law at Abbeville. At once he took a leading position in the Legislature. He had been in his seat but a few days when the Republican members, as the custom then was, met in caucus to nominate a President and Vice-President of the United States. For Mr. Madison the caucus was unanimous, but there was a difference with regard to the Vice-Presidency, then filled by the aged George Clinton of New York, who represented the anti-Virginian wing of the party in power. Mr. Calhoun, in a set speech, opposed the renomination of Governor Clinton, on the ground that in the imminency of a war with England the Republican party ought to present an unbroken front. He suggested the nomination of John Langdon of New Hampshire for the second office. At this late day we cannot determine whether this suggestion was original with Mr. Calhoun. We only know that the caucus affirmed it, and that the nomination was afterwards tendered to Mr. Langdon by the Republican party, and declined by him. Mr. Calhoun's speech on this occasion was the expression of Southern opinions as to the foreign policy of the country. The South was then nearly ready for war with England, while Northern Republicans still favored Mr. Jefferson's non-intercourse policy. In this instance, as in so many others, we find the Slave States, which used to plume themselves upon being the conservative element in an else unrestrainable democracy, ready for war first, though far from being the worst sufferers from England's piracies. We should have had *no* war from 1782 to 1865, but for them. We also find Mr. Calhoun, in this his first utterance as a public man, the mouth-piece of his " section." He has been styled the most inconsistent of our statesmen; but beneath the palpable contradictions of his speeches, there is to be noticed a deeper consistency. Whatever opinion, whatever policy, he may have advocated, he always spoke the sense of what Mr. Sumner used to call the Southern oligarchy. If *it* changed, *he* changed. If he appeared sometimes to lead it, it was by leading it in the direction in which it wanted to go. He was doubtless as sincere in this as any great special pleader is in a cause in which all his powers are enlisted. Calhoun's mind was narrow and provincial. He could not have been the citizen of a large place. As a statesman he was naturally the advocate of something special and sectional, something not the whole.

Distinguished in the Legislature, he was elected, late in 1810, by a very great majority, to represent his district in Congress. In May, 1811, he was married to a second-cousin, Floride Calhoun, who brought a considerable accession to his slender estate. November 4, 1811, he took his seat in the House of Representatives. Thus, at the early age of twenty-nine, he was fairly launched into public life, with the advantage, usually enjoyed then by Southern members, of being independent in his circumstances. Though unknown to the country, his fame had preceded him to Washington ; and the Speaker, Mr. Clay, gave him a place on the Committee on Foreign Relations. This Committee, considering that Congress had been summoned a month earlier than usual for the express purpose of dealing with foreign relations, was at once the most important and the most conspicuous committee of the House.

Mr. Calhoun's first session gave him national reputation, and made him a leader of the war party in Congress. We could perhaps say *the* leader, since Mr. Clay was not upon the floor. After surveying the novel scene around him for six weeks, he delivered his maiden speech, — a plain, forcible, not extraordinary argument in favor of preparing for war. It was prodigiously successful, so far as the reputation of the speaker was concerned. Members gathered round to congratulate the young orator ; and Father Ritchie (if he was a father then) "hailed this young Carolinian as one of the master spirits who stamp their names upon the age in which they live." This speech contains one passage which savors of the "chivalric" taint, and indicates the provincia. mind. In replying to the objection founded on the expenses of war, he said: "I enter my solemn protest against this low and calculating avarice' entering this hall of legislation. It is *only fit for shops and counting-houses*, and ought not to disgrace the seat of power by its squalid aspect. Whenever it touches sovereign power, the nation is ruined. It is too short-sighted to defend itself. It is a compromising spirit, always ready to yield a part to save the residue. It is too timid to have in itself the laws of self-preservation. Sovereign power is never safe but under the shield of honor." This was thought very fine talk in those simple days among the simple Southern country members.

As the session progressed, Mr. Calhoun spoke frequently, and with greater effect. Wisely he never spoke. In his best efforts we see that something which we know not what to name, unless we call it *Southernism*. If it were allowable to use a slang expression, we should style the passages to which we refer effective bosh. The most telling passage in the most telling speech which he delivered at this session may serve to illustrate our meaning. Imagine these short, vigorous sentences uttered with great rapidity, in a loud, harsh voice, and with energy the most intense: —

"Tie down a hero, and he feels the puncture of a pin; throw him into battle, and he is almost insensible to vital gashes. So in war. Impelled alternately by hope and fear, stimulated by revenge, depressed by shame, or elevated by victory, the people become invincible. No privation can shake their fortitude; no calamity break their spirit. Even when equally successful, the contrast between the two systems is striking. War and restriction may leave the country equally exhausted; but the latter not only leaves you poor, but, even when successful, dispirited, divided, discontented, with diminished patriotism, and the morals of a considerable portion of your people corrupted. Not so in war. In that state, the common danger unites all, strengthens the bonds of society, and feeds the flame of patriotism. The national character mounts to energy. In exchange for the expenses and privat'ons of war, you obtain military and naval skill, and a more perfect organization of such parts of your administration as are connected with the science of national defence. Sir, are these advantages to be counted as trifles in the present state of the world? Can they be measured by moneyed valuation? I would prefer a single victory over the enemy, by sea or land, to all the good we shall ever derive

from the continuation of the Non-importation act. I know not that
a victory would produce an equal pressure on the enemy; but I am
certain of what is of greater consequence, it would be accompanied by
more salutary effects to ourselves. The memory of Saratoga, Princeton, and Eutaw is immortal. It is there you will find the country's
boast and pride, — the inexhaustible source of great and heroic sentiments. But what will history say of restriction? What examples
worthy of imitation will it furnish to posterity? What pride, what
pleasure will our children find in the events of such times? Let me
not be considered romantic. This nation ought to be taught to rely on
its courage, its fortitude, its skill and virtue, for protection. These are
the only safeguards in the hour of danger. Man was endued with
these great qualities for his defence. There is nothing about him that
indicates that he is to conquer by endurance. He is not incrusted in
a shell; he is not taught to rely upon his insensibility, his passive suffering, for defence. No, sir; it is on the invincible mind, on a magnanimous nature, he ought to rely. Here is the superiority of our kind; it
is these that render man the lord of the world. Nations rise above
nations, as they are endued in a greater degree with these brilliant
qualities."

This passage is perfectly characteristic of Calhoun, whose
speeches present hundreds of such inextricable blendings of truth
and falsehood.

We have the written testimony of an honorable man, still living, Commodore Charles Stewart, U. S. N., that John C. Calhoun
was a conscious traitor to the Union as early as 1812. In December of that year, Captain Stewart's ship, the Constitution, was
refitting at the Washington Navy Yard, and the Captain was
boarding at Mrs. Bushby's, with Mr. Clay, Mr. Calhoun, and
many other Republican members. Conversing one evening with
the new member from South Carolina, he told him that he was
" puzzled " to account for the close alliance which existed between
the Southern planters and the Northern Democracy.

" You," said Captain Stewart, " in the South and Southwest, are decidedly the aristocratic portion of this Union; you are so in holding
persons in perpetuity in slavery; you are so in every domestic quality
so in every habit in your lives, living, and actions, so in habits, customs, intercourse, and manners; you neither work with your hands,
heads, nor any machinery, but live and have your living, not in ac-

cordance with the will of your Creator, but by the sweat of slavery, and yet you assume all the attributes, professions, and advantages of democracy."

Mr. Calhoun, aged thirty, replied thus to Captain Stewart, aged thirty-four: —

"I see you speak through the head of a young statesman, and from the heart of a patriot, but you lose sight of the politician and the sectional policy of the people. I admit your conclusions in respect to us Southrons. That we are essentially aristocratic, I cannot deny; but we can and do yield much to democracy. This is our sectional policy; we are from necessity thrown upon and solemnly wedded to that party, however it may occasionally clash with our feelings, for the conservation of our interests. It is through our affiliation with that party in the Middle and Western States that we hold power; but when we cease thus to control this nation through a disjointed democracy, or any material obstacle in that party which shall tend to throw us out of that rule and control, we shall then resort to the dissolution of the Union. The compromises in the Constitution, under the circumstances, were sufficient for our fathers, but, under the altered condition of our country from that period, leave to the South no resource but dissolution; for no amendments to the Constitution could be reached through a convention of the people under their three-fourths rule."

Probably all of our readers have seen this conversation in print before. But it is well for us to consider it again and again. It is the key to all the seeming inconsistencies of Mr. Calhoun's career. He came up to Congress, and took the oath to support the Constitution, secretly resolved to break up the country just as soon as the Southern planters ceased to control it for the maintenance of their peculiar interest. The reader will note, too, the distinction made by this young man, who was never youthful, between the "statesman" and the "politician," and between the "heart of a patriot" and "the sectional policy of the people."

Turning from his loathsome and despicable exposition to the Congressional career of Mr. Calhoun, we find no indication there of the latent traitor. He was merely a very active, energetic member of the Republican party; supporting the war by assiduous labors in committee, and by intense declamation of the kind of which we have given a specimen. In all his speeches there

6 *   I

is not a touch of greatness. He declared that Demosthenes was his model, — an orator who was a master of all the arts, all the artifices, and all the tricks by which a mass of ignorant and turbulent hearers can be kept attentive, but who has nothing to impart to a member of Congress who honestly desires to convince his equals. Mr. Calhoun's harangues in the supposed Demosthenean style gave him, however, great reputation out of doors, while his diligence, his dignified and courteous manners, gained him warm admirers on the floor. He was a messmate of Mr. Clay at this time. Besides agreeing in politics, they were on terms of cordial personal intimacy. Henry Clay, Speaker of the House, was but five years older than Calhoun, and in everything but years much younger. Honest patriots pointed to these young men with pride and hope, congratulating each other that, though the Revolutionary statesmen were growing old and passing away, the high places of the Republic would be filled, in due time, by men worthy to succeed them.

When the war was over, a strange thing was to be noted in the politics of the United States : the Federal party was dead, but the Republican party had adopted its opinions. The disasters of the war had convinced almost every man of the necessity of investing the government with the power to wield the resources of the country more readily ; and, accordingly, we find leading Republicans, like Judge Story, John Quincy Adams, and Mr. Clay, favoring the measures which had formerly been the special rallying-cries of the Federalists. Judge Story spoke the feeling of his party when he wrote, in 1815 : " Let us extend the national authority over the whole extent of power given by the Constitution. Let us have great military and naval schools, an adequate regular army, the broad foundations laid of a permanent navy, a national bank, a national bankrupt act," etc., etc. The strict-constructionists were almost silenced in the general cry, " Let us be a Nation." In the support of *all* the measures to which this feeling gave rise, especially the national bank, internal improvements, and a protective tariff, Mr. Calhoun went as far as any man, and farther than most ; for such at that time was the humor of the planters.

To the principle of a protective tariff he was peculiarly committed. It had not been his intention to take part in the debates on the Tariff Bill of 1816. On the 6th of April, while he was busy writing in a committee-room, Mr. Samuel D. Ingham of Pennsylvania, his particular friend and political ally, came to him and said that the House had fallen into some confusion while discussing the tariff bill, and added, that, as it was "difficult to rally so large a body when once broken on a tax bill," he wished Mr. Calhoun would speak on the question in order to keep the House together. "What can I say?" replied the member from South Carolina. Mr. Ingham, however, persisted, and Mr. Calhoun addressed the House. An amendment had just been introduced to leave cotton goods unprotected, a proposition which had been urged on the ground that Congress had no authority to impose any duty except for revenue. On rising to speak, Mr. Calhoun at once, and most unequivocally, committed himself to the protective principle. He began by saying, that, *if the right to protect had not been called in question, he would not have spoken at all.* It was solely to assist in establishing *that* right that he had been induced, without previous preparation, to take part in the debate. He then proceeded to deliver an ordinary protectionist speech; without, however, entering upon the question of constitutional right. He merely dwelt upon the great benefits to be derived from affording to our infant manufactures "immediate and ample protection." That the Constitution interposed no obstacle, was assumed by him throughout. He concluded by observing, that a flourishing manufacturing interest would "bind together more closely our widely-spread republic," since "it will greatly increase our mutual dependence and intercourse, and excite an increased attention to internal improvements, — a subject every way so intimately connected with the ultimate attainment of national strength and the perfection of our political institutions." He further observed, that "the liberty and union of this country are inseparable," and that the destruction of either would involve the destruction of the other. He concluded his speech with these words: "Disunion, — this single word comprehends almost the sum of our political dangers, and against t we ought to be perpetually guarded."

The time has passed for any public man to claim credit for "consistency." A person who, after forty years of public life, can truly say that he has never changed an opinion, must be either a demigod or a fool. We do not blame Mr. Calhoun for ceasing to be a protectionist and becoming a free-trader; for half the thinking world has changed sides on that question during the last thirty years. A growing mind must necessarily change its opinions. But there *is* a consistency from which no man, public or private, can ever be absolved, — the consistency of his statements with fact. In the year 1833, in his speech on the Force Bill, Mr. Calhoun referred to his tariff speech of 1816 in a manner which excludes him from the ranks of men of honor. He had the astonishing audacity to say: "I am constrained in candor to acknowledge, for I wish to disguise nothing, that the pro‧tective principle was recognized by the Act of 1816. How this was overlooked at the time, it is not in my power to say. *It escaped my observation*, which I can account for only on the ground that the principle was new, and that my attention was engaged by another important subject." The charitable reader may interpose here, and say that Mr. Calhoun may have forgotten his speech of 1816. Alas! no. He had that speech before him at the time. Vigilant opponents had unearthed it, and kindly presented a copy to the author. We do not believe that, in all the debates of the American Congress, there is another instance of flat falsehood as bad as this. It happens that the speech of 1816 and that of 1833 are both published in the same volume of the Works of Mr. Calhoun (Vol. II. pp. 163 and 197). We advise our readers who have the time and opportunity to read both, if they wish to see how a false position necessitates a false tongue. Those who take our advice will also discover why it was that Mr. Calhoun dared to utter such an impudent falsehood: his speeches are such appallingly dull reading, that there was very little risk of a busy people's comparing the interpretation with the text.

It was John C. Calhoun who, later in the same session, introduced the bill for setting apart the dividends and bonus of the United States Bank as a permanent fund for internal improvements, His speech on this bill, besides going all lengths in favor of the internal improvement system, presents some amusing contrasts with his later speeches on the same subject. His hearers of 1835 to 1850 must have smiled on reading in the speech of 1817 such sentences as these : —

"I am no advocate for *refined arguments* on the Constitution. The instrument was not intended as a thesis for the logician to exercise his ingenuity on. It ought to be construed with plain good-sense." "If we are restricted in the use of our money to the enumerated powers, on what principle can the purchase of Louisiana be justified ?" "The uniform sense of Congress and the country furnishes better evidence of the true interpretation of the Constitution than the most refined and subtle arguments."

Mark this, too : —

"In a country so extensive and so various in its interests, what is necessary for the common interest may apparently be opposed to the interest of particular sections. *It must be submitted to as the condition of our greatness.*"

Well might he say, in the same speech : —

"We may reasonably raise our eyes to a most splendid future, if we only act in a manner worthy of our advantages. If, however, neglecting them, we permit a low, sordid, selfish, *sectional* spirit to take possession of this House, this happy scene will vanish. We will divide ; and, in its consequences, will follow misery and despotism."

With this speech before him and before the country, Mr. Calhoun had not the candor to avow, in later years, a complete change of opinion. He could only go so far as to say, when opposing the purchase of the Madison Papers in 1837, that, "at his entrance upon public life, he had *inclined* to that interpretation of the Constitution which favored a latitude of powers." Inclined! He was a most enthusiastic and thorough-going champion of that interpretation. His scheme of internal improvements embraced a network of post-roads and canals from "Maine to Louisiana," and a system of harbors for lake and ocean. He kindled, he glowed, at the spectacle which his imagination conjured up, of the whole country rendered accessible, and of the distant farmer selling his produce at a price not seriously less than that which it brought on the coast. On this subject he became animated, interesting, almost eloquent. And, so far from this advocacy being confined to the period of his "entrance upon political life," he continued to be its very warmest exponent as late as 1819, when he had been ten years in public life. In that year, having to report upon the condition of military roads and fortifications, his flaming zeal for a grand and general system of roads and canals frequently bursts the bounds of the subject he had to treat. He tells Congress that the internal improvements which are best for peace are best for war also; and expatiates again upon his dazzling dream of "connecting Louisiana by a durable and well-finished road with Maine, and Boston with Savannah by a well-established line of internal navigation." The United States, he said, with its vast systems of lakes, rivers, and mountains, its treble line of sea-coast, its valleys large enough for empires, was "a world of itself," and needed nothing but to be rendered accessible. From what we know of the way things are managed in Congress, we should guess that he was invited to make this report for the very purpose of affording to the foremost champion of internal improvements an opportunity of lending a helping hand to pending bills.

Mr. Calhoun served six years in the House of Representatives, and grew in the esteem of Congress and the country at every session. As it is pleasing to see an old man at the theatre entering into the merriment of the play, since it shows that his heart has triumphed over the cares of life, and he has preserved a little of his youth, so is it eminently graceful in a young man to have something of the seriousness of age, especially when his conduct is even more austere than his demeanor. Mr. Clay at this time was addicted to gaming, like most of the Western and Southern members, and he was not averse to the bottle. Mr. Webster was reckless in expenditure, fond of his ease, and loved a joke better than an argument. In the seclusion of Washington, many members lived a very gay, rollicking life. Mr. Calhoun never gambled, never drank to excess, never jested, never quarrelled, cared nothing for his ease, and tempered the gravity of his demeanor by an admirable and winning courtesy. A deep and serious ambition impelled and restrained him.   Like boys at school, Clay and Webster were eager enough to get to the head of the class, but they did not brood over it all the time, and never feel comfortable unless they were conning their spelling-book; while little Calhoun expended all his soul in the business, and had no time or heart left for play.   Consequently he advanced rapidly for one of his size, and was universally pointed at as the model scholar.   Accidents, too, generally favor a rising man.   Mr. Calhoun made an extremely lucky hit in 1815, which gave members the highest opinion of his sagacity.   In opposing an ill-digested scheme for a national bank, he told the House that the bill was so obviously defective and unwise, that, if news of peace should arrive that day, it would not receive fifteen votes.   News of peace, which was totally unexpected, did arrive that very hour, and the bill was rejected the next day by about the majority which he had predicted.   At the next session, he won an immense reputation for firmness.   An act was passed changing the mode of compensating members of Congress from six dollars a day to fifteen hundred dollars a year.   We were a nation of rustics then; and this harmless measure excited a disgust in the popular mind so intense and general, that most of the members who had voted for it declined to present themselves for re-election.   Calhoun was one of the guilty ones.   Popular as he was in his district, supported by two powerful family connections, — his own and his wife's, — admired throughout the State as one who had done honor to it upon the conspicuous scene of Congressional debate, — even he was threatened with defeat.   Formidable candidates presented themselves.   In these circumstances he mounted the stump, boldly justified his vote, and defended the odious bill.   He was handsomely re-elected, and when the bill was up for repeal in the House he again supported it with all his former energy.   At the conclusion of his speech, a member from New York, Mr. Grosvenor, a political opponent, with whom Calhoun had not been on speaking terms for two years, sprang to his feet, enraptured, and began to express his approval of the speech in ordinary parliamentary language.   But his feelings could not be relieved in that manner.   He paused a moment, and then said: —

" Mr. Speaker, I will not be restrained.   No barrier shall exist which
I will not leap over for the purpose of offering to that gentleman my
thanks for the judicious, independent, and national course which he has
pursued in this House for the last two years, and particularly upon the
subject now before us.   Let the honorable gentleman continue with the
same manly independence, aloof from party views and local prejudices,
to pursue the great interests of his country, and fulfil the high destiny
for which it is manifest he was born.   The buzz of popular applause
may not cheer him on his way, but he will inevitably arrive at a high
and happy elevation in the view of his country and the world."

Such scenes as this enhance the prestige of a rising man.
Members weak at home envied at once and admired a man who
was strong enough to bring over his constituents to his opinion.
He was fortunate, too, in this, that a triumph so striking occurred
just before he left the House for another sphere of public life.
He had what the actors call a splendid exit.

The inauguration of Mr. Monroe on the 4th of March, 1817,
ushered in the era of good feeling, and gave to Henry Clay the
first of his long series of disappointments.   As Secretaries of
State had usually succeeded their chiefs in the Presidency, the
appointment of Mr. Adams to that office by Mr. Monroe was regarded almost in the light of a nomination to the succession.   To
add to Mr. Clay's mortification, he was tendered the post of Secretary of War, which he had declined a year before, and now
again declined.   The President next selected General Jackson,
then in the undimmed lustre of his military renown, and still
holding his Major-General's commission.   He received, however
a private notification that General Jackson would not accept a
place in the Cabinet.   The President then offered the post to the
aged Governor Isaac Shelby of Kentucky, who had the good
sense to decline it.   There appear to have been negotiations with
other individuals, but at length, in October, 1817, the place was
offered to Mr. Calhoun, who, after much hesitation, accepted it,
and entered upon the discharge of its duties in December.   His
friends, we are told, unanimously disapproved his going into office,
as they believed him formed to shine in debate rather than in the
transaction of business.

Fortune favored him again.   Entering the office after a long

vacancy, and when it was filled with the unfinished business of
the war, — fifty million dollars of deferred claims, for one item,
— he had the same easy opportunity for distinction which a steward has who takes charge of an estate just out of chancery, and
under a new proprietor who has plenty of money.   The sweeping up of the dead leaves, the gathering of the fallen branches, and
the weeding out of the paths, changes the aspect of the place, and
gives the passer-by a prodigious idea of the efficiency of the new
broom.   The country was alive, too, to the necessity of coast and
frontier defences, and there was much building of forts during the
seven years of Mr. Calhoun's tenure of place.   Respecting the
manner in which he discharged the multifarious and unusual duties of his office, we have never heard anything but commendation.   He was prompt, punctual, diligent, courteous, and firm.
The rules which he drew up for the regulation of the War Department remained in force, little changed, until the magnitude of
the late contest abolished or suspended all ancient methods.   The
claims of the soldiers were rapidly examined and passed upon.
It was Mr. Calhoun who first endeavored to collect considerable
bodies of troops for instruction at one post.   He had but six
thousand men in all, but he contrived to get together several companies of artillery at Fortress Monroe for drill.   He appeared to
take much interest in the expenditure of the ten thousand dollars
a year which Congress voted for the education of the Indians.
He reduced the expenses of his office, which was a very popular
thing at that day.   He never appointed nor removed a clerk for
opinion's sake.   In seven years he only removed two clerks,
both for cause, and to both were given in writing the reasons of
their removal.   There was no special merit in this, for at that
day to do otherwise would have been deemed infamous.

Mr. Calhoun, as a member of Mr. Monroe's Cabinet, still
played the part of a national man, and supported the measures
of his party without exception.   Scarcely a trace of the sectional
champion yet appears.   In 1819, he gave a written opinion favoring the cession of Texas in exchange for Florida; the motive of
which was to avoid alarming the North by the prospective increase
of Slave States.   In later years, Mr. Calhoun, of course, wished

to deny this; and the written opinions of Mr. Monroe's Cabinet on that question mysteriously disappeared from the archives of the State Department. We have the positive testimony of Mr. John Quincy Adams, that Calhoun, in common with most Southern men of that day, approved the Missouri Compromise of 1820, and gave a written opinion that it was a constitutional measure. That he was still an enthusiast for internal improvements, we have already mentioned.

The real difficulty of the War Department, however, as of the State Department, during the Monroe administration, was a certain Major-General Andrew Jackson, commanding the Military Department of the South. The popularity of the man who had restored the nation's self-love by ending a disastrous war with a dazzling and most unexpected victory, was something different from the respect which we all now feel for the generals distinguished in the late war. The first honors of the late war are divided among four chieftains, each of whom contributed to the final success at least one victory that was essential to it. But in 1815, among the military heroes of the war that had just closed General Jackson stood peerless and alone. His success in defending the Southwest, ending in a blaze of glory below New Orleans, utterly eclipsed all the other achievements of the war, excepting alone the darling triumphs on the ocean and the lakes. The deferential spirit of Mr. Monroe's letters to the General, and the readiness of every one everywhere to comply with his wishes, show that his popularity, even then, constituted him a power in the Republic. It was said in later times, that "General Jackson's popularity could stand anything," and in one sense this was true: it could stand anything that General Jackson was likely to do. Andrew Jackson could never have done a cowardly act, or betrayed a friend, or knowingly violated a trust, or broken his word, or forgotten a debt. He was always so entirely certain that he, Andrew Jackson, was in the right, his conviction on this point was so free from the least quaver of doubt, that he could always convince other men that he was right, and carry the multitude with him. His honesty, courage, and inflexible resolution, joined to his ignorance, narrowness, intensity, and liability to prejudice, rendered him at once the idol of his countrymen and the plague of all men with whom he had official connection. Drop an Andrew Jackson from the clouds upon any spot of earth inhabited by men, and he will have half a dozen deadly feuds upon his hands in thirty days.

Mr. Calhoun inherited a quarrel with Jackson from George Graham, his *pro tempore* predecessor in the War Department. This Mr. Graham was the gentleman ("spy," Jackson termed him) despatched by President Jefferson in 1806 to the Western country to look into the mysterious proceedings of Aaron Burr, which led to the explosion of Burr's scheme. This was enough to secure the bitterest enmity of Jackson, who wholly and always favored Burr's design of annihilating the Spanish power in North America, and who, as President of the United States, rewarded Burr's followers, and covertly assisted Houston to carry out part of Burr's project. Graham had sent orders to Jackson's subordinates directly, instead of sending them through the chief of the Department. Jackson, after due remonstrance, ordered his officers not to obey any orders but such as were communicated by or through himself. This was a high-handed measure; but Mr. Calhoun, on coming into power, passed it by without notice, and conceded the substance of Jackson's demand, — as he ought. This was so exquisitely pleasing to General Jackson, that he was well affected by it for many years towards Mr. Calhoun. Among the younger public men of that day, there was no one who stood so high in Jackson's regard as the Secretary of War.

The Florida war followed in 1818. When the report of General Jackson's invasion of Florida, and of the execution of Arbuthnot and Armbrister reached Washington, Mr. Calhoun was the only man in the Cabinet who expressed the opinion that General Jackson had transcended his powers, and ought to be brought before a court of inquiry. This opinion he supported with ardor, until it was overruled by the President, who was chiefly influenced by Mr. Adams, the Secretary of State. How keenly General Jackson resented the course of Mr. Calhoun on this occasion, when, eleven years afterwards, he discovered it, is sufficiently well known. We believe, however, that the facts justify Calhoun and condemn Jackson. Just before going to the seat of war, the General wrote privately to the President, strongly recommending the seizure of Florida, and added these words: "This can be done without implicating the government. Let it be signified to me through any channel (say, Mr. J. Rhea) that the possession of the Floridas would be desirable to the United States, and in sixty days it will be accomplished." General Jackson dwells, in his "Exposition" of this matter, upon the fact that Mr. Calhoun was the first man in Washington who read this letter. But he does not say that Mr. Calhoun was aware that Mr. Rhea had been commissioned to answer the letter, and had answered it in accordance with General Jackson's wishes. And if the Rhea correspondence justified the seizure of Florida, it did not justify the execution of the harmless Scottish trader Arbuthnot, who, so far from "instigating" the war, had exerted the whole of his influence to prevent it. It is an honor to Mr. Calhoun to have been the only man in the Cabinet to call for an inquiry into proceedings which disgraced the United States and came near involving the country in war. We have always felt it to be a blot upon the memory of John Quincy Adams, that he did not join Mr. Calhoun in demanding the trial of General Jackson; and we have not been able to attribute his conduct to anything but the supposed necessities of his position as a candidate for the succession.

Readers versed in political history need not be reminded that nearly every individual in the Cabinet of Mr. Monroe had hopes of succeeding him. Mr. Adams had, of course; for he was the premier. Mr. Crawford, of course; for it had been "arranged" at the last caucus that he was to follow Mr. Monroe, to whose claims he had deferred on that express condition. Henry Clay, the Speaker of the House of Representatives, and De Witt Clinton of New York, had expectations. All these gentlemen had "claims" which both their party and the public could recognize. Mr. Calhoun, too, who was forty-two years of age in Mr. Monroe's last year of service, boldly entered the lists; relying upon the united support of the South and the support of the manufacturing States of the North, led by Pennsylvania. Tha against such competitors he had any ground at all to hope for success, shows how rapid and how real had been his progress toward a first-rate national position. If our readers will turn to the letters of Webster, Story, Wirt, Adams, Jackson, and others of that circle of distinguished men, they will see many evidences of the extravagant estimation in which he was held in 1824. They appear to have all seen in him the material for a President, though not yet quite mature for the position. They all deemed him a man of unsullied honor, of devoted patriotism, of perfect sincerity, and of immense ability, — so assiduously had he played the part of the good boy.

How the great popularity of General Jackson was adroitly used by two or three invisible wire-pullers to defeat the aspirations of these too eager candidates, and how from the general wreck of their hopes Mr. Calhoun had the dexterity to emerge Vice-President of the United States, has been related with the amplest detail, and need not be repeated here. Mr. Calhoun's position seemed then to combine all the advantages which a politician of forty-three could desire or imagine. By withdrawing his name from the list of candidates in such a way as to lead General Jackson to suppose that he had done so in *his* favor, he seemed to place the General under obligations to him. By secretly manifesting a preference for Mr. Adams (which he really felt) when the election devolved upon the House of Representatives, he had gained friends among the adherents of the successful candidate. His withdrawal was accepted by the public as an evidence of modesty becoming the youngest candidate. Finally he was actually Vice-President, as John Adams had been, as Jefferson had been, before their elevation to the highest place. True, Henry Clay, as Secretary of State, was in the established line of succession; but, as time wore on, it became very manifest that the re-election of Mr. Adams, upon which Mr. Clay's hopes depended, was itself exceedingly doubtful; and we accordingly find Mr. Calhoun numbered in the ranks of the opposition. Toward the close of Mr. Adams's Presidency, the question of real interest in the inner circle of politicians was, not who should succeed John Quincy Adams in 1829, but who should succeed

Andrew Jackson in 1833; and already the choice was narrowing to two men, — Martin Van Buren and John C. Calhoun.

During Mr. Calhoun's first term in the Vice-Presidency, —
1825 to 1829, — a most important change took place in his political position, which controlled all his future career. While he
was Secretary of War, — 1817 to 1824, — he resided with his
family in Washington, and shared in the nationalizing influences
of the place. When he was elected Vice-President, he removed
to a plantation called Fort Hill, in the western part of South
Carolina, where he was once more subjected to the intense and
narrow provincialism of the planting States. And there was
nothing in the character or in the acquirements of his mind to
counteract that influence. Mr. Calhoun was not a student; he
probed nothing to the bottom; his information on all subjects
was small in quantity, and second-hand in quality. Nor was he
a patient thinker. Any stray fact or notion that he met with in
his hasty desultory reading, which chanced to give apparent support to a favorite theory or paradox of his own, he seized upon
eagerly, paraded it in triumph, but pondered it little; while the
weightiest facts which controverted his opinion he brushed aside
without the slightest consideration. His mind was as arrogant
as his manners were courteous. Every one who ever conversed
with him must remember his positive, peremptory, unanswerable
" *Not at all, not at all*," whenever one of his favorite positions was
assailed. He was wholly a special pleader; he never summed
up the testimony. We find in his works no evidence that
he had read the masters in political economy; not even Adam
Smith, whose reputation was at its height during the first half of
his public life. In history he was the merest smatterer, though
it was his favorite reading, and he was always talking about
Sparta, Athens, and Rome. The slenderness of his fortune prevented his travelling. He never saw Europe; and if he ever
visited the Northern States, after leaving college, his stay was
short. The little that he knew of life was gathered in three
places, all of which were of an exceptional and artificial character, — the city of Washington, the up-country of South Carolina
and the luxurious, reactionary city of Charleston. His mind

naturally narrow and intense, became, by revolving always in this narrow sphere and breathing a close and tainted atmosphere, more and more fixed in its narrowness and more intense in its operations.

This man, moreover, was consumed by a poor ambition : he lusted after the Presidency. The rapidity of his progress in public life, the high offices he had held, the extravagant eulogiums he had received from colleagues and the press, deceived him as to the real nature of his position before the country, and blinded him to the superior chances of other men. Five times in his life he made a distinct clutch at the bawble, but never with such prospect of success that any man could discern it but himself and those who used his eyes. It is a satisfaction to know that, of the Presidency seekers, — Clay, Webster, Calhoun, Douglas, Wise, Breckenridge, Tyler, Fillmore, Clinton, Burr, Cass, Buchanan, and Van Buren, — only two won the prize, and those two only by a series of accidents which had little to do with their own exertions. We can almost lay it down as a law of this Republic, that no man who makes the Presidency the principal object of his public life will ever be President. The Presidency is an accident, and such it will probably remain.

Mr. Vice-President Calhoun found his Carolina discontented in 1824, when he took up his abode at Fort Hill. Since the Revolution, South Carolina had never been satisfied, and had never had reason to be. The cotton-gin had appeased her for a while, but had not suspended the operation of the causes which produced the stagnation of the South. Profuse expenditure, unskilful agriculture, the costliest system of labor in the world, and no immigration, still kept *Irelandizing* the Southern States ; while the North was advancing and improving to such a degree as to attract emigrants from all lands. The contrast was painful ᴄ Southern men, and to most of them it was mysterious. Southern politicians came to the conclusion that the cause at once of Northern prosperity and Southern poverty was the protective tariff and the appropriations for internal improvements, but chiefly the tariff. In 1824, when Mr. Calhoun went home, the tariff on some leading articles had been increased, and the South

was in a ferment of opposition to the protective system. If **Mr**
Calhoun had been a wise and honest man, he would have reminded his friends that the decline of the South had been a subject of remark from the peace of 1783, and therefore could not
have been caused by the tariff of 1816, or 1820, or 1824.   He
would have told them that slavery, as known in the Southern
States, demands virgin lands, — must have, every few years, its
cotton-gin, its Louisiana, its Cherokee country, its *something*, to
give new value to its products or new scope for its operations. He
might have added that the tariff of 1824 was a grievance, did tend
to give premature development to a manufacturing system, and
was a fair ground for a national issue between parties.   The thing
which he did was this : he adopted the view of the matter which
was predominant in the extreme South, and accepted the leadership of the extreme Southern, anti-tariff, strict-constructionist wing
of the Democratic party.   He echoed the prevailing opinion, that
the tariff and the internal improvement system, to both of which
he was fully committed, were the *sole* causes of Southern stagnation ; since by the one their money was taken from them, and by
the other it was mostly spent where it did them no good.

He was, of course, soon involved in a snarl of contradictions,
from which he never could disentangle himself. Let us pass to
the year 1828, a most important one in the history of the country
and of Mr. Calhoun ; for then occurred the first of the long series
of events which terminated with the surrender of the last Rebel
army in 1865.   The first act directly tending to a war between
the South and the United States bears date December 6, 1828
and it was the act of John C. Calhoun.

It was the year of that Presidential election which placed Andrew Jackson in the White House, and re-elected Mr. Calhoun to
the Vice-Presidency.   It was the year that terminated the honorable part of Mr. Calhoun's career and began the dishonorable.
His political position in the canvass was utterly false, as he him
self afterwards confessed.   On the one hand, he was supporting
for the Presidency a man committed to the policy of protection
and on the other, he became the organ and mouthpiece of the
Southern party, whose opposition to the protective principle was

ending to the point of armed resistance to it. The tariff bill of 1828, which they termed the bill of abominations, had excited the most heated opposition in the cotton States, and especially in South Carolina. This act was passed in the spring of the very year in which those States voted for a man who had publicly indorsed the principle involved in it ; and we see Mr. Calhoun heading the party who were electioneering for Jackson, and the party who were considering the policy of nullifying the act which he had approved. His Presidential aspirations bound him to the support of General Jackson ; but the first, the fundamental necessity of his position was to hold possession of South Carolina.

The burden of Mr. Calhoun's later speeches was the reconciliation of the last part of his public life with the first. The task was difficult, for there is not a leading proposition in his speeches after 1830 which is not refuted by arguments to be found in his public utterances before 1828. In his speech on the Force Bill, in 1834, he volunteered an explanation of the apparent inconsistency between his support of General Jackson in 1828, and his authorship of the " South Carolina Exposition " in the same year. Falsehood and truth are strangely interwoven in almost every sentence of his later writings ; and there is also that vagueness in them which comes of a superfluity of words. He says, that for the strict-constructionist party to have presented a candidate openly and fully identified with their opinions would have been to court defeat ; and thus they were obliged either to abandon the contest, or to select a candidate " whose opinions were intermediate or doubtful on the subject which divided the two sections," — a candidate " who, at best, was but a choice of evils." Besides, General Jackson was a Southern man, and it was hoped that, notwithstanding his want of experience, knowledge, and self control, the advisers whom he would invite to assist him would compensate for those defects. Then Mr. Calhoun proceeds to state, that the contest turned chiefly upon the question of protection or free trade ; and the strife was, which of the two parties should go farthest in the advocacy of protection. The result was, he says, that the tariff bill of 1828 was passed, — " that disastrous measure which has brought so many calamities upon us,

7   J

and put in peril the liberty and union of the country," and "poured millions into the treasury beyond the most extravagant wants of the country."

The passage of this tariff bill was accomplished by the tact of Martin Van Buren, aided by Major Eaton, Senator from Tennessee. Mr. Van Buren was the predestined chief of General Jackson's Cabinet, and Major Eaton was the confidant, agent, and travelling manager of the Jacksonian wire-pullers, besides being the General's own intimate friend. The events of that session notified Mr. Calhoun that, however manageable General Jackson might be, he was not likely to fall into the custody of the Vice-President. General Jackson's election being considered certain, the question was alone interesting, who should possess him for the purposes of the succession. The prospect, as surveyed that winter from the Vice-President's chair, was not assuring to the occupant of that lofty seat. If General Jackson could not be used as a fulcrum for the further elevation of Mr. Calhoun, would it not be advisable to begin to cast about for another?

The tariff bill of 1828 was passed before the Presidential canvass had set in with its last severity. There was time for Mr. Calhoun to withdraw from the support of the man whose nearest friends had carried it through the Senate under his eyes. He did not do so. He went home, after the adjournment of Congress, to labor with all his might for the election of a protectionist, and to employ his leisure hours in the composition of that once famous paper called the "South Carolina Exposition," in which protection was declared to be an evil so intolerable as to justify the nullification of an act founded upon it. This Exposition was the beginning of our woe, — the baleful egg from which were hatched nullification, treason, civil war, and the desolation of the Southern States. Here is Mr. Calhoun's own account of the manner in which what he correctly styles "*the double operation*" was "pushed on" in the summer of 1828 : —

"This disastrous event [the passage of the tariff bill of 1828] opened our eyes (I mean myself and those immediately connected with me) as to the full extent of the danger and oppression of the protective system, and the hazard of failing to effect the reform it tended through

the election of General Jackson. With these disclosures, it became
necessary to seek some other ultimate, but more certain measure of
protection. We turned to the Constitution to find this remedy. We
directed a more diligent and careful scrutiny into its provisions, in order to understand fully the nature and character of our political system. We found a certain and effectual remedy in that great fundamental division of the powers of the system between this government
and its independent co-ordinates, the separate governments of the
States, — to be called into action to arrest the unconstitutional acts of
this government by the interposition of the States, — the paramount
source from which both governments derive their power. But in relying on this our ultimate remedy, we did not abate our zeal in the
Presidential canvass ; we still hoped that General Jackson, if elected, would effect the necessary reform, and thereby supersede the necessity for calling into action the sovereign authority of the State,
which we were anxious to avoid. With these views the two were
pushed with equal zeal at the same time ; which double operation
commenced in the fall of 1828, but a few months after the passage of
the tariff act of that year ; and at the meeting of the Legislature of
the State, at the same period, a paper known as the South Carolina
Exposition was reported to that body, containing a full development, as
well on the constitutional point as on the operation of the protective
system, preparatory to a state of things which might eventually render
the action of the State necessary in order to protect her rights and interest, and to stay a course of policy which we believed would, if not
arrested, prove destructive of liberty and the Constitution." — *Works*,
II. 396.

Mr. Calhoun omits, however, to mention that the Exposition
was not presented to the Legislature of South Carolina until
after the Presidential election had been decided. Nor did he
inform his hearers that the author of the paper was Mr. Vice-
President Calhoun. Either there was a great dearth of literary
ability in that body, or else Mr. Calhoun had little confidence in
it ; for nearly all the ponderous documents on nullification given
to the world in its name were penned by Mr. Calhoun, and appear in his collected works. If the Legislature addressed its
constituents or the people of the United States on *this* subject, it
was he who prepared the draft. The South Carolina Exposition
was found among his papers in his own handwriting, and it was

adopted by the Legislature with only a few alterations and sup-pressions.   There never was a piece of mischief more completely the work of one man than the nullification troubles of 1833 - 34.

The South Carolina Exposition, when Mr. Calhoun had com-pleted it, was brought before the public by one of the usual methods.   The Legislature of South Carolina passed the follow-ing resolutions : —

" *Resolved*, That it is expedient to protest against the unconstitu-tional and oppressive operation of the system of protective duties, and to have such protest entered on the journals of the Senate of the Unit-ed States.   Also, to make a public exposition of our wrongs, and of the remedies within our power, to be communicated to our sister States, with a request that they will co-operate with this State in pro-curing a repeal of the tariff for protection, and an abandonment of the principle ; and if the repeal be not procured, that they will co-operate in such measures as may be necessary for averting the evil.

" *Resolved*, That a committee of seven be raised to carry the fore-going resolution into effect."

The resolution having been carried, the following gentlemen were appointed to father Mr. Calhoun's paper : James Gregg, D. L. Wardlaw, Hugh S. Legaré, Arthur P. Hayne, William C. Preston, William Elliott, and R. Barnwell Smith.   The duty of this committee consisted in causing a copy of Mr. Calhoun's pa-per to be made and presenting it to the Legislature.   This was promptly done ; and the Exposition was adopted by the Legisla-ture on the 6th of December, 1828.   Whether any protest was forwarded to the Secretary of the United States Senate for in-sertion in the journal does not appear.   We only know that five thousand copies of this wearisome and stupid Exposition were ordered to be printed, and that in the hubbub of the incoming of a new administration it attracted scarcely any attention beyond the little knot of original nullifiers.   Indeed, Mr. Calhoun's writ-ings on this subject were " protected " by their own length and dulness.   No creature ever read one of them quite through, ex-cept for a special purpose.

The leading assertions of this Exposition are these : — 1. Ev ery duty imposed for protection is a violation of the Constitution, which empowers Congress to impose taxes for revenue only. 2. The *whole* burden of the protective system is borne by agriculture and commerce. 3. The *whole* of the advantages of protection accrue to the manufacturing States. 4. In other words, the South, the Southwest, and two or three commercial cities, support the government, and pour a stream of treasure into the coffers of manufacturers. 5. The result must soon be, that the people of South Carolina will have either to abandon the culture of rice and cotton, and remove to some other country, or else to become a manufacturing community, which would only be ruin in another form.

Lest the reader should find it impossible to believe that any man out of a lunatic asylum could publish such propositions as this last, we will give the passage. Mr. Calhoun is endeavoring to show that Europe will at length retaliate by placing high duties upon American cotton and rice. At least that appears to be what he is aiming at.

" We already see indications of a commercial warfare, the termination of which no one can conjecture, though our fate may easily be. The last remains of our great and once flourishing agriculture must be annihilated in the conflict. In the first instance we will * be thrown on the home market, which cannot consume a fourth of our products; and, instead of supplying the world, as we would with free trade, we would be compelled to abandon the cultivation of three fourths of what we now raise, and receive for the residue whatever the manufacturers, who would then have their policy consummated by the entire possession of our market, might choose to give. Forced to abandon our ancient and favorite pursuit, to which our soil, climate, habits, and peculiar labor are adapted, at an immense sacrifice of property, we would be compelled, without capital, experience, or skill, and with a population untried in such pursuits, to attempt to become the rivals, instead of the customers, of the manufacturing States. The result is not doubtful. If they, by superior capital and skill, should keep down successful competition on our part, we would be doomed to toil at our unprofitable agriculture, — selling at the prices which a single and very limited

---

* Mr. Calhoun had still Irish enough in his composition to use " will' for shall.'

market might give. But, on the contrary, if our necessity should triumph over their capital and skill, if, instead of raw cotton we should ship to the manufacturing States cotton yarn and cotton goods, the thoughtful must see that it would inevitably bring about a state of things which could not long continue. *Those who now make war on our gains would then make it on our labor.* They would not tolerate that those who now cultivate our plantations, and furnish them with the material and the market for the product of their arts, should, by becoming their rivals, take bread from the mouths of their wives and children. The committee will not pursue this painful subject; but as they clearly see that the system if not arrested, must bring the country to this hazardous extremity, neither prudence nor patriotism would permit them to pass it by without raising a warning voice against an evil of so menacing a character." — *Works*, VI. 12.

The only question which arises in the mind of present readers of such passages (which abound in the writings of Mr. Calhoun) is this: Were they the chimeras of a morbid, or the utterances of a false mind? Those who knew him differ in opinion on this point. For our part, we believe such passages to have been inserted for the sole purpose of alarming the people of South Carolina, so as to render them the more subservient to his will. It is the stale trick of the demagogue, as well as of the false priest, to subjugate the mind by terrifying it.

Mr. Calhoun concludes his Exposition by bringing forward his remedy for the frightful evils which he had conjured up. That remedy, of course, was nullification. The State of South Carolina, after giving due warning, must declare the protective acts "null and void" in the State of South Carolina after a certain date; and then, unless Congress repealed them in time, refuse obedience to them. Whether this should be done by the Legislature or by a convention called for the purpose, Mr. Calhoun would not say; but he evidently preferred a convention. He advised, however, that nothing be done hastily; that time should be afforded to the dominant majority for further reflection. Delay, he remarked, was the more to be recommended, because of "the great political revolution which will displace from power, on the 4th of March next, those who have acquired authority by setting the will of the people at defiance, and which will bring in an eminent citizen, distinguished for his services to his country and his justice and patriotism"; under whom, it was hoped, there would be " a complete restoration of the pure principles of our government." This passage Mr. Calhoun could write *after* witnessing the manœuvres of Mr. Van Buren and Mr. Eaton! If the friends of Mr. Adams had set the will of the people at defiance on the tariff question, what had the supporters of General Jackson done? In truth, this menace of nullification was the second string to the bow of the Vice-President. It was not yet ascertained which was going to possess and use General Jackson, — the placid and flexible Van Buren, or the headstrong, short-sighted, and uncomfortable Calhoun. Nullification, as he used daily to declare, was a " reserved power."

At the time of General Jackson's inauguration, it would have puzzled an acute politician to decide which of the two aspirants had the best chance of succeeding the General. The President seemed equally well affected toward both. One was Secretary of State, the other Vice-President. Van Buren, inheriting the political tactics of Burr, was lord paramount in the great State of New York, and Calhoun was all-powerful in his own State and very influential in all the region of cotton and rice. In the Cabinet Calhoun had two friends, and one tried and devoted ally (Ingham), while Van Buren could only boast of Major Eaton, Secretary of War; and the tie that bound them together was political far more than personal. In the public mind, Calhoun towered above his rival, for he had been longer in the national councils, had held offices that drew upon him the attention of the whole country, and had formerly been distinguished as an orator. If any one had been rash enough in 1829 to intimate to Mr. Calhoun that Martin Van Buren stood before the country on a par with himself, he would have pitied the ignorance of that rash man.

Under despotic governments, like those of Louis XIV. and Andrew Jackson, no calculation can be made as to the future of any public man, because his future depends upon the caprice of the despot, which cannot be foretold. Six short weeks — nay, not so much, not six — sufficed to estrange the mind of the

President from Calhoun, and implant within him a passion to promote the interests of Van Buren. Our readers, we presume, all know how this was brought to pass. It was simply that Mr Calhoun would *not*, and Mr. Van Buren *would*, call upon Mrs. Eaton. All the other influences that were brought to bear upon the President's singular mind were nothing in comparison with this. Daniel Webster uttered only the truth when he wrote, at the time, to his friend Dutton, that the "Aaron's serpent among the President's desires was a settled purpose of making out the lady, of whom so much has been said, a person of reputation"; and that this ridiculous affair would "probably determine who should be the successor to the present chief magistrate." It had precisely that effect. We have shown elsewhere the successive manœuvres by which this was effected, and how vigorously but unskilfully Calhoun struggled to avert his fate. We cannot and need not repeat the story; nor can we go over again the history of the Nullification imbroglio, which began with the South Carolina Exposition in 1828, and ended very soon after Calhoun had received a private notification that the instant news reached Washington of an overt act of treason in South Carolina, the author and fomenter of that treason would be arrested and held for trial as a traitor.

One fact alone suffices to prove that, in bringing on the Nullification troubles, Calhoun's motive was factious. When General Jackson saw the coming storm, he did two things. First, he prepared to maintain the authority of the United States by force. Secondly, he used all his influence with Congress to have the cause of Southern discontent removed. General Jackson felt that the argument of the anti-tariff men, in view of the speedy extinction of the national debt, was unanswerable. He believed it was absurd to go on raising ten or twelve millions a year more than the government could spend, merely for the sake of protecting Northern manufactures. Accordingly, a bill was introduced which aimed to do just what the nullifiers had been clamoring for, that is, to reduce the revenue to the amount required by the government. If Mr. Calhoun had supported this measure, he could have carried it. He gave it no support; but exerted all his influence in favor of the Clay Compromise, which was expressly intended to save as much of the protective system as could be saved, and which reduced duties gradually, instead of suddenly. Rather than permit the abhorred administration to have the glory of pacificating the country, this lofty Roman stooped to a coalition with his personal enemy, Henry Clay, the champion and the soul of the protectionist party.

No words can depict the bitterness of Calhoun's disappointment and mortification at being distanced by a man whom he despised so cordially as he did Van Buren. To comprehend it, his whole subsequent career must be studied. The numerous covert allusions to the subject in his speeches and writings are surcharged with rancor; and it was observed that, whenever his mind reverted to it, his manner, the tone of his voice, and every gesture testified to the intensity of his feelings. " Every Southern man," said he on one occasion, " who is true to the interests of his section, and faithful to the duties which Providence has allotted him, will be forever excluded from the honors and emoluments of this government, which will be reserved only for those who have qualified themselves by political prostitution for admission into the Magdalen Asylum." His face, too, from this time, assumed that haggard, cast-iron, intense, introverted aspect which struck every beholder.

Miss Martineau, in her Retrospect of Western Travel, has given us some striking and valuable glimpses of the eminent men of that period, particularly of the three most eminent, who frequently visited her during her stay in Washington. This passage, for example, is highly interesting.

" Mr. Clay sitting upright on the sofa, with his snuffbox ever in his hand, would discourse for many an hour in his even, soft, deliberate tone, on any one of the great subjects of American policy which we might happen to start, always amazing us with the moderation of estimate and speech which so impetuous a nature has been able to attain. Mr. Webster, leaning back at his ease, telling stories, cracking jokes, shaking the sofa with burst after burst of laughter, or smoothly discoursing to the perfect felicity of the logical part of one's constitution, would illuminate an evening now and then. Mr. Calhoun, the cast-iron man, who looks as if he had never been born and could never be

7 *

extinguished, would come in sometimes to keep our understandings on
a painful stretch for a short while, and leave us to take to pieces his
close, rapid, theoretical, illustrated talk, and see what we could make
of it. We found it usually more worth retaining as a curiosity, than
as either very just or useful. His speech abounds in figures, truly illustrative, if that which they illustrate were true also. But his theories
of government (almost the only subject upon which his thoughts are
employed), the squarest and compactest that ever were made, are composed out of limited elements, and are not, therefore, likely to stand
service very well. It is at first extremely interesting to hear Mr.
Calhoun talk ; and there is a never-failing evidence of power in all
that he says and does, which commands intellectual reverence ; but the
admiration is too soon turned into regret, into absolute melancholy. It
is impossible to resist the conviction, that all this force can be at best
but useless, and is but too likely to be very mischievous. *His mind
has long lost all power of communicating with any other.* I know of no
man who lives in such utter intellectual solitude. He meets men and
harangues by the fireside as in the Senate , he is wrought like a piece
of machinery, set going vehemently by a weight, and stops while you
answer ; he either passes by what you say, or twists it into a suitability
with what is in his head, and begins to lecture again. Of course, a
mind like this can have little influence in the Senate, except by virtue,
perpetually wearing out, of what it did in its less eccentric days ; but
its influence at home is to be dreaded. There is no hope that an intellect so cast in narrow theories will accommodate itself to varying circumstances ; and there is every danger that it will break up all that it
can in order to remould the materials in its own way. Mr. Calhoun
is as full as ever of his Nullification doctrines ; and those who know
the force that is in him, and his utter incapacity of modification by
other minds, (after having gone through as remarkable a revolution
of political opinion as perhaps any man ever experienced,) will no
more expect repose and self-retention from him than from a volcano
in full force. Relaxation is no longer in the power of his will. I never
saw any one who so completely gave me the idea of possession. Half
an hour's conversation with him is enough to make a necessitarian of
anybody. Accordingly, he is more complained of than blamed by his
enemies. His moments of softness by his family, and when recurring
to old college days, are hailed by all as a relief to the vehement working of the intellectual machine, — a relief equally to himself and others.
These moments are as touching to the observer as tears on the face of
a soldier."

Of his appearance in the Senate, and of h.s manner of speaking, Miss Martineau records her impressions also : —

"Mr. Calhoun's countenance first fixed my attention ; the splendid eye, the straight forehead, surmounted by a load of stiff, upright, dark hair, the stern brow, the inflexible mouth, — it is one of the most remarkable heads in the country."

"Mr. Calhoun followed, and impressed me very strongly. While he kept to the question, what he said was close, good, and moderate, though delivered in rapid speech, and with a voice not sufficiently modulated. But when he began to reply to a taunt of Colonel Benton's, that he wanted to be President, the force of his speaking became painful. He made protestations which it seemed to strangers had better have been spared, 'that he would not turn on his heel to be President,' and that 'he had given up all for his own brave, magnanimous little State of South Carolina.' While thus protesting, his eyes flashed, his brow seemed charged with thunder, his voice became almost a bark, and his sentences were abrupt, intense, producing in the auditory a sort of laugh which is squeezed out of people by the application of a very sudden mental force. I believe he knew not what a revelation he made in a few sentences. *They were to us strangers the key, not only to all that was said and done by the South Carolina party during the remainder of the session, but to many things at Charleston and Columbia which would otherwise have passed unobserved and unexplained.*"

This intelligent observer saw the chieftain on his native heath : —

"During my stay in Charleston, Mr. Calhoun and his family arrived from Congress, and there was something very striking in the welcome he received, like that of a chief returned to the bosom of his clan. He stalked about like a monarch of the little domain, and there was certainly an air of mysterious understanding between him and his followers."

What Miss Martineau says of the impossibility of Calhoun's mind communicating with another mind, is confirmed by an anecdote which we have heard related by Dr. Francis Lieber, who, as Professor in the College of South Carolina, was for several years the neighbor and intimate acquaintance of Mr. Calhoun. The learned Professor, upon his return from a visit to Europe, called upon him, and in the course of the interview Mr. Calhoun declared, in his positive manner, that the slaves in the Southern States were better lodged, fed, and cared for than the mechanics of Europe. Dr. Lieber, being fresh from that continent, assured the Secretary of State that such was not the fact, as he could testify from having resided in both lands. " Not at all, not at all," cried Calhoun dogmatically, and repeated his wild assertion. The Doctor saw that the poor man had reached the condition of absolute unteachableness, and dropped the subject. There could not well be a more competent witness on the point in dispute than Dr. Lieber ; for, besides having long resided in both continents, it was the habit and business of his life to observe and ponder the effect of institutions upon the welfare of those who live under them. Calhoun pushed him out of the witness-box, as though he were an idiot.

A survey of the last fifteen years of Calhoun's life discloses nothing upon which the mind can dwell with complacency. On the approach of every Presidential election, we see him making what we can only call a *grab* at a nomination, by springing upon the country some unexpected issue designed to make the South a unit in his support. From 1830 to 1836, he exhausted all the petty arts of the politician to defeat General Jackson's resolve to bring in Mr. Van Buren as his successor ; and when all had failed, he made an abortive attempt to precipitate the question of the annexation of Texas. This, too, being foiled, Mr. Van Buren was elected President. Then Mr. Calhoun, who had for ten years never spoken of Van Buren except with contempt, formed the notable scheme of winning over the President so far as to secure his support for the succession. He advocated all the test measures of Mr. Van Buren's administration, and finished by courting a personal reconciliation with the man whom he had a hundred times styled a fox and a political prostitute. This design coming to naught, through the failure of Mr. Van Buren to reach a second term, he made a wild rush for the prize by again thrusting forward the Texas question. Colonel Benton, who was the predetermined heir of Van Buren, has detailed the manner in which this was done in a very curious chapter of his " Thirty Years." The plot was successful, so far as plunging the country into a needless war was concerned; but it was Polk and Taylor, not Calhoun, who obtained the Presidency through it. Mr. Calhoun's struggles for a nomination in 1844 were truly pitiable, but they were not known to the public, who saw him, at a certain stage of the campaign, affecting to decline a nomination which there was not the slightest danger of his receiving.

We regret that we have not space to show how much the agitation of the slavery question, from 1835 to 1850, was the work of this one man. The labors of Mr. Garrison and Mr. Wendell Phillips might have borne no fruit during their lifetime, if Calhoun had not made it his business to supply them with material. " I mean to *force* the issue upon the North," he once wrote; and he did force it. On his return to South Carolina after the termination of the Nullification troubles, he said to his friends there, (so avers Colonel Benton, " Thirty Years," Vol. II. p. 786,) " that the South could never be united against the North on the tariff question; that the sugar interest of Louisiana would keep her out; and that the basis of Southern union must be shifted to the slave question." Here we have the key to the mysteries of all his subsequent career. The denial of the right of petition, the annexation of Texas, the forcing of slavery into the Territories, — these were among the issues upon which he hoped to unite the South in his favor, while retaining enough strength at the North to secure his election. Failing in all his schemes of personal advancement, he died in 1850, still protesting that slavery is divine, and that it must rule this country or ruin it. This is really the sum and substance of that last speech to the Senate, which he had not strength enough left to deliver.

We have run rapidly over Mr. Calhoun's career as a public man. It remains for us to notice his claims as a teacher of political philosophy, a character in which he influenced his countrymen more powerfully after he was in his grave than he did while living among them.

The work upon which his reputation as a thinker will rest with posterity is his Treatise on the Nature of Government. Written in the last year of his life, when at length all hope of further

personal advancement must have died within him, it may be
taken as the deliberate record or summary of his political opinions.   He did not live to revise it, and the concluding portion he
evidently meant to enlarge and illustrate, as was ascertained from
notes and memoranda in pencil upon the manuscript.   After the
death of the author in 1850, the work was published in a substantial and elegant form by the Legislature of South Carolina,
who ordered copies to be presented to individuals of note in
science and literature, and to public libraries.   We are, therefore, to regard this volume, not merely as a legacy of Mr. Calhoun to his countrymen, but as conveying to us the sentiments
of South Carolina with regard to her rights and duties as a member of the Union.   Events since its publication have shown us
that it is more even than this.   The assemblage of troublesome
communities which we have been accustomed to style "the
South," adopted this work as their political gospel.   From this
source the politicians of the Southern States have drawn all they
have chosen to present to the world in justification of their course
which bears the semblance of argument; for, in truth, Mr. Calhoun, since Jefferson and Madison passed from the stage, is almost the only thinking being the South has had.   His was a very
narrow, intense, and untrustworthy mind, but he was an angel of
light compared with the men who have been recently conspicuous
in the Southern States.

This treatise on government belongs to the same class of works
as Louis Napoleon's Life of Cæsar, having for its principal object
one that lies below the surface, and the effect of both is damaged
by the name on the title-page.   The moment we learn that Louis
Napoleon wrote that Life of Cæsar, the mind is intent upon discovering allusions to recent history, which the author has an
interest in misrepresenting.   The common conscience of mankind
condemns him as a perjured usurper, and the murderer of many
of his unoffending fellow-citizens.   No man, whatever the power
and splendor of his position, can rest content under the scorn of
mankind, unless his own conscience gives him a clear acquittal,
and assures him that one day the verdict of his fellow-men will
be reversed; and even in that case, it is not every man that can

possess his soul in patience. Every page of the Life of Cæsar was composed with a secret, perhaps half-unconscious reference to that view of Louis Napoleon's conduct which is expressed with such deadly power in Mr. Kinglake's History of the Crimean War, and which is so remarkably confirmed by an American eyewitness, the late Mr. Goodrich, who was Consul at Paris in 1848. Published anonymously, the Life of Cæsar might have had some effect. Given to the world by Napoleon III., every one reads it as he would a defence by an ingenious criminal of his own cause. The highest praise that can be bestowed upon it is, that it is very well done, considering the object the author had in view.

So, in reading Mr. Calhoun's disquisition upon government, we are constantly reminded that the author was a man who had only escaped trial and execution for treason by suddenly arresting the treasonable measures which he had caused to be set on foot. Though it contains but one allusion to events in South Carolina in 1833, the work is nothing but a labored, refined justification of those events. It has been even coupled with Edwards on the Will, as the two best examples of subtle reasoning which American literature contains. Admit his premises, and you are borne along, at a steady pace, in a straight path, to the final inferences: that the sovereign State of South Carolina possesses, by the Constitution of the United States, an absolute veto upon every act of Congress, and may secede from the Union whenever she likes; and that these rights of veto and secession do not merely constitute the strength of the Constitution, but *are* the Constitution, — and do not merely tend to perpetuate the Union, but are the Union's self, — the thing that binds the States together.

Mr. Calhoun begins his treatise by assuming that government is necessary. He then explains why it is necessary. It is necessary because man is more selfish than sympathetic, feeling more intensely what affects himself than what affects others. Hence he will encroach on the rights of others; and to prevent this, government is indispensable.

But government, since it must be administered by selfish men, will feel more intensely what affects itself than what affects **the** people governed. It is, therefore, the tendency of all governments to encroach on the rights of the people ; and they certainly will do so, if they can. The same instinct of self-preservation, the same love of accumulation, which tempts individuals to over-reach their neighbors, inclines government to preserve, increase, and consolidate its powers. Therefore, as individual selfishness requires to be held in check by government, so government **must** be restrained by *something*.

This something is the constitution, written or unwritten. **A** constitution is to the government what government is to the people : it is the restraint upon its selfishness. Mr. Calhoun assumes here that the relation between government and governed is naturally and inevitably " antagonistic." He does not perceive that government is the expression of man's love of justice, and the means by which the people cause justice to be done.

Government, he continues, must be powerful ; must have **at** command the resources of the country; must be so strong that it can, if it will, disregard the limitations of the constitution. The question is, How to compel a government, holding such powers, having an army, a navy, and a national treasury **at** command, to obey the requirements of a mere piece of printed paper ?

Power, says Mr. Calhoun, can only be resisted by power. Therefore, a proper constitution must leave to the governed the *power* to resist encroachments. This is done in free countries by universal suffrage and the election of rulers at frequent and fixed periods. This gives to rulers the strongest possible motive to please the people, which can only be done by executing their will.

So far, most readers will follow the author without serious dif-ficulty. But now we come to passages which no one could understand who was not acquainted with the Nullification imbroglio of 1833. A philosophic Frenchman or German, who should read this work with a view to enlightening his mind upon the nature of government, would be much puzzled after passing the thir

teenth page ; for at that point the hidden loadstone begins to op
erate upon the needle of Mr. Calhoun's compass, and he is as
Louis Napoleon writing the Life of Cæsar.

Universal suffrage, he continues, and the frequent election of
rulers, are indeed the primary and fundamental principles of a
constitutional government ; and they are sufficient to give the
people an effective control over those whom they have elected.
But this is all they can do. They cannot make rulers good, or
just, or obedient to the constitution, but only faithful representatives of the majority of the people and executors of the will of
that majority. The right of suffrage transfers the supreme authority from the rulers to the body of the community, and the
more perfectly it does this, the more perfectly it accomplishes its
object. Majority is king. But this king, too, like all others, is
selfish, and will abuse his power if he can.

So, we have been arguing in a circle, and have come back to
the starting-point. Government keeps within bounds the selfishness of the people ; the constitution restrains the selfishness of the
government ; but, in doing so, it has only created a despot as
much to be dreaded as the power it displaced. We are still,
therefore, confronted by the original difficulty. How are we to
limit the sway of tyrant Majority ?

If, says Mr. Calhoun, all the people had the same interests, so
that a law which oppressed one interest would oppress all interests, then the right of suffrage would itself be sufficient ; and the
only question would be as to the fitness of different candidates.
But this is not the case. Taxation, for example : no system of
taxation can be arranged that will not bear oppressively upon
some interests or section. Disbursements, also : some portions
of the country must receive back, in the form of governmental
disbursements, more money than they pay in taxes, and others
less ; and this may be carried so far, that one region may be utterly impoverished, while others are enriched. King Majority
may have his favorites. He may now choose to favor agriculture ;
now, commerce ; now, manufactures ; and so arrange the imports
as to crush one for the sake of promoting the others. "Crush"
is Mr. Calhoun's word. "One portion of the community," he

K

says, " may be crushed, and another elevated on its ruins, by systematically perverting the power of taxation and disbursement, for the purpose of aggrandizing or building up one portion of the community at the expense of the other." *May* be. But has not the most relentless despot an interest in the prosperity of his subjects? And can one interest be crushed without manifest and immediate injury to all the others? Mr. Calhoun says: That this fell power to crush important interests *will* be used, is exactly as certain as that it *can* be.

All this would be unintelligible to our foreign philosopher, but American citizens know very well what it means. Through this fine lattice-work fence they discern the shining countenance of the colored person.

But now, what remedy? Mr. Calhoun approaches this part of the subject with the due acknowledgment of its difficulty. The remedy, of course, is Nullification; but he is far from using a word so familiar. There is but one mode, he remarks, by which the majority of the whole people can be prevented from oppressing the minority, or portions of the minority, and that is this: " By taking the sense of each interest or portion of the community, which may be unequally and injuriously affected by the action of the government, separately, through its own majorty, or in some other way by which its voice can be expressed; and to require the consent of each interest, either to put or to keep the government in motion." And this can only be done by such an " organism " as will " give to each division or interest either a concurrent voice in making and executing the laws or *a veto on their execution.*"

This is perfectly intelligible when read by the light of the history of 1833. But no human being unacquainted with that history could gather Mr. Calhoun's meaning. Our studious foreigner would suppose by the word " interest," that the author meant the manufacturing interest, the commercial and agricultural interests, and that each of these should have its little congress concurring in or vetoing the acts of the Congress sitting at Washington. *We*, however, know that Mr. Calhoun meant that South Carolina should have the power to nullify acts of Congress and give law to the Union. He does not tell us how South Carolina's tyrant Majority is to be kept within bounds; but only how that majority is to control the majority of the whole country. He has driven his problem into a corner, and there he leaves it.

Having thus arrived at the conclusion, that a law, to be binding on all "interests," i. e. on all the States of the Union, must be concurred in by all, he proceeds to answer the obvious objection, that "interests" so antagonistic could never be brought to unanimous agreement. He thinks this would present no difficulty, and adduces some instances of unanimity to illustrate his point.

First, trial by jury. Here are twelve men, of different character and calibre, shut up in a room to agree upon a verdict, in a cause upon which able men have argued upon opposite sides. How unlikely that they should be able to agree unanimously! Yet they generally do, and that speedily. Why is this? Because, answers Mr. Calhoun, they go into their room knowing that nothing short of unanimity will answer; and consequently every man is *disposed* to agree with his fellows, and, if he cannot agree, to compromise. "Not at all." The chief reason why juries generally agree is, that they are not interested in the matter in dispute. The law of justice is so plainly written in the human heart, that the fair thing is usually obvious to disinterested minds, or can be made so. It is interest, it is rivalry, that blinds us to what is right; and Mr. Calhoun's problem is to render "antagonistic" interests unanimous. We cannot, therefore, accept this illustration as a case in point.

Secondly, Poland. Poland is not the country which an American would naturally visit to gain political wisdom. Mr. Calhoun, however, repairs thither, and brings home the fact, that in the turbulent Diet of that unhappy kingdom every member had an absolute veto upon every measure. Nay, more: no king could be elected without the unanimous vote of an assembly of one hundred and fifty thousand persons. Yet Poland lasted two centuries! The history of those two centuries is a sufficient comment upon Mr Calhoun's system, to say nothing of the final catastrophe, which Mr. Calhoun confesses was owing to "the extreme to which the principle was carried." A sound principle cannot be carried to an unsafe extreme; it is impossible for a man to be too right. If it is right for South Carolina to contro. and nullify the United States, it is right for any one man in South Carolina to control and nullify South Carolina. One of the tests of a system is to ascertain where it will carry us if it *is* pushed to the uttermost extreme. Mr. Calhoun gave his countrymen this valuable information when he cited the lamentable case of Poland.

From Poland the author descends to the Six Nations, the federal council of which was composed of forty-two members, each of whom had an absolute veto upon every measure. Nevertheless, this confederacy, he says, became the most powerful and the most united of all the Indian nations. He omits to add, that it was the facility with which this council could be wielded by the French and English in turn, that hastened the grinding of the Six Nations to pieces between those two millstones.

Rome is Mr. Calhoun's next illustration. The *Tribunus Plebis*, he observes, had a veto upon the passage of all laws and upon the execution of all laws, and thus prevented the oppression of the plebeians by the patricians. To show the inapplicability of this example to the principle in question, to show by what steps his tribunal, long useful and efficient, gradually absorbed the power of the government, and became itself, first oppressive, and then an instrument in the overthrow of the constitution, would be to write a history of Rome. Niebuhr is accessible to the public, and Niebuhr knew more of the *Tribunus Plebis* than Mr. Calhoun. We cannot find in Niebuhr anything to justify the author's aim to constitute patrician Carolina the *Tribunus Plebis* of the United States.

Lastly, England. England, too, has that safeguard of liberty ' an organism by which the voice of each order or class is taken through its appropriate organ, and which requires the concurring voice of all to constitute that of the whole community." These orders are King, Lords, and Commons. They must all concur in every law, each having a veto upon the action of the two others. The government of the United States is also so arranged that the President and the two Houses of Congress must concur

in every enactment; but then they all represent the *same* order
or interest, the people of the United States. The English government, says Mr. Calhoun, is so exquisitely constituted, that the
greater the revenues of the government, the more stable it is;
because those revenues, being chiefly expended upon the lords
and gentlemen, render them exceedingly averse to any radical
change. Mr. Calhoun does not mention that the majority of the
people of England are not represented in the government at all.
Perhaps, however, the following passage, in a previous part of
the work, was designed to meet their case: —

"It is a great and dangerous error to suppose that all people are
equally entitled to liberty. It is a reward to be earned, not a blessing
to be gratuitously lavished on all alike; — a reward reserved for the
intelligent, the patriotic, the virtuous, and deserving; and not a boon
to be bestowed on a people too ignorant, degraded, and vicious to be
capable either of appreciating or of enjoying it."

Mr. Calhoun does not tell us who is to *bestow* this precious
boon. He afterwards remarks, that the progress of a people
"rising" to the point of civilization which entitles them to freedom, is "necessarily slow." How very slow, then, it must be,
when the means of civilization are forbidden to them by law!

With his remarks upon England, Mr. Calhoun terminates his
discussion of the theory of government. Let us grant all that he
claims for it, and see to what it conducts us. Observe that his
grand position is, that a "numerical majority," like all other sovereign powers, will certainly tyrannize if it can. His remedy for
this is, that a local majority, the majority of each State, shall
have a veto upon the acts of the majority of the whole country.
But he omits to tell us how that local majority is to be kept within
bounds. According to his reasoning, South Carolina should have
veto upon acts of Congress. Very well; then each county of
South Carolina should have a veto upon the acts of the State
Legislature; each town should have a veto upon the behests of
the county; and each voter upon the decisions of the town. Mr.
Calhoun's argument, therefore, amounts to this: that one voter
in South Carolina should have the constitutional right to nullify

an act of Congress, and no law should be binding which has not received the assent of every citizen.

Having completed the theoretical part of his subject, the author proceeds to the practical. In his first essay he describes the " organism " that is requisite for the preservation of liberty ; and in his second, he endeavors to show that the United States *is* precisely such an organism, since the Constitution, rightly inter· preted, *does* confer upon South Carolina the right to veto the decrees of the numerical majority. Mr. Calhoun's understanding appears to much better advantage in this second discourse, which contains the substance of all his numerous speeches on nullification. It is marvellous how this morbid and intense mind had brooded over a single subject, and how it had subjugated all history and all law to its single purpose. But we cannot follow Mr. Calhoun through the tortuous mazes of his second essay ; nor, if we could, should we be able to draw readers after us. We can only say this : Let it be granted that there *are* two ways in which the Constitution can be fairly interpreted ; — one, the Websterian method ; the other, that of Mr. Calhoun. On one of these interpretations the Constitution will work, and on the other it will not. We prefer the interpretation that is practicable, and leave the other party to the enjoyment of their argument. Nations cannot be governed upon principles so recondite and refined, that not one citizen in a hundred will so much as follow a mere statement of them. The fundamental law must be as plain as the ten commandments, — as plain as the four celebrated propositions in which Mr. Webster put the substance of his speeches in reply to Mr. Calhoun's ingenious defence of his conduct in 1833.

The author concludes his essay by a prophetic glance at the future. He remarks, that with regard to the future of the United States, as then governed, only one thing could be predicted with absolute certainty, and that was, that the Republic could not last. It might lapse into a monarchy, or it might be dismembered, — no man could say which ; but that one of these things would happen was entirely certain. The rotation-in-office system, as introduced by General Jackson, and sanctioned by his subservient Congress, had rendered the Presidential office a prize so tempting, in which so large a number of men had an interest, that the contest would gradually cease to be elective, and would finally lose the elective form. *The incumbent would appoint his successor;* and " thus the absolute form of a popular, would end in the absolute form of a monarchical government," and there would be no possibility of even rendering the monarchy limited or constitutional. Mr. Calhoun does not mention here the name of General Jackson or of Martin Van Buren, but American readers know very well what he was thinking of when he wrote the passage.

Disunion, according to Mr. Calhoun, was another of our perils. In view of recent events, our readers may be interested in reading his remarks on this subject, written in 1849, among the last words he ever deliberately put upon paper: —

" The conditions impelling the government toward disunion are very powerful. They consist chiefly of two; — the one arising from the great extent of the country; the other, from its division into separate States, having local institutions and interests. The former, under the operation of the numerical majority, has necessarily given to the two great parties, in their contest for the honors and emoluments of the government, a geographical character, for reasons which have been fully stated. This contest must finally settle down into a struggle on the part of the stronger section to obtain the permanent control; and on the part of the weaker, to preserve its independence and equality as members of the Union. The conflict will thus become one between the States occupying the different sections, — that is, between organized bodies on both sides, — each, in the event of separation, having the means of avoiding the confusion and anarchy to which the parts would be subject without such organization. This would contribute much to increase the power of resistance on the part of the weaker section against the stronger in possession of the government. With these great advantages and resources, it is hardly possible that the parties occupying the weaker section would consent quietly, under any circumstances, to break down from independent and equal sovereignties into a dependent and colonial condition · and still less so, under circumstances that would revolutionize them *internally*, and put their very existence as a people at stake. Never was there an issue between independent States that involved greater calamity to the conquered, han is involved in that between the States which compose the two sections of the Union. The condition of the weaker, should it sink from a state of independence and equality to one of dependence and subjection, would be more calamitous than ever before befell a civilized people. It is vain to think that, with such consequences before them, they will not resist; especially, when resistance *may* save them, and cannot render their condition worse. That this will take place, unless the stronger section desists from its course, may be assumed as certain : and that, if forced to resist, the weaker section would prove successful, and the system end in disunion, is, to say the least, highly probable. But if it should fail, the great increase of power and patronage which must, in consequence, accrue to the government of the United States, would but render certain and hasten the termination in the other alternative. So that, at all events, to the one or to the other — to monarchy or disunion — it must come, if not prevented by strenuous or timely efforts."

This is a very instructive passage, and one that shows well the complexity of human motives. Mr. Calhoun betrays the secret that, after all, the contest between the two sections is a " contest for the honors and emoluments of the government," and that all the rest is but pretext and afterthought, — as General Jackson said it was. He plainly states that the policy of the South is rule or ruin. Besides this, he intimates that there is in the United States an "interest," an institution, the development of which is incompatible with the advancement of the general interest ; and either that one interest must overshadow and subdue all other interests, or all other interests must unite to crush that one. The latter has been done.

Mr. Calhoun proceeds to suggest the measures by which these calamities can be averted. The government must be " restored to its federal character " by the repeal of all laws tending to the annihilation of State sovereignty, and by a strict construction of the Constitution. The President's power of removal must be limited. In earlier times, these would have sufficed ; but at that day the nature of the disease was such that nothing could reach it short of an organic change, which should give the weaker section a negative on the action of the government. Mr. Calhoun was of opinion that this could best be done by our having two Presidents, — one elected by the North and the other by the South, —

the assent of both to be necessary to every act of Congress. Under such a system, he thought, —

" The Presidential election, instead of dividing the Union into hos
tile geographical parties, the stronger struggling to enlarge its powers,
and the weaker to defend its rights, as is now the case, would become
the means of restoring harmony and concord to the country and the
government. It would make the Union a union in truth, — a bond
of mutual affection and brotherhood ; and not a mere connection used
by the stronger as the instrument of dominion and aggrandizement,
and submitted to by the weaker only from the lingering remains
of former attachment, and the fading hope of being able to restore
the government to what it was originally intended to be, — a blessing
to all."

The utter misapprehension of the purposes and desires of the
Northern people which this passage betrays, and which pervades
all the later writings of Mr. Calhoun, can only be explained by
the supposition that he judged them out of his own heart. It is
astounding to hear the author of the annexation of Texas charg-
ing the North with the lust of dominion, and the great Nullifier
accusing Northern statesmen of being wholly possessed by the
mania to be President.

Webster, Clay, and Calhoun, — these were great names in their
day. When the last of them had departed, the country felt a
sense of bereavement, and even of self-distrust, doubting if ever
again such men would adorn the public councils. A close scrutiny into the lives of either of them would, of course, compel us to
deduct something from his contemporary renown, for they were
all, in some degree, at some periods, diverted from their true path
by an ambition beneath an American statesman, whose true glory
alone consists in serving his country well in that sphere to which
his fellow-citizens call him. From such a scrutiny the fame of
neither of those distinguished men would suffer so much as that
of Calhoun. His endowments were not great, nor of the most valuable kind ; and his early education, hasty and very incomplete, was
not continued by maturer study. He read rather to confirm his
impressions than to correct them. It was impossible that he
should ever have been wise, because he refused to admit his lia-

8

bility to error. Never was mental assurance more complete, and seldom less warranted by innate or acquired superiority. If his knowledge of books was slight, his opportunities of observing men were still more limited, since he passed his whole life in places as exceptional, perhaps, as any in the world, — Washington and South Carolina. From the beginning of his public career there was a canker in the heart of it; for, while his oath, as a member of Congress, to support the Constitution of the United States, was still fresh upon his lips, he declared that his attachment to the Union was conditional and subordinate. He said that the alliance between the Southern planters and Northern Democrats was a false and calculated compact, to be broken when the planters could no longer rule by it. While he resided in Washington, and acted with the Republican party in the flush of its double triumph, he appeared a respectable character, and won golden opinions from eminent men in both parties. But when he was again subjected to the narrowing and perverting influence of a residence in South Carolina, he shrunk at once to his original proportions, and became thenceforth, not the servant of his country, but the special pleader of a class and the representative of a section. And yet, with that strange judicial blindness which has ever been the doom of the defenders of wrong, he still hoped to attain the Presidency. There is scarcely any example of infatuation more remarkable than this. Here we have, lying before us at this moment, undeniable proofs, in the form of "campaign lives" and "campaign documents," that, as late as 1844 there was money spent and labor done for the purpose of placing him in nomination for the highest office.

Calhoun failed in all the leading objects of his public life, except one; but in that one his success will be memorable forever. He has left it on record (see Benton, II. 698) that his great aim, from 1835 to 1847, was to force the slavery issue on the North. "It is our duty," he wrote in 1847, " to force the issue on the North." "Had the South," he continued, "or even my own State, backed me, I would have forced the issue on the North in 1835"; and he welcomed the Wilmot Proviso in 1847 because, as he privately wrote, it would be the means of "ena bling us to force the issue on the North." In this design, at length, when he had been ten years in the grave, he succeeded. Had there been no Calhoun, it is possible — nay, it is not improbable — that that issue might have been deferred till the North had so outstripped the South in accumulating all the elements of power, that the fire-eaters themselves would have shrunk from submitting the question to the arbitrament of the sword. It was Calhoun who forced the issue upon the United States, and compelled us to choose between annihilation and war.

JOHN RANDOLPH.

JOHN RANDOLPH.

IN June, 1861, Dr Russell, the correspondent of the London Times, was ascending the Mississippi in a steamboat, on board of which was a body of Confederate troops, several of whom were sick, and lay along the deck helpless. Being an old campaigner, he had his medicine-chest with him, and he was thus enabled to administer to these men the medicines which he supposed their cases required. One huge fellow, attenuated to a skeleton by dysentery, who appears to have been aware of his benefactor's connection with the press, gasped out these words: "Stranger, remember, if I die, that I am Robert Tallon of Tishimingo County, and that I died for States' Rights. See, now, they put that in the papers, won't you? Robert Tallon died for States' Rights." Having thus spoken, he turned over on his blanket, and was silent. Dr. Russell assures his readers that this man only expressed the nearly unanimous feeling of the Southern people at the outbreak of the war. He had been ten weeks travelling in the Southern States, and he declared that the people had but one battle-cry, — "States' Rights, and death to those who make war upon them!" About the same time, we remember, there was a paragraph going the rounds of the newspapers which related a conversation said to have taken place between a Northern man and a Southern boy. The boy happening to use the word "country," the Northerner asked him, "What is your country?" To which the boy instantly and haughtily replied, "SOUTH CAROLINA!"

Such anecdotes as these were to most of us here at the North a revelation. The majority of the Northern people actually did not know of the *existence* of such a feeling as that expressed by the Carolina boy, nor of the doctrine enunciated by the dying soldier. If every boy in the Northern States old enough to understand the question had been asked, What is your country? every one of them, without a moment's hesitation, would have quietly answered in substance thus : " Why, the United States, of course " ; — and the only feeling excited by the question would have been one of surprise that it should have been asked. And with regard to that " battle-cry " of States' Rights, seven tenths of the voters of the North hardly knew what a Southern man meant when he pronounced the words. Thus we presented to the world the curious spectacle of a people so ignorant of one another, so little homogeneous, that nearly all on one side of an imaginary line were willing to risk their lives for an idea which the inhabitants on the other side of the line not only did not entertain, but knew nothing about. We observe something similar in the British empire. The ordinary Englishman does not know what it is of which Ireland complains, and if an Irishman is asked the name of his country, he does not pronounce any of the names which imply the merging of his native isle in the realm of Britain.

Few of us, even now, have a " realizing sense," as it is called, of the strength of the States' Rights feeling among the Southern people. Of all the Southern States in which we ever sojourned, the one that seemed to us most like a Northern State was North Carolina. We stayed some time at Raleigh, ten years ago, during the session of the Legislature, and we were struck with the large number of reasonable, intelligent, upright men who were members of that body. Of course, we expected to find Southern men all mad on one topic; but in the Legislature of North Carolina there were several individuals who could converse even on that in a rational and comfortable manner. We were a little surprised, therefore, the other day, to pick up at a book-stall in Nassau Street a work entitled : " The North Carolina Reader, Number III. Prepared with Special Reference to the Wants and Interests of North Carolina. Under the Auspices of the Superintendent of Common Schools. Containing Selections in Prose and Verse. By C. H. Wiley. New York : A. S

Barnes and Burr." The acute reader will at once surmise that the object of this series of school readers was to instil into the minds of the youth of North Carolina a due regard for the sacredness and blessed effects of our peculiar institution. But for once the acute reader is mistaken. No such purpose appears, at least not in Number III.; in which there are only one or two even distant allusions to that dread subject. Onesimus is not mentioned; there is no reference to Ham, nor is there any discourse upon long heels and small brains. The great, the only object of this Reader was to nourish in the children of the State the feeling which the boy expressed when he proudly said that his country was South Carolina. Nothing can exceed the innocent, childlike manner in which this design is carried out in Number III. First, the children are favored with a series of chapters descriptive of North Carolina, written in the style of a school geography, with an occasional piece of poetry on a North Carolina subject by a North Carolina poet. Once, however, the compiler ventures to depart from his plan by inserting the lines by Sir William Jones, "What constitutes a State?" To this poem he appends a note apologizing for "breaking the thread of his discourse," upon the ground that the lines were so "applicable to the subject," that it seemed as if the author "must have been describing North Carolina." When the compiler has done cataloguing the fisheries, the rivers, the mountains, and the towns of North Carolina, he proceeds to relate its history precisely in the style of our school history books. The latter half of the volume is chiefly occupied by passages from speeches, and poems from newspapers, written by natives of North Carolina. It is impossible for us to convey an idea of the innutritiousness and the inferiority of most of these pieces. North Carolina is the great theme of orator and poet.

"We live," says one of the legislators quoted, "in the most beautiful land that the sun of heaven ever shone upon. Yes, sir, I have heard the anecdote from Mr. Clay, that a preacher in Kentucky, when speaking of the beauties of paradise, when he desired to make his audience believe it was a place of bliss, said it was a Kentucky of a place. Sir, this preacher had never visited the western counties of North Carolina

8 *   L

I have spent days of rapture in looking at her scenery of unsurpassed grandeur, in hearing the roar of her magnificent waterfalls, second only to the great cataract of the North; and while I gazed for hours, lost in admiration at the power of Him who by his word created such a country, and gratitude for the blessings He had scattered upon it, I thought that if Adam and Eve, when driven from paradise, had been near this land, they would have thought themselves in the next best place to that they had left."

We do not aver that the contents of this collection are generally as ludicrous as this specimen; but we do say that the passage quoted gives a very fair idea of the spirit and quality of the book. There is scarcely one of the North Carolina pieces which a Northern man would not for one reason or another find extremely comic. One of the reading lessons is a note written fifteen years ago by Solon Robinson, the agricultural editor of the Tribune, upon the use of the long leaves of the *North Carolina* pine for braiding or basket-work; another is a note written to accompany a bunch of *North Carolina* grapes sent to an editor; and there are many other newspaper cuttings of a similar character. The editor seems to have thought nothing too trivial, nothing too ephemeral, for his purpose, provided the passage contained the name of his beloved State.

How strange all this appears to a Northern mind! Everywhere else in Christendom, teachers strive to enlarge the mental range of their pupils, readily assenting to Voltaire's well-known definition of an educated man: "One who is *not* satisfied to survey the universe from his parish belfry." Everywhere else, the intellectual class have some sense of the ill-consequences of "breeding in and in," and take care to infuse into their minds the vigor of new ideas and the nourishment of strange knowledge. How impossible for a Northern State to think of doing what Alabama did last winter, pass a law designed to limit the circulation in that State of Northern newspapers and periodicals! What Southern men mean by "State pride" is really not known in the Northern States. All men of every land are fond of their native place; but the pride that Northern people may feel in the State wherein they happened to be born is as subordinate to their national feeling, as the attachment of a Frenchman to his native province is to his pride in France.

Why this difference? It did not always exist. It cost New York and Massachusetts as severe a struggle to accept the Constitution of 1787 as it did Virginia. George Clinton, Governor of New York, had as much State pride as Patrick Henry, orator of Virginia, and parted as reluctantly with a portion of the sovereignty which he wielded. If it required Washington's influence and Madison's persuasive reasoning to bring Virginia into the new system, the repugnance of Massachusetts was only overcome by the combined force of Hancock's social rank and Samuel Adams's late, reluctant assent.

On this subject let us hear Samuel Adams for a moment as he wrote to a friend in 1788 : —

"I confess, as I enter the building I stumble at the threshold. I meet with a national government instead of a federal union of sovereign states. I am not able to conceive why the wisdom of the Convention led them to give the preference to the former before the latter. If the several States in the Union are to be one entire nation under one Legislature, the powers of which shall extend to every subject of legislation, and its laws be supreme and control the whole, the idea of sovereignty in these States must be lost. Indeed, I think, upon such a supposition, those sovereignties ought to be eradicated from the mind, for they would be *imperia in imperio*, justly deemed a solecism in politics, and they would be highly dangerous and destructive of the peace, union, and safety of the nation.

" And can this National Legislature be competent to make laws for the *free* internal government of one people, living in climates so remote, and whose habits and particular interests are, and probably always will be, so different? Is it to be expected that general laws can be adapted to the feelings of the more eastern and the more southern parts of so extensive a nation? It appears to me difficult, if practicable. Hence, then, may we not look for discontent, mistrust, disaffection to government, and frequent insurrections, which will require standing armies to suppress them in one place and another, where they may happen to arise. Or, if laws could be made adapted to the local habits, feelings, views, and interests of those distant parts, would they not cause jealousies of partiality in government, which would excite envy and other malignant passions productive of wars and fighting?

But should we continue distinct sovereign States, confederated for the purpose of mutual safety and happiness, each contributing to the federal head such a part of its sovereignty as would render the government fully adequate to those purposes and *no more*, the people would govern themselves more easily, the laws of each State being well adapted to its own genius and circumstances, and the liberties of the United States would be more secure than they can be, as I humbly conceive, under the proposed new constitution." — *Life of Samuel Adams*, Vol. III., p. 251.

This passage is one of the large number in the writings of that time to which recent events have given a new interest; nor is it now without salutary meaning for us, though we quote it only to show the reluctance of some of the best citizens of the North to come into a national system. Suppose, to-day, that the United States were invited to merge their sovereignty into a confederation of all the nations of America, which would require us to abolish the city of Washington, and send delegates to a general congress on the isthmus of Darien! A sacrifice of pride like that was demanded of the leading States of the Union in 1787 Severe was the struggle, but the sacrifice was made, and it cost the great States of the North as painful a throe as it did the great States of the South. Why, then, has State pride died away in the North, and grown stronger in the South? Why is it only in the Southern States that the doctrine of States' Rights is ever heard of? Why does the Northern man swell with national pride, and point with exultation to a flag bearing thirty-seven stars, feeling the remotest State to be as much his country as his native village, while the Southern man contracts to an exclusive love for a single State, and is willing to die on its frontiers in repelling from its sacred soil the national troops, and can see the flag under which his fathers fought torn down without regret?

The study of John Randolph of Virginia takes us to the heart of this mystery. He could not have correctly answered the question we have proposed, but he *was* an answer to it. Born when George Washington, Thomas Jefferson, George Mason, and James Madison were Virginia farmers, and surviving to the time when Andrew Jackson was President of the United States, he lived through the period of the decline of his race, and he was of that decline a conscious exemplification. He represented the decay of Virginia, himself a living ruin attesting by the strength and splendor of portions of it what a magnificent structure it was once. "Poor old Virginia! Poor old Virginia!" This was the burden of his cry for many a year. Sick, solitary, and half mad, at his lonely house in the wilderness of Roanoke, suffering from inherited disease, burdened with inherited debt, limited by inherited errors, and severed by a wall of inherited prejudice from the life of the modern world, he stands to us as the type of the palsied and dying State. Of the doctrine of States' Rights he was the most consistent and persistent champion; while of that feeling which the North Carolina Reader No. III. styles "State pride," we may call him the very incarnation. "When I speak of my country," he would say, "I mean the Commonwealth of Virginia." He was the first eminent man in the Southern States who was prepared in spirit for war against the government of the United States; for during the Nullification imbroglio of 1833, he not only was in the fullest accord with Calhoun, but he used to say, that, if a collision took place between the nullifiers and the forces of the United States, he, John Randolph of Roanoke, old and sick as he was, would have himself buckled on his horse, Radical, and fight for the South to his last breath.

But then he was a man of genius, travel, and reading. We find him, therefore, as we have said, a *conscious* witness of his Virginia's decline. Along with a pride in the Old Dominion that was fanatical, there was in this man's heart a constant and most agonizing sense of her inferiority to lands less beloved. By no tongue or pen — not by Sumner's tongue nor Olmstead's pen — have more terrible pictures been drawn of Virginia's lapse into barbarism, than are to be found in John Randolph's letters. At a time (1831) when he would not buy a pocket-knife made in New England, nor send a book to be bound north of the Potomac, we find him writing of his native State in these terms: —

"I passed a night in Farrarville, in an apartment which, in England, would not have been thought fit for my servant; nor on the Continent

did he ever occupy so mean a one. Wherever I stop it is the same,
walls black and filthy; bed and furniture sordid; furniture scanty and
mean, generally broken; no mirror; no fire-irons; in short, dirt and
discomfort universally prevail; and in most private houses the matter
is not mended. The cows milked a half a mile off, or not got up, and
no milk to be had at any distance, — no jordan; — in fact, all the old
gentry are gone, and the *nouveaux riches*, when they have the inclination, do not know how to live. *Biscuit*, not half *cuit;* everything
animal and vegetable smeared with butter and lard. Poverty stalking
through the land, while we are engaged in political metaphysics, and,
amidst our filth and vermin, like the Spaniard and Portuguese, look
down with contempt on other nations, — England and France especially. We hug our lousy cloak around us, take another *chaw of tub-
backer*, float the room with nastiness, or ruin the grate and fire-irons,
where they happen not to be rusty, and try conclusions upon constitutional points."

What truth and painting in this passage! But if we had
asked this suffering genius as to the cause of his "country's"
decline, he would have given us a mad answer indeed. He
would have said, in his wild way, that it was all Tom Jefferson's
doing, sir. Tom Jefferson abolished primogeniture in Virginia,
and thus, as John Randolph believed, destroyed the old families,
the life and glory of the State. Tom Jefferson was unfaithful to
the States' Rights and strict-constructionist creed, of which he
was the expounder and trustee, and thus let in the "American
system" of Henry Clay, with its protective tariff, which completed
the ruin of the agricultural States. This was his simple theory
of the situation. These were the reasons why he despaired of
ever again seeing, to use his own language, "the Nelsons, the
Pages, the Byrds, and Fairfaxes, living in their palaces, and
driving their coaches and sixes, or the good old Virginia gentlemen in the Assembly drinking their twenty and forty bowls of
rack punches, and madeira and claret, in lieu of a knot of deputy
sheriffs and hack attorneys, each with his cruet of whiskey before
him, and puddle of tobacco-spittle between his legs." He was as
far from seeing any relation of cause and effect between the
coaches, palaces, and bowls of punch, and the "knot of deputy
sheriffs," as a Fenian is from discerning any connection between

the Irish rackrenting of the last century, and the Irish beggary of this. Like conditions produce like characters. How interesting to discover in this republican, this native Virginian of English stock, a perfect and splendid specimen of a species of tory supposed to exist only in such countries as Poland, Spain, Ireland, and the Highlands of Scotland, but which in reality does abound in the Southern States of this Union, — the tory, conscious of his country's ruin, but clinging with fanatical and proud tenacity to the principles that ruined it.

Dear tobacco, virgin land, and cheap negroes gave the several families in Virginia, for three generations, a showy, delusive prosperity, which produced a considerable number of dissolute, extravagant men, and educated a few to a high degree of knowledge and wisdom. Of these families, the Randolphs were the most numerous, and among the oldest, richest, and most influential. The soldiers of the late army of the Potomac know well the lands which produced the tobacco that maintained them in baronial state. It was on Turkey Island (an island no more), twenty miles below Richmond, close to Malvern Hill of immortal memory, that the founder of the family settled in 1660, — a Cavalier of ancient Yorkshire race ruined in the civil wars. Few of our troops, perhaps, who rambled over Turkey Bend, were aware that the massive ruins still visible there, and which served as negro quarters seven years ago, are the remains of the great and famous mansion built by this Cavalier, turned tobacco-planter. This home of the Randolphs was so elaborately splendid, that a man served out the whole term of his apprenticeship to the trade of carpenter in one of its rooms. The lofty dome was for many years a beacon to the navigator. Such success had this Randolph in raising tobacco during the fifty-one years of his residence upon Turkey Island, that to each of his six sons he gave or left a large estate, besides portioning liberally his two daughters. Five of these sons reared families, and the sons of those sons were also thriving and prolific men; so that, in the course of three generations, Virginia was full of Randolphs. There was, we believe, not one of the noted controlling families that was not related to them by blood or marriage.

In 1773, when John Randolph was born, the family was still powerful; and the region last trodden by the Army of the Potomac was still adorned by the seats of its leading members. Cawsons, the mansion in which he was born, was situated at the junction of the James and Appomattox, in full view of City Point and Bermuda Hundred, and only an after-breakfast walk from Dutch Gap. The mansion long ago disappeared, and nothing now marks its site but negro huts. Many of those exquisite spots on the James and Appomattox, which we have seen men pause to admire while the shells were bursting overhead, were occupied sixty years ago by the sumptuous abodes of the Randolphs and families related to them. Mattoax, the house in which John Randolph passed much of his childhood, was on a bluff of the Appomattox, two miles above Petersburg; and Bizarre, the estate on which he spent his boyhood, lay above, on both sides of the same river. Over all that extensive and enchanting region, trampled and torn and laid waste by hostile armies in 1864 and 1865, John Randolph rode and hunted from the time he could sit a pony and handle a gun. Not a vestige remains of the opulence and splendor of his early days. Not one of the mansions inhabited or visited by him in his youth furnished a target for our cannoneers or plunder for our camps. A country better adapted to all good purposes of man, nor one more pleasing to the eye, hardly exists on earth; but before it was trodden by armies, it had become little less than desolate. The James River is as navigable as the Hudson, and flows through a region far more fertile, longer settled, more inviting, and of more genial climate; but there are upon the Hudson's banks more cities than there are rotten landings upon the James. The shores of this beautiful and classic stream are so unexpectedly void of even the signs of human habitation, that our soldiers were often ready to exclaim: " Can this be the river of Captain John Smith and Pocahontas? Was it here that Jamestown stood? Is it possible that white men have lived in this delightful land for two hundred and fifty-seven years? Or has not the captain of the steamboat made a mistake, and turned into the wrong river?"

One scene of John Randolph's boyhood reveals to us the entire political economy of the Old Dominion. He used to relate it himself, when denouncing the manufacturing system of Henry Clay. One ship, he would say, sufficed, in those happy days, for all the commerce of that part of Virginia with the Old World, and that ship was named the London Trader. When this ship was about to sail, all the family were called together, and each member was invited to mention the articles which he or she wanted from London. First, the mother of the family gave in her list; next the children, in the order of their ages; next, the overseer; then the *mammy*, the children's black nurse; lastly, the house servants, according to their rank, down even to their children. When months had passed, and the time for the ship's return was at hand, the weeks, the days, the hours were counted; and when the signal was at last descried, the whole household burst into exclamations of delight, and there was festival in the family for many days.

How picturesque and interesting! How satisfactory to the tory mind! But alas! this system of exhausting the soil in the production of tobacco by the labor of slaves, and sending for all manufactured articles to England, was more ruinous even than it was picturesque. No middle class could exist, as in England, to supply the waste of aristocratic blood and means; and in three generations, rich and beautiful Virginia, created for empire, was only another Ireland. But it was a picturesque system and John Randolph, poet and tory, revelled in the recollection of it. "Our Egyptian taskmasters," he would say, meaning the manufacturers of Pennsylvania, New York, New Jersey, and New England, "only wish to leave us the recollection of past times, and insist upon our purchasing their vile *domestic* stuffs; but it won't do: no wooden nutmegs for old Virginia."

His own pecuniary history was an illustration of the working of the system. His father left forty thousand acres of the best land in the world, and several hundred slaves, to his three boys; the greater part of which property, by the early death of the two elder brothers, fell to John. As the father died when John was but three years old, there was a minority of eighteen years, dur ing which the boy's portion should have greatly increased. So far from increasing, an old debt of his father's — a *London* debt, incurred for goods brought to a joyous household in the London Trader — remained undiminished at his coming of age, and hung about his neck for many years afterward. Working two large estates, with a force of negroes equivalent to one hundred and eighty full field hands, he could not afford himself the luxury of a trip to Europe until he was fifty years old. The amount of this debt we do not know, but he says enough about it for us to infer that it was not of very large amount in comparison with his great resources. One hundred and eighty stalwart negroes working the best land in the world, under a man so keen and vigilant as this last of the noble Randolphs, and yet making scarcely any headway for a quarter of a century!

The blood of this fine breed of men was also running low. Both the parents of John Randolph and both of his brothers died young, and he himself inherited weakness which early developed into disease. One of his half-brothers died a madman. "My whole name and race," he would say, " lie under a curse. I feel the curse clinging to me." He was a fair, delicate child, more like a girl than a boy, and more inclined, as a child, to the sports of girls than of boys. His mother, a fond, tender, gentle lady, nourished his softer qualities, powerless to govern him, and probably never attempting it. Nevertheless, he was no girl ; he was a genuine *son* of the South. Such was the violence of his passions, that, before he was four years old, he sometimes in a fit of anger fell senseless upon the floor, and was restored only after much effort. His step-father, who was an honorable man, seems never to have attempted either to control his passions or develop his intellect. He grew up, as many boys of Virginia did, and do, unchecked, unguided, untrained. Turned loose in a miscellaneous library, nearly every book he read tended to intensify his feelings or inflame his imagination. His first book was Voltaire's Charles XII., and a better book for a boy has never been written. Then he fell upon the Spectator. Before he was twelve he had read the Arabian Nights, Orlando, Robinson Crusoe, Smollett's Works, Reynard the Fox, Don Quixote, Gil Blas,

Tom Jones, Gulliver, Shakespeare, Plutarch's Lives, Pope's Homer, Goldsmith's Rome, Percy's Reliques, Thomson's Seasons, Young, Gray, and Chatterton, — a gallon of sack to a penny's worth of bread. A good steady drill in arithmetic, geography, and language might have given his understanding a chance ; but this ill-starred boy never had a steady drill in anything. He never remained longer at any one school than a year, and he learned at school very little that he needed most to know. In the course of his desultory schooling he picked up some Latin, a little Greek, a good deal of French, and an inconceivable medley of odds and ends of knowledge, which his wonderful memory enabled him to use sometimes with startling effect.

Everywhere else, in the whole world, children are taught that virtue is self-control. In the Southern States, among these tobacco-lords, boys learned just the opposite lesson, — that virtue is self-indulgence. This particular youth, thin-skinned, full of talent, fire, and passion, the heir to a large estate, fatherless, would have been in danger anywhere of growing up untrained, — a wild beast in broadcloth. In the Virginia of that day, in the circle in which he lived, there was nothing for him in the way either of curb or spur. He did what he pleased, and nothing else. All that was noble in his life, — those bursts of really fine oratory, his flashes of good sense, his occasional generosities, his hatred of debt, and his eager haste to pay it, — all these things were due to the original excellence of his race. In the very dregs of good wine there is flavor. We cannot make even good vinegar out of a low quality of wine.

His gentle mother taught him all the political economy he ever took to heart. "Johnny," said she to him one day, when they had reached a point in their ride that commanded an extensive view, "all this land belongs to you and your brother. It is your father's inheritance. When you get to be a man, you must not sell your land : it is the first step to ruin for a boy to part with his father's home. Be sure to keep it as long as you live. Keep your land, and your land will keep you." There never came a time when his mind was mature and masculine enough to *consider* this advice. He clung to his land as Charles Stuart clung to his prerogative.

All the early life of this youth was wandering and desultory. At fourteen, we find him at Princeton College in New Jersey, where, we are told, he fought a duel, exchanged shots twice with his adversary, and put a ball into his body which he carried all his life. By this time, too, the precocious and ungovernable boy had become, as he flattered himself, a complete atheist. One of his favorite amusements at Princeton was to burlesque the precise and perhaps ungraceful Presbyterians of the place. The library of his Virginian home, it appears, was furnished with a great supply of what the French mildly call the literature of incredulity, — Helvetius, Voltaire, Rousseau, Diderot, D'Alembert, and the rest. The boy, in his rage for knowledge, had read vast quantities of this literature, and, of course, embraced the theory of the writers that pushed denial farthest. For twenty-two years, he says in one of his letters, he never entered a church. Great pleasure it gave him to show how superior the Mahometan religion was to the Christian, and to recite specimens of what he took delight in styling Hebrew jargon. The Psalms of David were his special aversion.

Almost all gifted and fearless lads that have lived in Christendom during the last hundred years have had a fit of this kind between fifteen and twenty-five. The strength of the tendency to question the grounds of belief must be great indeed to bear away with it a youth like this, formed by Nature to believe. John Randolph had no more intellectual right to be a sceptic, than he had a moral right to be a republican. A person whose imagination is quick and warm, whose feelings are acute, and whose intellect is wholly untrained, can find no comfort except in belief. His scepticism is a mere freak of vanity or self-will. Coming upon the stage of life when unbelief was fashionable in high drawing-rooms, he became a sceptic. But Nature will have her way with us all, and so this atheist at fifteen was an Evangelical at forty-five.

His first political bias was equally at war with his nature. John Randolph was wholly a tory; there was not in his whole composition one republican atom. But coming early under the direct personal influence of Thomas Jefferson, whose every fibre was republican, he, too, the sympathetic tory of genius, espoused the people's cause. He was less than twenty-two years, however, in recovering from *this* false tendency.

Summoned from Princeton, after only a few months' residence, by the death of his mother, he went next to Columbia College, in the city of New York, where for a year or two he read Greek with a tutor, especially Demosthenes. At New York he saw the first Congress under the new Constitution assemble, and was one of the concourse that witnessed the scene of General Washington's taking the oath on the balcony of the old City Hall. It seemed to this Virginia boy natural enough that a Virginian should be at the head of the government; not so, that a Yankee should hold the second place and preside over the Senate. Forty years after, he recalled with bitterness a trifling incident, which, trifling as it was, appears to have been the origin of his intense antipathy to all of the blood of John Adams. The coachman of the Vice-President, it seems, told the brother of this little republican tory to stand back; or, as the orator stated it, forty years after, "I remember the manner in which my brother was spurned by the coachman of the Vice-President for coming too near the arms emblazoned on the vice-regal carriage."

Boy as he was, he had already taken sides with those who opposed the Constitution. The real ground of his opposition to it was, that it reduced the importance of Virginia, — great Virginia! Under the new Constitution, there was a man on the Western Continent of more consequence than the Governor of Virginia, there were legislative bodies more powerful than the Legislature of Virginia. This was the secret of the disgust with which he heard it proposed to style the President " His Highness " and " His Majesty." *This* was the reason why it kindled his ire to read, in the newspapers of 1789, that " the most honorable Rufus King " had been elected Senator. It was only Jefferson and a very few other of the grand Virginians who objected for higher and larger reasons.

In March, 1790, Mr. Jefferson reached New York, after his return from France, and entered upon his new office of Secretary of State under General Washington. He was a distant relative of our precocious student, then seventeen years of age ; and the two families had just been brought nearer together by the marriage of one of Mr. Jefferson's daughters to a Randolph. The reaction against republican principles was at full tide; and no one will ever know to what lengths it would have gone, had not Thomas Jefferson so opportunely come upon the scene. At his modest abode, No. 57 Maiden Lane, the two Randolph lads — John, seventeen, Theodorick, nineteen — were frequent visitors. Theodorick was a roistering blade, much opposed to his younger brother's reading habits, caring himself for nothing but pleasure. John was an eager politician. During the whole period of the reaction, first at New York, afterward at Philadelphia, finally in Virginia, John Randolph sat at the feet of the great Democrat of America, fascinated by his conversation, and generally convinced by his reasoning. It is a mistake, however, to suppose that he was a blind follower of Mr. Jefferson, even then. On the question of States' Rights, he was in the most perfect accord with him. But when, in 1791, the eyes of all intelligent America were fixed upon the two combatants, Edmund Burke and Thomas Paine, Burke condemning, Paine defending, the French Revolution, the inherited instincts of John Randolph asserted themselves, and he gave all his heart to Burke. Lord Chatham and Edmund Burke were the men who always held the first place in the esteem of this kindred spirit. Mr. Jefferson, of course, sympathized with the view of his friend Paine, and never wavered in his belief that the French Revolution was necessary and beneficial. A generous and gifted nation strangled, moved him to deeper compassion than a class proscribed. He dwelt more upon the long and bitter provocation, than upon the brief frenzy which was only one of its dire results. Louis XIV. and Louis XV., picturesque as they were, excited within him a profounder horror than ugly Marat and Robespierre. He pitied haggard, distracted France more than graceful and high-bred Marie Antoinette. In other words, he was not a tory.

There was a difference, too, between Mr. Jefferson and his young kinsman on the points upon which they agreed. Jefferson was a States' Rights man, and a strict constructionist, because he was a republican ; Randolph, because he was a Virginian. Jefferson thought the government should be small, that the people might be great ; John Randolph thought the government should be small, that Virginia might be great. Pride in Virginia was John Randolph's ruling passion, not less in 1790 than in 1828. The welfare and dignity of man were the darling objects of Thomas Jefferson's great soul, from youth to hoary age.

Here we have the explanation of the great puzzle of American politics, — the unnatural alliance, for sixty years, between the plantation lords of the South and the democracy of the North, both venerating the name of Jefferson, and both professing his principles. It was not, as many suppose, a compact of scurvy politicians for the sake of political victory. Every great party, whether religious or political, that has held power long in a country, has been founded upon conviction, — disinterested conviction. Some of the cotton and tobacco lords, men of intellect and culture, were democrats and abolitionists, like Jefferson himself. Others took up with republicanism because it was the reigning affectation in their circle, as it was in the chateaux and drawing-rooms of France. But their State pride it was that bound them as a class to the early Republican party. The Southern aristocrat saw in Jefferson the defender of the sovereignty of his State : the "smutched artificer" of the North gloried in Jefferson as the champion of the rights of man. While the Republican party was in opposition, battling with unmanageable John Adams, with British Hamilton, and with a foe more powerful than both of those men together, Robespierre, — while it had to contend with Washington's all but irresistible influence, and with the nearly unanimous opposition of educated and orthodox New England, — this distinction was not felt. Many a tobacco aristocrat cut off his pig-tail and wore trousers down to his ankles, which were then the outward signs of the inward democratic grace. But time tries all. It is now apparent to every one that the strength of the original Democratic party in the South was the States' Rights portion of its platform, while in the North it was the sentiment of republicanism that kept the party together

Young politicians should study this period of their country's history. If ever again a political party shall rule the United States for sixty years, or for twenty years, it will be, we think, a party resembling the original Republican party, as founded in America by Franklin, and organized under Jefferson. Its platform will be, perhaps, something like this : simple, economical government machinery ; strict construction of the Constitution : the rights of the States scrupulously observed ; the suffrage open to all, without regard to color or sex, — *open* to all, but *conferred* only upon men and women capable of exercising it.

John Randolph agreed upon another point with Mr. Jefferson he was an abolitionist. But for the English debt which he inherited, it is extremely probable that he would have followed the example of many of the best Virginians of his day, and emancipated his slaves. He would, perhaps, have done so when that debt was discharged, instead of waiting to do it by his last will, but for the forlorn condition of freedmen in a Slave State. His eldest brother wrote, upon the division of the estate, in 1794 : "I want not a single negro for any other purpose than his immediate emancipation. I shudder when I think that such an insignificant animal as I am is invested with this monstrous, this horrid power." He told his guardian that he would give up all his land rather than own a slave. There was no moment in the whole life of John Randolph when he did not sympathize with this view of slavery, and he died expressing it. But though he was, if possible, a more decided abolitionist than Jefferson, he never for a moment doubted the innate superiority of a Virginia gentleman to all the other inhabitants of America. He had not even the complaisance to take his hair out of queue, nor hide his thin legs in pantaloons. He was not endowed by nature with understanding enough to rise superior to the prejudices that had come down to him through generations of aristocrats. He was weak enough, indeed, to be extremely vain of the fact that a grandfather of his had married one of the great-granddaughters of Pocahontas, who, it was believed, performed the act that renders her famous at Point of Rocks on the Appomattox, within walking distance of one of the Randolph mansions. It is interesting to observe who an unquestioning, childlike faith he always had in the superiority of his caste, of his State, and of his section. He once got so far as to speak favorably of the talents of Daniel Webster; but he was obliged to conclude by saying that he was the best debater he had ever known *north of the Potomac.*

This singular being was twenty-six years of age before any one suspected, least of all himself, that he possessed any of the talents which command the attention of men. His life had been desultory and purposeless. He had studied law a little, attended a course or two of medical lectures, travelled somewhat, dipped into hundreds of books, read a few with passionate admiration, had lived much with the ablest men of that day, — a familiar guest at Jefferson's fireside, and no stranger at President Washington's stately table. Father, mother, and both brothers were dead. He was lonely, sad, and heavily burdened with property, with debt, and the care of many dependants. His appearance was even more singular than his situation. At twenty-three he had still the aspect of a boy. He actually grew half a head after he was twenty-three years of age. "A tall, gawky-looking, flaxen-haired stripling, apparently of the age of sixteen or eighteen, with complexion of a good parchment color, beardless chin, and as much assumed self-consequence as any two-footed animal I ever saw." So he was described by a Charleston bookseller, who saw him in his store in 1796, carelessly turning over books. "At length," continues this narrator, "he hit upon something that struck his fancy; and never did I witness so sudden, so perfect a change of the human countenance. That which was before dull and heavy in a moment became animated, and flashed with the brightest beams of intellect. He stepped up to the old gray-headed gentleman (his companion), and giving him a thundering slap on the shoulder, said, 'Jack, look at this!'" Thus was he described at twenty-three. At twenty-six he was half a head taller, and quite as slender as before. His light hair was then combed back into an elegant queue. His eye of hazel was bright and restless. His chin was still beardless. He wore a frock-coat of light blue cloth, yellow breeches, silk stockings, and top-boots. Great was the love he bore his horses, which were

9   M

numerous, and as good as Virginia could boast. It is amusing to notice that the horse upon which this pattern aristocrat used to scamper across the country, in French-Revolution times, was named *Jacobin!*

It was in March, 1799, the year before the final victory of the Republicans over the Federal party, that the neighbors of John Randolph and John Randolph himself discovered, to their great astonishment, that he was an orator. He had been nominated for Representative in Congress. Patrick Henry, aged and infirm, had been so adroitly manipulated by the Federalists, that he had at length agreed to speak to the people in support of the hateful administration of John Adams. John Randolph, who had never in his life addressed an audience, nor, as he afterwards declared, had ever imagined that he could do so, suddenly determined, the very evening before the day named for the meeting, to reply to Patrick Henry. It was an open-air meeting. No structure in Virginia could have contained the multitude that thronged to hear the transcendent orator, silent for so many years, and now summoned from his retirement by General Washington himself to speak for a Union imperilled and a government assailed. He spoke with the power of other days, for he was really alarmed for his country; and when he had finished his impassioned harangue, he sunk back into the arms of his friends, as one of them said, "like the sun setting in his glory." For the moment he had all hearts with him. The sturdiest Republican in Virginia could scarcely resist the spell of that amazing oratory.

John Randolph rose to reply. His first sentences showed not only that he could speak, but that he knew the artifices of an old debater; for he began by giving eloquent expression to the veneration felt by his hearers for the aged patriot who had just addressed them. He spoke for three hours, it is said; and if we may judge from the imperfect outline of his speech that has come down to us, he spoke as well that day as ever he did. States' Rights was the burden of his speech. That the Alien and Sedition Law was an outrage upon human nature, he may have believed; but what he *felt* was, that it was an outrage upon the Commonwealth of Virginia. He may have thought it desirable that all governments should confine themselves to the simple business of compelling the faithful performance of contracts; but what he *insisted upon* was, that the exercise by the government of the United States of any power not expressly laid down in the letter of the Constitution was a wrong to Virginia. If John Adams is right, said he, in substance, then Virginia has gained nothing by the Revolution but a change of masters, — New England for Old England, — which he thought was *not* a change for the better.

It was unnecessary, in the Virginia of 1799, for the head of the house of Randolph to be an orator in order to secure an election to the House of Representatives. He was elected, of course. When he came forward to be sworn in, his appearance was so youthful, that the Clerk of the House asked him, with the utmost politeness, whether he had attained the legal age. His reply was eminently characteristic of the tobacco lord: " Go, sir, and ask my constituents : they sent me here." As there was no one present authorized by the Constitution to box the ears of impudent boys on the floor of the House, he was sworn without further question. It has often occurred to us that this anecdote, which John Randolph used to relate with much satisfaction, was typical of much that has since occurred. The excessive courtesy of the officer, the insolence of the Virginia tobacconist, the submission of the Clerk to that insolence, — who has not witnessed such scenes in the Capitol at Washington?

It was in December, 1799, that this fiery and erratic genius took his seat in the House of Representatives. John Adams had still sixteen months to serve as target for the sarcasm of the young talent of the nation. To calm readers of the present day, Mr. Adams does really seem a strange personage to preside over a government; but the calm reader of the present day cannot realize the state of things in the year 1800. We cannot conceive what a fright the world had had in the excesses of the French Revolution, and the recent usurpation of General Bonaparte. France had made almost every timid man in Christendom a tory. Serious and respectable people, above forty, and enjoying a comfortable income, felt that there was only one thing left for a de cent person to do, — to assist in preserving the *authority* of government. John Adams, by the constitution of his mind, was as much a tory as John Randolph; for he too possessed imagination and talent disproportioned to his understanding. To be a democrat it is necessary to have a little pure intellect; since your democrat is merely a person who can, occasionally, see things and men as they are. New England will always be democratic enough as long as her boys learn mental arithmetic; and Ireland will always be the haunt of tories as long as her children are brought up upon songs, legends, and ceremonies. To make a democratic people, it is only necessary to accustom them to use their minds.

Nothing throws such light upon the state of things in the United States in 1800, as the once famous collision between these two natural tories, John Adams and John Randolph, which gave instantaneous celebrity to the new member, and made him an idol of the Republican party. In his maiden speech, which was in opposition to a proposed increase of the army, he spoke disparagingly of the troops already serving, using the words *ragamuffins* and *mercenaries*. In this passage of his speech, the partisan spoke, not the man. John Randolph expressed the real feeling of his nature toward soldiers, when, a few years later, on the same floor, he said: "If I must have a master, let him be one with epaulets; something which I can look up to; but not a master with a quill behind his ear." In 1800, however, it pleased him to style the soldiers of the United States ragamuffins and mercenaries; which induced two young officers to push, hustle, and otherwise discommode and insult him at the theatre. Strange to relate, this hot Virginian, usually so prompt with a challenge to mortal combat, reported the misconduct of these officers to the President of the United States. This eminently proper act he did in an eminently proper manner, thanks to his transient connection with the Republican party. Having briefly stated the case, he concluded his letter to the President thus: "The independence of the legislature has been attacked, and the majesty of the people, of which you are the principal representative, insulted, and your authority contemned. In their name, I demand that a provision commensurate with the evil be made, and which will be calculated to deter others from any future attempt to introduce the reign of terror into our country. In addressing you in this plain language of man, I give you, sir the best proof I can afford of the estimation in which I hold your office and your understanding; and I assure you with truth, that I am, with respect, your fellow-citizen, John Randolph."

This language so well accords with our present sense of the becoming, that a person unacquainted with that period would be unable to point to a single phrase calculated to give offence. In the year 1800, however, the President of the United States saw in every expression of the letter contemptuous and calculated insult. "The majesty of the people," forsooth! The President merely their "representative"! "plain language of man"! and "with respect, your fellow-citizen"! To the heated imaginations of the Federalists of 1800, language of this kind, addressed to the President, was simply prophetic of the guillotine. So amazed and indignant was Mr. Adams, that he submitted the letter to his Cabinet, requesting their opinion as to what should be done with it. Still more incredible is it, that four members of the Cabinet, in writing, declared their opinion to be, that "the contemptuous language therein adopted requires a public censure." They further said, that, "if such addresses remain unnoticed, we are apprehensive that a precedent will be established which must necessarily destroy the ancient, respectable, and urbane usages of this country." Some lingering remains of good-sense in the other member of the Cabinet prevented the President from acting upon their advice; and he merely sent the letter to the House, with the remark that he "submitted the whole letter and its tendencies" to their consideration, "without any other comments on its matter and style."

This affair, trivial as it was, sufficed in that mad time to lift the young member from Virginia into universal notoriety, and caused him to be regarded as a shining light of the Republican party. The splendor of his talents as an orator gave him at once the ear of the House and the admiration of the Republican side of it; while the fury of his zeal against the President rendered him most efficient in the Presidential canvass. No young man, per-haps, did more than he toward the election of Jefferson and Burr in 1800. He was indeed, at that time, before disease had wasted him, and while still enjoying the confidence of the Republican leaders and subject to the needed restraints of party, a most effec-tive speaker, whether in the House or upon the stump. He had something of Burke's torrent-like fluency, and something of Chatham's spirit of command, with a piercing, audacious sarcasm all his own. He was often unjust and unreasonable, but never dull. He never spoke in his life without being at least atten-tively listened to.

Mr. Jefferson came into power; and John Randolph, triumph-antly re-elected to Congress, was appointed Chairman of the Committee of Ways and Means, — a position not less important then than now. He was the leader of the Republican majority in the House. His social rank, his talents, his position in the House of Representatives, the admiration of the party, the confi-dence of the President, all united to render him the chief of the young men of the young nation. It was captivating to the popu-lar imagination to behold this heir of an ancient house, this pos-sessor of broad lands, this orator of genius, belonging to the party of the people. He aided to give the Republican party the only element of power which it lacked, — social consideration. The party had numbers and talent; but it had not that which could make a weak, rich man vain of the title of Republican. At the North, clergy, professors, rich men, were generally Federalists, and it was therefore peculiarly pleasing to Democrats to point to this eminent and brilliant Virginian as a member of their party He discharged the duties of his position well, showing ability as a man of business, and living in harmony with his colleagues. As often as he reached Washington, at the beginning of a ses-sion, he found the President's card (so Colonel Benton tells us) awaiting him for dinner the next day at the White House, when the great measures of the session were discussed. It was he who moved the resolutions of respect for the memory of that consum mate republican, that entire and perfect democrat, Samuel Adams of Massachusetts. It was he who arranged the financial measures required for the purchase of Louisiana, and made no objection to the purchase. During the first six years of Mr. Jefferson's Presidency, he shrank from no duty which his party had a right to claim from him. Whatever there might be narrow or erroneous in his political creed was neutralized by the sentiment of nationality which the capital inspires, and by the practical views which must needs be taken of public affairs by the Chairman of the Committee of Ways and Means.

These were the happy years of his life, and the most honorable ones. Never, since governments have existed, has a country been governed so wisely, so honestly, and so economically as the United States was governed during the Presidency of Thomas Jefferson. Randolph himself, after twenty years of opposition to the policy of this incomparable ruler, could still say of his administration, that it was the only one he had ever known which "seriously and in good faith was disposed to give up its patronage," and which desired to go further in depriving itself of power than the people themselves had thought. "Jefferson," said John Randolph in 1828, "was the only man I ever knew or heard of who really, truly, and honestly, not only said, *Nolo episcopari*, but actually refused the mitre."

For six years, as we have said, Mr. Randolph led the Republican party in the House of Representatives, and supported the measures of the administration, — all of them. In the spring of 1807, without apparent cause, he suddenly went into opposition, and from that time opposed the policy of the administration, — the whole of it.

Why this change? If there were such a thing as going apprentice to the art of discovering truth, a master in that art could not set an apprentice a better preliminary lesson than this: Why did John Randolph go into opposition in 1807? The gossips of that day had no difficulty in answering the question. Some said he had asked Mr. Jefferson for a foreign mission, and been refused. Others thought it was jealousy of Mr. Madison, who was known to be the President's choice for the succession. Others surmised that an important state secret had been revealed to other members of the House, but not to him. These opinions our tyro would find very positively recorded, and he would also, in the course of his researches, come upon the statement that Mr Randolph himself attributed the breach to his having beaten the President at a game of chess, which the President could not forgive.

The truth is, that John Randolph bolted for the same reason that a steel spring resumes its original bent the instant the restraining force is withdrawn. His position as leader of a party was irksome, because it obliged him to work in harness, and he had never been broken to harness. His party connection bound him to side with France in the great contest then raging between France and England, and yet his whole soul sympathized with England. This native Virginian was more consciously and positively English than any native of England ever was. English literature had nourished his mind; English names captivated his imagination; English traditions, feelings, instincts, habits, prejudices, were all congenial to his nature. How hard for such a man to side officially with Napoleon in those gigantic wars! Abhorring Napoleon with all a Randolph's force of antipathy, it was nevertheless expected of him, as a good Republican, to interpret leniently the man who, besides being the armed soldier of democracy, had sold Louisiana to the United States. Randolph, moreover, was an absolute aristocrat. He delighted to tell the House of Representatives that he, being a Virginian slaveholder, was *not* obliged to curry favor with his coachman or his shoeblack, lest when he drove to the polls the coachman should dismount from his box, or the shoeblack drop his brushes, and neutralize their master's vote by voting on the other side. How he exulted in the fact that in Virginia none but freeholders could vote! How happy he was to boast, that, in all that Commonwealth, there was no such thing as a ballot-box! "May I never live to see the day," he would exclaim, "when a Virginian shall be ashamed to declare aloud at the polls for whom he casts his vote!" What pleasure he took in speaking of his Virginia wilderness as a "barony," and signing his name "John Randolph of Roanoke," and in wearing the garments that were worn in Virginia when the great tobacco lords were running through their estates in the fine old picturesque and Irish fashion!

Obviously, an antique of this pattern was out of place as a leader in the Republican party. For a time the spell of Jefferson's winning genius, and the presence of a powerful opposition, kept him in some subjection; but in 1807 that spell had spent its force, and the Federal party was not formidable. John Randolph was himself again. The immediate occasion of the rupture was, probably, Mr. Jefferson's evident preference of James Madison as his successor. We have a right to infer this, from the extreme and lasting rancor which Randolph exhibited toward Mr. Madison, who he used to say was as mean a man for a Virginian as John Quincy Adams was for a Yankee. Nor ought we ever to speak of this gifted and unhappy man without considering his physical condition. It appears from the slight notices we have of this vital matter, that about the year 1807 the stock of vigor which his youth had acquired was gone, and he lived thenceforth a miserable invalid, afflicted with diseases that sharpen the temper and narrow the mind. John Randolph *well* might have outgrown inherited prejudices and limitations, and attained to the stature of a modern, a national, a republican man. John Randolph *sick* — radically and incurably sick — ceased to grow just when his best growth would naturally have begun.

The sudden defection of a man so conspicuous and considerable, at a time when the Republican party was not aware of its strength, struck dismay to many minds, who felt, with Jefferson, that to the Republican party in the United States were confided the best interests of human nature. Mr. Jefferson was not in the least alarmed, because he knew the strength of the party and the weakness of the man. The letter which he wrote on this subject to Mr. Monroe ought to be learned by heart by every politician in the country, — by the self-seekers, for the warning which it gives them, and by the patriotic, for the comfort which it affords them in time of trouble. Some readers, perhaps, will be reminded by it of events which occurred at Washington not longer ago than last winter.*

" Our old friend Mercer broke off from us some time ago ; at first, professing to disdain joining the Federalists; yet, from the habit of

* 1865 – 6.

voting togethe , becoming soon identified with them. Without carrying over with him one single person, he is now in a state of as perfect
obscurity as if his name had never been known. Mr. J. Randolph is
in the same track, and will end in the same way. His course has excited considerable alarm. Timid men consider it as a proof of the
weakness of our government, and that it is to be rent in pieces by
demagogues and to end in anarchy. I survey the scene with a different eye, and draw a different augury from it. In a House of Representatives of a great mass of good sense, Mr. Randolph's popular eloquence gave him such advantages as to place him unrivalled as the
leader of the House ; and, although not conciliatory to those whom he
led, principles of duty and patriotism induced many of them to swallow
humiliations he subjected them to, and to vote as was right, as long as
he kept the path of right himself. The sudden departure of such a
man could not but produce a momentary astonishment, and even dismay ; but for a moment only. The good sense of the House rallied
around its principles, and, without any leader, pursued steadily the business of the session, did it well, and by a strength of vote which has
never before been seen. . . . . The augury I draw from this is, that
there is a steady good sense in the legislature and in the body of the
nation, joined with good intentions, which will lead them to discern
and to pursue the public good under all circumstances which can arise,
and that no *ignis fatuus* will be able to lead them long astray."

Mr. Jefferson predicted that the lost sheep of the Republican
fold would wander off to the arid wastes of Federalism ; but he
never did so. His defection was not an inconsistency, but a return
to consistency. He presented himself in his true character
thenceforth, which was that of a States' Rights fanatic. He opposed the election of Mr. Madison to the Presidency, as he said,
because Mr. Madison was weak on the sovereignty of the States.
He opposed the war of 1812 for two reasons : — 1. Offensive
war was in itself unconstitutional, being a *national* act. 2. War
was nationalizing. A hundred times before the war, he foretold
that, if war occurred, the sovereignty of the States was gone forever, and we should lapse into nationality. A thousand times
after the war, he declared that this dread lapse had occurred.
At a public dinner, after the return of peace, he gave the once
celebrated toast, " States' Rights, — *De mortuis nil nisi bonum.*"
As before the war he sometimes affected himself to tears while

dwelling upon the sad prospect of kindred people imbruing their hands in one another's blood, so during the war he was one of the few American citizens who lamented the triumphs of their country's arms. In his solitude at Roanoke he was cast down at the news of Perry's victory on the lake, because he thought it would prolong the contest; and he exulted in the banishment of Napoleon to Elba, although it let loose the armies and fleets of Britain upon the United States. "That insolent coward," said he, "has met his deserts at last." This Virginia Englishman would not allow that Napoleon possessed even military talent ' but stoutly maintained, to the last, that he was the merest sport of fortune. When the work of restoration was in progress, under the leadership of Clay and Calhoun, John Randolph was in his element, for he could honestly oppose every movement and suggestion of those young orators, — national bank, protective tariff, internal improvements, everything. He was one of the small number who objected to the gift of land and money to Lafayette, and one of the stubborn minority who would have seen the Union broken up rather than assent to the Missouri Compromise, or to *any* Missouri compromise. The question at issue in all these measures, he maintained, was the same, and it was this: Are we a nation or a confederacy?

Talent, too, is apt to play the despot over the person that possesses it. This man had such a power of witty vituperation in him, with so decided a histrionic gift, that his rising to speak was always an interesting event; and he would occasionally hold both the House and the galleries attentive for three or four hours. He became accustomed to this homage; he craved it; it became necessary to him. As far back as 1811, Washington Irving wrote of him, in one of his letters from Washington: "There is no speaker in either House that excites such universal attention as Jack Randolph. But they listen to him more to be delighted by his eloquence and entertained by his ingenuity and eccentricity, than to be convinced by sound doctrine and close argument." As he advanced in age, this habit of startling the House by unexpected dramatic exhibitions grew upon him. One of the most vivid pictures ever painted in words of a par liamentary scene is that in which the late Mr. S. G. Goodrich records his recollection of one of these displays. It occurred in 1820, during one of the Missouri debates. A tall man, with a little head and a small oval face, like that of an aged boy, rose and addressed the chairman.

"He paused a moment," wrote Mr. Goodrich, "and I had time to study his appearance. His hair was jet-black, and clubbed in a queue; his eye was black, small, and painfully penetrating. His complexion was a yellowish-brown, bespeaking Indian blood. I knew at once that it must be John Randolph. As he uttered the words, 'Mr. Speaker!' every member turned in his seat, and, facing him, gazed as if some portent had suddenly appeared before them. 'Mr. Speaker,' said he, in a shrill voice, which, however, pierced every nook and corner of the hall, 'I have but one word to say, — one word, sir, and that is to state a fact. The measure to which the gentleman has just alluded originated in a dirty trick!' These were his precise words. The subject to which he referred I did not gather, but the coolness and impudence of the speaker were admirable in their way. I never saw better acting, even in Kean. His look, his manner, his long arm, his elvish fore-finger, — like an exclamation-point, punctuating his bitter thought, — showed the skill of a master. The effect of the whole was to startle everybody, as if a pistol-shot had rung through the hall." — *Recollections*, Vol. II. p. 395.

Such anecdotes as these, which are very numerous, both in and out of print, convey an inadequate idea of his understanding; for there was really a great fund of good sense in him and n his political creed. Actor as he was, he was a very honest man, and had a hearty contempt for all the kinds of falsehood which he had no inclination to commit. No man was more restive under debt than he, or has better depicted its horrors. Speaking once of those Virginia families who gave banquets and kept up expensive establishments, while their estates were covered all over with mortgages, he said: "I always think I can see the anguish under the grin and grimace, like old Mother Cole's dirty flannel peeping out beneath her Brussels lace." He was strong in the opinion that a man who is loose in money matters is not trustworthy in anything, — an opinion which is shared by every one who knows either life or history. "The time was, he wrote, "when I was fool enough to believe that a man might be negligent of pecuniary obligations, and yet be a very good fellow; but long experience has convinced me that he who is lax in this respect is utterly unworthy of trust in any other." He discriminated well between those showy, occasional acts of so-called generosity which such men perform, and the true, habitual, self-denying benevolence of a solvent and just member of society. "Despise the usurer and the miser as much as you will," he would exclaim, "but the spendthrift is more selfish than they." But his very honesty was most curiously blended with his toryism. One of his friends relates the following anecdote: —

"Just before we sailed, the Washington papers were received, announcing the defeat of the Bankrupt Bill by a small majority. At that moment, I forgot that Randolph had been one of its most determined opponents, and I spoke with the feelings of a merchant when I said to him, —

" 'Have you heard the very bad news from Washington this morning?'

" 'No, sir,' replied he, with eagerness; 'what is it?'

" 'Why, sir, I am sorry to tell you that the House of Representatives has thrown out the Bankrupt Bill by a small majority.'

" 'Sorry, sir!' exclaimed he; and then, taking off his hat and looking upwards, he added, most emphatically, 'Thank God for all his mercies!'

" After a short pause he continued: 'How delighted I am to think that I helped to give that hateful bill a kick. Yes, sir, this very day week I spoke for three hours against it, and my friends, who forced me to make the effort, were good enough to say that I never had made a more successful speech; it must have had *some* merit, sir; for I assure you, whilst I was speaking, although the Northern mail was announced, not a single member left his seat to look for letters, — a circumstance which had not occurred before during the session!'

" I endeavored to combat his objections to a Bankrupt Bill subsequently, but, of course, without any success: *he felt as a planter, and was very jealous of the influence of merchants as legislators.*"

There are flashes of sense and touches of pathos in some of his most tory passages. As he was delivering in the House one of his emphatic predictions of the certain failure of our experiment of freedom on this continent, he broke into an apology for so doing, that brought tears to many eyes. "It is an infirmity of my nature," said he, "to have an obstinate constitutional pref erence of the true over the agreeable; and I am satisfied, that, if I had had an only son, or what is dearer, an only daughter, — which God forbid! — I say, God forbid, for she might bring her father's gray hairs with sorrow to the grave; she might break my heart, or worse than that — what? Can anything be worse than that? Yes, sir, *I might break hers!*" His fable, too, of the caterpillar and the horseman was conceived in arrogance, but it was pretty and effective. Every tory intellect on earth is pleased to discourse in that way of the labors of the only men who greatly help their species, — the patient elaborators of truth. A caterpillar, as we learn from this fable, had crawled slowly over a fence, which a gallant horseman took at a single leap. "Stop," says the caterpillar, "you are too flighty; you want con nection and continuity; it took me an hour to get over; you can't be as sure as I am that you have really overcome the difficulty, and are indeed over the fence." To which, of course, the gallant horseman makes the expected contemptuous reply. This is precisely in the spirit of Carlyle's sneers at the politi cal economists, — the men who are not content to sit down and howl in this wilderness of a modern world, but bestir them selves to discover methods by which it can be made less a wil derness.

There is so much truth in the doctrines of the original States' Rights party, — the party of Jefferson, Madison, and Patrick Henry, — that a very commonplace man, who learned his politics in that school, is able to make a respectable figure in the public counsels. The mere notion that government, being a necessary evil, is to be reduced to the minimum that will answer the pur poses of government, saves from many false steps. The doctrine that the central government is to confine itself to the duties as signed it in the Constitution, is a guiding principle suited to the limited human mind. A vast number of claims, suggestions, and petitions are excluded by it even from consideration. If an elo quent Hamiltonian proposes to appropriate the public money for the purpose of enabling American manufacturers to exhibit their

products at a Paris Exhibition, the plainest country member of
the Jeffersonian school perceives at once the inconsistency of such
a proposition with the fundamental principle of his political creed.
He has a compass to steer by, and a port to sail to, instead of
being afloat on the waste of waters, the sport of every breeze
that blows.   It is touching to observe that this unhappy, sick, and
sometimes mad John Randolph, amid all the vagaries of his later
life, had always a vein of soundness in him, derived from his
early connection with the enlightened men who acted in politics
with Thomas Jefferson.   The phrase "masterly inactivity" is
Randolph's ; and it is something only to have given convenient
expression to a system of conduct so often wise.   He used to say
that Congress could scarcely do too little.   His ideal of a session
was one in which members should make speeches till every man
had fully expressed and perfectly relieved his mind, then pass
the appropriation bills, and go home.   And we ought not to
forgot that, when President John Quincy Adams brought forward his schemes for covering the continent with magnificent
works at the expense of the treasury of the United States, and
of uniting the republics of both Americas into a kind of holy
alliance, it was Randolph's piercing sarcasm which, more than
anything else, made plain to new members the fallacy, the peril,
of such a system.   His opposition to this wild federalism involved his support of Andrew Jackson ; but there was no other
choice open to him.

   Seldom did he display in Congress so much audacity and ingenuity as in defending General Jackson while he was a candidate for the Presidency against Mr. Adams.   The two objections
oftenest urged against Jackson were that he was a military chieftain, and that he could not spell.   Mr. Randolph discoursed on
these two points in a most amusing manner, displaying all the impudence and ignorance of the tory, inextricably mingled with the
good sense and wit of the man.   " General Jackson cannot write,"
said a friend.   " Granted," replied he.   ' General Jackson cannot write because he was never taught ; but his competitor
cannot write because he was not teachable."   He made a bold
remark in one of his Jacksonian harangues.   " The talent which

enables a man to write a book or make a speech has no more
relation to the leading of an army or a senate, than it has to the
dressing of a dinner." He pronounced a fine eulogium on the
Duke of Marlborough, one of the worst spellers in Europe, and
then asked if gentlemen would have had that illustrious man
"superseded by a Scotch schoolmaster." It was in the same
ludicrous harangue that he uttered his famous joke upon those
schools in which young ladies were said to be "finished." "Yes,"
he exclaimed, "*finished* indeed; finished for all the duties of a
wife, or mother, or mistress of a family." Again he said: "There
is much which it becomes a second-rate man to know, which a first-
rate man ought to be ashamed to know. No head was ever clear
and sound that was stuffed with book-learning. My friend, W.
R. Johnson, has many a groom that can clean and dress a race-
horse, and ride him too, better than he can." He made the
sweeping assertion, that no man had ever presided over a government with advantage to the country governed, who had not in
him the making of a good general; for, said he, "the talent for
government lies in these two things, — sagacity to perceive, and
decision to act." Really, when we read this ingenious apology
for, or rather eulogy of, ignorance, we cease to wonder that General Jackson should have sent him to Russia.

The religious life of Randolph is a most curious study. He
experienced in his lifetime four religious changes, or conversions.
His gentle mother, whose name he seldom uttered without adding with tender emphasis, "God bless her!" was such a member
of the Church of England as gentle ladies used to be before an
"Evangelical" party was known in it. She taught his infant
lips to pray; and, being naturally trustful and affectionate, he
was not an unapt pupil. But in the library of the old mansion
on the Appomattox, in which he passed his forming years, there
was a "wagon-load" of what he terms "French infidelity,"
though it appears there were almost as many volumes of Hobbes,
Shaftesbury, Collins, Hume, and Gibbon, as there were of
Diderot, D'Alembert, Helvetius, and Voltaire. These works he
read in boyhood; and when he came to mingle among men, he
found that the opinions of such authors prevailed in the circles

which he most frequented. Just as he, a natural tory, caught some tincture of republicanism from Jefferson and his friends, so he, the natural believer, adopted the fashion of scepticism, which then ruled the leading minds of all lands; and just as he lapsed back into toryism when the spell which drew him away from it had spent its force, so he became, in the decline of his powers, a prey to religious terrors. For twenty-two years, as we have said, he held aloof from religion, its ministers, and its temples. The disease that preyed upon him so sharpened his temper, and so perverted his perceptions of character, that, one after another, he alienated all the friends and relations with whom he ought to have lived; and he often found himself, between the sessions of Congress, the sole white tenant of his lonely house at Roanoke,— the sick and solitary patriarch of a family of three hundred persons. He sought to alleviate this horrid solitude by adopting and rearing the orphaned sons of old friends; to whom, when he was himself, he was the most affectionate and generous of guardians. But even they could not very long endure him; for, in his adverse moods, he was incarnate Distrust, and, having conceived a foul suspicion, his genius enabled him to give it such withering expression that it was not in the nature of a young man to pass it by as the utterance of transient madness. So they too left him, and he was utterly alone in the midst of a crowd of black dependants. We see from his letters, that, while he saw the impossibility of his associating with his species, he yet longed and pined for their society and love. Perhaps there never lived a more unhappy person. Revering women, and formed to find his happiness in domestic life, he was incapable of being a husband; and if this had not been the case, no woman could have lived with him. Yearning for companionship, but condemned to be alone, his solace was the reflection that, so long as there was no one near him, he was a torment only to himself. "Often," he writes in one of his letters, " I mount my horse and sit upon him for ten or fifteen minutes, wishing to go somewhere, but not knowing where to ride; for I would escape anywhere from the incubus that weighs me down, body and soul; but the fiend follows me *en croupe*. . . . . The strongest considerations of duty

N

are barely sufficient to prevent me from absconding to some distant country, where I might live and die unknown."

A mind in such a state as this is the natural prey of superstition. A dream, he used to say, first recalled his mind to the
consideration of religion. This was about the year 1810, at the
height of those hot debates that preceded the war of 1812. For
nine years, he tells us, the subject gradually gained upon him, so
that, at last, it was his first thought in the morning and his last at
night. From the atheism upon which he had formerly plumed
himself, he went to the opposite extreme. For a long time he
was plunged into the deepest gloom, regarding himself as a sinner
too vile to be forgiven. He sought for comfort in the Bible, in
the Prayer-book, in conversation and correspondence with religious friends, in the sermons of celebrated preachers. He
formed a scheme of retiring from the world into some kind of
religious retreat, and spending the rest of his life in prayers and
meditation. Rejecting this as a cowardly desertion of the post
of duty, he had thoughts of setting up a school for children, and
becoming himself a teacher in it. This plan, too, he laid aside,
as savoring of enthusiasm. Meanwhile, this amiable and honest
gentleman, whose every error was fairly attributable to the natural limitations of his mind or to the diseases that racked his body,
was tormented by remorse, which would have been excessive if
he had been a pirate. He says that, after three years of continual striving, he still dared not partake of the Communion, feeling
himself "unworthy." "I was present," he writes, "when Mr.
Hoge invited to the table, and I would have given all I was
worth to have been able to approach it." Some inkling of his
condition, it appears, became known to the public, and excited
great good-will towards him on the part of many persons of similar
belief.

Some of his letters written during this period contain an almost
ludicrous mixture of truth and extravagance. He says in one of
them, that his heart has been softened, and he "*thinks* he has
succeeded in forgiving all his enemies"; then he adds, "There is
not a human being that I would hurt if it were in my power, —
not even Bonaparte." In another place he remarks that the

world is a vast mad-house, and, "if what is to come be anything like what has passed, it would be wise to abandon the hulk to the underwriters, — the worms." In the whole of his intercourse with mankind, he says he never met with but three persons whom he did not, on getting close to their hearts, discover to be unhappy ; and they were the only three he had ever known who had a religion. He expresses this truth in language which limits it to one form or kind of religion, the kind which he heard expounded in the churches of Virginia in 1819. Give it broader expression, and every observer of human life will assent to it. It is indeed most true, that no human creature gets much out of life who has no religion, no sacred object, to the furtherance of which his powers are dedicated.

He obtained some relief at length, and became a regular communicant of the Episcopal Church. But although he ever after manifested an extreme regard for religious things and persons, and would never permit either to be spoken against in his presence without rebuke, he was very far from edifying his brethren by a consistent walk. At Washington, in the debates, he was as incisive and uncharitable as before. His denunciations of the second President Adams's personal character were as outrageous as his condemnation of parts of his policy was just. Mr. Clay, though removed from the arena of debate by his appointment to the Department of State, was still the object of his bitter sarcasm ; and at length he included the President and the Secretary in that merciless philippic in which he accused Mr. Clay of forgery, and styled the coalition of Adams and Clay as " the combination of the Puritan and the Blackleg." He used language, too, in the course of this speech, which was understood to be a defiance to mortal combat, and it was so reported to Mr. Clay. The reporters, however, misunderstood him, as it was not his intention nor his desire to fight. Nevertheless, to the astonishment and sorrow of his religious friends, he accepted Mr. Clay's challenge with the utmost possible promptitude, and bore himself throughout the affair like (to use the poor, lying, tory cant of the last generation) " a high-toned Virginia gentleman." Colonel Benton tells us that Mr. Randolph invented an ingenious excuse for the enormous inconsistency of his conduct on this occasion. A duel, he maintained, was private war, and was justifiable on the same ground as a war between two nations. Both were lamentable, but both were allowable when there was no other way of getting redress for insults and injuries. This was plausible, but it did not deceive *him*. He knew very well that his offensive language respecting a man whom he really esteemed was wholly devoid of excuse. He had the courage requisite to expiate the offence by standing before Mr. Clay's pistol; but he could not stand before his countrymen and confess that his abominable antithesis was but the spurt of mingled ill-temper and the vanity to shine. Any good tory can fight a duel with a respectable degree of composure; but to own one's self, in the presence of a nation, to have outraged the feelings of a brother-man, from the desire to startle and amuse an audience, requires the kind of valor which tories do not know. "Whig and tory," says Mr. Jefferson, "belong to natural history." But then there is such a thing, we are told, as the regeneration of the natural man; and we believe it, and cling to it as a truth destined one day to be resuscitated and purified from the mean interpretations which have made the very word sickening to the intelligence of Christendom. Mr. Randolph had not achieved the regeneration of his nature. He was a tory still. In the testing hour, the "high-toned Virginia gentleman" carried the day, without a struggle, over the communicant.

During the last years of his life, the monotony of his anguish was relieved by an occasional visit to the Old World. It is interesting to note how thoroughly at home he felt himself among the English gentry, and how promptly they recognized him as a man and a brother. He was, as we have remarked, *more* English than an Englishman; for England does advance, though slowly, from the insular to the universal. Dining at a great house in London, one evening, he dwelt with pathetic eloquence upon the decline of Virginia. Being asked what he thought was the reason of her decay, he startled and pleased the lords and ladies present by attributing it all to the repeal of the law of primogeniture. One of the guests tells us that this was deemed "a strange remark from a *Republican*," and that, before the party

broke up, the company had " almost taken him for an aristocrat."
It happened sometimes, when he was conversing with English
politicians, that it was the American who defended the English
system against the attacks of Englishmen; and so full of British
prejudice was he, that, in Paris, he protested that a decent dinner
could not be bought for money. Westminster Abbey woke all
his veneration. He went into it, one morning, just as service
was about beginning, and took his place among the worshippers.
Those of our readers who have attended the morning service at
an English cathedral on a week-day cannot have forgotten the
ludicrous smallness of the congregation compared with the imposing array of official assistants. A person who has a little tincture
of the Yankee in him may even find himself wondering how it
can "pay" the British empire to employ half a dozen reverend
clergymen and a dozen robust singers to aid seven or eight unim-
portant members of the community in saying their prayers. But
John Randolph of Roanoke had not in him the least infusion of
Yankee. Standing erect in the almost vacant space, he uttered
the responses in a tone that was in startling contrast to the low
mumble of the clergyman's voice, and that rose above the melodious amens of the choir. He took it all in most serious earnest.
When the service was over, he said to his companion, after lamenting the hasty and careless manner in which the service had
been performed, that he esteemed it an honor to have worshipped
God in Westminster Abbey. As he strolled among the tombs,
he came, at last, to the grave of two men who had often roused
his enthusiasm. He stopped, and spoke: "I will not say, Take
off your shoes, for the ground on which you stand is holy; but,
look, sir, do you see those simple letters on the flagstones beneath
your feet, — W. P. and C. J. F. Here lie, side by side, the remains of the two great rivals, Pitt and Fox, whose memory so
completely lives in history. No marble monuments are necessary to mark the spot where *their* bodies repose. There is more
simple grandeur in those few letters than in all the surrounding
monuments, sir." How more than English was all this! England had been growing away from and beyond Westminster
Abbey, William Pitt, and Charles James Fox; but this Virginia

Englishman, living alone in his woods, with his slaves and his overseers, severed from the progressive life of his race, was living still in the days when a pair of dissolute young orators could be deemed, and with some reason too, the most important persons in a great empire. A friend asked him how he was pleased with England. He answered with enthusiasm, — " There never was such a country on the face of the earth as England, and it is utterly impossible that there can be any combination of circumstances hereafter to make such another country as Old England now is ! "

We ought not to have been surprised at the sympathy which the English Tories felt during the late war for their brethren in the Southern States of America. It was as natural as it was for the English Protestants to welcome the banished Huguenots. It was as natural as it was for Louis XIV. to give an asylum to the Stuarts. The traveller who should have gone, seven years ago, straight from an English agricultural county to a cotton district of South Carolina, or a tobacco county of Virginia, would have felt that the differences between the two places were merely external. The system in both places and the spirit of both were strikingly similar. In the old parts of Virginia, the Carolinas, Tennessee, and Kentucky, you had only to get ten miles from a railroad to find yourself among people who were English in their feelings, opinions, habits, and even in their accent. New England differs from Old England, because New England has grown: Virginia was English, because she had been stationary. Happening to be somewhat familiar with the tone of feeling in the South, — the *real* South, or, in other words, the South ten miles from a railroad, — we were fully prepared for Mr. Russell's statement with regard to the desire so frequently expressed in 1861 for one of the English princes to come and reign over a nascent Confederacy. Sympathies and antipathies are always mutual when they are natural; and never was there a sympathy more in accordance with the nature of things, than that which so quickly manifested itself between the struggling Southern people and the majority of the ruling classes of Great Britain.

Mr. Randolph took leave of public life, after thirty years o' service, not in the most dignified manner. He furnished another illustration of the truth of a remark made by a certain queen of Denmark, — " The lady doth protest too much." Like many other gentlemen in independent circumstances, he had been particularly severe upon those of his fellow-citizens who earned their subsistence by serving the public. It pleased him to speak of members of the Cabinet as "the drudges of the departments," and to hold gentlemen in the diplomatic service up to contempt as forming " the tail of the *corps diplomatique* in Europe." He liked to declaim upon the enormous impossibility of *his* ever exchanging a seat in Congress for " the shabby splendors" of an office in Washington, or in a foreign mission " to dance attendance abroad instead of at home." When it was first buzzed about in Washington, in 1830, that General Jackson had tendered the Russian mission to John Randolph, the rumor was not credited. An appointment so exquisitely absurd was supposed to be beyond even Andrew Jackson's audacity. The offer had been made, however. Mr. Randolph's brilliant defence of General Jackson's bad spelling, together with Mr. Van Buren's willingness to place an ocean between the new administration and a master of sarcasm, to whom opposition had become an unchangeable habit, had dictated an offer of the mission, couched in such seductive language that Mr. Randolph yielded to it as readily as those ladies accept an offer of marriage who have often announced their intention never to marry. Having reached the scene of his diplomatic labors at the beginning of August, he began to perform them with remarkable energy. In a suit of black, the best, he declared, that London could furnish, he was presented to the Emperor and to the Empress, having first submitted his costume to competent inspection. Resolute to do his whole duty, he was not content to send his card to the diplomatic corps, but, having engaged a handsome coach and four, he called upon each member of the diplomatic body, from the ambassadors to the secretaries of legation. Having performed these labors, and having discovered that a special object with which he was charged could not then be accomplished, he had leisure to observe that St. Petersburg, in the month of August, is not a pleasant residence to an invalid of sixty. He describes the climate in these terms: —

" Heat, dust impalpable, pervading every part and pore. . . . Insects of all nauseous descriptions, bugs, fleas, mosquitoes, flies innumerable, gigantic as the empire they inhabit, who will take no denial. This is the land of Pharaoh and his plagues, — Egypt and its ophthalmia and vermin, without its fertility, — Holland, without its wealth, improvements, or cleanliness."

He endured St. Petersburg for the space of ten days, then sailed for England, and never saw Russia again. When the appropriation bill was before Congress at the next session, opposition members did not fail to call in question the justice of requiring the people of the United States to pay twenty thousand dollars for Mr. Randolph's ten days' work, or, to speak more exactly, for Mr. Randolph's apology for the President's bad spelling; but the item passed, nevertheless. During the reign of Andrew Jackson, Congress was little more than a board of registry for the formal recording of his edicts. There are those who think, at the present moment, that what a President hath done, a President may do again.

It was fortunate that John Randolph was in retirement when Calhoun brought on his Nullification scheme. The presence in Congress of a man so eloquent and so reckless, whose whole heart and mind were with the Nullifiers, might have prevented the bloodless postponement of the struggle. He was in constant correspondence with the South Carolina leaders, and was fully convinced that it was the President of the United States, not " the Hamiltons and Haynes " of South Carolina, who ought to seize the first pretext to concede the point in dispute. No citizen of South Carolina was more indignant than he at General Jackson's Proclamation. He said that, if the people did not rouse themselves to a sense of their condition, and " put down this wretched old man," the country was irretrievably ruined; and he spoke of the troops despatched to Charleston as " mercenaries," to whom he hoped " no quarter would be given." The " wretched old man " whom the people were to " put down " was Andrew Jackson, not John C. Calhoun.

We do not forget that, when John Randolph uttered these words, he was scarcely an accountable being. Disease had re-

duced him to a skeleton, and robbed him of almost every attribute of man except his capacity to suffer. But even in his madness he was a representative man, and spoke the latent feeling
of his class. The diseases which sharpened his temper unloosed
his tongue; he revealed the tendency of the Southern mind, as a
petulant child reveals family secrets. In his good and in his evil
he was an exaggerated Southerner of the higher class. He was
like them, too, in this: they are not criminals to be punished, but
patients to be cured. Sometimes, of late, we have feared that
they resemble him also in being incurable.

As long as Americans take an interest in the history of their
country, they will read with interest the strange story of this sick
and suffering representative of sick and suffering Virginia. To
the last, old Virginia wore her ragged robes with a kind of grandeur which was not altogether unbecoming, and which to the
very last imposed upon tory minds. Scarcely any one could
live among the better Southern people without liking them and
few will ever read Hugh Garland's Life of John Randolph, without more than forgiving all his vagaries, impetuosities, and foibles.
How often, upon riding away from a Southern home, have we
been ready to exclaim, " What a pity such good people should be
so accursed!" Lord Russell well characterized the evil to which
we allude as " that fatal gift of the poisoned garment which was
flung around them from the first hour of their establishment."

The last act of John Randolph's life, done when he lay dying
at a hotel in Philadelphia, in June, 1833, was to express once
more his sense of this blighting system. Some years before, he
had made a will by which all his slaves were to be freed at his
death. He would probably have given them their freedom before his death, but for the fact, too evident, that freedom to a
black man in a Slave State was not a boon. The slaves freed
by his brother, forty years before, had not done well, because (as
he supposed) no land had been bequeathed for their support.
Accordingly, he left directions in his will that a tract of land,
which might be of four thousand acres, should be set apart for the
maintenance of his slaves, and that they should be transported
to it and established upon it at the expense of his estate. " I

10

give my slaves their freedom," said he in his will, " to which my conscience tells me they are justly entitled." On the last day of his life, surrounded by strangers, and attended by two of his old servants, his chief concern was to make distinctly known to as many persons as possible that it was really his will that his slaves should be free. Knowing, as he did, the aversion which his fellow-citizens had to the emancipation of slaves, and even to the presence in the State of free blacks, he seemed desirous of taking away every pretext for breaking his will. A few hours before his death, he said to the physician in attendance : " I confirm every disposition in my will, especially that concerning my slaves whom I have manumitted, and for whom I have made provision." The doctor, soon after, took leave of him, and was about to depart. " You must not go," said he, " you cannot, you shall not leave me." He told his servant not to let the doctor go, and the man immediately locked the door and put the key in his pocket. The doctor remonstrating, Mr. Randolph explained, that, by the laws of Virginia, in order to manumit slaves by will, it was requisite that the master should *declare* his will in that particular in the presence of a white witness, who, after hearing the declaration, must never lose sight of the party until he is dead. The doctor consented, at length, to remain, but urged that more witnesses should be sent for. This was done. At ten in the morning, four gentlemen were ranged in a semicircle round his bed. He was propped up almost in a sitting posture, and a blanket was wrapped round his head and shoulders. His face was yellow, and extremely emaciated ; he was very weak, and it required all the remaining energy of his mind to endure the exertion he was about to make. It was evident to all present that his whole soul was in the act, and his eye gathered fire as he performed it. Pointing toward the witnesses with that gesture which for so many years had been familiar to the House of Representatives, he said, slowly and distinctly : " I confirm all the directions in my will respecting my slaves, and direct them to be enforced, particularly in regard to a provision for their support." Then, raising his hand and placing it upon the shoulder of his servant, he added, " Especially for this man." Having performed this act, his mind appeared relieved, but his strength immediately left him, and in two hours he breathed his last.

The last of the Randolphs, and one of the best representatives of the original masters of Virginia, the high-toned Virginia gentleman, was no more. Those men had their opportunity, but they had not strength of character equal to it. They were tried and found wanting. The universe, which loves not the high-toned, even in violins, disowned them, and they perished. Cut off from the life-giving current of thought and feeling which kept the rest of Christendom advancing, they came to love stagnation, and looked out from their dismal, isolated pool with lofty contempt at the gay and active life on the flowing stream. They were not teachable, for they despised the men who could have taught them. But we are bound always to consider that they were subjected to a trial under which human virtue has always given way, and will always. Sudden wealth is itself sufficient to spoil any but the very best men, — those who can instantly set it at work for the general good, and continue to earn an honest livelihood by faithful labor. But those tobacco lords of Virginia, besides making large fortunes in a few years, were the absolute, irresponsible masters of a submissive race. And when these two potent causes of effeminacy and pride had worked out their proper result in the character of the masters, then, behold! their resources fail. Vicious agriculture exhausts the soil, false political economy prevents the existence of a middle class, and the presence of slaves repels emigration. Proud, ignorant, indolent, dissolute, and in debt, the dominant families, one after another, passed away, attesting to the last, by an occasional vigorous shoot, the original virtue of the stock. All this poor John Randolph represented and was.

Virginia remains. Better men will live in it than have ever yet lived there; but it will not be in this century, and possibly not in the next. It cannot be that so fair a province will not be one day inhabited by a race of men who will work according to the laws of nature, and whom, therefore, the laws of nature will co-operate with and preserve. How superior will such Virginians be to what Dr. Francis Lieber styles the "provincial egotism" of State sovereignty!

STEPHEN GIRARD

AND HIS COLLEGE.

STEPHEN GIRARD AND HIS COLLEGE.

WITHIN the memory of many persons still alive, "old Girard," as the famous banker was usually styled, a short, stout, brisk old gentleman, used to walk, in his swift, awkward way, the streets of the lower part of Philadelphia. Though everything about him indicated that he had very little in common with his fellow-citizens, he was the marked man of the city for more than a generation. His aspect was rather insignificant and quite unprepossessing. His dress was old-fashioned and shabby; and he wore the pig-tail, the white neck-cloth, the wide-brimmed hat, and the large-skirted coat of the last century. He was blind of one eye; and though his bushy eyebrows gave some character to his countenance, it was curiously devoid of expression. He had also the absent look of a man who either had no thoughts or was absorbed in thought; and he shuffled along on his enormous feet, looking neither to the right nor to the left. There was always a certain look of the old mariner about him, though he had been fifty years an inhabitant of the town. When he rode it was in the plainest, least comfortable gig in Philadelphia, drawn by an ancient and ill-formed horse, driven always by the master's own hand at a good pace. He chose still to live where he had lived for fifty years, in Water Street, close to the wharves, in a small and inconvenient house, darkened by tall storehouses, amid the bustle, the noise, and the odors of commerce. His sole pleasure was to visit once a day a little farm which be possessed a few miles out of town, where he was wont to take off his coat, roll up his shirt-sleeves, and personally labor in the field and in the barn, hoeing corn, pruning trees, tossing hay, and not disdaining even to assist in butchering

the animals which he raised for market.   It was no mere orna·
mental or experimental farm.   He made it pay.   All of its produce was carefully, nay, scrupulously husbanded, sold, recorded,
and accounted for.   He loved his grapes, his plums, his pigs, and
especially his rare breed of Canary-birds; but the people of
Philadelphia had the full benefit of their increase, — at the highest market rates.

Many feared, many served, but none loved this singular and
lonely old man.   If there was among the very few who habitually
conversed with him one who understood and esteemed him, there
was but one ; and he was a man of such abounding charity, that,
like Uncle Toby, if he had heard that the Devil was hopelessly
damned, he would have said, "I am sorry for it."   Never was
there a person more destitute than Girard of the qualities which
win the affection of others.   His temper was violent, his presence
forbidding, his usual manner ungracious, his will inflexible, his
heart untender, his imagination dead.   He was odious to many
of his fellow-citizens, who considered him the hardest and mean-
est of men.   He had lived among them for half a century, but
he was no more a Philadelphian in 1830 than in 1776.   He still
spoke with a French accent, and accompanied his words with a
French shrug and French gesticulation.   Surrounded with Christian churches which he had helped to build, he remained a sturdy
unbeliever, and possessed the complete works of only one man,
Voltaire.   He made it a point of duty to labor on Sunday, as a
good example to others.   He made no secret of the fact, that he
considered the idleness of Sunday an injury to the people, moral
and economical.   He would have opened his bank on Sundays,
if any one would have come to it.   For his part, he required no
rest, and would have none.   He never travelled.   He never attended public assemblies or amusements.   He had no affections
to gratify, no friends to visit, no curiosity to appease, no tastes to
indulge.   What he once said of himself appeared to be true, that
he rose in the morning with but a single object, and that was to
labor so hard all day as to be able to sleep all night.   The world
was absolutely nothing to him but a working-place.   He scorned
and scouted the opinion, that old men should cease to labor, and

should spend the evening of their days in tranquillity. "No," he would say, "labor is the price of life, its happiness, its everything; to rest is to rust; every man should labor to the last hour of his ability." Such was Stephen Girard, the richest man who ever lived in Pennsylvania.

This is an unpleasing picture of a citizen of polite and amiable Philadelphia. It were indeed a grim and dreary world in which should prevail the principles of Girard. But see what this man has done for the city that loved him not! Vast and imposing structures rise on the banks of the Schuylkill, wherein, at this hour, six hundred poor orphan boys are fed, clothed, trained, and taught, upon the income of the enormous estate which he won by this entire consecration to the work of accumulating property. In the ample grounds of Girard College, looking up at its five massive marble edifices, strolling in its shady walks or by its verdant play-grounds, or listening to the cheerful cries of the boys at play, the most sympathetic and imaginative of men must pause before censuring the sterile and unlovely life of its founder. And if he should inquire closely into the character and career of the man who willed this great institution into being, he would perhaps be willing to admit that there was room in the world for one Girard, though it were a pity there should ever be another. Such an inquiry would perhaps disclose that Stephen Girard was endowed by nature with a great heart as well as a powerful mind, and that circumstances alone closed and hardened the one, cramped and perverted the other. It is not improbable that he was one of those unfortunate beings who desire to be loved, but whose temper and appearance combine to repel affection. His marble statue, which adorns the entrance to the principal building. if it could speak, might say to us, "Living, you could not understand nor love me; dead, I compel at least your respect." Indeed, he used to say, when questioned as to his career, "Wait till I am dead; my deeds will show what I was."

Girard's recollections of his childhood were tinged with bitterness. He was born at Bordeaux in 1750. He was the eldest of the five children of Captain Pierre Girard, a mariner of substance and respectability. He used to complain that, while his

10 *   o

younger brothers were taught at college, his own education was neglected, and that he acquired at home little more than the ability to read and write. He remembered, too, that at the age of eight years he discovered, to his shame and sorrow, that one of his eyes was blind, — a circumstance that exposed him to the taunts of his companions. The influence of a personal defect, and of the ridicule it occasions, upon the character of a sensitive child, can be understood only by those whose childhood was embittered from that cause; but such cases as those of Byron and Girard should teach those who have the charge of youth the crime it is to permit such defects to be the subject of remark. Girard also early lost his mother, an event which soon brought him under the sway of a step-mother. Doubtless he was a wilful, arbitrary, and irascible boy, since we know that he was a wilful, arbitrary, and irascible man. Before he was fourteen, having chosen the profession of his father, he left home, with his father's consent, and went to sea in the capacity of cabin-boy. He used to boast, late in life, that he began the world with sixpence in his pocket. Quite enough for a cabin-boy.

For nine years he sailed between Bordeaux and the French West Indies, returning at length with the rank of first mate, or, as the French term it, lieutenant of his vessel. He had well improved his time. Some of the defects of his early education he had supplied by study, and it is evident that he had become a skilful navigator. It was then the law of France that no man should command a vessel who was not twenty-five years old, and had not sailed two cruises in a ship of the royal navy. Girard was but twenty-three, and had sailed in none but merchant-vessels. His father, however, had influence enough to procure him a dispensation; and in 1773 he was licensed to command. He appears to have been scarcely just to his father when he wrote, sixty-three years after: " I have the proud satisfaction of knowing that my conduct, my labor, and my economy have enabled me to do one hundred times more for my relations than they all together have ever done for me since the day of my birth." In the mere amount of money expended, this may have been true but it is the *start* toward fortune that is so difficult. His father besides procuring the dispensation, assisted him to purchase goods for his first commercial venture. At the age of twenty-four, we find him sailing to the West Indies ; not indeed in command of the vessel, but probably as mate and supercargo, and part owner of goods to the value of three thousand dollars. He never trod his native land again. Having disposed of his cargo and taken on board another, he sailed for New York, which he reached in July, 1774. The storm of war, which was soon to sweep commerce from the ocean, was already muttering below the horizon, when Stephen Girard, " mariner and merchant," as he always delighted to style himself, first saw the land wherein his lot was to be cast. For two years longer, however, he continued to exercise his twofold vocation. An ancient certificate, preserved among his papers, informs the curious explorer, that, " in the year 1774, Stephen Girard sailed as mate of a vessel from New York to [New] Orleans, and that he continued to sail out of the said port until May, 1776, when he arrived in Philadelphia commander of a sloop," of which the said Stephen Girard was part owner.

Lucky was it for Girard that he got into Philadelphia just when he did, with all his possessions with him. He had the narrowest escape from capture. On his way from New Orleans to a Canadian port, he had lost himself in a fog at the entrance of Delaware Bay, swarming then with British cruisers, of whose presence Captain Girard had heard nothing. His flag of distress brought alongside an American captain, who told him where he was, and assured him that, if he ventured out to sea, he would never reach port except as a British prize. " *Mon Dieu!* " exclaimed Girard in great panic, " what shall I do ? " " You have no chance but to push right up to Philadelphia," replied the captain. " How am I to get there ? " said Girard ; " I have no pilot, and I don't know the way " A pilot was found, who, however, demanded a preliminary payment of five dollars, which Girard had not on board. In great distress, he implored the captain to be his security for the sum. He consented, a pilot took charge of the sloop, the anchor was heaved, and the vessel sped on her way. An hour later while they were still in sight of the anchorage, a British man-of-war came within the capes. But Dr. Franklin, with his oared galleys, his *chevaux de frise*, his forts, and his signal-stations, had made the Delaware a safe harbor of refuge ; and Girard arrived safely at Philadelphia on one of the early days of May, 1776. Thus it was a mere chance of war that gave Girard to the Quaker City. In the whole world he could not have found a more congenial abode, for the Quakers were the only religious sect with which he ever had the slightest sympathy. Quakers he always liked and esteemed, partly because they had no priests, partly because they disregarded ornament and reduced life to its simplest and most obvious utilities, partly because some of their opinions were in accord with his own. He had grown up during the time when Voltaire was sovereign lord of the opinions of Continental Europe. Before landing at Philadelphia, he was already a republican and an unbeliever, and such he remained to the last. The Declaration of Independence was impending : he was ready for it. The " Common Sense " of Thomas Paine had appeared : he was the man of all others to enjoy it. It is, however, questionable if at that time he had English enough to understand it in the original, since the colloquy just reported with the American captain took place in French. He was slow in becoming familiar with the English language, and even to the end of his life seemed to prefer conversing in French.

He was a mariner no more. The great fleet of Lord Howe arrived at New York in July. Every harbor was blockaded, and all commerce was suspended. Even the cargoes of tobacco despatched by Congress to their Commissioners in France, for the purchase of arms and stores, were usually captured before they had cleared the Capes. Captain Girard now rented a small store in Water Street, near the spot where he lived for nearly sixty years, in which he carried on the business of a grocer and wine-bottler. Those who knew him at this time report that he was a taciturn, repulsive young man, never associating with men of his own age and calling, devoted to business, close in his dealings, of the most rigorous economy, and preserving still the tough clothing and general appearance of a sailor. Though but

twenty-six years of age, he was called " old Girard.   He
seemed conscious of his inability to please, but bore the derision of
his neighbors with stoical equanimity, and plodded on.

War favors the skilful and enterprising business-man.   Girard
had a genius for business.   He was not less bold in his operations
than prudent ; and his judgment as a man of business was well-
nigh infallible.   Destitute of all false pride, he bought whatever
he thought he could sell to advantage, from a lot of damaged cord-
age to a pipe of old port ; and he labored incessantly with his
own hands.   He was a thriving man during the first year of his
residence in Philadelphia ; his chief gain, it is said, being derived from his favorite business of bottling wine and cider.

The romance, the mystery, the tragedy of his life now occurred.
Walking along Water Street one day, near the corner of Vine
Street, the eyes of this reserved and ill-favored man were caught
by a beautiful servant-girl going to the pump for a pail of water.
She was an enchanting brunette of sixteen, with luxuriant black
locks curling and clustering about her neck.   As she tripped
along with bare feet and empty pail, in airy and unconscious
grace, she captivated the susceptible Frenchman, who saw in her
the realization of the songs of the forecastle and the reveries of
the quarter-deck.   He sought her acquaintance, and made himself at home in her kitchen.   The family whom she served, mis-
interpreting the designs of the thriving dealer, forbade him the
house ; when he silenced their scruples by offering the girl his
hand in marriage.   Ill-starred Polly Lumm !   Unhappy Girard !
She accepted his offer ; and in July, 1777, the incongruous two,
being united in matrimony, attempted to become one.

The war interrupted their brief felicity.   Philadelphia, often
threatened, fell into the hands of Lord Howe in September,
1777 ; and among the thousands who needlessly fled at his approach were " old Girard " and his pretty young wife.   He
bought a house at Mount Holly, near Burlington, in New Jersey,
for five hundred dollars, to which he removed, and there continued to bottle claret and sell it to the British officers, until the
departure of Lord Howe, in June, 1778, permitted his return to
Philadelphia.   The gay young officers, it is said, who came to his

house at Mount Holly to drink his claret, were far from being in sensible to the charms of Mrs. Girard; and tradition further reports that on one occasion a dashing colonel snatched a kiss, which the sailor resented, and compelled the officer to apologize for.

Of all miserable marriages this was one of the most miserable. Here was a young, beautiful, and ignorant girl united to a close, ungracious, eager man of business, devoid of sentiment, with a violent temper and an unyielding will. She was an American, he a Frenchman; and that alone was an immense incompatibility. She was seventeen, he twenty-seven. She was a woman; he was a man without imagination, intolerant of foibles. She was a beauty, with the natural vanities of a beauty; he not merely had no taste for decoration, he disapproved it on principle. These points of difference would alone have sufficed to endanger their domestic peace; but time developed something that was fatal to it. Their abode was the scene of contention for eight years; at the expiration of which period Mrs. Girard showed such symptoms of insanity that her husband was obliged to place her in the Pennsylvania Hospital. In these distressing circumstances, he appears to have spared no pains for her restoration. He removed her to a place in the country, but without effect. She returned to his house only to render life insupportable to him. He resumed his old calling as a mariner, and made a voyage to the Mediterranean; but on his return he found his wife not less unmanageable than before. In 1790, thirteen years after their marriage, and five after the first exhibition of insanity, Mrs. Girard was placed permanently in the hospital; where, nine months after, she gave birth to a female child. The child soon died; the mother never recovered her reason. For twenty-five years she lived in the hospital, and, dying in 1815, was buried in the hospital grounds after the manner of the Quakers. The coffin was brought to the grave, followed by the husband and the managers of the institution, who remained standing about it in silence for several minutes. It was then lowered to its final resting-place, and again the company remained motionless and silent for a while. Girard looked at the coffin once more, then turned to an acquaintance and said, as he walked away, 'It is very well." A green mound, without headstone or monument, still marks the spot where the remains of this unhappy woman repose. Girard, both during his lifetime and after his death, was a liberal, though not lavish, benefactor of the institution which had so long sheltered his wife

Fortunes were not made rapidly in the olden time. After the Revolution, Girard engaged in commerce with the West Indies, in partnership with his brother John; and he is described in an official paper of the time as one who "carried on an extensive business as a merchant, and is a considerable owner of real estate." But on the dissolution of the partnership in 1790, when he had been in business, as mariner and merchant, for sixteen years, his estate was valued at only thirty thousand dollars. The times were troubled. The French Revolution, the massacre at St. Domingo, our disturbed relations with England, and afterwards with France, the violence of our party contests, all tended to make merchants timid, and to limit their operations. Girard, as his papers indicate, and as he used to relate in conversation, took more than a merchant's interest in the events of the time. From the first, he had formally cast in his lot with the struggling Colonists, as we learn from a yellow and faded document left among his papers: —

"I do hereby certify that Stephen Girard, of the city of Philadelphia, merchant, hath voluntarily taken the oath of allegiance and fidelity, as directed by an act of the General Assembly of Pennsylvania, passed the 13th day of June, A. D. 1777. Witness my hand and seal, the 27th day of October, A. D. 1778.

"JNO. ORD.

"No. 1678."

The oath was repeated the year following. When the French Revolution had divided the country into two parties, the Federalists and the Republicans, Girard was a Republican of the radical school. He remembered assisting to raise a liberty-pole in the Presidency of John Adams; and he was one of Mr. Jefferson's most uncompromising adherents at a time when men of substance were seldom found in the ranks of the Democracy. As long as he lived, he held the name of Thomas Jeffer son in veneration.

We have now to contemplate this cold, close, ungainly, ungra cious man in a new character. We are to see that a man may seem indifferent to the woes of individuals, but perform sublime acts of devotion to a community. We are to observe that there are men of sterling but peculiar metal, who only shine when the furnace of general affliction is hottest. In 1793, the malignant yellow-fever desolated Philadelphia. The consternation of the people cannot be conceived by readers of the present day, be cause we cannot conceive of the ignorance which then prevailed respecting the laws of contagion, because we have lost in some degree the habit of panic, and because no kind of horror can be as novel to us as the yellow-fever was to the people of Philadel phia in 1793. One half of the population fled. Those who re mained left their houses only when compelled. Most of the churches, the great Coffee-House, the Library, were closed. Of four daily newspapers, only one continued to be published. Some people constantly smoked tobacco, — even women and children did so; others chewed garlic; others exploded gun powder; others burned nitre or sprinkled vinegar; many as siduously whitewashed every surface within their reach; some carried tarred rope in their hands, or bags of. camphor round their necks; others never ventured abroad without a handker chief or a sponge wet with vinegar at their noses. No one ven tured to shake hands. Friends who met in the streets gave each other a wide berth, eyed one another askance, exchanged nods. and strode on. It was a custom to walk in the middle of the street, to get as far from the houses as possible. Many of the sick died without help, and the dead were buried without cere mony. The horrid silence of the streets was broken only by the tread of litter-bearers and the awful rumble of the dead-wagon. Whole families perished, — perished without assistance, their fate unknown to their neighbors. Money was powerless to buy at tendance, for the operation of all ordinary motives was sus pended. From the 1st of August to the 9th of November, in a population of twenty-five thousand, there were four thousand and thirty-one burials, — about one in six.

Happily for the honor of human nature, there are always, in times like these, great souls whom base panic cannot prostrate A few brave physicians, a few faithful clergymen, a few high-minded citizens, a few noble women, remembered and practised what is due to humanity overtaken by a calamity like this. On the 10th of September, a notice, without signature, appeared in the only paper published, stating that all but three of the Visitors of the Poor were sick, dead, or missing, and calling upon all who were willing to help to meet at the City Hall on the 12th. From those who attended the meeting, a committee of twenty-seven was appointed to superintend the measures for relief, of whom Stephen Girard was one. On Sunday, the 15th, the committee met; and the condition of the great hospital at Bush Hill was laid before them. It was unclean, ill-regulated, crowded, and ill-supplied. Nurses could not be hired at any price, for even to approach it was deemed certain death. Then, to the inexpressible astonishment and admiration of the committee, two men of wealth and importance in the city offered personally to take charge of the hospital during the prevalence of the disease. Girard was one of these, Peter Helm the other. Girard appears to have been the first to offer himself. "Stephen Girard," records Matthew Carey, a member of the committee, "sympathizing with the wretched situation of the sufferers at Bush Hill, voluntarily and unexpectedly offered himself as a manager to superintend that hospital. The surprise and satisfaction excited by this extraordinary effort of humanity can be better conceived than expressed."

That very afternoon, Girard and Helm went out to the hospital, and entered upon their perilous and repulsive duty. Girard chose the post of honor. He took charge of the interior of the hospital, while Mr. Helm conducted its out-door affairs. For sixty days he continued to perform, by day and night, all the distressing and revolting offices incident to the situation. In the great scarcity of help, he used frequently to receive the sick and dying at the gate, assist in carrying them to their beds, nurse them, receive their last messages, watch for their last breath, and then, wrapping them in the sheet they had died upon, carry them out to the burial-ground, and place them in the trench. He had a vivid recollection of the difficulty of finding any kind of fabric in which to wrap the dead, when the vast number of interments had exhausted the supply of sheets. "I would put them," he would say, "in any old rag I could find." If he ever left the hospital, it was to visit the infected districts, and assist in removing the sick from the houses in which they were dying without help. One scene of this kind, witnessed by a merchant, who was hurrying past with camphored handkerchief pressed to his mouth, affords us a vivid glimpse of this heroic man engaged in his sublime vocation. A carriage, rapidly driven by a black man, broke the silence of the deserted and grass-grown street. It stopped before a frame house ; and the driver, first having bound a handkerchief over his mouth, opened the door of the carriage, and quickly remounted to the box. A short, thick-set man stepped from the coach and entered the house. In a minute or two, the observer, who stood at a safe distance watching the proceedings, heard a shuffling noise in the entry, and soon saw the stout little man supporting with extreme difficulty a tall, gaunt, yellow-visaged victim of the pestilence. Girard held round the waist the sick man, whose yellow face rested against his own; his long, damp, tangled hair mingled with Girard's ; his feet dragging helpless upon the pavement. Thus he drew him to the carriage door, the driver averting his face from the spectacle, far from offering to assist. Partly dragging, partly lifting, he succeeded, after long and severe exertion, in getting him into the vehicle. He then entered it himself, closed the door, and the carriage drove away towards the hospital.

A man who can do such things at such a time may commit errors and cherish erroneous opinions, but the essence of that which makes the difference between a good man and a bad man must dwell within him. Twice afterwards Philadelphia was visited by yellow-fever, in 1797 and 1798. On both occasions, Girard took the lead, by personal exertion or gifts of money, in relieving the poor and the sick. He had a singular taste for nursing the sick, though a sturdy unbeliever in medicine. According to him, nature, not doctors, is the restorer, — nature aided by good nursing. Thus, after the yellow-fever of 1798, he wrote to a friend in France: "During all this frightful time, I have constantly remained in the city; and, without neglecting my public duties, I have played a part which will make you smile. Would you believe it, my friend, that I have visited as many as fifteen sick people in a day? and what will surprise you still more, I have lost only one patient, an Irishman, who would drink a little. I do not flatter myself that I have cured one single person; but you will think with me, that in my quality of Philadelphia physician I have been very moderate, and that not one of my *confrères* has killed fewer than myself."

It is not by nursing the sick, however, that men acquire colossal fortunes. We revert, therefore, to the business career of this extraordinary man. Girard, in the ancient and honorable acceptation of the term, was a merchant; i. e. a man who sent his own ships to foreign countries, and exchanged their products for those of his own. Beginning in the West India trade, with one small schooner built with difficulty and managed with caution, he expanded his business as his capital increased, until he was the owner of a fleet of merchantmen, and brought home to Philadelphia the products of every clime. Beginning with single voyages, his vessels merely sailing to a foreign port and back again, he was accustomed at length to project great mercantile cruises, extending over long periods of time, and embracing many ports. A ship loaded with cotton and grain would sail, for example, to Bordeaux, there discharge, and take in a cargo of wine and fruit; thence to St. Petersburg, where she would exchange her wine and fruit for hemp and iron; then to Amsterdam, where the hemp and iron would be sold for dollars; to Calcutta next for a cargo of tea and silks, with which the ship would return to Philadelphia. Such were the voyages so often successfully made by the Voltaire, the Rousseau, the Helvetius, and the Montesquieu; ships long the pride of Girard and the boast of Philadelphia, their names being the tribute paid by the merchant to the literature of his native land. He seldom failed to make very large profits. He rarely, if ever, lost a ship.

His neighbors, the merchants of Philadelphia, deemed him a

lucky man. Many of them thought they could do as well as he, if they only had his luck. But the great volumes of his letters and papers, preserved in a room of the Girard College, show that his success in business was not due, in any degree whatever, to good fortune. Let a money-making generation take note, that Girard principles inevitably produce Girard results. The grand, the fundamental secret of his success, as of all success, was that *he understood his business.* He had a personal, familiar knowledge of the ports with which he traded, the commodities in which he dealt, the vehicles in which they were carried, the dangers to which they were liable, and the various kinds of men through whom he acted. He observed everything, and forgot nothing. He had done everything himself which he had occasion to require others to do. His directions to his captains and supercargoes, full, minute, exact, peremptory, show the hand of a master. Every possible contingency was foreseen and provided for; and he demanded the most literal obedience to the maxim, "Obey orders, though you break owners." He would dismiss a captain from his service forever, if he saved the whole profits of a voyage by departing from his instructions. He did so on one occasion. Add to this perfect knowledge of his craft, that he had a self-control which never permitted him to anticipate his gains or spread too wide his sails; that his industry knew no pause; that he was a close, hard bargainer, keeping his word to the letter, but exacting his rights to the letter; that he had no vices and no vanities; that he had no toleration for those calamities which result from vices and vanities; that his charities, though frequent, were bestowed only upon unquestionably legitimate objects, and were never profuse; that he was as wise in investing as skilful in gaining money; that he made his very pleasures profitable to himself in money gained, to his neighborhood in improved fruits and vegetables; that he had no family to maintain and indulge; that he held in utter aversion and contempt the costly and burdensome ostentation of a great establishment, fine equipages, and a retinue of servants; that he reduced himself to a money-making machine, run at the minimum of expense; — and we have an explanation of his rapidly acquired wealth. He used to boast, after he was a millionnaire, of wearing the same overcoat for fourteen winters; and one of his clerks, who saw him every day for twenty years, declares that he never remembered having seen him wear a new-looking garment but once. Let us note, too, that he was an adept in the art of getting men to serve him with devotion. He paid small salaries, and was never known in his life to bestow a gratuity upon one who served him; but he knew how to make his humblest clerk feel that the master's eye was upon him always. Violent in his outbreaks of anger, his business letters are singularly polite, and show consideration for the health and happiness of his subordinates.

Legitimate commerce makes many men rich; but in Girard's day no man gained by it ten millions of dollars. It was the war of 1812, which suspended commerce, that made this merchant so enormously rich. In 1811, the charter of the old United States Bank expired; and the casting-vote of Vice-President George Clinton negatived the bill for rechartering it. When war was imminent, Girard had a million dollars in the bank of Baring Brothers in London. This large sum, useless then for purposes of commerce, — in peril, too, from the disturbed condition of English finance, — he invested in United States stock and in stock of the United States Bank, both being depreciated in England. Being thus a large holder of the stock of the bank, the charter having expired, and its affairs being in liquidation, he bought out the entire concern; and, merely changing the name to Girard's Bank, continued it in being as a private institution, in the same building, with the same coin in its vaults, the same bank-notes, the same cashier and clerks. The banking-house and the house of the cashier, which cost three hundred and fifty thousand dollars, he bought for one hundred and twenty thousand. The stock, which he bought at four hundred and twenty, proved to be worth, on the winding up of the old bank, four hundred and thirty-four. Thus, by this operation, he extricated his property in England, invested it wisely in America, established a new business in place of one that could no longer be carried on, and saved the mercantile community from a considerable part of the loss and embarrassment which the total annihilation of the bank would have occasioned.

His management of the bank perfectly illustrates his singular and apparently contradictory character. Hamilton used to say of Burr, that he was great in little things, and little in great things. Girard in little things frequently seemed little, but in great things he was often magnificently great. For example: the old bank had been accustomed to present an overcoat to its watchman every Christmas; Girard forbade the practice as extravagant; — the old bank had supplied penknives gratis to its clerks; Girard made them buy their own; — the old bank had paid salaries which were higher than those given in other banks; Girard cut them down to the average rate. To the watchman and the clerks this conduct, doubtless, seemed little. Without pausing to argue the question with them, let us contemplate the new banker in his great actions. He was the very sheet-anchor of the government credit during the whole of that disastrous war. If advances were required at a critical moment, it was Girard who was promptest to make them. When all other banks and houses were contracting, it was Girard who stayed the panic by a timely and liberal expansion. When all other paper was depreciated, Girard's notes, and his alone, were as good as gold. In 1814, when the credit of the government was at its lowest ebb, when a loan of five millions, at seven per cent interest and twenty dollars bonus, was up for weeks, and only procured twenty thousand dollars, it was "old Girard" who boldly subscribed for the whole amount; which at once gave it market value, and infused life into the paralyzed credit of the nation. Again, in 1816, when the subscriptions lagged for the new United States Bank, Girard waited until the last day for receiving subscriptions, and then quietly subscribed for the whole amount not taken, which was three million one hundred thousand dollars. And yet again, in 1829, when the enormous expenditures of Pennsylvania upon her canals had exhausted her treasury and impaired her credit, it was Girard who prevented the total suspension of the public works by a loan to the Governor, which the assembling Legislature might or might not reimburse.

Once, during the war, the control of the coin in the bank procured him a signal advantage. In the spring of 1813, his fine ship, the Montesquieu, crammed with tea and fabrics from China, was captured by a British shallop when she was almost within Delaware Bay. News of the disaster reaching Girard, he sent orders to his supercargo to treat for a ransom. The British admiral gave up the vessel for one hundred and eighty thousand dollars in coin; and, despite this costly ransom, the cargo yielded a larger profit than that of any ship of Girard's during the whole of his mercantile career. Tea was then selling at war prices. Much of it brought, at auction, two dollars and fourteen cents a pound, more than four times its cost in China. He appears to have gained about half a million of dollars.

From the close of the war to the end of his life, a period of sixteen years, Girard pursued the even tenor of his way, as keen and steady in the pursuit of wealth, and as careful in preserving it, as though his fortune were still insecure. Why was this? We should answer the question thus : Because his defective education left him no other resource. We frequently hear the "success" of such men as Astor and Girard adduced as evidence of the uselessness of early education. On the contrary, it is precisely such men who prove its necessity; since, when they have conquered fortune, they know not how to avail themselves of its advantages. When Franklin had, at the age of forty-two, won a moderate competence, he could turn from business to science, and from science to the public service, using money as a means to the noblest ends. Strong-minded but unlettered men, like Girard, who cannot be idle, must needs plod on to the end, adding superfluous millions to their estates. In Girard's case, too, there was another cause of this entire devotion to business. His domestic sorrows had estranged him from mankind, and driven him into himself. Mr. Henry W. Arey, the very able and high-minded Secretary of Girard College, in whose custody are Girard's papers, is convinced that it was not the love of money which kept him at work early and late to the last days of his life.

"No one," he remarks, "who has had access to his private papers, ran fail to become impressed with the belief that these early disappointments furnish the true key to his entire character. Originally of warm and generous impulses, the belief in childhood that he had not been given his share of the love and kindness which were extended to others changed the natural current of his feelings, and, acting on a warm and passionate temperament, alienated him from his home, his parents, and his friends. And when in after time there were super-added the years of bitter anguish resulting from his unfortunate and ill-adapted marriage, rendered even more poignant by the necessity of concealment, and the consequent injustice of public sentiment, and marring all his cherished expectations, it may be readily understood why constant occupation became a necessity, and labor a pleasure."

Girard himself confirms this opinion. In one of his letters of 1820, to a friend in New Orleans, he says : —

"I observe with pleasure that you have a numerous family, that you are happy and in the possession of an honest fortune. This is all that a wise man has the right to wish for. As to myself, I live like a gal-ley-slave, constantly occupied, and often passing the night without sleep-ing. I am wrapped up in a labyrinth of affairs, and worn out with care. I do not value fortune. The love of labor is my highest ambi-tion. You perceive that your situation is a thousand times preferable to mine."

In his lifetime, as we have remarked, few men loved Girard, still fewer understood him. He was considered mean, hard, avaricious. If a rich man goes into a store to buy a yard of cloth, no one expects that he will give five dollars for it when the price is four. But there is a universal impression that it is "handsome" in him to give higher wages than other people to those who serve him, to bestow gratuities upon them, and, espe-cially, to give away endless sums in charity. The truth is, how-ever, that one of the duties which a rich man owes to society is to be careful *not* to disturb the law of supply and demand by giving more money for anything than a fair price, and *not* to encourage improvidence and servility by inconsiderate and profuse gifts. Girard rescued his poor relations in France from want, and edu-cated nieces and nephews in his own house ; but his gifts to them were not proportioned to his own wealth, but to their circum-stances. His design evidently was to help them as much as would do them good, but not so much as to injure them as self-sustaining members of society. And surely it was well for every clerk in his bank to know that all he had to expect from the rich

Girard was only what he would have received if he had served another bank. The money which in loose hands might have relaxed the arm of industry and the spirit of independence, which might have pampered and debased a retinue of menials, and drawn around the dispenser a crowd of cringing beggars and expectants, was invested in solid houses, which Girard's books show yielded him a profit of three per cent, but which furnished to many families comfortable abodes at moderate rents. To the most passionate entreaties of failing merchants for a loan to help them over a crisis, he was inflexibly deaf. They thought it meanness. But we can safely infer from Girard's letters and conversation that he thought it an injury to the community to avert from a man of business the consequences of extravagance and folly, which, in his view, were the sole causes of failure. If there was anything that Girard utterly despised and detested, it was that vicious mode of doing business which, together with extravagant living, causes seven business men in ten to fail every ten years. We are enabled to state, however, on the best authority, that he was substantially just to those whom he employed, and considerately kind to his own kindred. At least he meant to be kind; he did for them what he really thought was for their good. To little children, and to them only, he was gracious and affectionate in manner. He was never so happy as when he had a child to caress and play with.

After the peace of 1815, Girard began to consider what he should do with his millions after his death. He was then sixty-five, but he expected and meant to live to a good age. "The Russians," he would say, when he was mixing his *olla podrida* of a Russian salad, "understand best how to eat and drink; and I am going to see how long, by following their customs, I can live." He kept an excellent table; but he became abstemious as he grew older, and lived chiefly on his salad and his good claret. Enjoying perfect health, it was not until about the year 1828, when he was seventy-eight years of age, that he entered upon the serious consideration of a plan for the final disposal of his immense estate. Upon one point his mind had been long made up. "No man," said he, "shall be a gentleman on *my* money." He often

11   P

said that, even if he had had a son, he should have been brought up to labor, and should not, by a great legacy, be exempted from the necessity of labor. " If I should leave him twenty thousand dollars," he said, " he would be lazy or turn gambler." Very likely. The son of a man like Girard, who was virtuous without being able to make virtue engaging, whose mind was strong but rigid and ill-furnished, commanding but uninstructive, is likely to have a barren mind and rampant desires, the twin causes of debauchery. His decided inclination was to leave the bulk of his property for the endowment of an institution of some kind for the benefit of Philadelphia. The only question was, what kind of institution it should be.

William J. Duane* was his legal adviser then, — that honest and intrepid William J. Duane who, a few years later, stood calmly his ground on the question of the removal of the deposits against the infuriate Jackson, the Kitchen Cabinet, and the Democratic party. Girard felt all the worth of this able and honorable lawyer. With him alone he conversed upon the projected institution ; and Mr. Duane, without revealing his purpose, made inquiries among his travelled friends respecting the endowed establishments of foreign countries. For several months before sitting down to prepare the will, they never met without conversing upon this topic, which was also the chief subject of discourse between them on Sunday afternoons, when Mr. Duane invariably dined at Mr. Girard's country-house. A home for the education of orphans was at length decided upon, and then the will was drawn. For three weeks the lawyer and his client were closeted, toiling at the multifarious details of that curious document.

The minor bequests were speedily arranged, though they were numerous and well considered. He left to the Pennsylvania Hospital, thirty thousand dollars ; to the Deaf and Dumb Asylum, twenty thousand ; to the Orphan Asylum, ten thousand ; to the Lancaster public schools, the same sum ; the same for providing fuel for the poor in Philadelphia ; the same to the Society for the Relief of Distressed Sea-Captains and their families ; to the

---

* The facts which follow I received from the lips and from the papers of this revered man, now no more. — J. P.

Freemasons of Pennsylvania, for the relief of poor members twenty thousand; six thousand for the establishment of a free school in Passyunk, near Philadelphia; to his surviving brother, and to his eleven nieces, he left sums varying from five thousand dollars to twenty thousand; but to one of his nieces, who had a very large family, he left sixty thousand dollars. To each of the captains who had made two voyages in his service, and who should bring his ship safely into port, he gave fifteen hundred dollars; and to each of his apprentices, five hundred. To his old servants, he left annuities of three hundred and five hundred dollars each. A portion of his valuable estates in Louisiana he bequeathed to the corporation of New Orleans, for the improvement of that city. Half a million he left for certain improvements in the city of Philadelphia; and to Pennsylvania, three hundred thousand dollars for her canals. The whole of the residue of his property, worth then about six millions of dollars, he devoted to the construction and endowment of a College for Orphans.

Accustomed all his life to give minute directions to those whom he selected to execute his designs, he followed the same system in that part of his will which related to the College. The whole will was written out three times, and some parts of it more than three. He strove most earnestly, and so did Mr. Duane, to make every paragraph so clear that no one could misunderstand it. No candid person, sincerely desirous to understand his intentions, has ever found it difficult to do so. He directed that the buildings should be constructed of the most durable materials, "avoiding useless ornament, attending chiefly to the strength, convenience, and neatness of the whole." *That*, at least, is plain. He then proceeded to direct precisely what materials should be used, and how they should be used; prescribing the number of buildings, their size, the number and size of the apartments in each, the thickness of each wall, giving every detail of construction, as he would have given it to a builder. He then gave briefer directions as to the management of the institution. The orphans were to be plainly but wholesomely fed, clothed, and lodged; instructed in the English branches, in geometry, natural philosophy, the French and Spanish languages, and whatever else might be deemed suitable and beneficial to them. "I would have them," says the will, "taught facts and things, rather than words or signs." At the conclusion of the course, the pupils were to be apprenticed to "suitable occupations, as those of agriculture, navigation, arts, mechanical trades, and manufactures."

The most remarkable passage of the will is the following. The Italics are those of the original document.

"I enjoin and require that *no ecclesiastic, missionary, or minister of any sect whatsoever, shall ever hold or exercise any station or duty whatever in the said College; nor shall any such person ever be admitted for any purpose, or as a visitor, within the premises appropriated to the purposes of the said College.* In making this restriction, I do not mean to cast any reflection upon any sect or person whatsoever; but as there is such a multitude of sects, and such a diversity of opinion amongst them, I desire to keep the tender minds of the orphans, who are to derive advantage from this bequest, free from the excitement which clashing doctrines and sectarian controversy are so apt to produce; my desire is, that all the instructors and teachers in the College shall take pains to instil into the minds of the scholars *the purest principles of morality,* so that, on their entrance into active life, they may, *from inclination and habit,* evince *benevolence toward their fellow-creatures,* and *a love of truth, sobriety, and industry,* adopting at the same time such religious tenets as their *matured reason* may enable them to prefer."

When Mr. Duane had written this passage at Girard's dictation, a conversation occurred between them, which revealed, perhaps, one of the old gentleman's reasons for inserting it. "What do you think of that?" asked Girard. Mr. Duane, being unprepared to comment upon such an unexpected injunction, replied, after a long pause, "I can only say now, Mr. Girard, that I think it will make a great sensation." Girard then said, "I can tell you something else it will do, — it will please the Quakers." He gave another proof of his regard for the Quakers by naming three of them as the executors of his will; the whole number of the executors being five.

In February, 1830, the will was executed, and deposited in Mr. Girard's iron safe. None but the two men who had drawn the will, and the three men who witnessed the signing of it, were aware of its existence; and none but Girard and Mr. Du ane had the least knowledge of its contents. There never was such a keeper of his own secrets as Girard, and never a more faithful keeper of other men's secrets than Mr. Duane. And here we have another illustration of the old man's character. He had just signed a will of unexampled liberality to the public; and the sum which he gave the able and devoted lawyer for his three weeks' labor in drawing it was three hundred dollars!

Girard lived nearly two years longer, always devoted to business, and still investing his gains with care. An accident in the street gave a shock to his constitution, from which he never fully recovered; and in December, 1831, when he was nearly eighty-two years of age, an attack of influenza terminated his life. True to his principles, he refused to be cupped, or to take drugs into his system, though both were prescribed by a physician whom he respected.

Death having dissolved the powerful spell of a presence which few men had been able to resist, it was to be seen how far his will would be obeyed, now that he was no longer able personally to enforce it. The old man lay dead in his house in Water Street. While the public out of doors were curious enough to learn what he had done with his money, there was a smaller number within the house, the kindred of the deceased, in whom this curiosity raged like a mania. They invaded the cellars of the house, and, bringing up bottles of the old man's choice wine, kept up a continual carouse. Surrounding Mr. Duane, who had been present at Mr. Girard's death, and remained to direct his funeral, they demanded to know if there was a will. To silence their indecent clamor, he told them there was, and that he was one of the executors. On hearing this, their desire to learn its contents rose to fury. In vain the executors reminded them that decency required that the will should not be opened till after the funeral. They even threatened legal proceedings if the will were not immediately produced; and at length, to avoid a public scandal, the executors consented to have it read. These affectionate relatives being assembled in a parlor of the house in which the body of their benefactor lay, the will was taken from the iron safe by one of the executors.*

* Mr. Duane.

When he had opened it, and was about to begin to read, he chanced to look over the top of the document at the company seated before him. No artist that ever held a brush could depict the passion of curiosity, the frenzy of expectation, expressed in that group of pallid faces. Every individual among them expected to leave the apartment the conscious possessor of millions, for no one had dreamed of the probability of his leaving the bulk of his estate to the public. If they had ever heard of his saying that no one should be gentleman upon his money, they had forgotten or disbelieved it. The opening paragraphs of the will all tended to confirm their hopes, since the bequests to existing institutions were of small amount. But the reader soon reached the part of the will which assigned to ladies and gentlemen present such trifling sums as five thousand dollars, ten thousand, twenty thousand; and he arrived erelong at the sections which disposed of millions for the benefit of great cities and poor children. Some of them made not the slightest attempt to conceal their disappointment and disgust. Men were there who had married with a view to share the wealth of Girard, and had been waiting years for his death. Women were there who had looked to that event as the beginning of their enjoyment of life. The imagination of the reader must supply the details of a scene which we might think dishonored human nature, if we could believe that human nature was meant to be subjected to such a strain. It had been better, perhaps, if the rich man, in his own lifetime, had made his kindred partakers of his superabundance, especially as he had nothing else that he could share with them. They attempted, on grounds that seem utterly frivolous, to break the will, and employed the most eminent counsel to conduct their cause, but without effect. They did, however, succeed in getting the property acquired after the execution of the will; which Girard, disregarding the opinion of Mr. Duane, attempted by a postscript to include in the will. "It will not stand," said the lawyer. "Yes it will," said Girard. Mr. Duane, knowing his man, was silent; and the courts have since decided that his opinion was correct.

Thirty-three years have passed since the city of Philadelphia entered upon the possession of the enormous and growing estate with which Mr. Girard intrusted it. It is a question of general interest how the trust has been administered. No citizen of Philadelphia needs to be informed, that, in some particulars, the government of their city has shown little more regard to the manifest will of Girard than his nephews and nieces did. If he were to revisit the banks of the Schuylkill, would he recognize, in the splendid Grecian temple that stands in the centre of the College grounds, the home for poor orphans, devoid of needless ornament, which he directed should be built there? It is singular that the very ornaments which Girard particularly disliked are those which have been employed in the erection of this temple; namely, pillars. He had such an aversion to pillars, that he had at one time meditated taking down those which supported the portico of his bank. Behold his College surrounded with thirty-four Corinthian columns, six feet in diameter and fifty-nine in height, of marble, with capitals elaborately carved, each pillar having cost thirteen thousand dollars, and the whole colonnade four hundred and forty thousand! And this is the abode of poor little boys, who will leave the gorgeous scene to labor in shops, and to live in such apartments as are usually assigned to apprentices!

Now there is probably no community on earth where the number of honorable men bears a larger proportion to the whole population than in Philadelphia. Philadelphia is a community of honest dealers and faithful workmen. It is a matter of the highest interest to know how it could happen that, in such a city, a bequest for such a purpose should be so monstrously misappropriated.

The magnitude of the bequest was itself one cause of its misappropriation, and the habits of the country were another. When we set about founding an institution, our first proceeding is to erect a vast and imposing edifice. When we pronounce the word College, a vision of architecture is called up. It was natural, therefore, that the people of Philadelphia, bewildered by the unprecedented amount of the donation, should look to see the monotony of their city relieved by something novel and stupendous in the way of a building; and there appears to have been no one to remind them that the value of a school depends wholly upon the teachers who conduct it, provided those teachers are free to execute their plans. The immediate cause, however, of the remarkable departure from the will in the construction of the principal edifice was this: the custody of the Girard estate fell into the hands of the politicians of the city, who regarded the patronage appertaining thereunto as part of the " spoils " of victory at the polls. As we live at a time when honest lovers of their country frequently meditate on the means of rescuing important public interests from the control of politicians, we shall not deem a little of our space ill bestowed in recounting the history of the preposterous edifice which Girard's money paid for, and which Girard's will forbade.

On this subject we can avail ourselves of the testimony of the late Mr. Duane. During his own lifetime he would not permit the following narrative to be published, though he allowed it to be used as a source of information. We can now give it in his own words : —

" In relation to the Girard College, *the whole community of Philadelphia, and all political parties in it,* are culpable. At the time of Mr. Girard's death there was a mixture of Democrats and Federalists in our Councils: the former preponderating in number. It is said that of all steps the first is the most important, and that the first proceeding has either a good or a bad influence in all that follow. Now, what was the first step of the Democratic Councils, after Mr. Girard's death, in relation to the College ? Were they satisfied with the plan of it as described in his will ? Did they scout the project of building a palace for poor orphans ? Were there no views to offices and profits under the trust ? As I was in the Select Council at the time myself, I can partly answer these questions. Instead of considering the plan of a College given in the will a good one, the Democratic Councils offered rewards to architects for other plans. And as to offices, some members of Councils looked forward to them, to say nothing of aspirants out of doors.

" I have ever been a Democrat in principle myself, but not so much of a modern one in practice as to pretend that the Democratic party are free from blame as to the College. If they had been content with Mr. Girard's plain plan, would they have called in architects for others

If they had been opposed to pillars and ornaments, why did they invite scientific men to prepare pictures and plans almost inevitably ornamental? If they had been so careful of the trust funds, why did they stimulate the community, by presenting to them architectural drawings, to prefer some one of them to the simple plan of Girard himself? Besides, after they had been removed from power, and saw preparations made for a temple surrounded with costly columns, why did they not invoke the Democratic Legislature to arrest that proceeding.? If they at any time whatever did make such an appeal, I have no recollection of it. For party effect, much may have been said and done on an election day, but I am not aware that otherwise any resistance was made. No doubt there were many good men in the Democratic party in 1831–2, and there always have been many good men in it; but I doubt whether those who made the most noise about the College on election days were either the best Democrats or the best men. The leaders, as they are called, were just as factious as the leaders of their opponents. *The struggle of both for the Girard Fund was mainly with a view to party influence.* How much at variance with Mr. Girard's wishes this course was, may readily be shown.

"Immediately after his death in 1831, his will was published in the newspapers, in almanacs, and in other shapes likely to make its contents universally known. In it he said: 'In relation to the organization of the College and its appurtenances, I leave necessarily many details to the mayor, aldermen, and citizens of Philadelphia, and their successors; and I do so with the more confidence, as, from the nature of my bequests and the benefit to result from them, I trust that my fellow-citizens will observe and evince especial care and anxiety in selecting members for their City Councils and other agents.'

"What appeal could have been more emphatic than this? How could the testator have more delicately, but clearly, indicated his anxiety that his estate should be regarded as a sacred provision for poor orphans, and not 'spoils' for trading politicians?

"In this city, however, as almost everywhere else, to the public discredit and injury, our social affairs had been long mingled with the party questions of the Republic. At each rise or fall of one or the other party, the 'spoils' were greedily sought for. Even scavengers, unless of the victorious party, were deemed unworthy to sweep our streets. Mr. Girard's estate, therefore very soon became an object of desire with each party, in order to increase its strength and favor its adherents. Instead of selecting for the Councils the best men of the whole community, as Mr. Girard evidently desired, the citizens of Phi-

11*

adelphia persisted in preserving factious distinctions, and in October 1832, the Federal candidates prevailed.

" The triumphant party soon manifested a sense of their newly ac-quired power. Without making any trial whatever of the efficiency of the rules prepared by their predecessors for the management of the Girard trusts, they at once abolished them, and there were various other analogous evidences of intolerance.

" Without asserting that party passions actuated them, certain it is, that those who were now in power placed none of Mr. Girard's inti-mate friends in any position where they could aid in carrying out his views. No serious application was ever made, to my knowledge, to one of them for explanation on any point deemed doubtful. On the contrary, objections made by myself and others to the erection of a gorgeous temple, instead of a plain building for orphans, were utterly disregarded.

" A majority of the citizens of Philadelphia as a political class, and not a majority as a social community, as trustees of a fund for orphans, having thus got entire control of the Girard estate, they turned their attention to the plans of a College collected by their Democratic pre-decessors. Neither of the parties appears to have originally considered whether the plan described in the will ought not to be followed, if that could be done practically. The main desire of both so far seems to have been to build in the vicinity of this city a more magnificent edifice than any other in the Union.

" At this time, Mr. Nicholas Biddle was in the zenith of his power. Hundreds of persons, who at the present day find fault with him, were then his worshippers. He could command any post which he was will-ing to fill. I do not pretend that he sought any post, but it suited his inclinations to be at the head of those who were intrusted by Coun-cils with the construction of the College. Over his colleagues in this, as in another memorable instance, he seems to have had an absolute control. The architect, also, whose plan had been preferred, appears to have considered himself bound to adapt it to Mr. Biddle's concep-tions of true excellence. And you now behold the result, — a splendid temple in an unfinished state, instead of the unostentatious edifice con-templated by Mr. Girard.

" Is all this surprising? Why should Democrats think it so? It was by them that plans and pictures of architects were called for. Why should their opponents be astonished? It was by them that a *carte blanche* seems to have been given to Mr. Biddle in relation to the plans and the College. Is Mr. Biddle culpable? Is there no excuse for one

AND HIS COLLEGE.251

so strongly tempted as he was, not merely to produce a splendid edifice, but to connect his name, in some measure, with that of its founder? While I am not an apologist for Mr. Biddle, I am not willing to
cast blame upon him alone for the waste of time and money that we
have witnessed. As a classical scholar, a man of taste, and a traveller
abroad, it was not unnatural that he should desire to see near his native city the most magnificent edifice in North America. Having all
the pride and sense of power which adulation is calculated to produce,
the plain house described in his will may have appeared to him a prof-
anation of all that is beautiful in architecture, and an outrage at once
against all the Grecian orders. In short, the will of Mr. Girard to the
contrary, Mr. Biddle, like another distinguished person, may have
said, ' I take the responsibility!'

" It is true that this responsibility was a serious one, but less so to
Mr. Biddle than to the City Councils. They were the trustees, and
ought to have considered Mr. Girard's will as law to them. They
should have counted the cost of departing from it. They ought to
have reflected that by departing from it many orphans would be excluded from the benefits of education. They should have considered
whether a Grecian temple would be such a place as poor orphans
destined to labor ought to be reared in. The Councils of 1832–3,
therefore, have no apology to offer. But Mr. Biddle may well say to
all our parties: ' You are all more in fault than I am. You Democrats gave rewards for plans. You Federalists submitted those plans
to me, and I pointed out the one I thought the best, making improvements upon it. A very few persons, Mr. Ronaldson, Mr. Duane, and
one or two others alone objected; while the majority of my fellow-
citizens, the Councils, and the Legislature, all looked on at what I was
doing, and were silent.' "

While erecting an edifice the most opposite to Girard's intentions that could be contrived by man, the architect was permitted
to follow the directions of the will in minor particulars, that rendered the building as inconvenient as it was magnificent. The
vaulted ceilings of those spacious rooms reverberated to such a
degree, that not a class could say its lesson in them till they were
hung with cotton cloth. The massive walls exuded dampness
continually. The rooms of the uppermost story, lighted only
from above, were so hot in the summer as to be useless; and the
lower rooms were so cold in winter as to endanger the health of

the inmates. It has required ingenuity and expense to render the main building habitable; but even now the visitor cannot but smile as he compares the splendor of the architecture with the homely benevolence of its purpose. The Parthenon was a suitable dwelling-place for a marble goddess, but the mothers of Athens would have shuddered at the thought of consigning their little boys to dwell in its chilling grandeurs.

We can scarcely overstate the bad effect of this first mistake. It has constantly tended to obscure Mr. Girard's real purpose, which was to afford a plain, comfortable home, and a plain, substantial education to poor orphans, destined to gain their livelihood by labor. Always there have been two parties in the Board of Directors: one favoring a scheme which would make the College a *college;* the other striving to keep it down to the modest level of the founder's intentions. That huge and dazzling edifice seems always to have been exerting a powerful influence against the stricter constructionists of the will. It is only within the last two years that this silent but ponderous argument has been partially overcome by the resolute good-sense of a majority of the Directors. Not the least evil consequent upon the erection of this building was, that the delay in opening the College caused the resignation of its first President, Alexander D. Bache, a gentleman who had it in him to organize the institution aright, and give it a fair start. It is a curious fact, that the extensive report by this gentleman of his year's observation of the orphan schools of Europe has not been of any practical use in the organization of Girard College. Either the Directors have not consulted it, or they have found nothing in it available for their purpose.

The first class of one hundred pupils was admitted to the College on the first day of the year 1848. The number of inmates is now six hundred. The estate will probably enable the Directors to admit at length as many as fifteen hundred. It will be seen, therefore, that Girard College, merely from the number of its pupils, is an institution of great importance.

Sixteen years have gone by since the College was opened, but it cannot yet be said that the policy of the Directors is fixed. These Directors, appointed by the City Councils, are eighteen in number, of whom six go out of office every year, while the Councils themselves are annually elected. Hence the difficulty of settling upon a plan, and the greater difficulty of adhering to one. Sometimes a majority has favored the introduction of Latin or Greek; again, the manual-labor system has had advocates; some have desired a liberal scale of living for the pupils; others have thought it best to give them Spartan fare. Four times the President has been changed, and there have been two periods of considerable length when there was no President. There have been dissensions without and trouble within. As many as forty-four boys have run away in a single year. Meanwhile, the Annual Reports of the Directors have usually been so vague and so reticent, that the public was left utterly in the dark as to the condition of the institution. Letters from masters to whom pupils have been apprenticed were published in the Reports, but only the letters which had nothing but good to say of the apprentices. Large numbers of the boys, it is true, have done and are doing credit to the College; but the public have no means of judging whether, upon the whole, the training of the College has been successful.

Nevertheless, we believe we may say with truth that invaluable experience has been gained, and genuine progress has been made. To maintain and educate six hundred boys, even if those boys had enlightened parents to aid in the work, is a task which would exhaust the wisdom and the tact of the greatest educator that ever lived. But these boys are all fatherless, and many of them motherless; the mothers of many are ignorant and unwise, of some are even vicious and dissolute. A large number of the boys are of very inferior endowments, have acquired bad habits, have inherited evil tendencies. It would be hard to overstate the difficulty of the work which the will of Girard has devolved upon the Directors and teachers of Girard College. Mistakes have been made, but perhaps they have not been more serious or more numerous than we ought to expect in the forming of an institution absolutely unique, and composed of material the most unmanageable.

There are indications, too, that the period of experiment draws to an end, and that the final plan of the College, on the basis of common-sense, is about to be settled. Mr. Richard Vaux, the present head of the Board of Directors, writes Reports in a style most eccentric, and not always intelligible to remote readers ; but it is evident that his heart is in the work, and that he belongs to the party who desire the College to be the useful, unambitious institution that Girard wished it to be. His Reports are not written with rose-water. They say *something*. They confess some failures, as well as vaunt some successes. We would earnestly advise the Directors never to shrink from taking the public into their confidence. The public is wiser and better than any man or any board. A plain statement every year of the real condition of the College, the real difficulties in the way of its organization, would have been far better than the carefully uttered nothings of which the Annual Reports have generally consisted. It was to Philadelphia that Girard left his estate. The honor of Philadelphia is involved in its faithful adminis tration. Philadelphia has a right to know how it is adminis tered.

The President of the College is Major Richard Somers Smith, a graduate of West Point, where he was afterwards a Professor. He has served with distinction in the Army of the Potomac, in which he commanded a brigade. To learn how to be an efficient President of Girard College is itself a labor of years and Major Smith is only in the second year of his incumbency The highest hopes are indulged, however, that under his energetic rule, the College will become all that the public ought to expect. He seems to have perceived at once the weak point of the institution.

" I find in the College," he says in one of his monthly reports, "a certain degree of impatience of study, an inertness, a dragging along, an infection of ' young-Americanism,' a disposition to flounder along through duties half done, hurrying to reach — what is never attained — an ' easy success '; and I observe that this state of things is confined to the higher departments of study. In the elementary departments there is life ; but as soon as the boy has acquired the rudiments of his English or common-school education, he begins to chafe, and to fee that it is time for him to *go out,* and to make haste to 'finish (!) his studies,' — which of course he does without much heart."

And again : —

" The ' poor white male orphan,' dwelling for eight or ten years in comfort almost amounting to luxury, waited upon by servants and machinery in nearly all his domestic requirements, unused to labor, or laboring only occasionally, with some reward in view in the form of extra privileges, finds it hard to descend from his fancied elevation to the lot of a simple apprentice ; and his disappointment is not soothed by the discovery that with all his learning he has not learned wherewithal to give ready satisfaction to his master."

It has been difficult, also, to induce the large manufacturers to take apprentices ; they are now accustomed to place boys at once upon the footing of men, paying them such wages as they are worth. Men who employ forty boys will not generally undertake the responsibilities involved in receiving them as bound apprentices for a term of years.

To remedy all these evils, Major Smith proposes to add to the College a Manual Labor Department, in which the elder boys shall acquire the rudiments of the arts and trades to which they are destined. This will alleviate the tedium of the College routine, assist the physical development of the boys, and send them forth prepared to render more desirable help to their employers. The present Board of Directors favor the scheme.

In one particular the College has fulfilled the wishes of its founder. He said in his will, " I desire that by every proper means, a pure attachment to our republican institutions, and to the sacred rights of conscience, as guaranteed by our happy Constitution, shall be formed and fostered in the minds of the scholars." Three fourths of the whole number of young men, out of their time, who were apprenticed from Girard College, have joined the Union army. We must confess, also, that a considerable number of its apprentices, *not* out of their time, have run away for the same purpose. With regard to the exclusion of ecclesiastics, it is agreed on all hands that no evil has resulted from that singular injunction of the will. On the contrary, it has served to call particular attention to the religious instruction of the pupils. The only effect of the clause is, that the morning prayers and the Sunday services are conducted by gentlemen who have not undergone the ceremony of ordination.

The income of the Girard estate is now about two hundred thousand dollars a year, and it is increasing. Supposing that only one half of this revenue is appropriated to the College, it is still, we believe, the largest endowment in the country for an educational purpose. The means of the College are therefore ample. To make those means effective in the highest degree, some mode must be devised by which the politics of the city shall cease to influence the choice of Directors. In other words, " Girard College must be taken out of politics." The Board of Directors should, perhaps, be a more permanent body than it now is. At the earliest possible moment a scheme of instruction should be agreed upon, which should remain unchanged, in its leading features, long enough for it to be judged by its results. The President must be clothed with ample powers, and held responsible, not for methods, but results. He must be allowed, at least, to nominate all his assistants, and to recommend the removal of any for reasons given; and both his nominations and his recommendations of removal, so long as the Directors desire to retain his services, should be ratified by them. He must be made to feel strong in his place; otherwise, he will be tempted to waste his strength upon the management of committees, and general whitewashing. Human nature is so constituted, that a gentleman with a large family will not willingly give up an income of three thousand dollars a year, with lodging in a marble palace. If he is a strong man and an honorable, he will do it, rather than fill a post the duties of which an ignorant or officious committee prevent his discharging. If he is a weak or dishonest man, he will cringe to that committee, and expend all his ingenuity in making the College show well on public days. It might even be well, in order to strengthen the President, to give him the right of appeal to the Mayor and Councils, in case of an irreconcilable difference of opinion between him and the Directors. Everything depends upon the President. Given the right President, with power enough and time enough, and the success or the College is assured. Given a bad President, or a good one hampered by committees, or too dependent upon a board, and the College will be the reproach of Philadelphia.

It is a question with political economists, whether, upon the whole, such endowments as this are a good or an evil to a community. There is now a considerable party in England, among whom are several clergymen of the Established Church, who think it would be better for England if every endowment were swept away, and thus to each succeeding generation were restored the privilege of supporting all its poor, caring for all its sick, and educating all its young. Dr. Chalmers appears to have been inclined to an opinion like this. It will be long, however, before this question becomes vital in America. Girard College must continue for generations to weigh heavily on Philadelphia, or to lighten its burdens. The conduct of those who have charge of it in its infancy will go far to determine whether it shall be an argument for or against the utility of endowments. Meanwhile, we advise gentlemen who have millions to leave behind them not to impose difficult conditions upon the future, which the future may be unable or unwilling to fulfil; but either to bestow their wealth for some object that can be immediately and easily accomplished, or else imitate the conduct of that respectable and public-spirited man who left five pounds towards the discharge of his country's debt.

JAMES GORDON BENNETT

AND

THE NEW YORK HERALD

JAMES GORDON BENNETT AND THE NEW YORK HERALD.

A FEW years ago it seemed probable that the people of the United States would be supplied with news chiefly through the agency of newspapers published in the city of New York. We were threatened with a paper despotism similar to that formerly exercised in Great Britain by the London Times; since, when one city furnishes a country with newspapers, one newspaper is sure, at length, to gain such a predominance over others that its proprietor, if he is equal to his position, wields a power greater than ought to be intrusted to an individual. There have been periods when the director of the London Times appeared to be as truly the monarch of Great Britain as Henry VIII. once was, or as William Pitt during the Seven Years' War. It was, we believe, the opinion of the late Mr. Cobden, which Mr. Kinglake confirms, that the editor of the London Times could have prevented the Crimean War. Certainly he conducted it. Demosthenes did not more truly direct the resources of Athens against Philip, than did this invisible and anonymous being those of the British Empire against Russia. The first John Walter, who was to journalism what James Watt was to the steam-engine, had given this man daily access to the ear of England; and to that ear he addressed, not the effusions of his own mind, but the whole purchasable eloquence of his country. He had relays of Demosthenes. The man controlling such a press, and fit to control it, can bring the available and practised intellect of his country to bear upon the passions of his countrymen; for it is a fact, that nearly the whole literary talent of a nation is at the command of any honorable man who has money enough, with tact enough The editor who expends fifty guineas a day in the purchase of three short essays can have them written by the men who can do them best. What a power is this, to say three things every morning to a whole nation, — to say them with all the force which genius, knowledge, and practice united can give, — and to say them without audible contradiction! Fortunate for England is it that this power is no longer concentrated in a single man, and that the mighty influence once wielded by an individual will henceforth be exerted by a profession.

We in America have escaped all danger of ever falling under the dominion of a paper despot. There will never be a Times in America. Twenty years ago the New York news and the New York newspaper reached distant cities at the same moment; but since the introduction of the telegraph, the news outstrips the newspaper, and is given to the public by the local press. It is this fact which forever limits the circulation and national importance of the New York press. The New York papers reach a village in Vermont late in the afternoon, — six, eight, ten hours after a carrier has distributed the Springfield Republican; and nine people in ten will be content with the brief telegrams of the local centre. At Chicago, the New York paper is forty hours behind the news; at San Francisco, thirty days; in Oregon, forty. Before California had been reached by the telegraph, the New York newspapers, on the arrival of a steamer, were sought with an avidity of which the most ludicrous accounts have been given. If the news was important and the supply of papers inadequate, nothing was more common than for a lucky newsboy to dispose of his last sheets at five times their usual price. All this has changed. A spirited local press has anticipated the substance of the news, and most people wait tranquilly for the same local press to spread before them the particulars when the tardy mail arrives. Even the weekly and semi-weekly editions issued by the New York daily press have probably reached their maximum of importance; since the local daily press also publishes weekly and semi-weekly papers, many of which are of high excellence and are always improving, and have the additional attraction of full local intelligence. If some bold Yankee should invent a method by which a bundle of newspapers could be shot from New York to Chicago in half an hour, it would certainly enhance the importance of the New York papers, and diminish that of the rapidly expanding and able press of Chicago. Such an invention is possible; nay, we think it a probability. But even in that case, the local news, and, above all, the local advertising, would still remain as the basis of a great, lucrative, honorable, and very attractive business.

We believe, however, that if the local press were annihilated, and this whole nation lived dependent upon the press of a single city, still we should be safe from a paper despotism; because the power of the editorial lessens as the intelligence of the people increases. The prestige of the editorial is gone. Just as there is a party in England who propose the omission of the sermon from the church service as something no longer needed by the people, so there are journalists who think the time is at hand for the abolition of editorials, and the concentration of the whole force of journalism upon presenting to the public the history and picture of the day. The time for this has not come, and may never come; but our journalists already know that editorials neither make nor mar a daily paper, that they do not much influence the public mind, nor change many votes, and that the power and success of a newspaper depend finally upon its success in getting and its skill in exhibiting the news. The word *newspaper* is the exact and complete description of the thing which the true journalist aims to produce. The news is his work; editorials are his play. The news is the point of rivalry; it is that for which nineteen twentieths of the people buy newspapers; it is that which constitutes the power and value of the daily press; it is that which determines the rank of every newspaper in every free country.

No editor, therefore, will ever reign over the United States, and the newspapers of no one city will attain universal currency. Hence the importance of journalism in the United States. By the time a town has ten thousand inhabitants, it usually has a daily paper, and in most large cities there is a daily paper for every twenty thousand people. In many of the Western cities there are daily newspapers conducted with great energy, and on a scale of expenditure which enables them to approximate real excellence. Many of our readers will live to see the day when there will be in Chicago, St. Louis, New Orleans, Cincinnati, and San Francisco daily newspapers more complete, better executed, and produced at greater expense than any newspaper now existing in the United States. This is a great deal to say, in view of the fact, that, during the late war, one of the New York papers ex pended in war correspondence alone two thousand dollars a week Nevertheless, we believe it. There will never be *two* newspapers in any one city that can sustain such an expenditure; but in fif- teen years from to-day there will be one, we think, in each of our great cities, and besides that one there will be four or five strug- gling to supplant it, as well as one or two having humbler aims and content with a lowlier position.

It is plain that journalism will henceforth and forever be an important and crowded profession in the United States. The daily newspaper is one of those things which are rooted in the ne- cessities of modern civilization. The steam-engine is not more essential to us. The newspaper is that which connects each in- dividual with the general life of mankind, and makes him part and parcel of the whole; so that we can almost say, that those who neither read newspapers nor converse with people who do read them are not members of the human *family;* — though, like the negroes of Guinea, they may become such in time. They are beyond the pale ; they have no hold of the electric chain, and therefore do not receive the shock.

There are two mornings of the year on which newspapers have not hitherto been published in the city of New York, — the 5th of July, and the 2d of January. A shadow appears to rest on he world during those days, as when there is an eclipse of the sun. We are separated from our brethren, cut off, lost, alone ; vague apprehensions of evil creep over the mind. We feel, in some degree, as husbands feel who, far from wife and children, say to themselves, shuddering, " What things *may* have happened, and I not know it ! " Nothing quite dispels the gloom until the Evening Post — how eagerly seized — assures us hat nothing very particular has happened since our last. It is amusing to notice how universal is the habit of reading a morning paper. Hundreds of vehicles and vessels convey the business men of New York to that extremity of Manhattan Island which may be regarded as the counting-house of the Western Continent. It is not uncommon for every individual in a cabin two hundred feet long to be sitting absorbed in his paper, like boys conning their lessons on their way to school. Still more striking is it to observe the torrent of workingmen pouring down town, many of them reading as they go, and most of them provided with a newspaper for dinner-time, not less as a matter of course than the tin kettle which contains the material portion of the repast. Notice, too, the long line of hackney-coaches on a stand, nearly every driver sitting on his box reading his paper. Many of our Boston friends have landed in New York at five o'clock in the morning, and ridden up town in the street cars, filled, at that hour, with women and boys, folding newspapers and throwing off bundles of them from time to time, which are caught by other boys and women in waiting. Carriers are flitting in every direction, and the town is alive with the great business of getting two hundred thousand papers distributed before breakfast.

All this is new, but it is also permanent. Having once had daily papers, we can never again do without them; so perfectly does this great invention accord with the genius of modern life. The art of journalism is doubtless destined to continuous improvement for a long time to come; the newspapers of the future will be more convenient, and better in every way, than those of the present day; but the art remains forever an indispensable auxiliary to civilization. And this is so, not by virtue of editorial essays, but because journalism brings the events of the time to bear upon the instruction of the time. An editorial essayist is a man addressing men; but the skilled and faithful journalist, recording with exactness and power the thing that has come to pass, is Providence addressing men. The thing that has actually happened, — to know that is the beginning of wisdom. All else is theory and conjecture, which may be right and may be wrong

While it is true that the daily press of the city of New York

12

ıs limited by the telegraph, it has nevertheless a very great, an unapproached, national importance. We do not consider it certain that New York is always to remain the chief city of the United States; but it holds that rank now, and must for many years. Besides being the source of a great part of our news, it was the first city that afforded scope for papers conducted at the incredible expense which modern appliances necessitate. Consequently its daily papers reach the controlling minds of the country. They are found in all reading-rooms, exchanges, bank parlors, insurance-offices, counting-rooms, hotels, and wherever else the ruling men of the country congregate. But, above all, they are, and must be, in all newspaper offices, subject to the scissors. This is the chief source of their importance. Not merely that in this way their contents are communicated to the whole people. The grand reason why the New York papers have national importance is, that it is chiefly through them that the art of journalism in the United States is to be perfected. They set daily copies for all editors to follow. The expenditure necessary for the carrying on of a complete daily newspaper is so immense, that the art can only be improved in the largest cities. New York is first in the field; it has the start of a quarter of a century or more; and it therefore devolves upon the journalists of that city to teach the journalists of the United States their vocation. It is this fact which invests the press of New York with such importance, and makes it so well worth considering.

It is impossible any longer to deny that the chief newspaper of that busy city is the New York Herald. No matter how much we may regret this fact, or be ashamed of it, no journalist can deny it. We do not attach much importance to the fact that Abraham Lincoln, the late lamented President of the United States, thought it worth while, during the dark days of the summer of 1864, to buy its support at the price of the offer of the French mission. He was mistaken in supposing that this paper had any considerable power to change votes; which was shown by the result of the Presidential election in the city of New York, where General McClellan had the great majority of thirty-seven thousand. Influence over opinion no paper can have which has

itself no opinion, and cares for none. It is not as a vehicle of opinion that the Herald has importance, but solely as a vehicle of
news. It is for its excellence. real or supposed, in this particular,
that eighty thousand people buy it every morning.   Mr. Lincoln
committed, as we cannot help thinking, a most egregious error
and fault in his purchase of the editor of this paper, though he is
in some degree excused by the fact that several leading Republicans, who were in a position to know better, advised or sanctioned the bargain, and leading journalists agreed not to censure
it.   Mr. Lincoln could not be expected to draw the distinction
between the journalist and the writer of editorials. He perceived
the strength of this carrier-pigeon's pinions, but did not note the
trivial character of the message tied to its leg.   Thirty or forty
war correspondents in the field, a circulation larger than any of
its rivals, an advertising patronage equalled only by that of the
London Times, the popularity of the paper in the army, the frequent utility of its maps and other elucidations, — these things
imposed upon his mind; and his wife could tell him from personal
observation, that the proprietor of this paper lived in a style of
the most profuse magnificence, — maintaining costly establishments in town and country, horses, and yachts, to say nothing
of that most expensive appendage to a reigning house, an heir
apparent.

Our friends in the English press tell us, that the Herald was
one of the principal obstacles in their attempts to guide English
opinions aright during the late struggle. Young men in the press
would point to its editorials and say : "This is the principal
newspaper in the Northern States; this is the Times of America;
can a people be other than contemptible who prefer such a newspaper as this to journals so respectable and so excellent as the
Times and Tribune, published in the same city?" "As to
(American) journalism," says Professor Goldwin Smith, "the
New York Herald is always kept before our eyes." That is to
say, the editorial articles in the Herald; not that variety and fulness of intelligence which often compelled men who hated it most
to get up at the dawn of day to buy it. A paper which can de-
tach two or three men, after a battle, to collect the names of the

killed and wounded, with orders to do only that, cannot lack pur-chasers in war time. Napoleon assures us that the whole art of war consists in having the greatest force at the point of contact. This rule applies to the art of journalism; the editor of the Herald knew it, and had the means to put it in practice.

Even here, at home, we find two opinions as to the cause of the Herald's vast success as a business. One of these opinions is this, — the Herald takes the lead because it is such a bad paper. The other opinion is, — the Herald takes the lead because it is such a good paper. It is highly important to know which of these two opinions is correct; or, in other words, whether it is the Herald's excellences as a newspaper, or its crimes as a public teacher, which give it such general currency. Such success as this paper has obtained is a most influential fact upon the journal-ism of the whole country, as any one can see who looks over a file of our most flourishing daily papers. It is evident that our daily press is rapidly becoming Heraldized; and it is well known that the tendency of imitation is to reproduce all of the copy except-ing alone that which made it worth copying. It is honorable to the American press that this rule has been reversed in the pres-ent instance. Some of the more obvious good points of the Herald have become universal, while as yet no creature has been found capable of copying the worst of its errors.

If there are ten bakers in a town, the one that gives the best loaf for sixpence is sure, at last, to sell most bread. A man may puff up his loaves to a great size, by chemical agents, and so deceive the public for a time; another may catch the crowd for a time by the splendor of his gilt sheaf, the magnitude of his signs, and the bluster of his advertising; and the intrinsically best baker may be kept down, for a time, by want of tact, or capital, or some personal defect. But let the competition last thirty years! The gilt sheaf fades, the cavities in the big loaf are observed; but the ugly little man round the corner comes steadily into favor, and all the town, at length, is noisy in the morning with the rattle of his carts. The particular caterer for our morning repast, now under consideration, has achieved a success of this kind, against every possible obstacle, and under every possible disadvantage. He had no friends at the start, he has made none since, and he has none now. He has had the support of no party or sect. On the contrary, he has won his object in spite of the active opposition of almost every organized body in the country, and the fixed disapproval of every public-spirited human being who has lived in the United States since he began his career. What are we to say of this? Are we to say that the people of the United States are competent to judge of bread, but not of newspapers? Are we to say that the people of the United States prefer evil to good? We cannot assent to such propositions.

Let us go back to the beginning, and see how this man made his way to his present unique position. We owe his presence in this country, it seems, to Benjamin Franklin; and he first smelt printer's ink in Boston, near the spot where young Ben Franklin blackened his fingers with it a hundred years before. Born and reared on the northeastern coast of Scotland, in a Roman Catholic family of French origin, he has a French intellect and Scotch habits. Frenchmen residing among us can seldom understand why this man should be odious, so French is he. A French naval officer was once remonstrated with for having invited him to a ball given on board a ship of war in New York harbor. "Why, what has he done?" inquired the officer. "Has he committed murder? Has he robbed, forged, or run away with somebody's wife?" "No." "Why then should we not invite him?" "He is the editor of the New York Herald." "Ah!" exclaimed the Frenchman, — "the Herald! it is a delightful paper, — it reminds me of my gay Paris." This, however, was thirty years ago, when Bennett was almost as French as Voltaire. He was a Frenchman also in this: though discarding, in his youth, the doctrines of his Church, and laughing them to scorn in early manhood, he still maintained a kind of connection with the Catholic religion. The whole of his power as a writer consists in his detection of the evil in things that are good, and of the falsehood in things that are true, and of the ridiculous in things that are important. He began with the Roman Catholic Church, — "the holy Roman Catholic Church," as he once styled it, — adding in a parenthesis, "all of us Catholics are devilish holy." Another French indication is, that his early tastes were romantic literature *and* political economy, — a conjunction very common in France from the days of the "philosophers" to the present time. During our times of financial collapse, we have noticed, among the nonsense which he daily poured forth, some gleams of a superior understanding of the fundamental laws of finance. He appears to have understood 1837 and 1857 better than most of his contemporaries.

In a Catholic seminary he acquired the rudiments of knowledge, and advanced so far as to read Virgil. He also picked up a little French and Spanish in early life. The real instructors of his mind were Napoleon, Byron, and Scott. It was their fame, however, as much as their works, that attracted and dazzled him. It is a strange thing, but true, that one of the strongest desires of one of the least reputable of living men was, and is, to be admired and held in lasting honor by his fellow-men. Nor has he now the least doubt that he deserves their admiration, and will have it. In 1817, an edition of Franklin's Autobiography was issued in Scotland. It was his perusal of that little book that first directed his thoughts toward America, and which finally decided him to try his fortune in the New World. In May, 1819, being then about twenty years of age, he landed at Halifax, with less than five pounds in his purse, without a friend on the Western Continent, and knowing no vocation except that of book-keeper.

Between his landing at Halifax and the appearance of the first number of the Herald sixteen years elapsed; during most of which he was a very poor, laborious, under-valued, roving writer for the daily press. At Halifax, he gave lessons in book-keeping for a few weeks, with little profit, then made his way along the coast to Portland, whence a schooner conveyed him to Boston. He was then, it appears, a soft, romantic youth, alive to the historic associations of the place, and susceptible to the varied, enchanting loveliness of the scenes adjacent, on land and sea. He even expressed his feelings in verse, in the Childe Harold manner, — verse which does really show a poetic habit of feeling with an occasional happiness of expression. At Boston he experienced the last extremity of want. Friendless and alone he wandered about the streets, seeking work and finding none; until, his small store of money being all expended, he passed two whole days without food, and was then only relieved by finding a shilling on the Common. He obtained at length the place of salesman in a bookstore, from which he was soon transferred to the printing-house connected therewith, where he performed the duties of proof-reader. And here it was that he received his first lesson in the art of catering for the public mind. The firm in whose employment he was were more ambitious of glory than covetous of profit, and consequently published many works that were in advance of the general taste. Bankruptcy was their reward. The youth noted another circumstance at Boston. The newspaper most decried was Buckingham's Galaxy; but it was also the most eagerly sought and the most extensively sold. Buckingham habitually violated the traditional and established decorums of the press; he was familiar, chatty, saucy, anecdotical, and sadly wanting in respect for the respectabilities of the most respectable town in the universe. Every one said that he was a very bad man, *but* every one was exceedingly curious every Saturday to see " what the fellow had to say this week." If the youth could have obtained a sight of a file of James Franklin's Courant, of 1722, in which the youthful Benjamin first addressed the public, he would have seen a still more striking example of a journal generally denounced and universally read.

Two years in Boston. Then he went to New York, where he soon met the publisher of a Charleston paper, who engaged him as translator from the Spanish, and general assistant. During the year spent by him at Charleston he increased his knowledge of the journalist's art. The editor of the paper with which he was connected kept a sail-boat, in which he was accustomed to meet arriving vessels many miles from the coast, and bring in his files of newspapers a day in advance of his rivals. The young assistant remembered this, and turned it to account in after years. At Charleston he was confronted, too, with the late peculiar institution, and saw much to approve in it, nothing to condemn. From that day to this he has been but in one thing consistent, — contempt for the negro and for all white men interested in his welfare, approving himself in this a thorough Celt.   If, for one brief period, he forced himself, for personal reasons, to veil this feeling, the feeling remained rooted within him, and soon resumed its wonted expression.   He liked the South, and the people of the South, and had a true Celtic sympathy with their aristocratic pretensions.   The salary of an assistant editor at that time was something between the wages of a compositor and those of an office-boy.   Seven dollars a week would have been considered rather liberal pay ; ten, munificent ; fifteen, lavish.

Returning to New York, he endeavored to find more lucrative employment, and advertised his intention to open, near the site of the present Herald office, a " Permanent Commercial School," in which all the usual branches were to be taught " in the inductive method."   His list of subjects was extensive, — " reading, elocution, penmanship, and arithmetic ; algebra, astronomy, history, and geography ; moral philosophy, commercial law, and political economy ; English grammar, and composition ; and also, if required, the French and Spanish languages, by natives of *those countries.*"   Application was to be made to " J. G. B., 148 Fulton Street."   Applications, however, were not made in sufficient number, and the school, we believe, never came into existence.   Next, he tried a course of lectures upon Political Economy, at the old Dutch Church in Ann Street, then not far from the centre of population.   The public did not care to hear the young gentleman upon that abstruse subject, and the pecuniary result of the enterprise was not encouraging.   He had no resource but the ill-paid, unhonored drudgery of the press.

For the next few years he was a paragraphist, reporter, scissorer, and man-of-all-work for the New York papers, daily and weekly, earning but the merest subsistence.   He wrote then in very much the same style as when he afterwards amused and shocked the town in the infant Herald ; only he was under restraint, being a subordinate, and was seldom allowed to violate decorum.   In point of industry, sustained and indefatigable industry, he had no equal, and has never since had but one.   One thing is to be specially noted as one of the chief and indispensable causes of his success. *He had no vices.* He never drank to excess, nor gormandized, nor gambled, nor even smoked, nor in any other way wasted the vitality needed for a long and tough grapple with adverse fortune. What he once wrote of himself in the early Herald was strictly true : " I eat and drink to live, — not live to eat and drink. Social glasses of wine are my aversion; public dinners are my abomination ; all species of gormandizing, my utter scorn and contempt. When I am hungry, I eat ; when thirsty, drink. Wine or viands taken for society, or to stimulate conversation, tend only to dissipation, indolence, poverty, contempt, and death." This was an immense advantage, which he had in common with several of the most mischievous men of modern times, — Calhoun, Charles XII., George III., and others. Correct bodily habits are of themselves such a source of power, that the man who has them will be extremely likely to gain the day over competitors of ten times his general worth who have them not. Dr. Franklin used to say, that if Jack Wilkes had been as exemplary in this particular as George III., he would have turned the king out of his dominions. In several of the higher kinds of labor, such as law, physic, journalism, authorship, art, when the competition is close and keen, and many able men are near the summit, the question, who shall finally stand upon it, often resolves itself into one of physical endurance. This man Bennett would have lived and died a hireling scribe, if he had ad even one of the common vices. Everything was against his rising, except alone an enormous capacity for labor, sustained by strictly correct habits.

He lived much with politicians during these years of laborious poverty. Gravitating always towards the winning side, he did much to bring into power the worst set of politicians we ever had, — those who " availed " themselves of the popularity of Andrew Jackson, and who were afterwards used by him for the purpose of electing Martin Van Buren. He became perfectly familiar with all that was petty and mean in the political strifes of the day, but without ever suspecting that there was anything in politics not petty and mean. He had no convictions of his

12 *   R

own, and therefore not the least belief that any politician had. If the people were in earnest about the affairs of their country, (*their* country, not his,) it was because the people were not behind the scenes, were dupes of their party leaders, were a parcel of fools. In short, he acquired his insight into political craft in the school of Tammany Hall and the Kitchen Cabinet. His value was not altogether unappreciated by the politicians. He was one of those whom they use and flatter during the heat of the contest, and forget in the distribution of the spoils of victory.

He made his first considerable hit as a journalist in the spring of 1828, when he filled the place of Washington correspondent to the New York Enquirer. In the Congressional Library, one day, he found an edition of Horace Walpole's Letters, which amused him very much. " Why not," said he to himself, " try a few letters on a similar plan from this city, to be published in New York ? " The letters appeared. Written in a lively manner, full of personal allusions, and describing individuals respecting whom the public are always curious, — free also from offensive personalities, — the letters attracted much notice and were generally copied in the press. It is said that some of the ladies whose charms were described in those letters were indebted to them for husbands. Personalities of this kind were a novelty then, and mere novelty goes a great way in journalism. At this period he produced almost every kind of composition known to periodical literature, — paragraphs and leading articles, poetry and love-stories, reports of trials, debates, balls, and police cases ; his earnings ranging from five dollars a week to ten or twelve. If there had been then in New York one newspaper publisher who understood his business, the immense possible value of this man as a journalist would have been perceived, and he would have been secured, rewarded, and kept under some restraint. But there was no such man. There were three or four forcible writers for the press, but not one journalist.

During the great days of " The Courier and Inquirer," from 1829 to 1832, when it was incomparably the best newspaper on the continent, James Gordon Bennett was its most efficient hand. It lost him in 1832, when the paper abandoned General Jackson.

and took up Nicholas Biddle ; and in losing him lost its chance of retaining the supremacy among American newspapers to this day. We can truly say, that at that time journalism, as a thing by itself and for itself, had no existence in the United States. Newspapers were mere appendages of party ; and the darling object of each journal was to be recognized as the organ of the party it supported. As to the public, the great public, hungry for interesting news, no one thought of it. Forty years ago, in the city of New York, a copy of a newspaper could not be bought for money. If any one wished to see a newspaper, he had either to go to the office and subscribe, or repair to a bar-room and buy a glass of something to drink, or bribe a carrier to rob one of his customers. The circulation of the Courier and Inquirer was considered something marvellous when it printed thirty-five hundred copies a day, and its business was thought immense when its daily advertising averaged fifty-five dollars. It is not very unusual for a newspaper now to receive for advertising, in one day, six hundred times that sum. Bennett, in the course of time, had a chance been given to him, would have made the Courier and Inquirer powerful enough to cast off all party ties ; and this he would have done merely by improving it as a vehicle of news. But he was kept down upon one of those ridiculous, tantalizing, corrupting salaries, which are a little more than a single man needs, but not enough for him to marry upon. This salary was increased by the proprietors giving him a small share in the small profits of the printing-office ; so that, after fourteen years of hard labor and Scotch economy, he found himself, on leaving the great paper, a capitalist to the extent of a few hundred dollars. The chief editor of the paper which he now abandoned sometimes lost as much in a single evening at the card-table. It probably never occurred to him that this poor, ill-favored Scotchman was destined to destroy his paper and all the class of papers to which it belonged. Any one who now examines a file of the Courier and Inquirer of that time, and knows its interior circumstances, will see plainly enough that the possession of this man was the vital element in its prosperity. He alone knew the rudiments of his trade. He alone had the physical stamina, the inde fatigable industry, the sleepless vigilance, the dexterity, tact, and audacity, needful for keeping up a daily newspaper in the face of keen competition.

Unweaned yet from the politicians, he at once started a cheap party paper, " The Globe," devoted to Jackson and Van Buren. The party, however, did not rally to its support, and it had to contend with the opposition of party papers already existing, upon whose manor it was poaching. The Globe expired after an existence of thirty days. Its proprietor, still untaught by such long experience, invested the wreck of his capital in a Philadelphia Jackson paper, and struggled desperately to gain for it a footing in the party. He said to Mr. Van Buren and to other leaders, Help me to a loan of twenty-five hundred dollars for two years, and I can establish my Pennsylvanian on a self-supporting basis. The application was politely refused, and he was compelled to give up the struggle. The truth is, he was not implicitly trusted by the Jackson party. They admitted the services he had rendered ; but, at the same time, they were a little afraid of the vein of mockery that broke out so frequently in his writings. He was restive in harness. He was devoted to the party, but he was under no party illusions. He was fighting in the ranks as an adventurer or soldier of fortune. He fought well ; but would it do to promote a man to high rank who knew the game so well, ـnd upon whom no man could get any *hold?* To him, in his secret soul, Martin Van Buren was nothing (as he often said) but a country lawyer, who, by a dexterous use of the party machinery, the well-timed death of De Witt Clinton, and General Jackson's frenzy in behalf of Mrs. Eaton, had come to be the chosen successor of the fiery chieftain. The canny Scotchman saw this with horrid clearness, and saw nothing more. Political chiefs do ـot like subalterns of this temper. Underneath the politician in Martin Van Buren there was the citizen, the patriot, the gentleman, and the man, whose fathers were buried in American soil, whose children were to live under American institutions, who had, necessarily, an interest in the welfare and honor of the country, and whose policy, upon the whole, was controlled by that natural interest in his country's welfare and honor. To our mocking Celt nothing of this was apparent, nor has ever been.

His education as a journalist was completed by the failure of his Philadelphia scheme. Returning to New York, he resolved to attempt no more to rise by party aid, but henceforth have no master but the public. On the 6th of May, 1835, appeared the first number of the Morning Herald, price one cent. It was born in a cellar in Wall Street, — not a basement, but a veritable cellar. Some persons are still doing business in that region who remember going down into its subterranean office, and buying copies of the new paper from its editor, who used to sit at a desk composed of two flour-barrels and a piece of board, and who occupied the only chair in the establishment. For a considerable time his office contained absolutely nothing but his flour-barrel desk, one wooden chair, and a pile of Heralds. " I remember," writes Mr. William Gowans, the well-known bookseller of Nassau Street, " to have entered the subterranean office of its editor early in its career, and purchased a single copy of the paper, for which I paid the sum of one cent United States currency. On this occasion the proprietor, editor, and vendor was seated at his desk, busily engaged writing, and appeared to pay little or no attention to me as I entered. On making known my object in coming in, he requested me to put my money down on the counter, and help myself to a paper ; all this time he continuing his writing operations. The office was a single oblong underground room ; its furniture consisted of a counter, which also served as a desk, constructed from two flour-barrels, perhaps empty, standing apart from each other about four feet, with a single plank covering both ; a chair, placed in the centre, upon which sat the editor busy at his vocation, with an inkstand by his right hand ; on the end nearest the door were placed the papers for sale."

Everything appeared to be against his success. It was one poor man in a cellar against the world. Already he had failed three times ; first, in 1825, when he attempted to establish a Sunday paper ; next, in 1832, when he tried a party journal recently, in Philadelphia. With great difficulty, and after many rebuffs, he had prevailed upon two young printers to print his paper and share its profits or losses, and he possessed about enough money to start the enterprise and sustain it ten days. The cheap-

ness of his paper was no longer a novelty, for there was already
a penny paper with a paying circulation. He had cut loose from
all party ties, and he had no influential friends except those who
had an interest in his failure. The great public, to which he
made this last desperate appeal, knew him not even by name.
The newsboy system scarcely existed; and all that curious machinery by which, in these days, a "new candidate for public
favor" is placed, at no expense, on a thousand news-stands, had
not been thought of. There he was alone in his cellar, without
clerk, errand-boy, or assistant of any kind. For many weeks he
did with his own hands everything, — editorials, news, reporting,
receiving advertisements, and even writing advertisements for
persons "unaccustomed to composition." He expressly announced that advertisers could have their advertisements written
for them at the office, and this at a time when there was no one
to do it but himself. The extreme cheapness of the paper rendered him absolutely dependent upon his advertisers, and yet
he dared not charge more than fifty cents for sixteen lines, and
he offered to insert sixteen lines for a whole year for thirty dollars.

He at once produced an eminently salable article. If just
such a paper were to appear to-day, or any day, in any large
city of the world, it would instantly find a multitude of readers.
It was a very small sheet, — four little pages of four columns
each, — much better printed than the Herald now is, and not a
waste line in it. Everything *drew*, as the sailors say. There
was not much scissoring in it, — the scissors have never been
much esteemed in the Herald office, — but the little that there
was all told upon the general effect of the sheet. There is a
story current in newspaper offices that the first few numbers of
the Herald were strictly decorous and "respectable," but that the
editor, finding the public indifferent and his money running low,
changed his tactics, and filled his paper with scurrility and indecency, which immediately made it a paying enterprise. No such
thing. The first numbers were essentially of the same character
as the number published this morning. They had the same excellences and the same defects: in the news department, immense

industry, vigilance, and tact; in the editorial columns, the vein of Mephistophelean mockery which has puzzled and shocked so many good people at home and abroad. A leading topic then was a certain Matthias, one of those long-bearded religious impostors who used to appear from time to time. The first article in the first number of the Herald was a minute account of the origin and earlier life of the fellow, — just the thing for the paper, and the sure method of exploding *him*. The first editorial article, too, was perfectly in character: —

"In *débuts* of this kind," said the editor, " many talk of principle — political principle, party principle — as a sort of steel-trap to catch the public. We mean to be perfectly understood on this point, and therefore openly disclaim all steel-traps, — all principle, as it is called, — all party, — all politics. Our only guide shall be good, sound, practical common-sense, applicable to the business and bosoms of men engaged in every-day life. We shall support no party, be the organ of no faction or coterie, and care nothing for any election or any candidate, from President down to constable. We shall endeavor to record facts on every public and proper subject, stripped of verbiage and coloring, with comments, when suitable, just, independent, fearless, and good-tempered. If the Herald wants the mere expansion which many journals possess, we shall try to make it up in industry, good taste, brevity, variety, point, piquancy, and cheapness."

He proceeded immediately to give a specimen of the "comments" thus described, in the form of a review of an Annual Register just published. The Register informed him that there were 1,492 "rogues in the State Prison." His comment was: " But God only knows how many out of prison, preying upon he community, in the shape of gamblers, blacklegs, speculators, and politicians." He learned from the Register that the poorhouse contained 6,547 paupers; to which he added, "and double the number going there as fast as indolence and intemperance can carry them." The first numbers were filled with nonsense and gossip about the city of New York, to which his poverty confined him. He had no boat with which to board arriving ships, no share in the pony express from Washington, and no correspondents in other cities. All he could do was to catch the floating gossip, scandal, and folly of the town, and present as much of them every day as one man could get upon paper by sixteen hours' labor. He laughed at everything and everybody, — not excepting himself and his squint eye, — and, though his jokes were not always good, they were generally good enough. People laughed, and were willing to expend a cent the next day to see what new folly the man would commit or relate. We all like to read about our own neighborhood: this paper gratified the propensity.

The man, we repeat, really had a vein of poetry in him, and the first numbers of the Herald show it. He had occasion to mention, one day, that Broadway was about to be paved with wooden blocks. This was not a very promising subject for a poetical comment; but he added: "When this is done, every vehicle will have to wear sleigh-bells as in sleighing times, and Broadway will be so quiet that you can pay a compliment to a lady, in passing, and she will hear you." This was nothing in itself; but here was a man wrestling with fate in a cellar, who could turn you out two hundred such paragraphs a week, the year round. Many men. can growl in a cellar; this man could laugh, and keep laughing, and make the floating population of a city laugh with him. It must be owned, too, that he had a little real insight into the nature of things around him, — a little Scotch sense, as well as an inexhaustible fund of French vivacity. Alluding, once, to the "hard money" cry, by which the lying politicians of the day carried elections, he exploded that nonsense in two lines: "If a man gets the wearable or the eatable he wants, what cares he whether he has gold or paper-money?" He devoted two sentences to the Old School and New School Presbyterian controversy: "Great trouble among the Presbyterians just now. The question in dispute is, whether or not a man can do anything towards saving his own soul." He had, also, an article upon the Methodists, in which he said that the two religions nearest akin were the Methodist and the Roman Catholic. We should add to these trifling specimens the fact, that he uniformly maintained, from 1835 to the crash of 1837, that the prosperity of the country was unreal, and would end in disaster Perhaps we can afford space for a single specimen of his way of treating this subject; although it can be fully appreciated only by those who are old enough to remember the rage for land speculation which prevailed in 1836: —

"THE RICH POOR — THE POOR RICH. — 'I have made $ 50,000 since last January' said one of these real-estate speculators to a friend.

"'The deuce you nave,' said the other, looking up in astonishment. 'Why, last January you were not worth a twenty-dollar bill.'

"'I know that; but I now calculate I'm worth full $ 50,000, if not $ 60,000.'

"'How have you made it?'

"'By speculating in real estate. I bought three hundred lots at Goose Island at $ 150 apiece; they are now worth $ 400. I would not sell them for $ 350 apiece, I assure you.'

"'Do you think so?'

"'Sartain. I have two hundred and fifty lots at Blockhead's Point, worth $ 150 a piece; some on them are worth $ 200. I have one hundred lots at Jackass Inlet, worth at least $ 100, at the very lowest calculation. In short, I'm worth a hull $ 60,000.'

"'Well, I'm glad to hear it. You can pay me now the $ 500 you nave owed me for these last four years. There's your note, I believe, said he, handing the speculator a worn piece of paper that had a piece of writing upon it.

"The speculator looked blank at this. 'Oh! yes — my — now — I'd like — suppose,' but the words could not form themselves into a perfect sentence.

"'I want the money very much, said the other; 'I have some payments to make to-morrow.'

"'Why, you don't want cash for it surely.'

"'Yes, but I do. You say you are worth $ 60,000, — surely $ 500 is but a trifle to pay; do let me have the cash on the nail, if you please.'

"'Oh. — by — well — now — do tell — really, I have not got the money at present.'

"'So you can't pay it, eh? A man worth $ 60,000, and can't pay an old debt of $ 500?'

"'Oh! yes I can — I'll — I'll — just give you my note for it at ninety days.'

"'The D—l you will! A man worth $ 60,000, and can t pay $ 500 for ninety days! what do you mean?'

"'Well now, my dear sir, I'm worth what I say.. I can pay you. There's my property,' spreading out half a dozen very beautiful lithographs; 'but really I can't raise that amount at present. Yesterday I had to give three per cent a month for $ 4,000 to save my whole fortune. I had to look out for the mortgages. Take my note; you can get it discounted for three per cent.'

"'No, I can't. If you will give me $ 250 for the debt, I shall give the other half to pay the interest on your mortgages.' . , . .

"Whether the proposition has been accepted we shall know to-morrow; but we have many such rich people." — *Herald*, Oct. 28, 1836.

But it was not such things as these that established the Herald. Confined as he was to the limits of a single town, and being compelled to do everything with his own hands, he could not have much in his columns that we should now call "news." But what is news? The answer to that question involves the whole art, mystery, and history of journalism. The time was when news signified the doings of the king and his court. This was the staple of the first news-letter writers, who were employed by great lords, absent from court, to send them court intelligence. To this was soon added news of the doings of other kings and courts; and from that day to this the word *news* has been continually gaining increase of meaning, until now it includes all that the public are curious to know, which may be told without injury to the public or injustice to individuals. While this man was playing fantastic tricks before high Heaven, his serious thoughts were absorbed in schemes to make his paper the great vehicle of news. Early in the second month, while he was still losing money every day, he hit upon a new kind of news, which perhaps had more to do with the final success of the Herald than any other single thing. His working day, at that time, was sixteen or seventeen hours. In the morning, from five to eight, he was busy, in the quiet of his room, with those light, nonsensical paragraphs and editorials which made his readers smile in spite of themselves. During the usual business hours of the morning, he was in his cellar, over his flour-barrel desk, engaged in the ordinary routine of editorial work; not disdaining to sell the morning paper, write advertisements, and take the money for them

About one o'clock, having provided abundant copy for the compositors, he sallied forth into Wall Street, picking up material for his stock-tables and subjects for paragraphs. From four to six he was at his office again, winding up the business of the day. In the evening he was abroad, — at theatre, concert, ball, or public meeting, — absorbing fresh material for his paper. He con- verted himself, as it were, into a medium through which the gossip, scandal, fun, and nonsense of this great town were daily conveyed back to it for its amusement; just as a certain popular preacher is reported to do, who spends six days in circulating among his parishioners, and on the seventh tells them all that they have taught him.

Now Wall Street, during the years that General Jackson was disturbing the financial system by his insensate fury against the United States Bank, was to journalism what the Army of the Potomac was in the year 1864. The crash of 1837 was full two years in coming on, during which the money market was always deranged, and moneyed men were anxious and puzzled. The public mind, too, was gradually drawn to the subject, until Wall Street was the point upon which all eyes were fixed. The editor of the Herald was the first American journalist to avail himself of this state of things. It occurred to him, when his paper had been five weeks in existence, to give a little account every day of the state of affairs in Wall Street, — the fluctuations of the money market and their causes, — the feeling and gossip of the street. He introduced this feature at the moment when General Jackson's embroilment with the French Chambers was at its height, and when the return of the American Minister was hourly expected. Some of our readers may be curious to see the first " money article " ever published in the United States. It was as follows : —

" COMMERCIAL.

" Stocks yesterday maintained their prices during the session of the Board, several going up. Utica went up 2 per cent ; the others sta- tionary. Large quantities were sold. After the Board adjourned and the news from France was talked over, the fancy stocks generally went down 1 to 1½ per cent ; other stocks quite firm. A rally was made by the bulls in the evening, under the trees, but it did not succeed. There will be a great fight in the Board to-day. The good people up town are anxious to know what the brokers think of Mr. Livingston. We shall find out, and let them know.

" The cotton and flour market rallied a little. The rise of cotton in Liverpool drove it up here a cent or so. The last shippers will make $2\frac{1}{2}$ per cent. Many are endeavoring to produce a belief that there will be a war. If the impression prevails, naval stores will go up a good deal. Every eye is outstretched for the Constitution. Hudson, of the Merchants' News Room, says he will hoist out the first flag. Gilpin, of the Exchange News Room, says he will have her name down in his Room one hour before his competitor. The latter claims having beat Hudson yesterday by an hour and ten minutes in chronicling the England." — *Herald*, June 13, 1835.

This was his first attempt. The money article constantly lengthened and increased in importance. It won for the little paper a kind of footing in brokers' offices and bank parlors, and provided many respectable persons with an excuse for buying it.

At the end of the third month, the daily receipts equalled the daily expenditures. A cheap police reporter was soon after engaged. In the course of the next month, the printing-office was burnt, and the printers, totally discouraged, abandoned the enterprise. The editor — who felt that he had caught the public ear, as he had — contrived, by desperate exertions, to " rake the Herald out of the fire," as he said, and went on alone. Four months after, the great fire laid Wall Street low, and all the great business streets adjacent. Here was his first real opportunity as a journalist; and how he improved it! — spending one half of every day among the ruins, note-book in hand, and the other half over his desk, writing out what he had gathered. He spread before the public reports so detailed, unconventional, and graphic, that a reader sitting at his ease in his own room became, as it were, an eyewitness of those appalling scenes. His accounts of that fire, and of the events following it, are such as Defoe would have given if he had been a New York reporter. Still struggling for existence, he went to the expense (great then) of publishing a picture of the burning Exchange, and a map of the burnt district. American journalism was born amid the roaring flames of the gieat fire of 1835; and no true journalist will deny, that from that day to this, whenever any very remarkable event has taken place in the city of New York, the Herald reports of it have generally been those which cost most money and exhibited most of the spirit and detail of the scene. For some years every dollar that the Herald made was expended in news, and, to this hour, no other journal equals it in daily expenditure for intelligence. If, to-morrow, we were to have another great fire, like that of thirty years ago, this paper would have twenty-five men in the streets gathering particulars.

But so difficult is it to establish a daily newspaper, that at the end of a year it was not yet certain that the Herald could continue. A lucky contract with a noted pill-vender gave it a great lift about that time; * and in the fifteenth month, the editor ven-

---

* We copy the following from Mr. Gowan's narrative: " Dr. Benjamin Brandreth, of well and wide-spread reputation, and who has made more happy and comfortable, for a longer or shorter time, as the case may be, by his prescriptions than any other son of Æsculapius, hailed me one day as I jumped from a railroad car passing up and along the shores of the Hudson River, and immediately commenced the following narrative. He held in his hand a copy of the New York Herald. 'Do you know,' said he, holding up the paper to my face, 'that it was by and through your agency that this paper ever became successful?' I replied in the negative. 'Then,' continued he, 'I will unfold the secret to you of how you became instrumental in this matter. Shortly after my arrival in America, I began looking about me how I was to dispose of my pills by agents and other means. Among others, I called upon you, then a bookseller in Chatham Street. After some conversation on the subject of my errand, a contract was soon entered into between us, — you to sell and I to furnish the said pills; but,' continued he, ' these pills will be of no use to me or any one else unless they can be made known to the public, or rather the great herd of the people; and that can only be done by advertising through some paper which goes into the hands of the many. Can you point out to me any such paper, published in the city?' After a short pause I in substance said that there had lately started a small penny paper, which had been making a great noise during its existence; and I had reason to believe it had obtained a very considerable circulation among that class of people which he desired to reach by advertising, and so concluded that it would be the best paper in the city for his purpose, provided he could make terms with the owner, who, I had no doubt, would be well disposed, as in all probability he stood in need of patronage of this kind. I immediately,' continued the doctor, 'adopted your advice, went directly to Mr. Bennett, made terms with him for advertising, and for a long time paid him a very considerable sum weekly for the use of his columns, which tended greatly to add to both his and my own treasury. The editor of the Herald

tured to raise his price to two cents. From that day he had a business, and nothing remained for him but to go on as he had begun. He did so. The paper exhibits now the same qualities as it did then, — immense expenditure and vigilance in getting news, and a reckless disregard of principle, truth, and decency in its editorials.

Almost from the first month of its existence, this paper was deemed infamous by the very public that supported it. We can well remember when people bought it on the sly, and blushed when they were caught reading it, and when the man in a country place who subscribed for it intended by that act to distinctly enroll himself as one of the ungodly. Journalists should thoroughly consider this most remarkable fact. We have had plenty of infamous papers, but they have all been short-lived but this. This one has lasted. After thirty-one years of life, it appears to be almost as flourishing to-day as ever. The foremost of its rivals has a little more than half its circulation, and less than half its income. A marble palace is rising to receive it, and its proprietor fares as sumptuously every day as the ducal family who furnished him with his middle name.

Let us see how the Herald acquired its ill name. We shall then know why it is still so profoundly odious; for it has never changed, and can never change, while its founder controls it. Its peculiarities are *his* peculiarities.

He came into collision, first of all, with the clergy and people of his own Church, the Roman Catholic. Thirty years ago, as some of our readers may remember, Catholics and Protestants had not yet learned to live together in the same community with perfect tolerance of one another's opinions and usages; and there were still some timid persons who feared the rekindling of the fagot, and the supremacy of the Pope in the United States. A controversy growing out of these apprehensions had been pro-

afterwards acknowledged to me that but for his advertising patronage he would have been compelled to collapse. Hence,' said he, 'had I never called on you in all probability I should not have had my attention turned to the New York Herald; and, as a consequence, that sheet would never have had my advertising; and that paper would have been a thing of the past, and perhaps entirely forgotten.' "

ceeding for some time in the newspapers when this impudent little Herald first appeared. The new-comer joined in the fray, and sided against the Church in which he was born; but laid about him in a manner which disgusted both parties. For example : —

"As a Catholic, we call upon the Catholic Bishop and clergy of New York to come forth from the darkness, folly, and superstition of the tenth century. They live in the nineteenth. There can be no mistake about it, — they will be convinced of this fact if they look into the almanac. . . . .

" But though we want a thorough reform, we do not wish them to discard their greatest absurdities at the first breath. We know the difficulty of the task. Disciples, such as the Irish are, will stick with greater pertinacity to absurdities and nonsense than to reason and common sense. We have no objection to the doctrine of Transubstantiation being tolerated for a few years to come. We may for a while indulge ourselves in the delicious luxury of creating and eating our Divinity. A peculiar taste of this kind, like smoking tobacco or drinking whiskey, cannot be given up all at once. The ancient Egyptians, for many years after they had lost every trace of the intellectual character of their religion, yet worshipped and adored the ox, the bull, and the crocodile. They had not discovered the art, as we Catholics have done, of making a God out of bread, and of adoring and eating him at one and the same moment. This latter piece of sublimity or religious cookery (we don't know which) was reserved for the educated and talented clergy from the tenth up to the nineteenth century. Yet we do not advise the immediate disturbance of this venerable piece of rottenness and absurdity. It must be retained, as we would retain carefully the tooth of a saint or the jawbone of a martyr, till the natural progress of reason in the Irish mind shall be able, silently and imperceptibly, to drop it among the forgotten rubbish of his early loves, or his more youthful riots and rows.

" There must be a thorough reformation and revolution in the American Catholic Church. Education must be more attended to. We never knew one priest who believed that he ate the Divinity when he took the Eucharist. If we must have a Pope, let us have a Pope of our own, — an American Pope, an intellectual, intelligent, and moral Pope, — not such a decrepit, licentious, stupid, Italian blockhead as the College of Cardinals at Rome condescends to give the Christian world of Europe."

This might be good advice; but no serious Protestant, at that day, could relish the tone in which it was given. Threatening letters were sent in from irate and illiterate Irishmen; the Herald was denounced from a Catholic pulpit; its carriers were assaulted on their rounds; but the paper won no friends from the side which it affected to espouse. Every one felt that to this man *nothing* was sacred, or august, or venerable, or even serious. He was like an unbeliever in a party composed of men of various sects. The Baptist could fairly attack an Episcopalian, because he had convictions of his own that could be assaulted; but this stranger, who believed nothing and respected nothing, could not be hit at all. The result would naturally be, that the whole company would turn upon him as upon a common foe.

So in politics. Perhaps the most serious and sincere article he ever wrote on a political subject was one that appeared in November, 1836, in which he recommended the subversion of republican institutions and the election of an emperor. If he ever had a political conviction, we believe he expressed it then. After a rigmarole of Roman history and Augustus Cæsar, he proceeded thus : —

"Shall we not profit by these examples of history? Let us, for the sake of science, art, and civilization, elect at this election General Jackson, General Harrison, Martin Van Buren, Hugh White, or Anybody, we care not whom, the EMPEROR of this great REPUBLIC for life, and have done with this eternal turmoil and confusion. Perhaps Mr. Van Buren would be the best Augustus Cæsar. He is sufficiently corrupt, selfish, and heartless for that dignity. He has a host of favorites that will easily form a Senate. He has a court in preparation, and the Prætorian bands in array. He can pick up a Livia anywhere. He has violated every pledge, adopted and abandoned every creed, been for and against every measure, is a believer in all religions by turns, and, like the first Cæsar, has always been a republican and taken care of number one. He has called into action all the ragged adventurers from every class, and raised their lands, stocks, lots, and places without end. He is smooth, agreeable, oily, as Octavianus was. He has a couple of sons, also, who might succeed him and preserve the imperial line. We may be better off under an Emperor, — we could not be worse off as a nation than we are now. Besides, who knows but Van Buren is of the blood of the great Julius himself? That great man conquered all Gaul and Helvetia, which in those days comprised Holland. Caius Julius Cæsar may thus have laid the foundation of a royal line to be transmitted to the West. There is a prophecy in Virgil's 'Pollio' evidently alluding to Van. But of this another day.

A man who writes in this way may have readers, but he can have no friends. An event occurred in his first year which revealed this fact to him in an extremely disagreeable manner. There was then upon the New York stage a notoriously dissolute actor, who, after outraging the feelings of his wife in all the usual modes, completed his infamy by denouncing her from the stage of a crowded theatre. The Herald took her part, which would naturally have been the popular side. But when the actor retorted by going to the office of the Herald and committing upon its proprietor a most violent and aggravated assault, accompanying his blows with acts of peculiar indecency, it plainly appeared, that the sympathies of the public were wholly with the actor, — not with the champion of an injured woman. His hand had been against every man, and in his hour of need, when he was greatly in the right, every heart was closed against him. Not the less, however, did the same public buy his paper, because it contained what the public wanted, i. e. the news of the day, vividly exhibited.

The course of this curious specimen of our kind during the late war was perfectly characteristic. During the first two years of the war he was inclined to think that the Rebels would be successful so far as to win over the Democratic party to their side, and thus constitute Jefferson Davis President of the United States. If he had any preference as to the result of the contest, it was probably this. If the flag of the United States had been trailed in the mud of Nassau Street, followed by hooting ruffians from the Sixth Ward, and the symbol of the Rebellion had floated in its stead from the cupola of the City Hall, saluted by Captain Rynders's gun, it would not have cost this isolated alien one pang, — unless, perchance, a rival newspaper had been the first to announce the fact. *That*, indeed, would have cut him to the heart. Acting upon the impression that the Rebellion, in some way, would triumph, he gave it all the support possible, and continued

13

to do so until it appeared certain that, whatever the issue of the strife, the South was lost for a long time as a patron of New York papers.

The key to most of the political vagaries of this paper is given in a single sentence of one of its first numbers: *"We have never been in a minority, and we never shall be."* In his endeavors to act upon this lofty principle, he was sadly puzzled during the war, — so difficult was it to determine which way the cat would finally jump. He held himself ready, however, to jump with it, whichever side the dubious animal might select. At the same time, he never for an instant relaxed his endeavors to obtain the earliest and fullest intelligence from the seat of war. Never perhaps did any journal in any country maintain so great an expenditure for news. Every man in the field representing that paper was more than authorized — he was encouraged and commanded — to incur any expense whatever that might be necessary either in getting or forwarding intelligence. There were no rigid or grudging scrutiny of reporters' drafts; no minute and insulting inquiries respecting the last moments of a horse ridden to death in the service; no grumbling about the precise terms of a steamboat charter, or a special locomotive. A reporter returning from the army laden with information, procured at a lavish expense, was received in the office like a conqueror coming home from a victorious campaign, and he went forth again full of courage and zeal, knowing well that every man employed on the Herald was advancing himself when he served the paper well. One great secret of success the proprietor of the Herald knows better than most; — he knows how to get out of those who serve him all there is in them; he knows how to reward good service; he knows a man's value to him. There is no newspaper office in the world where real journalistic efficiency is more certain to meet prompt recognition and just reward than in this. Not much may be said to a laborious reporter about the hits he is making; but, on some Saturday afternoon, when he draws his salary, he finds in his hands a larger amount than usual. He hands it back to have the mistake corrected, and he is informed that his. salary is raised.

The Herald, too, systematically prepares the way for its re-porters. Some of our readers may remember how lavishly this paper extolled General McClellan during the time of his glory, and indeed as long as he held the chief command. One of the results of this policy was, that, while the reporters of other papers were out in the cold, writing in circumstances the most incon-venient, those of the Herald, besides being supplied with the best information, were often writing in a warm apartment or commo-dious tent, not far from head-quarters or at head-quarters. As long as General Butler held a command which gave him control over one of the chief sources of news, the Herald hoarded its private grudge against him; but the instant he was removed from command, the Herald was after him in full cry. If, to-morrow, the same General should be placed in a position which should render his office a source of important intelligence, we should prob-ably read in the Herald the most glowing eulogiums of his career and character.

What are we to think of a man who is at once so able and so false? It would be incorrect to call him a liar, because he is wanting in that sense of truth by violating which a man makes himself a liar. We cannot call him a traitor, for his heart knows no country; nor an infidel, for all the serious and high concerns of man are to him a jest. *Defective* is the word to apply to such as he. As far as he goes, he is good; and if the commodity in which he deals were cotton or sugar, we could commend his en-terprise and tact. He is like the steeple of a church in New York, which was built up to a certain height, when the material gave out, and it was hastily roofed in, leaving the *upper half* of the architect's design unexecuted. That region of the mind where conviction, the sense of truth and honor, public spirit and patriot-ism have their sphere, is in this man mere vacancy. But, we re-peat, as far as he *is* built up, he is very well constructed. Visit him: you see before you a quiet-mannered, courteous, and good-natured old gentleman, who is on excellent terms with himself and with the world. If you are a poor musician, about to give a concert, no editor is more likely than he to lend a favorable ear to your request for a few lines of preliminary notice. The per

sons about him have been very long in his employment, and to
some of them he has been munificently liberal. The best of them
appear to be really attached to his person, as well as devoted to
his service, and they rely on him as sailors rely on a captain who
has brought them safe through a thousand storms. He has the
Celtic virtue of standing by those who stand by him developed to
the uttermost degree. Many a slight favor bestowed upon him
in his days of obscurity he has recompensed a thousand-fold since
he has had the power to do so. We cannot assign a very exalted
rank in the moral scale to a trait which some of the lowest races
possess in an eminent degree, and which easily runs into narrowness and vice ; nevertheless, it is akin to nobleness, and is the
nearest approach to a true generosity that some strong natures
can attain.

What are we to say of the public that has so resolutely sustained this paper, which the outside world so generally condemns?
We say this. Every periodical that thrives supplies the public
with a certain description of intellectual commodity, which the
public is willing to pay for. The New York Ledger, for example, exists by furnishing stories and poetry adapted to the taste of
the greatest number of the people. Our spirited friends of The
Nation and Round Table supply criticism and that portion of the
news which is of special interest to the intellectual class. The
specialty of the daily newspaper is to give that part of the news
of the day which interests the whole public. A complete newspaper contains more than this ; but it ranks in the world of journalism exactly in the degree to which it does *this*. The grand
object of the true journalist is to be fullest, promptest, and most
correct on the one uppermost topic of the hour. That secured,
he may neglect all else. The paper that does this oftenest is the
paper that will find most purchasers ; and no general excellence,
no array of information on minor or special topics, will ever atone
for a deficiency on the subject of most immediate and universal
interest. During the war this fundamental truth of journalism
was apparent to every mind. In time of peace, it is less apparent, but not less a truth. In the absence of an absorbing topic,
general news rises in importance, until, in the dearth of the dog

days, the great cucumber gets into type; but the great point of competition is still the same, — to be fullest, quickest, and most correct upon the subject *most* interesting at the moment.

But every periodical, besides its specialty on which it lives, gives its readers something more. It need not, but it does. The universal Ledger favors its readers with many very excellent essays, written for it by distinguished clergymen, editors, and authors, and gives its readers a great deal of sound advice in other departments of the paper. It need not do this; these features do not materially affect the sale of the paper, as its proprietor well knows. The essays of such men as Mr. Everett and Mr. Bancroft do not increase the sale of the paper one hundred copies a week. Those essays are read and admired, and contribute their quota toward the education of the people, and reflect honor upon the liberal and enterprising man who publishes them; but scarcely any one buys the paper for their sake. People almost universally buy a periodical for the special thing which it has undertaken to furnish; and it is by supplying this special thing that an editor attains his glorious privilege and opportunity of addressing a portion of the people on other topics. This opportunity he may neglect; he may abuse it to the basest purposes, or improve it to the noblest, but whichever of these things he does, it does not materially affect the prosperity of his paper, — always supposing that his specialty is kept up with the requisite vigor. We have gone over the whole history of journalism, and we find this to be its Law of Nature, to which there are only apparent exceptions.

All points to this simple conclusion, which we firmly believe to be the golden rule of journalism: — that daily newspaper which has the best corps of reporters, and handles them best, *necessarily* takes the lead of all competitors.

There are journalists who say (we have often heard them in conversation) that this is a low view to take of their vocation. It is of no importance whether a view is high or low, provided it is correct. But we cannot agree with them that this is a low view. We think it the highest possible. Regarded as instructors of the people, they wield for our warning and rebuke, for our encouragement and reward, an instrument which is like the dread thunderbolt of Jove, at once the most terrible and the most beneficent, — *publicity.* Some years ago, a number of ill-favored and prurient women and a number of licentious men formed themselves into a kind of society for the purpose of devising and promulgating a theory to justify the gratification of unbridled lust. They were called Free-Lovers. To have assailed their nightly gatherings in thundering editorial articles would have only advertised them; but a detailed *report* of their proceedings in the Tribune scattered these assemblies in a few days, to meet no more except in secret haunts. Recently, we have seen the Fenian wind-bag first inflated, then burst, by mere publicity. The Strong Divorce Case, last year, was a nauseous dose, which we would have gladly kept out of the papers; but since it had to appear, it was a public benefit to have it given, Herald-fashion, with all its revolting particulars. What a punishment to the guilty! what a lesson to the innocent! what a warning to the un-detected! How much beneficial reflection and conversation it ex-cited! How necessary, in an age of sensation morals and free-love theories, to have self-indulgence occasionally exhibited in all its hideous nastiness, and without any of its fleeting, deceptive, imaginary charms! The instantaneous detection of the Otero murderers last autumn, and of the robbers of Adams's express-car last winter, as related in the daily papers, and the picture presented by them of young Ketchum seated at work in the shoe-shop of Sing-Sing Prison, were equivalent to the addition of a thousand men to the police force. Herein lies the power of such a slight person as the editor of the Herald. It is not merely that he impudently pulls your nose, but he pulls it in the view of a million people.

Nor less potent is publicity as a means of reward. How many brave hearts during the late war felt themselves far more than repaid for all their hardships in the field and their agony in the hospital by reading their names in despatches, or merely in the list of wounded, and thinking of the breakfast-tables far away at which that name had been spied out and read with mingled ex-ultation and pity. "Those who love me know that I did my duty, — it is enough."

Our whole observation of the daily press convinces us that its power to do good arises chiefly from its giving the news of the day ; and its power to do harm chiefly from its opportunity to comment upon the news. Viewed only as a vehicle of intelligence, the Herald has taught the journalists of the United States the greater part of all that they yet know of their profession ; regarded as an organ of opinion, it has done all that it was ever possible for a newspaper to do in perverting public opinion, debauching public taste, offending public morals, and dishonoring the national character.

The question arises, Why has not this paper been long ago outdone in giving the news? It has always been possible to suppress it by surpassing it. Its errors have given its rivals an immense advantage over it; for it has always prospered, not in consequence of its badness, but of its goodness. We are acquainted with two foolish young patriots who were wrought up to such a frenzy of disgust by its traitorous course during the first half of our late war, that they seriously considered whether there was any way in which they could so well serve their country in its time of need, as by slaying that pernicious and insolent editor ; but both of those amiable lunatics were compelled occasionally to buy the paper. Of late, too, we have seen vast audiences break forth into wild hootings at the mention of its name ; but not the less did the hooters buy it the next morning. Nevertheless, as soon as there exists a paper which to the Herald's good points adds the other features of a complete newspaper, and avoids its faults, from that hour the Herald wanes and falls speedily to the second rank.

Two men have had it in their power to produce such a newspaper, — Horace Greeley and Henry J. Raymond. In 1841, when the Herald was six years old, the Tribune appeared, edited by Mr. Greeley, with Mr. Raymond as his chief assistant. Mr. Greeley was then, and is now, the best writer of editorials in the United States; that is, he can produce a greater quantity of telling editorial per annum than any other individual. There never lived a man capable of working more hours in a year than he. Strictly temperate in his habits, and absolutely devoted to his work, he threw himself into this enterprise with an ardor never surpassed since Adam first tasted the sweets of honorable toil. Mr. Raymond, then recently from college, very young, wholly inexperienced, was endowed with an admirable aptitude for the work of journalism, and a power of getting through its routine labors, — a sustained, calm, swift industry, — unsurpassed at that time in the American press. The business of the paper was also well managed by Mr. McElrath. In the hands of these able men, the new paper made such rapid advances, that, in the course of a few months, it was fairly established, and in a year or two it had reached a circulation equal to that of the Herald. One after another, excellent writers were added to its corps ; — the vigorous, prompt, untiring Dana ; George Ripley, possessing that blend ing of scholarship and tact, that wisdom of the cloister and knowledge of the world, which alone could fit a man of great learning and talent for the work of a daily newspaper ; Margaret Fuller, whose memory is still green in so many hearts ; Bayard Taylor, the versatile, and others, less universally known.

Why, then, did not this powerful combination supplant the Herald ? If mere ability in the writing of a newspaper ; if to have given an impulse to thought and enterprise ; if to have won the admiration and gratitude of a host of the best men and wom en in America ; if to have inspired many thousands of young men with better feelings and higher purposes than they would else have attained ; if to have shaken the dominion of superstition, and made it easier for men to think freely, and freely utter their thought ; if to have produced a newspaper more interesting than any other in the world to certain classes in the community ; — if all these things had sufficed to give a daily paper the first position in the journalism of a country, then the Tribune would long ago have attained that position ; for all these things, and many more, the Tribune did. But they do not suffice. Such things may be incidental to a great success : they cannot cause it Great journalism — journalism pure and simple — alone can give a journal the first place. If Mr. Raymond had been ten years older, and had founded and conducted the paper, with Mr. Greeley as his chief writer of editorials, — that is, if the *journalist* had been the master of the journal, instead of the writer, the politician, and the philanthropist, — the Tribune might have won the splendid prize. Mr. Greeley is not a great journalist. He has regarded journalism rather as a disagreeable necessity of his vocation, and uniformly abandoned the care of it to others. An able man generally gets what he ardently seeks. Mr. Greeley produced just such a paper as he himself would have liked to take, but not such a paper as the public of the island of Manhattan prefers. He regards this as his glory. We cannot agree with him, because his course of management left the field to the Herald, the suppression of which was required by the interests of civilization.

The Tribune has done great and glorious things for us. Not free, of course, from the errors which mark all things human, it has been, and is, a civilizing power in this land. We hope to have the pleasure of reading it every day for the rest of our lives. One thing it has failed to do, — to reduce the Herald to insignificance by surpassing it in the particulars in which it is excellent. We have no right to complain. We only regret that the paper representing the civilization of the country should not yet have attained the position which would have given it the greatest power.

Mr. Raymond, also, has had it in his power to render this great service to the civilization and credit of the United States. The Daily Times, started in 1852, retarded for a while by a financial error, has made such progress toward the goal of its proprietors' ambition, that it is now on the home stretch, only a length or two behind. The editor of this paper is a journalist; he sees clearly the point of competition; he knows the great secret of his trade. The prize within his reach is splendid. The position of chief journalist gives power enough to satisfy any reasonable ambition wealth enough to glut the grossest avarice, and opportunity of doing good sufficient for the most public-spirited citizen. What is there in political life equal to it? We have no right to remark upon any man's choice of a career ; but this we may say, — that the man who wins the first place in the journalism of a free country must concentrate all his powers upon that one work, and

13 *

as an editor, owe no allegiance to party. He must stand above all parties, and serve all parties, by spreading before the public that full and exact information upon which sound legislation is based.

During the present (1865–6) session of Congress we have had daily illustration of this truth. The great question has been, What is the condition of the Southern States and the feeling of the Southern people? All the New York morning papers have expended money and labor, each according to its means and enterprise, in getting information from the South. This was well. But every one of these papers has had some party or personal bias, which has given it a powerful interest to make out a case. The World and News excluded everything which tended to show the South dissatisfied and disloyal. The Tribune, on the other hand, diligently sought testimony of that nature. The Times, also, being fully committed to a certain theory of reconstruction, naturally gave prominence to every fact which supported that theory, and was inclined to suppress information of the opposite tendency. The consequence was, that an inhabitant of the city of New York who simply desired to know the truth was compelled to keep an eye upon four or five papers, lest something material should escape him. This is pitiful. This is utterly beneath the journalism of 1866. The final pre-eminent newspaper of America will soar far above such needless limitations as these, and present the truth in *all* its aspects, regardless of its effects upon theories, parties, factions, and Presidential campaigns.

Presidential campaigns, — that is the real secret. The editors of most of these papers have selected their candidate for 1868; and, having done that, can no more help conducting their journals with a view to the success of that candidate, than the needle of a compass can help pointing awry when there is a magnet hidden in the binnacle. Here, again, we have no right to censure or complain. Yet we cannot help marvelling at the hallucination which can induce able men to prefer the brief and illusory honors of political station to the substantial and lasting power within the grasp of the successful journalist. He, if any one, — he more than any one else, — is the master in a free country. Have we not seen almost every man who has held or run for the Presidency during the last ten or fifteen years paying assiduous and servile court, directly or indirectly, or both, to the editor of the Herald? If it were proper to relate to the public what is known on this subject to a few individuals, the public would be exceedingly astonished. And yet this reality of power an editor is ready to jeopard for the sake of gratifying his family by exposing them in Paris! Jeopard, do we say? He has done more: he has thrown it away. He has a magnet in his binnacle. He has, for the time, sacrificed what it cost him thirty years of labor and audacity to gain. Strange weakness of human nature!

The daily press of the United States has prodigiously improved in every respect during the last twenty years. To the best of our recollection, the description given of it, twenty-three years ago, by Charles Dickens, in his American Notes, was not much exaggerated; although that great author did exaggerate its effects upon the morals of the country. His own amusing account of the rival editors in Pickwick might have instructed him on this latter point. It does not appear that the people of Eatanswill were seriously injured by the fierce language employed in "that false and scurrilous print, the Independent," and in "that vile and slanderous calumniator, the Gazette." Mr. Dickens, however, was too little conversant with our politics to take the atrocious language formerly so common in our newspapers "in a Pickwickian sense"; and we freely confess that in the alarming picture which he drew of our press there was only too much truth.

"The foul growth of America," wrote Mr. Dickens, "strikes its fibres deep in its licentious press.

"Schools may be erected, east, west, north, and south; pupils be taught, and masters reared, by scores upon scores of thousands; colleges may thrive, churches may be crammed, temperance may be diffused, and advancing knowledge in all other forms walk through the land with giant strides; but while the newspaper press of America is in or near its present abject state, high moral improvement in that country is hopeless. Year by year it must and will go back; year by year the tone of public feeling must sink lower down; year by year the Congress and the Senate must become of less account before all decent men ; and, year by year, the memory of the great fathers of the Revolution must be outraged more and more in the bad life of their degenerate child.

" Among the herd of journals which are published in the States, there are some, the reader scarcely need be told, of character and credit. From personal intercourse with accomplished gentlemen connected with publications of this class I have derived both pleasure and profit. But the name of these is Few, and of the others Legion ; and the influence of the good is powerless to counteract the mortal poison of the bad.

" Among the gentry of America, among the well-informed and moderate, in the learned professions, at the bar and on the bench, there is, as there can be, but one opinion in reference to the vicious character of these infamous journals. It is sometimes contended — I will not say strangely, for it is natural to seek excuses for such a disgrace — that their influence is not so great as a visitor would suppose. I must be pardoned for saying that there is no warrant for this plea, and that every fact and circumstance tends directly to the opposite conclusion.

" When any man, of any grade of desert in intellect or character, can climb to any public distinction, no matter what, in America, without first grovelling down upon the earth, and bending the knee before this monster of depravity ; when any private excellence is safe from its attacks, and when any social confidence is left unbroken by it, or any tie of social decency and honor is held in the least regard ; when any man in that free country has freedom of opinion, and presumes to think for himself, and speak for himself, without humble reference to a censorship which, for its rampant ignorance and base dishonesty, he utterly loathes and despises in his heart; when those who most acutely feel its infamy and the reproach it casts upon the nation, and who most denounce it to each other, dare to set their heels upon and crush it openly, in the sight of all men, — then I will believe that its influence is lessening, and men are returning to their manly senses. But while that Press has its evil eye in every house, and its black hand in every appointment in the state, from a President to a postman, — while, with ribald slander for its only stock in trade, it is the standard literature of an enormous class, who must find their reading in a newspaper, or they will not read at all, — so long must its odium be upon the country's head, and so long must the evil it works be plainly visible in the Republic.

" To those who are accustomed to the leading English journals, or to the respecta.ie journals of the Continent of Europe, to those who are accustomed to anything else in print and paper, it would be impossible, without an amount of extract for which I have neither space nor inclination, to convey an adequate idea of this frightful engine in America. But if any man desire confirmation of my statement on this head, let him repair to any place in this city of London where scattered numbers of these publications are to be found, and there let him form his own opinion."

From a note appended to this passage, we infer that the newspaper which weighed upon the author's mind when he wrote it was the New York Herald. The direct cause, however, of the general license of the press at that time, was not the Herald's bad example, but Andrew Jackson's debauching influence. The same man who found the government pure, and left it corrupt, made the press the organ of his own malignant passions by bestowing high office upon the editors who lied most recklessly about his opponents. In 1843 the press had scarcely begun to recover from this hateful influence, and was still the merest tool of politicians. The Herald, in fact, by demonstrating that a newspaper can flourish in the United States without any aid from politicians, has brought us nearer the time when no newspaper of any importance will be subject to party, which has been the principal cause of the indecencies of the press.

The future is bright before the journalists of America. The close of the war, by increasing their income and reducing their expenses, has renewed the youth of several of our leading journals, and given them a better opportunity than they have ever had before. The great error of the publishers of profitable journals hitherto has been the wretched compensation paid to writers and reporters. To this hour there is but one individual connected with the daily press of New York, not a proprietor, who receives a salary sufficient to keep a tolerable house and bring up a family respectably and comfortably; and if any one would find that individual, he must look for him, alas! in the office of the Herald. To be plainer: decent average housekeeping in the city of New York now costs a hundred dollars a week; and there is but one salary of that amount paid in New York to a journalist who owns no property in his journal. The consequence is, that there is scarcely an individual connected with a daily paper who is not compelled or tempted to eke out his ridiculous salary by other writing, to the injury of his health and the constant deterioration of his work. Every morning the public comes fresh and eager to the newspaper : fresh and eager minds should alone minister to it. No work done on this earth consumes vitality so fast as carefully executed composition, and consequently one of the main conditions of a man's writing his best is that he should write little and rest often. A good writer, moreover, is one of Nature's peculiar and very rare products. There is a mystery about the art of composition. Who shall explain to us why Charles Dickens can write about a three-legged stool in such a manner that the whole civilized world reads with pleasure ; while another man of a hundred times his knowledge and five times his quantity of mind cannot write on any subject so as to interest anybody ? The laws of supply and demand do not apply to this rarity ; for one man's writing cannot be compared with another's, there being no medium between valuable and worthless. How many overworked, under-paid men have we known in New York, really gifted with this inexplicable knack at writing, who, well commanded and justly compensated, lifted high and dry out of the slough of poor-devilism in which their powers were obscured and impaired, could almost have made the fortune of a newspaper ! Some of these Reporters of Genius are mere children in all the arts by which men prosper. A Journalist of Genius would know their value, understand their case, take care of their interest, secure their devotion, restrain their ardor, and turn their talent to rich account. We are ashamed to say, that for example of this kind of policy we should have to repair to the office named a moment since.

This subject, however, is beginning to be understood, and of late there has been some advance in the salaries of members of the press. Just as fast as the daily press advances in real independence and efficiency, the compensation of journalists will increase, until a great reporter will receive a reward in some slight degree proportioned to the rarity of the species and to the great ness of the services of which he is the medium. By reporters, we mean, of course, the entire corps of news-givers, from the youth who relates the burning of a stable, to the philosopher who chronicles the last vagary of a German metaphysician. These laborious men will be appreciated in due time. By them all the great hits of journalism have been made, and the whole future of journalism is theirs.

So difficult is the reporter's art, that we can call to mind only two series of triumphant efforts in this department, — Mr. Russell's letters from the Crimea to the London Times, and N. P. Willis's " Pencillings by the Way," addressed to the New York Mirror. Each of these masters chanced to have a subject perfectly adapted to his taste and talents, and each of them made the most of his opportunity. Charles Dickens has produced a few exquisite reports. Many ignorant and dull men employed on the New York Herald have written good reports *because* they were dull and ignorant. In fact, there are two kinds of good reporters, — those who know too little, and those who know too much, to wander from the point and evolve a report from the depths of their own consciousness. The worst possidle reporter is one who has a little talent, and depends upon that to make up for the meagreness of his information. The best reporter is he whose sole object is to relate his event exactly as it occurred, and describe his scene just as it appeared ; and this kind of excellence is attainable by an honest plodder, and by a man of great and well-controlled talent. If we were forming a corps of twenty-five reporters, we should desire to have five of them men of great and highly trained ability, and the rest indefatigable, unimaginative, exact short-hand chroniclers, caring for nothing but to get their fact and relate it in the plainest English.

There is one custom, a relic of the past, still in vogue in the offices of daily papers, which is of an absurdity truly exquisite. It is the practice of paying by the column, or, in other words, paying a premium for verbosity, and imposing a fine upon conciseness. It will often happen that information which cost three days to procure can be well related in a paragraph, and which, if related in a paragraph, would be of very great value to the newspaper printing it. But if the reporter should compress his facts into that space, he would receive for his three days' labor about what he expended in omnibus fare. Like a wise man, therefore, he spreads them out into three columns, and thus receives a compensation upon which life can be supported. If matter must be paid for by the column, we would respectfully suggest the following rates: For half a column, or less, twenty dollars; for one column, ten dollars; for two columns, five dollars; for three columns, nothing; for any amount beyond three columns, no insertion.

To conclude with a brief recapitulation: —

The commodity in which the publishers of daily newspapers deal is news, i. e. information respecting recent events in which the public take an interest, or in which an interest can be excited.

Newspapers, therefore, rank according to their excellence as *newspapers;* and no other kind of excellence can make up for any deficiency in the one thing for which they exist.

Consequently, the art of editorship consists in forming, handling, and inspiring a corps of reporters; for inevitably that newspaper becomes the chief and favorite journal which has the best corps of reporters, and uses them best.

Editorial articles have their importance. They can be a powerful means of advancing the civilization of a country, and of hastening the triumph of good measures and good men; and upon the use an editor makes of his opportunity of addressing the public in this way depends his title to our esteem as a man and fellow-citizen. But, in a mere business point of view, they are of inferior importance. The best editorials cannot make, nor the worst editorials mar, the fortune of a paper. Burke and Macaulay would not add a tenth part as many subscribers to a daily paper as the addition to its corps of two well-trained, ably-commanded reporters.

It is not law which ever renders the press free and independent. Nothing is free or independent in this world which is not power ful. Therefore, the editor who would conquer the opportunity of speaking his mind freely, must do it by making his paper so excellent as a vehicle of news that the public will buy it though it is a daily disgust to them.

The Herald has thriven beyond all its competitors, because its proprietor comprehended these simple but fundamental truths of his vocation, and, upon the whole, has surpassed his rivals both in the getting and in the display of intelligence. We must pronounce him the best journalist and the worst editorialist this continent has ever known; and accordingly his paper is generally read and its proprietor universally disapproved.

And finally, this bad, good paper cannot be reduced to secondary rank except by being outdone in pure journalism. The interests of civilization and the honor of the United States require that this should be done. There are three papers now existing — the Times, the Tribune, and the World — which ought to do it; but if the conductors of neither of these able and spirited papers choose to devote themselves absolutely to this task, then we trust that soon another competitor may enter the field, conducted by a journalist proud enough of his profession to be satisfied with its honors. There were days last winter on which it eemed as if the whole force of journalism in the city of New York was expended in tingeing and perverting intelligence on the greatest of all the topics of the time. We have read numbers of the World (which has talent and youthful energy enough for a splendid career) of which almost the entire contents — correspondence, telegrams, and editorials — were spoiled for all useful purposes by the determination of the whole corps of writers to make the news tell in favor of a political party. We can truly aver, that journalism, pure and simple, — journalism for its own sake, — journalism, the dispassionate and single-eyed servant of the whole public, — does not exist in New York during a session of Congress. It ought to exist.

CHARLES GOODYEAR.

CHARLES GOODYEAR.

THE copy before us, of Mr. Goodyear's work upon "Gum-Elastic and its Varieties," presents at least something unique in the art of book-making. It is self-illustrating; inasmuch as, treating of India-rubber, it is made of India-rubber. An unobservant reader, however, would scarcely suspect the fact before reading the Preface, for the India-rubber covers resemble highly polished ebony, and the leaves have the appearance of ancient paper worn soft, thin, and dingy by numberless perusals. The volume contains six hundred and twenty pages; but it is not as thick as copies of the same work printed on paper, though it is a little heavier. It is evident that the substance of which this book is composed cannot be India-rubber in its natural state. Those leaves, thinner than paper, can be stretched only by a strong pull, and resume their shape perfectly when they are let go. There is no smell of India-rubber about them. We first saw this book in a cold room in January, but the leaves were then as flexible as old paper; and when, since, we have handled it in warm weather, they had grown no softer.

Some of our readers may have heard Daniel Webster relate the story of the India-rubber cloak and hat which one of his New York friends sent him at Marshfield in the infancy of the manufacture. He took the cloak to the piazza one cold morning, when it instantly became as rigid as sheet-iron. Finding that it stood alone, he placed the hat upon it, and left the articles standing near the front door. Several of his neighbors who passed, seeing a dark and portly figure there, took it for the lord of the mansion, and gave it respectful salutation. The same articles were liable to an objection still more serious. In the sun, even in cool weather, they became sticky, while on a hot day they would melt entirely away to the consistency of molasses. Every one remembers the thick and ill-shaped India-rubber shoes of twenty years ago, which had to be thawed out under the stove before they could be put on, and which, if left under the stove too long, would dissolve into gum that no household art could ever harden again. Some decorous gentlemen among us can also remember that, in the nocturnal combats of their college days, a flinty India rubber shoe, in cold weather, was a missive weapon of a highly effective character.

This curious volume, therefore, cannot be made of the unmanageable stuff which Daniel Webster set up at his front door. So much is evident at a glance. But the book itself tells us that it can be subjected, without injury, to tests more severe than summer's sun and winter's cold. It can be soaked six months in a pail of water, and still be as good a book as ever. It can be boiled; it can be baked in an oven hot enough to cook a turkey; it can be soaked in brine, lye, camphene, turpentine, or oil; it can be dipped into oil of vitriol, and still no harm done. To crown its merits, no rat, mouse, worm, or moth has ever shown the slightest inclination to make acquaintance with it. The office of a Review is not usually provided with the means of subjecting literature to such critical tests as lye, vitriol, boilers, and hot ovens. But we have seen enough elsewhere of the ordeals to which India-rubber is now subjected to believe Mr. Goodyear's statements. Remote posterity will enjoy the fruit of his labors, unless some one takes particular pains to destroy this book; for it seems that time itself produces no effect upon the India-rubber which bears the familiar stamp, "GOODYEAR'S PATENT." In the dampest corner of the dampest cellar, no mould gathers upon it, no decay penetrates it. In the hottest garret, it never warps or cracks.

The principal object of the work is to relate how this remarkable change was effected in the nature of the substance of which it treats. It cost more than two millions of dollars to do it. I' cost Charles Goodyear eleven most laborious and painful years. His book is written without art or skill, but also without guile

He was evidently a laborious, conscientious, modest man, neither learned nor highly gifted, but making no pretence to learning or gifts, doing the work which fell to him with all his might, and with a perseverance never surpassed in all the history of invention and discovery. Who would have thought to find a romance in the history of India-rubber? We are familiar with the stories of poor and friendless men, possessed with an idea and pursuing their object, amid obloquy, neglect, and suffering, to the final triumph; of which final triumph other men reaped the substantial reward, leaving to the discoverer the barren glory of his achievement, — and that glory obscured by detraction. Columbus is the representative man of that illustrious order. We trust to be able to show that Charles Goodyear is entitled to a place in it. Whether we consider the prodigious and unforeseen importance of his discovery, or his scarcely paralleled devotion to his object, in the face of the most disheartening obstacles, we feel it to be due to his memory, to his descendants, and to the public, that his story should be told. Few persons will ever see his book, of which only a small number of copies were printed for private circulation. Still fewer will be at the pains to pick out the material facts from the confused mass of matter in which they are hidden. Happily for our purpose, no one now has an interest to call his merits in question. He rests from his labors, and the patent, which was the glory and misery of his life, has expired.

Our great-grandfathers knew India-rubber only as a curiosity, and our grandfathers only as a means of erasing pencil-marks. The first specimens were brought to Europe in 1730; and as late as 1770 it was still so scarce an article, that in London it was only to be found in one shop, where a piece containing half a cubic inch was sold for three shillings. Dr. Priestley, in his work on perspective, published in 1770, speaks of it as a new article, and recommends its use to draughtsmen. This substance, however, being one of those of which nature has provided an inexhaustible supply, greater quantities found their way into the commerce of the world; until, in 1820, it was a drug in all markets, and was frequently brought as ballast merely. About this time 't began to be subjected to experiments with a view to rendering it available in the arts. It was found useful as an ingredient of blacking and varnish. Its elasticity was turned to account in France in the manufacture of suspenders and garters, — threads of India-rubber being inserted in the web. In England, Mackintosh invented his still celebrated water-proof coats, which are made of two thin cloths with a paste of India-rubber between them. In chemistry, the substance was used to some extent, and its singular properties were much considered. In England and France, the India-rubber manufacture had attained considerable importance before the material had attracted the attention of American experimenters. The Europeans succeeded in rendering it useful because they did not attempt too much. The French cut the imported sheets of gum into shreds, without ever attempting to produce the sheets themselves. Mackintosh exposed no surface of India-rubber to the air, and brought no surfaces of India-rubber into contact. No one had discovered any process by which India-rubber once dissolved could be restored to its original consistency. Some of our readers may have attempted, twenty years ago, to fill up the holes in the sole of an India-rubber shoe. Nothing was easier than to melt a piece of India-rubber for the purpose ; but, when applied to the shoe, it would not harden. There was the grand difficulty, the complete removal of which cost so much money and so many years.

The ruinous failure of the first American manufacturers arose from the fact that they began their costly operations in ignorance of the existence of this difficulty. They were too fast. They proceeded in the manner of the inventor of the caloric engine, who began by placing one in a ship of great magnitude, involving an expenditure which ruined the owners.

It was in the year 1820 that a pair of India-rubber shoes was seen for the first time in the United States. They were covered with gilding, and resembled in shape the shoes of a Chinaman. They were handed about in Boston only as a curiosity. Two or three years after, a ship from South America brought to Boston five hundred pairs of shoes, thick, heavy, and ill shaped, which sold so readily as to invite further importations. The business increased until the annual importation reached half a million pairs, and India-rubber shoes had become an article of general use. The manner in which these shoes were made by the natives of South America was frequently described in the newspapers, and seemed to present no difficulty. They were made much as farmers' wives made candles. The sap being collected from the trees, clay lasts were dipped into the liquid twenty or thirty times, each layer being smoked a little. The shoes were then hung up to harden for a few days; after which the clay was removed, and the shoes were stored for some months to harden them still more. Nothing was more natural than to suppose that Yankees could do this as well as Indians, if not far better. The raw India-rubber could then be bought in Boston for five cents a pound, and a pair of shoes made of it brought from three to five dollars. Surely here was a promising basis for a new branch of manufacture in New England. It happened too, in 1830, that vast quantities of the raw gum reached the United States. It came covered with hides, in masses, of which no use could be made in America; and it remained unsold, or was sent to Europe.

Patent-leather suggested the first American attempt to turn India-rubber to account. Mr. E. M. Chaffee, foreman of a Boston patent-leather factory conceived the idea, in 1830, of spreading India-rubber upon cloth, hoping to produce an article which should possess the good qualities of patent-leather, with the additional one of being water-proof. In the deepest secrecy he experimented for several months. By dissolving a pound of India rubber in three quarts of spirits of turpentine, and adding lampblack enough to give it the desired color, he produced a composition which he supposed would perfectly answer the purpose. He invented a machine for spreading it, and made some specimens of cloth, which had every appearance of being a very useful article. The surface, after being dried in the sun, was firm and smooth; and Mr. Chaffee supposed, and his friends agreed with him, that he had made an invention of the utmost value. At this point he invited a few of the solid men of Roxbury to look at his specimens and listen to his statements. He convinced

14

them.   The result of the conference was the Roxbury India-rubber Company, incorporated in February, 1833, with a capital of thirty thousand dollars.

The progress of this Company was amazing.   Within a year its capital was increased to two hundred and forty thousand dollars. Before another year had expired, this was increased to three hundred thousand; and in the year following, to four hundred thousand. The Company manufactured the cloth invented by Mr. Chaffee, and many articles made of that cloth, such as coats, caps, wagon-curtains and coverings.   Shoes, made without fibre, were soon introduced.   Nothing could be better than the appearance of these articles when they were new.   They were in the highest favor, and were sold more rapidly than the Company could manufacture them.   The astonishing prosperity of the Roxbury Company had its natural effect in calling into existence similar establishments in other towns.   Manufactories were started at Boston, Framingham, Salem, Lynn, Chelsea, Troy, and Staten Island, with capitals ranging from one hundred thousand dollars to half a million; and all of them appeared to prosper.   There was an India-rubber mania in those years similar to that of petroleum in 1864. Not to invest in India-rubber stock was regarded by some shrewd men as indicative of inferior business talents and general dulness of comprehension.   The exterior facts were certainly well calculated to lure even the most wary.   Here was a material worth only a few cents a pound, out of which shoes were quickly made, which brought two dollars a pair!   It was a plain case.   Besides, there were the India-rubber Companies, all working to their extreme capacity, and selling all they could make.

It was when the business had reached this flourishing stage that Charles Goodyear, a bankrupt hardware merchant of Philadelphia, first had his attention directed to the material upon which it was founded.   In 1834, being in New York on business, he chanced to observe the sign of the Roxbury Company, which then had a depot in that city.   He had been reading in the newspapers, not long before, descriptions of the new life preservers made of India-rubber, an application of the gum that was much extolled.   Curiosity induced him to enter the store to examine

the life preservers. He bought one and took it home with him.
A native of Connecticut, he possessed in full measure the Yankee
propensity to look at a new contrivance, first with a view to understand its principle, and next to see if it cannot be improved.
Already he had had some experience both of the difficulty of introducing an improved implement, and of the profit to be derived
from its introduction. His father, the head of the firm of A.
Goodyear and Sons, of which he was a member, was the first to
manufacture hay-forks of spring steel, instead of the heavy,
wrought-iron forks made by the village blacksmith; and Charles
Goodyear could remember the time when his father reckoned it
a happy day on which he had persuaded a farmer to accept a few
of the new forks as a gift, on the condition of giving them a trial.
But it was also very fresh in his recollection that those same
forks had made their way to almost universal use, had yielded
large profits to his firm, and were still a leading article of its trade,
when, in 1830, the failure of Southern houses had compelled it to
suspend. He was aware, too, that, if anything could extricate
the house of A. Goodyear and Sons from embarrassment, it was
their possession of superior methods of manufacturing and their
sale of articles improved by their own ingenuity.

Upon examining his life-preserver, an improvement in the in-
flating apparatus occurred to him. When he was next in New
York he explained his improvement to the agent of the Roxbury
Company, and offered to sell it. The agent, struck with the ingenuity displayed in the new contrivance, took the inventor into
his confidence, partly by way of explaining why the Company
could not then buy the improved tube, but principally with a view
to enlist the aid of an ingenious mind in overcoming a difficulty
that threatened the Company with ruin. He told him that the
prosperity of the India-rubber Companies in the United States
was wholly fallacious. The Roxbury Company had manufactured vast quantities of shoes and fabrics in the cool months of
1833 and 1834, which had been readily sold at high prices; but
during the following summer, the greater part of them had
melted. Twenty thousand dollars' worth had been returned, reduced to the consistency of common gum, and emitting an odor

so offensive that they had been obliged to bury it. New ingredients had been employed, new machinery applied, but still the articles would dissolve. In some cases, shoes had borne the heat of one summer, and melted the next. The wagon-covers became sticky in the sun, and rigid in the cold. The directors were at their wits' end ; — since it required two years to test a new process, and meanwhile they knew not whether the articles made by it were valuable or worthless. If they stopped manufacturing, that was certain ruin. If they went on, they might find the product of a whole winter dissolving on their hands. The capital of the Company was already so far exhausted, that, unless the true method were speedily discovered, it would be compelled to wind up its affairs. The agent urged Mr. Goodyear not to waste time upon minor improvements, but to direct all his efforts to finding out the secret of successfully working the material itself. The Company could not buy his improved inflator ; but let him learn how to make an India-rubber that would stand the summer's heat, and there was scarcely any price which it would not gladly give for the secret.

The worst apprehensions of the directors of this Company were realized. The public soon became tired of buying India-rubber shoes that could only be saved during the summer by putting them into a refrigerator. In the third year of the mania, India-rubber stock began to decline, and Roxbury itself finally fell to two dollars and a half. Before the close of 1836, all the Companies had ceased to exist, their fall involving many hundreds of families in heavy loss. The clumsy, shapeless shoes from South America were the only ones which the people would buy. It was generally supposed that the secret of their resisting heat was that they were smoked with the leaves of a certain tree, peculiar to South America, and that nothing else in nature would answer the purpose.

The two millions of dollars lost by these Companies had one result which has proved to be worth many times that sum ; it led Charles Goodyear to undertake the investigation of India-rubber That chance conversation with the agent of the Roxbury Company fixed his destiny. If he were alive to read these lines, he

would, however, protest against the use of such a word as *chance*
in this connection. He really appears to have felt himself "called"
to study India-rubber. He says himself : —

" From the time that his attention was first given to the subject, a
strong and abiding impression was made upon his mind, that an object
so desirable and important, and so necessary to man's comfort, as the
making of gum-elastic available to his use, was most certainly placed
within his reach. Having this presentiment, of which he could not di-
vest himself under the most trying adversity, he was stimulated with
the hope of ultimately attaining this object.

" Beyond this he would refer the whole to the great Creator, who
directs the operations of mind to the development of the properties of
matter, in his own way, at the time when they are specially needed,
influencing some mind for every work or calling. . . . . Were he to
refrain from expressing his views thus briefly, he would ever feel that
he had done violence to his sentiments."

This is modestly said, but his friends assure us that he felt it
earnestly and habitually. It was, indeed, this steadfast conviction
of the possibility of attaining his object, and his religious devotion
to it, that constituted his capital in his new business. He had
little knowledge of chemistry, and an aversion to complicated cal-
culations. He was a ruined man ; for, after a long struggle with
misfortune, the firm of A. Goodyear and Sons had surrendered
their all to their creditors, and still owed thirty thousand dollars.
He had a family, and his health was not robust. Upon returning
home after conversing with the agent of the Roxbury Company,
he was arrested for debt, and compelled to reside within the prison
limits. He melted his first pound of India-rubber while he was
living within those limits, and struggling to keep out of the jail
itself. Thus he began his experiments in circumstances as little
favorable as can be imagined. There were only two things in
his favor. One was his conviction that India-rubber *could* be
subjugated, and that he was the man destined to subjugate it.
The other was, that, India-rubber having fallen to its old price,
he could continue his labors as long as he could raise five cents
and procure access to a fire. The very odium in which business-
men held India-rubber, though it long retarded his final triumph,
placed an abundance of the native gum within the means even of

an inmate of the debtor's prison, in which he often was during the whole period of his experimenting. He was seldom out of jail a whole year from 1835 to 1841, and never out of danger of arrest.

In a small house in Philadelphia, in the winter of 1834 – 35 he began his investigations. He melted his gum by the domestic fire, kneaded it with his own hands, spread it upon a marble slab, and rolled it with a rolling-pin. A prospect of success flattered him from the first and lured him on. He was soon able to produce sheets of India-rubber which appeared as firm as those imported, and which tempted a friend to advance him a sum of money sufficient to enable him to manufacture several hundred pairs of shoes. He succeeded in embossing his shoes in various patterns, which gave them a novel and elegant appearance. Mindful, however, of the disasters of the Roxbury Company, he had the prudence to store his shoes until the summer. The hot days of June reduced them all to soft and stinking paste. His friend was discouraged, and refused him further aid. For his own part, such experiences as this, though they dashed his spirits for a while, stimulated him to new efforts.

It now occurred to him, that perhaps it was the turpentine used in dissolving the gum, or the lampblack employed to color it, that spoiled his product. He esteemed it a rare piece of luck to procure some barrels of the sap not smoked, and still liquid. On going to the shed where the precious sap was deposited, he was accosted by an Irishman in his employ, who, in high glee, informed him that he had discovered the secret, pointing to his overalls, which he had dipped into the sap, and which were nicely coated with firm India-rubber. For a moment he thought that Jerry might have blundered into the secret. The man, however, sat down on a barrel near the fire, and, on attempting to rise found himself glued to his seat and his legs stuck together. He had to be cut out of his overalls. The master proceeded to experiment with the sap, but soon discovered that the handsome white cloth made of it bore the heat no better than that which was produced in the usual manner.

It is remarkable, that inventors seldom derive direct aid from

the science of their day. James Watt modestly ascribes to
Professor Black part of the glory of his improvements in the
steam-engine ; but it seems plain from his own narrative, that
he made his great invention of the condenser without any assistance. Professor Black assisted to instruct and form him ; but
the flash of genius, which made the steam-engine what we now
see it, was wholly his own. The science of Glasgow was diligently questioned by him upon the defects of the old engine, but
it gave him no hint of the remedy. It was James Watt, mathe-
matical-instrument maker, earning fourteen shillings a week, who
brooded over his little model until the conception of the condenser
burst upon him, as he was taking his Sunday afternoon stroll on
Glasgow Green. Goodyear had a similar experience. Philadelphia has always been noted for its chemists and its chemical
works, and that city still supplies the greater part of the country
with manufactured drugs and chemists' materials. Nevertheless,
though Goodyear explained his difficulties to professors, physicians, and chemists, none of them could give him valuable information ; none suggested an experiment that produced a useful
result. We know not, indeed, whether science has ever explained
his final success.

Satisfied that nothing could be done with India-rubber pure
and simple, he concluded that a compound of some substance
with India-rubber could alone render the gum available. He
was correct in this conjecture, but it remained to be discovered
whether there was such a substance in nature. He tried everything he could think of. For a short time he was elated with
the result of his experiments with magnesia, mixing half a pound
of magnesia with a pound of gum. This compound had the
advantage of being whiter than the pure sap. It was so firm
that he used it as leather in the binding of a book. In a few
weeks, however, he had the mortification of seeing his elegant
white book-covers fermenting and softening. Afterwards, they
grew as hard and brittle as shell, and so they remain to this day.

By this time, the patience of his friends and his own little fund
of money were both exhausted ; and, one by one, the relics of
his former prosperity, even to his wife's trinkets, found their way

to the pawnbroker. He was a sanguine man, as inventors need to be, always feeling that he was on the point of succeeding. The very confidence with which he announced a new conception served at length to close all ears to his solicitations. In the second year of his investigation he removed his family to the country, and went to New York, in quest of some one who had still a little faith in India-rubber. His credit was then at so low an ebb that he was obliged to deposit with the landlord a quantity of linen, spun by his excellent wife. It was never redeemed. It was sold at auction to pay the first quarter's rent; and his furniture also would have been seized, but that he had taken the precaution to sell it himself in Philadelphia, and had placed in his cottage articles of too little value to tempt the hardest creditor.

In New York, — the first resort of the enterprising and the last refuge of the unfortunate, — he found two old friends; one of whom lent him a room in Gold Street for a laboratory, and the other, a druggist, supplied him with materials on credit. Again his hopes were flattered by an apparent success. By boiling his compound of gum and magnesia in quicklime and water, an article was produced which seemed to be all that he could desire. Some sheets of India-rubber made by this process drew a medal at the fair of the American Institute in 1835, and were much commended in the newspapers. Nothing could exceed the smoothness and firmness of the surface of these sheets; nor have they to this day been surpassed in these particulars. He obtained a patent for the process, manufactured a considerable quantity, sold his product readily, and thought his difficulties were at an end. In a few weeks his hopes were dashed to the ground. He found that a drop of weak acid, such as apple-juice or vinegar and water, instantly annihilated the effect of the lime, and made the beautiful surface of his cloth sticky.

Undaunted, he next tried the experiment of mixing quicklime with pure gum. He tells us that, at this time, he used to prepare a gallon jug of quicklime at his room in Gold Street, and carry it on his shoulder to Greenwich Village, distant three miles, where he had access to horse-power for working his compound. This experiment, too, was a failure. The lime in a short time appeared to consume the gum with which it was mixed, leaving a substance that crumbled to pieces.

Accident suggested his next process, which, though he knew it not, was a step toward his final success. Except his almost unparalleled perseverance, the most marked trait in the character of this singular man was his love for beautiful forms and colors. An incongruous garment or decoration upon a member of his family, or anything tawdry or ill-arranged in a room, gave him positive distress. Accordingly, we always find him endeavoring to decorate his India-rubber fabrics. It was in bronzing the surface of some India-rubber drapery that the accident happened to which we have referred. Desiring to remove the bronze from a piece of the drapery, he applied aquafortis for the purpose, which did indeed have the effect desired, but it also discolored the fabric and appeared to spoil it. He threw away the piece as useless. Several days after, it occurred to him that he had not sufficiently examined the effect of the aquafortis, and, hurrying to his room, he was fortunate enough to find it again. A remarkable change appeared to have been made in the India-rubber. He does not seem to have been aware that aquafortis is two fifths sulphuric acid. Still less did he ever suspect that the surface of his drapery had really been "vulcanized." All he knew was, that India-rubber cloth "cured," as he termed it, by aquafortis, was incomparably superior to any previously made, and bore a degree of heat that rendered it available for many valuable purposes.

He was again a happy man. A partner, with ample capital, joined him. He went to Washington and patented his process. He showed his specimens to President Jackson, who expressed in writing his approval of them. Returning to New York, he prepared to manufacture on a great scale, hired the abandoned India-rubber works on Staten Island, and engaged a store in Broadway for the sale of his fabrics. In the midst of these grand preparations, his zeal in experimenting almost cost him his life. Having generated a large quantity of poisonous gas in his close room, he was so nearly suffocated that it was six weeks before he recovered his health. Before he had begun to produce his fabrics in any considerable quantity, the commercial storm of 1836 swept

14 *   U

away the entire property of his partner, which put a complete stop to the operations in India-rubber, and reduced poor Goodyear to his normal condition of beggary. Beggary it literally was; for he was absolutely dependent upon others for the means of sustaining life. He mentions that, soon after this crushing blow, his family having previously joined him in New York, he awoke one morning to discover that he had neither an atom of food for them, nor a cent to buy it with. Putting in his pocket an article that he supposed a pawnbroker would value, he set out in the hope of procuring enough money to sustain them for one day. Before reaching the sign, so familiar to him, of the three Golden Balls, he met a terrible being to a man in his situation, — a creditor! Hungry and dejected, he prepared his mind for a torrent of bitter reproaches; for this gentleman was one whose patience he felt he had abused. What was his relief when his creditor accosted him gayly with, " Well, Mr. Goodyear, what can I do for you to-day?" His first thought was, that an insult was intended, so preposterous did it seem that this man could really desire to aid him further. Satisfied that the offer was well meant, he told his friend that he had come out that morning in search of food for his family, and that a loan of fifteen dollars would greatly oblige him. The money was instantly produced, which enabled him to postpone his visit to the pawnbroker for several days. The pawnbroker was still, however, his frequent resource all that year, until the few remains of his late brief prosperity had all disappeared.

But he never for a moment let go his hold upon India-rubber. A timely loan of a hundred dollars from an old friend enabled him to remove his family to Staten Island, near the abandoned India-rubber factory. Having free access to the works, he and his wife contrived to manufacture a few articles of his improved cloth, and to sell enough to provide daily bread. His great object there was to induce the directors of the suspended Company to recommence operations upon his new process. But so completely sickened were they of the very name of a material which had involved them in so much loss and discredit, that during the six months of his residence on the Island he never succeeded in persuading one man to do so much as come to the factory and look at his specimens. There were thousands of dollars' worth of machinery there, but not a single shareholder cared even to know the condition of the property. This was the more remarkable, since he was unusually endowed by nature with the power to inspire other men with his own confidence. The magnates of Staten Island, however, involved as they were in the general shipwreck of property and credit, were inexorably deaf to his eloquence.

As he had formerly exhausted Philadelphia, so now New York seemed exhausted. He became even an object of ridicule. He was regarded as an India-rubber monomaniac. One of his New York friends having been asked how Mr. Goodyear could be recognized in the street, replied: "If you see a man with an India-rubber coat on, India-rubber shoes, an India-rubber cap, and in his pocket an India-rubber purse, with not a cent in it, that is he." He was in the habit then of wearing his material in every form, with the twofold view of testing and advertising it.

In September, 1836, aided again by a small loan, he packed a few of his best specimens in his carpet-bag, and set out alone for the cradle of the India-rubber manufacture, — Roxbury. The ruin of the great Company there was then complete, and the factory was abandoned. All that part of Massachusetts was suffering from the total depreciation of the India-rubber stocks. There were still, however, two or three persons who could not quite give up India-rubber. Mr. Chaffee, the originator of the manufacture in America, welcomed warmly a brother experimenter, admired his specimens, encouraged him to persevere, procured him friends, and, what was more important, gave him the use of the enormous machinery standing idle in the factory. A brief, delusive prosperity again relieved the monotony of misfortune. By his new process, he made shoes, piano-covers, and carriage-cloths, so superior to any previously produced in the United States as to cause a temporary revival of the business, which enabled him to sell rights to manufacture under his patents. His profits in a single year amounted to four or five thousand dollars. Again he had his family around him, and felt a boundless confidence in the future.

An event upon which he had depended for the completeness of his triumph plunged him again into ruin. He received an order from the government for a hundred and fifty India-rubber mail-bags. Having perfect confidence in his ability to execute this order, he gave the greatest possible publicity to it. All the world should now see that Goodyear's India-rubber was all that Goodyear had represented it. The bags were finished; and beautiful bags they were, — smooth, firm, highly polished, well-shaped, and indubitably water-proof. He had them hung up all round the factory, and invited every one to come and inspect them. They were universally admired, and the maker was congratulated upon his success. It was in the summer that these fatal bags were finished. Having occasion to be absent for a month, he left them hanging in the factory. Judge of his consternation when, on his return, he found them softening, fermenting, and dropping off their handles. The aquafortis did indeed " cure " the surface of his India-rubber, but only the sur-face. Very thin cloth made by this process was a useful and somewhat durable article; but for any other purpose, it was valueless. The public and signal failure of the mail-bags, together with the imperfection of all his products except his thinnest cloth, suddenly and totally destroyed his rising busi-ness. Everything he possessed that was salable was sold at auction to pay his debts. He was again penniless and destitute, with an increased family and an aged father dependent upon him.

His friends, his brothers, and his wife now joined in dissuad-ing him from further experiments. Were not four years of such vicissitude enough? Who had ever touched India-rubber without loss? Could he hope to succeed, when so many able and enterprising men had failed? Had he a right to keep his family in a condition so humiliating and painful? He had succeeded in the hardware business; why not return to it? There were those who would join him in any rational under taking; but how could he expect that any one would be will ing to throw more money into a bottomless pit that had already ingulfed millions without result? These arguments he could not answer, and we cannot; the friends of all the great inventors have had occasion to use the same. It seemed highly absurd to the friends of Fitch, Watt, Fulton, Wedgwood, Whitney, Arkwright, that they should forsake the beaten track of business to pursue a path that led through the wilderness to nothing but wilderness. Not one of these men, perhaps, could have made a reasonable reply to the remonstrances of their friends. They only felt, as poor Goodyear felt, that the steep and thorny path which they were treading was the path they *must* pursue. A power of which they could give no satisfactory account urged them on. And when we look closely into the lives of such men, we observe that, in their dark days, some trifling circumstance was always occurring that set them upon new inquiries and gave them new hopes. It might be an *ignis fatuus* that led them farther astray, or it might be genuine light which brought them into the true path.

Goodyear might have yielded to his friends on this occasion, for he was an affectionate man, devoted to his family, had not one of those trifling events occurred which inflamed his curiosity anew. During his late transient prosperity, he had employed a man, Nathaniel Hayward by name, who had been foreman of one of the extinct India-rubber companies. He found him in charge of the abandoned factory, and still making a few articles on his own account by a new process. To harden his India-rubber, he put a very small quantity of sulphur into it, or sprinkled sulphur upon the surface and dried it in the sun. Mr. Goodyear was surprised to observe that this process seemed to produce the same effect as the application of aquafortis. It does not appear to have occurred to him that Hayward's process and his own were essentially the same. A chemical dictionary would have informed him that sulphuric acid enters largely into the composition of aquafortis, from which he might have inferred that the only difference between the two methods was, that Hayward employed the sun, and Goodyear nitric acid, to give the sulphur effect. Hayward's goods, however, were liable to a serious objection: the smell of the sul phur, in warm weather, was intolerable. Hayward, it appears, was a very illiterate man; and the only account he could give of his invention was, that it was revealed to him in a dream. His process was of so little use to him, that Goodyear bought his patent for a small sum, and gave him employment at monthly wages until the mail-bag disaster deprived him of the means of doing so.

In combining sulphur with India-rubber, Goodyear had approached so near his final success that one step more brought him to it. He was certain that he was very close to the secret. He saw that sulphur had a mysterious power over India-rubber when a union could be effected between the two substances. True, there was an infinitesimal quantity of sulphur in his mail-bags, and they had melted in the shade; but the surface of his cloth, powdered with the sulphur and dried in the sun, bore the sun's heat. Here was a mystery. The problem was, how to produce in a *mass* of India-rubber the change effected on the surface by sulphur and sun? He made numberless experiments. He mixed with the gum large quantities of sulphur, and small quantities. He exposed his compound to the sun, and held it near a fire. He felt that he had the secret in his hands; but for many weary months it eluded him.

And, after all, it was an accident that revealed it; but an accident that no man in the world but Charles Goodyear could have interpreted, nor he, but for his five years' previous investigation. At Woburn one day, in the spring of 1839, he was standing with his brother and several other persons near a very hot stove. He held in his hand a mass of his compound of sulphur and gum, upon which he was expatiating in his usual vehement manner, — the company exhibiting the indifference to which he was accustomed. In the crisis of his argument he made a violent gesture, which brought the mass in contact with the stove, which was hot enough to melt India-rubber instantly; upon looking at it a moment after, he perceived that his compound had not melted in the least degree! It had charred as leather chars, but no part of the surface had dissolved. There was not a sticky place upon it To say that he was astonished at this would but faintly express his ecstasy of amazement. The result was absolutely new to all ex perience, — India-rubber not melting in contact with red-hot iron! A man must have been five years absorbed in the pursuit of an object to comprehend his emotions. He felt as Columbus felt when he saw the land-bird alighting upon his ship, and the drift-wood floating by. But, like Columbus, he was surrounded with an unbelieving crew. Eagerly he showed his charred India-rubber to his brother, and to the other bystanders, and dwelt upon the novelty and marvellousness of his fact. They regarded it with complete indifference. The good man had worn them all out. Fifty times before, he had run to them, exulting in some new discovery, and they supposed, of course, that this was another of his chimeras.

He followed the new clew with an enthusiasm which his friends would have been justified in calling frenzy, if success had not finally vindicated him. He soon discovered that his compound would not melt at any degree of heat. It next occurred to him to ascertain at how low a temperature it would char, and whether it was not possible to *arrest* the combustion at a point that would leave the India-rubber elastic, but deprived of its adhesiveness. A single experiment proved that this was possible. After toasting a piece of his compound before an open fire, he found that, while part of it was charred, a rim of India-rubber round the charred portion was elastic still, and even more elastic than pure gum. In a few days he had established three facts ; — first, that this rim of India-rubber would bear a temperature of two hundred and seventy-eight degrees without charring; second, that it would not melt or soften at any heat; third, that, placed between blocks of ice and left out of doors all night, it would not stiffen in the least degree. He had triumphed, and he knew it. He tells us that he now " felt himself amply repaid for the past, and quite indifferent as to the trials of the future." It was well he was so, for his darkest days were before him, and he was still six years from a practicable success. He had, indeed, proved that a compound of sulphur and India-rubber, in proper proportions and in certain conditions, being subjected for a certain time to a certain degree of heat, undergoes a change which renders it perfectly available for all the uses to which he had before attempted in vain to apply it. But it remained to be ascertained what were those proper proportions, what were those conditions, what was that degree of heat, what was that certain time, and by what means the heat could be best applied.

The difficulty of all this may be inferred when we state that at the present time it takes an intelligent man a year to learn how to conduct the process with certainty, though he is provided, from the start, with the best implements and appliances which twenty years' experience has suggested. And poor Goodyear had now reduced himself, not merely to poverty, but to isolation. No friend of his could conceal his impatience when he heard him pronounce the word India-rubber. Business-men recoiled from the name of it. He tells us that two entire years passed, after he had made his discovery, before he had convinced one human being of its value. Now, too, his experiments could no longer be carried on with a few pounds of India-rubber, a quart of turpentine, a phial of aquafortis, and a little lampblack. He wanted the means of producing a high, uniform, and controllable degree of heat, — a matter of much greater difficulty than he anticipated. We catch brief glimpses of him at this time in the volumes of testimony. We see him waiting for his wife to draw the loaves from her oven, that he might put into it a batch of India-rubber to bake, and watching it all the evening, far into the night, to see what effect was produced by one hour's, two hours', three hours', six hours' baking. We see him boiling it in his wife's saucepans, suspending it before the nose of her teakettle, and hanging it from the handle of that vessel to within an inch of the boiling water. We see him roasting it in the ashes and in hot sand, toasting it before a slow fire and before a quick fire, cooking it for one hour and for twenty-four hours, changing the proportions of his compound and mixing them in different ways. No success rewarded him while he employed only domestic utensils. Occasionally, it is true, he produced a small piece of perfectly vulcanized India-rubber; but upon subjecting other pieces to precisely the same process, they would blister or char.

Then we see him resorting to the shops and factories in the neighborhood of Woburn, asking the privilege of using an oven after working hours, or of hanging a piece of India-rubber in the "man-hole" of the boiler. The foremen testify that he was a great plague to them, and smeared their works with his sticky compound; but, though they all regarded him as little better than a troublesome lunatic, they all appear to have helped him very willingly. He frankly confesses that he lived at this time on charity; for, although *he* felt confident of being able to repay the small sums which pity for his family enabled him to borrow, his neighbors who lent him the money were as far as possible from expecting payment. Pretending to lend, they meant to give. One would pay his butcher's bill or his milk bill; another would send in a barrel of flour; another would take in payment some articles of the old stock of India-rubber; and some of the farmers allowed his children to gather sticks in their fields to heat his hillocks of sand containing masses of sulphurized India-rubber. If the people of New England were not the most "neighborly" people in the world, his family must have starved, or he must have given up his experiments. But, with all the generosity of his neighbors, his children were often sick, hungry, and cold, without medicine, food, or fuel. One witness testifies: "I found (in 1839) that they had not fuel to burn nor food to eat, and did not know where to get a morsel of food from one day to another, unless it was sent in to them." We can neither justify nor condemn their father. Imagine Columbus within sight of the new world, and his obstinate crew declaring it was only a mirage, and refusing to row him ashore! Never was mortal man surer that he had a fortune in his hand, than Charles Goodyear was when he would take a piece of scorched and dingy India-rubber from his pocket and expound its marvellous properties to a group of incredulous villagers. Sure also was he that he was just upon the point of a practicable success. Give him but an oven, and would he not turn you out fire-proof and cold-proof India-rubber, as fast as a baker can produce loaves of bread? Nor was it merely the hope of deliverance from his pecuniary straits that urged him on. In all the records of his career, we perceive traces of something nobler than this. His health being always infirm, he was haunted with the dread of dying before he had reached a point in his discoveries where other men, influenced by ordinary motives, could render them available.

By the time that he had exhausted the patience of the foremen of the works near Woburn, he had come to the conclusion that an oven was the proper means of applying heat to his compound. An oven he forthwith determined to build. Having obtained the use of a corner of a factory yard, his aged father, two of his brothers, his little son, and himself sallied forth, with pickaxe and shovels, to begin the work: and when they had done all that unskilled labor could effect towards it, he induced a mason to complete it, and paid him in bricklayers' aprons made of aquafortized India-rubber. This first oven was a tantalizing failure. The heat was neither uniform nor controllable. Some of the pieces of India-rubber would come out so perfectly "cured" as to demonstrate the utility of his discovery; but others, prepared in precisely the same manner, as far as he could discern, were spoiled, either by blistering or charring. He was puzzled and distressed beyond description; and no single voice consoled or encouraged him. Out of the first piece of cloth which he succeeded in vulcanizing he had a coat made for himself, which was not an ornamental garment in its best estate; but, to prove to the unbelievers that it would stand fire, he brought it so often in contact with hot stoves, that at last it presented an exceedingly dingy appearance. His coat did not impress the public favorably, and it served to confirm the opinion that he was laboring under a mania.

In the midst of his first disheartening experiments with sulphur, he had an opportunity of escaping at once from his troubles. A house in Paris made him an advantageous offer for the use of his aquafortis process. From the abyss of his misery the honest man promptly replied, that that process, valuable as it was, was about to be superseded by a new method, which he was then perfecting, and as soon as he had developed it sufficiently he should be glad to close with their offers. Can we wonder that his neighbors thought him mad?

It was just after declining the French proposal that he endured his worst extremity of want and humiliation. It was in the winter of 1839 – 40. One of those long and terrible snow-storms for which New England is noted had been raging for many hours, and he awoke one morning to find his little cottage half buried in snow, the storm still continuing, and in his house not an atom of fuel nor a morsel of food. His children were very young, and he was himself sick and feeble. The charity of his neighbors was exhausted, and he had not the courage to face their reproaches. As he looked out of the window upon the dreary and tumultuous scene, " fit emblem of his condition," he remarks, he called to mind that, a few days before, an acquaintance, a mere acquaintance, who lived some miles off, had given him upon the road a more friendly greeting than he was then accustomed to receive. It had cheered his heart as he trudged sadly by, and it now returned vividly to his mind. To this gentleman he determined to apply for relief, if he could reach his house. Terrible was his struggle with the wind and the deep drifts. Often he was ready to faint with fatigue, sickness, and hunger, and he would be obliged to sit down upon a bank of snow to rest. He reached the house and told his story, not omitting the oft-told tale of his new discovery, — that mine of wealth, if only he could procure the means of working it! The eager eloquence of the inventor was seconded by the gaunt and yellow face of the man His generous acquaintance entertained him cordially, and lent him a sum of money, which not only carried his family through the worst of the winter, but enabled him to continue his experiments on a small scale. O. B. Coolidge, of Woburn, was the name of this benefactor.

On another occasion, when he was in the most urgent need of materials, he looked about his house to see if there was left one relic of better days upon which a little money could be borrowed. There was nothing except his children's school-books, — the last things from which a New-Englander is willing to part. There was no other resource. He gathered them up and sold them for five dollars, with which he laid in a fresh stock of gum and sulphur, and kept on experimenting.

Seeing no prospect of success in Massachusetts, he now resolved to make a desperate effort to get to New York, feeling confident

that the specimens he could take with him would convince some
one of the superiority of his new method.   He was beginning to
understand the causes of his many failures, but he saw clearly
that his compound could not be worked with certainty without
expensive apparatus.   It was a very delicate operation, requiring
exactness and promptitude.   The conditions upon which success
depended were numerous, and the failure of one spoiled all.   To
vulcanize India-rubber is about as difficult as to make perfect
bread ; but the art of bread-making was the growth of ages, and
Charles Goodyear was only ten years and a half in perfecting
his process.   Thousands of ingenious men and women, aided by
many happy accidents, must have contributed to the successive
invention of bread ; but he was only one man, poor and sick.   It
cost him thousands of failures to learn that a little acid in his
sulphur caused the blistering ; that his compound must be heated
almost immediately after being mixed, or it would never vulcanize ; that a portion of white lead in the compound greatly facili-
tated the operation and improved the result; and when he had
learned these facts, it still required costly and laborious experiments to devise the best methods of compounding his ingredients,
the best proportions, the best mode of heating, the proper duration of the heating, and the various useful effects that could be
produced by varying the proportions and the degree of heat.   He
tells us that many times, when, by exhausting every resource, he
had prepared a quantity of his compound for heating, it was
spoiled because he could not, with his inadequate apparatus, apply the heat soon enough.

To New York, then, he directed his thoughts.   Merely to get
there cost him a severer and a longer effort than men in general
are capable of making.   First he walked to Boston, ten miles
distant, where he hoped to be able to borrow from an old acquaintance fifty dollars, with which to provide for his family and
pay his fare to New York.   He not only failed in this, but he
was arrested for debt and thrown into prison.   Even in prison,
while his father was negotiating to secure his release, he labored
to interest men of capital in his discovery, and made proposals for
founding a factory in Boston.   Having obtained his liberty, he

went to a hotel, and spent a week in vain efforts to effect a small loan. Saturday night came, and with it his hotel bill, which he had no means of discharging. In an agony of shame and anxiety, he went to a friend, and entreated the sum of five dollars to enable him to return home. He was met with a point-blank refusal. In the deepest dejection, he walked the streets till late in the night, and strayed at length, almost beside himself, to Cambridge, where he ventured to call upon a friend and ask shelter for the night. He was hospitably entertained, and the next morning walked wearily home, penniless and despairing. At the door of his house a member of his family met him with the news that his youngest child, two years of age, whom he had left in perfect health, was dying. In a few hours he had in his house a dead child, but not the means of burying it, and five living dependants without a morsel of food to give them. A storekeeper near by had promised to supply the family, but, discouraged by the unforeseen length of the father's absence, he had that day refused to trust them further. In these terrible circumstances, he applied to a friend upon whose generosity he knew he could rely, one who had never failed him. He received in reply a letter of severe and cutting reproach, enclosing seven dollars, which his friend explained was given only out of pity for his innocent and suffering family. A stranger, who chanced to be present when this letter arrived, sent them a barrel of flour, — a timely and blessed relief. The next day the family followed on foot the remains of the little child to the grave.

A relation in a distant part of the country, to whom Goodyear revealed his condition, sent him fifty dollars, which enabled him to get to New York. He had touched bottom. The worst of his trials were over. In New York, he had the good fortune to make the acquaintance of two brothers, William Rider and Emory Rider, men of some property and great intelligence, who examined his specimens, listened to his story, believed in him, and agreed to aid him to continue his experiments, and to supply his family until he had rendered his discovery available. From that time, though he was generally embarrassed in his circumstances, his family never wanted bread, and he was never obliged to sus-

pend his experiments.   Aided by the capital, the sympathy, and
the ingenuity of the brothers Rider, he spent a year in New York
in the most patient endeavors to overcome the difficulties in
heating his compound.   Before he had succeeded, their resources
failed.   But he had made such progress in demonstrating the
practicability of his process, that his brother-in-law, William De.
Forrest, a noted woollen manufacturer, took hold of the project
in earnest, and aided him to bring it to perfection.   Once more,
however, he was imprisoned for debt.   This event conquered his
scruples against availing himself of the benefit of the bankrupt
act, which finally delivered him from the danger of arrest.   We
should add, however, that, as soon as he began to derive income
from his invention, he reassumed his obligations to his old creditors, and discharged them gradually.

   It was not till the year 1844, more than ten years after he
began to experiment, and more than five years after discovering
the secret of vulcanization, that he was able to conduct his process with absolute certainty, and to produce vulcanized India-
rubber with the requisite expedition and economy.   We can form
some conception of the difficulties overcome by the fact, that the
advances of Mr. De Forrest in aid of the experiment reached
the sum of forty-six thousand dollars, — an amount the inventor
did not live long enough to repay.

   His triumph had been long deferred, and we have seen in part
how much it had cost him.   But his success proved to be richly
worth its cost.   He had added to the arts, not a new material
merely, but a new class of materials, applicable to a thousand
diverse uses.   His product had more than the elasticity of India-
rubber, while it was divested of all those properties which had
lessened its utility.   It was still India-rubber, but its surfaces
would not adhere, nor would it harden at any degree of cold, nor
soften at any degree of heat.   It was a cloth impervious to water.
It was paper that would not tear.   It was parchment that would
not crease.   It was leather which neither rain nor sun would injure.   It was ebony that could be run into a mould.   It was ivory
that could be worked like wax.   It was wood that never cracked,
shrunk, nor decayed.   It was metal, "elastic metal," as Daniel

Webster termed it, that could be wound round the finger or tied into a knot, and which preserved its elasticity almost like steel. Trifling variations in the ingredients, in the proportions, and in the heating, made it either as pliable as kid, tougher than ox-hide, as elastic as whalebone, or as rigid as flint.

All this is stated in a moment, but each of these variations in the material, as well as every article made from them, cost this indefatigable man days, weeks, months, or years of experiment. It cost him, for example, several years of most expensive trial to obviate the objection to India-rubber fabrics caused by the liability of the gum to peel from the cloth. He tried every known textile fabric, and every conceivable process before arriving at the simple expedient of mixing fibre with the gum, by which, at length, the perfect India-rubber cloth was produced. This invention he considered only second in value to the discovery of vulcanization. The India-rubber shoe, as we now have it, is an admirable article, — light, strong, elegant in shape, with a fibrous sole that does not readily wear, cut, or slip. As the shoe is made and joined before vulcanization, a girl can make twenty-five pairs in a day. They are cut from the soft sheets of gum and joined by a slight pressure of the hand. But almost every step of this process, now so simple and easy, was patiently elaborated by Charles Goodyear. A million and a half of pairs per annum is now the average number made in the United States by his process, though the business languishes somewhat from the high price of the raw materials. The gum, which, when Goodyear began his experiments, was a drug at five cents a pound, has recently been sold at one dollar and twenty cents a pound, with all its impurities. Even at this high price the annual import ranges at from four to five millions of pounds.

Poor Richard informs us that Necessity never makes a good bargain. Mr. Goodyear was always a prey to necessity. Nor was he ever a good man of business. He was too entirely an inventor to know how to dispose of his inventions to advantage; and he could never feel that he had accomplished his mission with regard to India-rubber. As soon as he had brought his shoemaking process to the point where other men could make it profitable, he withdrew from manufacturing, and sold rights to manufacture for the consideration of half a cent per pair. Five cents had been reasonable enough, and would have given him ample means to continue his labors. Half a cent kept him subject to necessity, which seemed to compel him to dispose of other rights at rates equally low. Thus it happened that, when the whole India-rubber business of the country paid him tribute, or ought to have paid it, he remained an embarrassed man. He had, too, the usual fate of inventors, in having to contend with the infringers of his rights, — men who owed their all to his ingenuity and perseverance. We may judge, however, of the rapidity with which the business grew, by the fact that, six years after the completion of his vulcanizing process, the holders of rights to manufacture shoes by that process deemed it worth while to employ Daniel Webster to plead their cause, and to stimulate his mind by a fee of twenty-five thousand dollars. It is questionable if Charles Goodyear ever derived that amount from his patents, if we deduct from his receipts the money spent in further developing his discovery. His ill-health obliged him to be abstemious, and he had no expensive tastes. It was only in his laboratory that he was lavish, and there he was lavish indeed.

His friends still smiled at his zeal, or reproached him for it. It has been only since the mighty growth of the business in his products that they have acknowledged that he was right and that they were wrong. They remember him, sick, meagre, and yellow, now coming to them with a walking-stick of India-rubber exulting in the new application of his material, and predicting its general use, while they objected that his stick had cost him fifty dollars; now running about among the comb factories, trying to get reluctant men to try their tools upon hard India-rubber, and producing at length a set of combs that cost twenty times the price of ivory ones; now shutting himself up for months, endeavoring to make a sail of India-rubber fabric, impervious to water that should never freeze, and to which no sleet or ice should ever cling; now exhibiting a set of cutlery with India-rubber handles, or a picture set in an India-rubber frame, or a book with India-rubber covers, or a watch with an India-rubber case; now exper imenting with India-rubber tiles for floors, which he hoped to make as brilliant in color as those of mineral, as agreeable to the tread as carpet, and as durable as an ancient floor of oak. There is nothing in the history of invention more remarkable than the devotion of this man to his object. No crusader was ever so devoted to his vow, no lover to his mistress, as he was to his purpose of showing mankind what to do with India-rubber. The doorplate of his office was made of it; his portrait was painted upon and framed with it; his book, as we have seen, was wholly composed of it; and his mind, by night and day, was surcharged with it. He never went to sleep without having within reach writing materials and the means of making a light, so that, if he should have an idea in the night, he might be able to secure it. Some of his best ideas, he used to say, were saved to mankind by this precaution.

It is not well for any man to be thus absorbed in his object. To Goodyear, whose infirm constitution peculiarly needed repose and recreation, it was disastrous, and at length fatal. It is well with no man who does not play as well as work. Fortunately, we are all beginning to understand this. We are beginning to see that a devotion to the business of life which leaves no reserve of force and time for social pleasures and the pursuit of knowledge, diminishes even our power to conduct business with the sustained and intelligent energy requisite for a safe success. That is a melancholy passage in one of Theodore Parker's letters, written in the premature decline of his powers, in which he laments that he had not, like Franklin, joined a club, and taken an occasional ramble with young companions in the country, and played billiards with them in the evening. He added, that he intended to lead a better life in these particulars for the future; but who can reform at forty-seven? And the worst of it is, that ill-health, the natural ally of all evil, favors intensity, lessening both our power and our inclination to get out of the routine that is destroying us. Goodyear, always sick, had been for so many years the slave of his pursuit, he had been so spurred on by necessity, and lured by partial success, that, when at last he might have rested, he could not.

15

It does not become us, however, who reap the harvest, to censure him who wore himself out in sowing the seed. The harvest is great, — greater than any but he anticipated. His friends know now that he never over-estimated the value of his invention. They know now what he meant when he said that no one but himself would take the trouble to apply his material to the thousand uses of which it was capable, because each new application demanded a course of experiments that would discourage any one who entered upon it only with a view to profit. The India-rubber manufacture, since his death, has increased greatly in extent, but not much in other respects, and some of the ideas which he valued most remain undeveloped. He died, for example, in the conviction that sails of India-rubber cloth would finally supersede all others. He spent six months and five thousand dollars in producing one or two specimens, which were tried and answered their purpose well; but he was unable to bring his sail-making process to an available perfection. The sole difficulty was to make his sails as light as those of cloth. He felt certain of being able to accomplish this; but in the multiplicity of his objects and the pressure of his embarrassments, he was compelled to defer the completion of his plans to a day that never came.

The catalogue of his successful efforts is long and striking. The second volume of his book is wholly occupied with that catalogue. He lived to see his material applied to nearly five hundred uses, to give employment in England, France, Germany and the United States to sixty thousand persons, who annually produced merchandise of the value of eight millions of dollars. A man does much who only founds a new kind of industry; and he does more when that industry gives value to a commodity that before was nearly valueless. But we should greatly undervalue the labors of Charles Goodyear, if we regarded them only as opening a new source of wealth; for there have been found many uses of India-rubber, as prepared by him, which have an importance far superior to their commercial value. Art, science, and humanity are indebted to him for a material which serves the purposes of them all, and serves them as no other known material could.

Some of our readers have been out on the picket-line during the war. They know what it is to stand motionless in a wet and miry rifle-pit, in the chilling rain of a Southern winter's night. Protected by India-rubber boots, blanket, and cap, the picket-man performs in comparative comfort a duty which, without that protection, would make him a cowering and shivering wretch, and plant in his bones a latent rheumatism to be the torment of his old age. Goodyear's India-rubber enables him to come in from his pit as dry as he was when he went into it, and he comes in to lie down with an India-rubber blanket between him and the damp earth. If he is wounded, it is an India-rubber stretcher, or an ambulance provided with India-rubber springs, that gives him least pain on his way to the hospital, where, if his wound is serious, a water-bed of India-rubber gives ease to his mangled frame, and enables him to endure the wearing tedium of an unchanged posture. Bandages and supporters of India-rubber avail him much when first he begins to hobble about his ward. A piece of India-rubber at the end of his crutch lessens the jar and the noise of his motions, and a cushion of India-rubber is comfortable to his armpit. The springs which close the hospital door, the bands which exclude the drafts from doors and windows, his pocket-comb and cup and thimble, are of the same material. From jars hermetically closed with India-rubber he receives the fresh fruit that is so exquisitely delicious to a fevered mouth. The instrument-case of his surgeon and the store-room of his matron contain many articles whose utility is increased by the use of it, and some that could be made of nothing else. His shirts and sheets pass through an India-rubber clothes-wringer, which saves the strength of the washerwoman and the fibre of the fabric. When the government presents him with an artificial leg, a thick heel and elastic sole of India-rubber give him comfort every time he puts it to the ground. An India-rubber pipe with an inserted bowl of clay, a billiard-table provided with India-rubber cushions and balls, can solace his long convalescence.

In the field, this material is not less strikingly useful. During this war, armies have marched through ten days of rain, and slept through as many rainy nights, and come out dry into the return-

ing sunshine, with its artillery untarnished and its ammunition un
injured, because men and munitions were all under India-rubber
When Goodyear's ideas are carried out, it will be by pontoons of
inflated India-rubber that rivers will be crossed. A pontoon-train
will then consist of one wagon drawn by two mules ; and if the
march is through a country that furnishes the wooden part of the
bridge, a man may carry a pontoon on his back in addition to his
knapsack and blanket.

In the naval service we meet this material in a form that at-
tracts little attention, though it serves a purpose of perhaps unequalled utility. Mechanics are aware, that, from the time of
James Watt to the year 1850, the grand desideratum of the en-
gine-builder was a perfect joint, — a joint that would not admit
the escape of steam. A steam-engine is all over joints and valves,
from most of which some steam sooner or later would escape,
since an engine in motion produces a continual jar that finally
impaired the best joint that art could make. The old joint-mak-
ing process was exceedingly expensive. The two surfaces of
iron had to be most carefully ground and polished, then screwed
together, and the edges closed with white lead. By the use of a
thin sheet of vulcanized India-rubber, placed between the iron
surfaces, not only is all this expense saved, but a joint is produced
that is absolutely and permanently perfect. It is not even necessary to rub off the roughness of the casting, for the rougher the
surface, the better the joint. Goodyear's invention supplies an
article that Watt and Fulton sought in vain, and which would
seem to put the finishing touch to the steam-engine, — if, in these
days of improvement, anything whatever could be considered
finished. At present, all engines are provided with these joints
and valves, which save steam, diminish jar, and facilitate the
separation of the parts. It is difficult to compute the value of
this improvement, in money. We are informed, however, by
competent authority, that a steamer of two thousand tons saves
ten thousand dollars a year by its use. Such is the demand for
the engine-packing, as it is termed, that the owners of the factory
where it is chiefly made, after constructing the largest water-
wheel in the world, found it insufficient for their growing business

and were obliged to add to it a steam-engine of two hundred horse-power. The New York agent of this company sells about a million dollars' worth of packing per annum.

Belting for engines is another article for which Goodyear's compound is superior to any other, inasmuch as the surface of the India-rubber clings to the iron wheel better than leather or fabric. Leather polishes and slips; India-rubber does not polish, and holds to the iron so firmly as to save a large percentage of power. It is no small advantage merely to save leather for other uses, since leather is an article of which the supply is strictly limited. It is not uncommon for India-rubber belts to be furnished, which, if made of leather, would require more than a hundred hides. Emery-wheels of this material have been recently introduced. They were formerly made of wood coated with emery, which soon wore off. In the new manufacture, the emery is kneaded into the entire mass of the wheel, which can be worn down till it is all consumed. On the same principle the instruments used to sharpen scythes are also made. Of late we hear excellent accounts of India-rubber as a basis for artificial teeth. It is said to be lighter, more agreeable, less expensive, than gold or platina, and not less durable. We have seen also some very pretty watch-cases of this material, elegantly inlaid with gold.

It thus appears, that the result of Mr. Goodyear's long and painful struggles was the production of a material which now ranks with the leading compounds of commerce and manufacture, such as glass, brass, steel, paper, porcelain, paint. Considering its peculiar and varied utility, it is perhaps inferior in value only to paper, steel, and glass. We see, also, that the use of the new compound lessens the consumption of several commodities, such as ivory, bone, ebony, and leather, which it is desirable to save, because the demand for them tends to increase faster than the supply. When a set of ivory billiard-balls costs fifty dollars, and civilization presses upon the domain of the elephant, it is well to make our combs and our paper-knives of something else.

That inventions so valuable should be disputed and pirated was something which the history of all the great inventions might have taught Mr. Goodyear to expect. We need not revive those

disputes which embittered his life and wasted his substance and
his time. The Honorable Joseph Holt, the Commissioner who
granted an extension to the vulcanizing patent in 1858, has suffi
ciently characterized them in one of the most eloquent papers
ever issued from the Patent Office : —

"No inventor probably has ever been so harassed, so trampled upon,
so plundered by that sordid and licentious class of infringers known in
the parlance of the world, with no exaggeration of phrase, as 'pirates.'
The spoliations of their incessant guerilla warfare upon his defenceless
rights have unquestionably amounted to millions. In the very front
rank of this predatory band stands one who sustains in this case the
double and most convenient character of contestant and witness; and
it is but a subdued expression of my estimate of the deposition he has
lodged, to say that this Parthian shaft — the last that he could hurl at
an invention which he has so long and so remorselessly pursued — is a
fitting finale to that career which the public justice of the country has
so signally rebuked."

Mr. Holt paid a noble tribute to the class of men of whose
rights he was the official guardian : —

"All that is glorious in our past or hopeful in our future is indissolu-
bly linked with that cause of human progress of which inventors are
the *preux chevaliers*. It is no poetic translation of the abiding sentiment of the country to say, that they are the true jewels of the nation
to which they belong, and that a solicitude for the protection of their
rights and interests should find a place in every throb of the national
heart. Sadly helpless as a class, and offering, in the glittering creations
of their own genius, the strongest temptations to unscrupulous cupidity,
they, of all men, have most need of the shelter of the public law, while,
in view of their philanthropic labors, they are of all men most entitled
to claim it. The schemes of the politician and of the statesman may
subserve the purposes of the hour, and the teachings of the moralist
may remain with the generation to which they are addressed, but all
this must pass away; while the fruits of the inventor's genius will
endure as imperishable memorials, and, surviving the wreck of creeds
and systems, alike of politics, religion, and philosophy, will diffuse
their blessings to all lands and throughout all ages."

When Mr. Goodyear had seen the manufacture of shoes and
fabrics well established in the United States, and when his rights
appeared to have been placed beyond controversy by the Trenton

decision of 1852, being still oppressed with debt, he went to Europe to introduce his material to the notice of capitalists there. The great manufactories of vulcanized India-rubber in England, Scotland, France, and Germany are the result of his labors ; but the peculiarities of the patent laws of those countries, or else his own want of skill in contending for his rights, prevented him from reaping the reward of his labors. He spent six laborious years abroad. At the Great Exhibitions of London and Paris, he made brilliant displays of his wares, which did honor to his country and himself, and gave an impetus to the prosperity of the men who have grown rich upon his discoveries. At the London Exhibition, he had a suite of three apartments, carpeted, furnished, and decorated only with India-rubber. At Paris, he made a lavish display of India-rubber jewelry, dressing-cases, work-boxes, picture-frames, which attracted great attention. His reward was, a four days' sojourn in the debtors' prison, and the cross of the Legion of Honor. The delinquency of his American licensees procured him the former, and the favor of the Emperor the latter.

We have seen that his introduction to India-rubber was through the medium of a life-preserver. His last labors, also, were consecrated to life-saving apparatus, of which he invented or suggested a great variety. His excellent wife was reading to him one evening, in London, an article from a review, in which it was stated that twenty persons perished by drowning every hour. The company, startled at a statement so unexpected, conversed upon it for some time, while Mr. Goodyear himself remained silent and thoughtful. For several nights he was restless, as was usually the case with him when he was meditating a new application of his material. As these periods of incubation were usually followed by a prostrating sickness, his wife urged him to forbear, and endeavor to compose his mind to sleep. "Sleep!" said he, "how can I sleep while twenty human beings are drowning every hour, and I am the man who can save them?" It was long his endeavor to invent some article which every man, woman, and child would necessarily wear, and which would make it impossible for them to sink

He experimented with hats, cravats, jackets, and petticoats and, though he left his principal object incomplete, he contrived many of those means of saving life which now puzzle the occupants of state-rooms. He had the idea that every article on board a vessel seizable in the moment of danger, every chair, table, sofa, and stool, should be a life-preserver.

He returned to his native land a melancholy spectacle to his friends, — yellow, emaciated, and feeble, — but still devoted to his work. He lingered and labored until July, 1860, when he died in New York, in the sixtieth year of his age. Almost to the last day of his life he was busy with new applications of his discovery. After twenty-seven years of labor and investigation, after having founded a new branch of industry, which gave employment to sixty thousand persons, he died insolvent, leaving to a wife and six children only an inheritance of debt. Those who censure him for this should consider that his discovery was not profitable to himself for more than ten years, that he was deeply in debt when he began his experiments, that his investigations could be carried on only by increasing his indebtedness, that all his bargains were those of a man in need, that the guilelessness of his nature made him the easy prey of greedy, dishonorable men, and that his neglect of his private interests was due, in part, to his zeal for the public good.

Dr. Dutton of New Haven, his pastor and friend, in the Sermon dedicated to his memory, did not exaggerate when he spoke of him as

"one who recognized his peculiar endowment of inventive genius as a divine gift, involving a special and defined responsibility, and considered himself called of God, as was Bezaleel, to that particular course of invention to which he devoted the chief part of his life. This he often expressed, though with his characteristic modesty, to his friends, especially his religious friends. . . . . His inventive work was his religion, and was pervaded and animated by religious faith and devotion. He felt like an apostle commissioned for that work; and he said to his niece and her husband, who went, with his approbation and sympathy as missionaries of the Gospel to Asia, that he was God's missionary as truly as they were."

Nothing more true. The demand for the raw gum, almost

created by him, in introducing abundance and developing in
dustry in the regions which produce it. As the culture of cot
ton seems the predestined means of improving Africa, so the
gathering of caoutchouc may procure for the inhabitants of the
equatorial regions of both continents such of the blessings of
civilization as they are capable of appropriating.

An attempt was made last winter to procure an act of Congress extending the vulcanizing patent for a further period of
seven years, for the benefit of the creditors and the family of the
inventor. The petition seemed reasonable. The very low tariff
paid by the manufacturers could have no perceptible effect upon
the price of articles, and the extension would provide a competence for a worthy family who had claims upon the gratitude of
the nation, if not upon its justice. The manufacturers generally
favored the extension, since the patent protected them, in the
deranged condition of our currency, from the competition of the
foreign manufacturer, who pays low wages and enjoys a sound
currency. The extension of the patent would have harmed no
one, and would have been an advantage to the general interests
of the trade. The son of the inventor, too, in whose name the
petition was offered, had spent his whole life in assisting his
father, and had a fair claim upon the consideration of Congress.
But the same unscrupulous and remorseless men who had plundered poor Goodyear living, hastened to Washington to oppose
the petition of his family. A cry of " monopoly " was raised in
the newspapers to which they had access. The presence in
Washington of Mrs. Goodyear, one of the most retiring of women,
and of her son, a singularly modest young man, who were aided
by one friend and one professional agent, was denounced as " a
powerful lobby, male and female," who, having despoiled the
public of " twenty millions," were boring Congress for a grant of
twenty millions more, — all to be wrung from an India-rubber-
consuming public. The short session of Congress is unfavorable
to private bills, even when they are unopposed. These arts
sufficed to prevent the introduction of the bill desired, and the
patent has since expired.

The immense increase in the demand for the gum has fre
15 *

quently suggested the inquiry whether there is any danger of the supply becoming unequal to it. There are now in Europe and America more than a hundred and fifty manufactories of India-rubber articles, employing from five to five hundred operatives each, and consuming more than ten millions of pounds of gum per annum. The business, too, is considered to be still in its infancy. Certainly, it is increasing. Nevertheless, there is no possibility of the demand exceeding the supply. The belt of land round the globe, five hundred miles north and five hundred miles south of the equator, abounds in the trees producing the gum, and they can be tapped, it is said, for twenty successive seasons. Forty-three thousand of these trees were counted in a tract of country thirty miles long and eight wide. Each tree yields an average of three table-spoonfuls of sap daily, but the trees are so close together that one man can gather the sap of eighty in a day. Starting at daylight, with his tomahawk and a ball of clay, he goes from tree to tree, making five or six incisions in each, and placing under each incision a cup made of the clay which he carries. In three or four hours he has completed his circuit and comes home to breakfast. In the afternoon he slings a large gourd upon his shoulder, and repeats his round to collect the sap. The cups are covered up at the roots of the tree, to be used again on the following day. In other regions the sap is allowed to exude from the tree, and is gathered from about the roots. But, however it is collected, the supply is superabundant; and the countries which produce it are those in which the laborer needs only a little tapioca, a little coffee, a hut, and an apron. In South America, from which our supply chiefly comes, the natives subsist at an expense of three cents a day. The present high price of the gum in the United States is principally due to the fact that greenbacks are not current in the tropics; but in part, to the rapidity with which the demand has increased. Several important applications of the vulcanized gum have been deferred to the time when the raw material shall have fallen to what Adam Smith would style its "natural price."

Charles Goodyear's work, therefore, is a permanent addition to the resources of man. The latest posterity will be indebted to him.

HENRY WARD BEECHER

AND HIS CHURCH.

HENRY WARD BEECHER AND HIS CHURCH.

IS there anything in America more peculiar to America, or more curious in itself, than one of our "fashionable" Protestant churches, — such as we see in New York, on the Fifth Avenue and in the adjacent streets? The lion and the lamb in the Millennium will not lie down together more lovingly than the Church and the World have blended in these singular establishments. We are far from objecting to the coalition, but note it only as something curious, new, and interesting.

We enter an edifice, upon the interior of which the upholsterer and the cabinet-maker have exhausted the resources of their trades. The word "subdued" describes the effect at which those artists have aimed. The woods employed are costly and rich, but usually of a sombre hue, and, though elaborately carved, are frequently unpolished. The light which comes through the stained windows, or through the small diamond panes, is of that description which is eminently the "*dim*, religious." Every part of the floor is thickly carpeted. The pews differ little from sofas, except in being more comfortable, and the cushions for the feet or the knees are as soft as hair and cloth can make them. It is a fashion, at present, to put the organ out of sight, and to have a clock so unobtrusive as not to be observed. Galleries are now viewed with an unfriendly eye by the projectors of churches, and they are going out of use. Everything in the way of conspicuous lighting apparatus, such as the gorgeous and dazzling chandeliers of fifteen years ago, and the translucent globes of later date, is discarded, and an attempt is sometimes made to hide the vulgar fact that the church is ever open in the evening. In a word the design of the fashionable church-builder of the present mo-

ment is to produce a richly furnished, quietly adorned, dimly il-
luminated, ecclesiastical parlor, in which a few hundred ladies
and gentlemen, attired in kindred taste, may sit perfectly at their
ease, and see no object not in harmony with the scene around
them.

To say that the object of these costly and elegant arrangements is to repel poor people would be a calumny. On the contrary, persons who show by their dress and air that they exercise
the less remunerative vocations are as politely shown to seats as
those who roll up to the door in carriages, and the presence of
such persons is desired, and, in many instances, systematically
sought. Nevertheless, the poor are repelled. They know they
cannot pay their proportion of the expense of maintaining such
establishments, and they do not wish to enjoy what others pay
for. Everything in and around the church seems to proclaim it
a kind of exclusive ecclesiastical club, designed for the accommodation of persons of ten thousand dollars a year, and upward.
Or it is as though the carriages on the Road to Heaven were divided into first-class, second-class, and third-class, and a man
either takes the one that accords with his means, or denies himself the advantage of travelling that road, or prefers to trudge
along on foot, an independent wayfarer.

It is Sunday morning, and the doors of this beautiful drawing-
room are thrown open. Ladies dressed with subdued magnificence glide in, along with some who have not been able to leave
at home the showier articles of their wardrobe. Black silk, black
velvet, black lace, relieved by intimations of brighter colors, and
by gleams from half-hidden jewelry, are the materials most employed. Gentlemen in uniform of black cloth and white linen
announce their coming by the creaking of their boots, quenched
in the padded carpeting. It cannot be said of these churches, as
Mr. Carlyle remarked of certain London ones, that a pistol could
be fired into a window across the church without much danger of
hitting a Christian. The attendance is not generally very large;
but as the audience is evenly distributed over the whole surface,
it looks larger than it is. In a commercial city everything is apt
to be measured by the commercial standard, and accordingly a

church numerically weak, but financially strong, ranks, in the estimation of the town, not according to its number of souls, but its number of dollars. We heard a fine young fellow, last summer full of zeal for everything high and good, conclude a glowing account of a sermon by saying that it was the direct means of adding to the church a capital of one hundred and seventy-five thousand dollars. He meant nothing low or mercenary; he honestly exulted in the fact that the power and influence attached to the possession of one hundred and seventy-five thousand dollars were thenceforward to be exerted on behalf of objects which he esteemed the highest. If therefore the church before our view cannot boast of a numerous attendance, it more than consoles itself by the reflection, that there are a dozen names of talismanic power in Wall Street on its list of members.

"But suppose the Doctor should leave you?" objected a friend of ours to a trustee, who had been urging him to buy a pew in a fashionable church.

"Well, my dear sir," was the business-like reply; "suppose he should. We should immediately engage the very first talent which money can command."

We can hardly help taking this simple view of things in rich commercial cities. Our worthy trustee merely put the thing on the correct basis. He frankly *said* what every church *does*, ought to do, and must do. He stated a universal fact in the plain and sensible language to which he was accustomed. In the same way these business-like Christians have borrowed the language of the Church, and speak of men who are " good " for a million.

The congregation is assembled. The low mumble of the organ ceases. A female voice rises melodiously above the rustle of dry-goods and the whispers of those who wear them. So sweet and powerful is it, that a stranger might almost suppose it borrowed from the choir of heaven; but the inhabitants of the town recognize it as one they have often heard at concerts or at the opera; and they listen critically, as to a professional performance, which it is. It is well that highly artificial singing prevents the hearer from catching the words of the song; for it *would* have rather an odd effect to hear rendered, in the modern Italian style, such plain straightforward words as these: —

" Can sinners hope for heaven
Who love this world so well?
Or dream of future happiness
While on the road to hell? "

The performance, however, is so exquisite that we do not think
of these things, but listen in rapture to the voice alone. When
the lady has finished her stanza, a noble barytone, also recognized
as professional, takes up the strain, and performs a stanza, solo ;
at the conclusion of which, four voices, in enchanting accord
breathe out a third. It is evident that the "first talent that
money can command" has been "engaged" for the entertainment
of the congregation ; and we are not surprised when the information is proudly communicated that the music costs a hundred and
twenty dollars per Sunday.

What is very surprising and well worthy of consideration is,
that this beautiful music does not " draw." In our rovings about
among the noted churches of New York, — of the kind which
" engage the first talent that money can command," — we could
never see that the audience was much increased by expensive
professional music. On the contrary, we can lay it down as a
general rule, that the costlier the music, the smaller is the average attendance. The afternoon service at Trinity Church, for
example, is little more than a delightful gratuitous concert of
boys, men, and organ ; and the spectacle of the altar brilliantly
lighted by candles is novel and highly picturesque. The sermon
also is of the fashionable length, — twenty minutes ; and yet the
usual afternoon congregation is about two hundred persons.
Those celestial strains of music, — well, they enchant the ear,
if the ear happens to be within hearing of them ; but somehow
they do not furnish a continuous attraction.

When this fine prelude is ended, the minister's part begins ;
and, unless he is a man of extraordinary bearing and talents,
every one present is conscious of a kind of lapse in the tone of
the occasion. Genius composed the music ; the " first talent "
executed it ; the performance has thrilled the soul, and exalted
expectation ; but the voice now heard may be ordinary, and the
words uttered may be homely, or even common. No one unac

customed to the place can help feeling a certain incongruity between the language heard and the scene witnessed. Everything
we see is modern; the words we hear are ancient. The preacher
speaks of "humble believers," and we look around and ask,
Where are they? Are these costly and elegant persons humble
believers? Far be it from us to intimate that they are not; we
are speaking only of their appearance, and its effect upon a cas
ual beholder. The clergyman reads,

"Come let *us* join in sweet accord,"

and straightway four hired performers execute a piece of difficult
music to an audience sitting passive. He discourses upon the
"pleasures of the world," as being at war with the interests of
the soul; and while a severe sentence to this effect is coming
from his lips, down the aisle marches the sexton, showing some
stranger to a seat, who is a professional master of the revels. He
expresses, perchance, a fervent desire that the heathen may be
converted to Christianity, and we catch ourselves saying, "Does
he mean *this* sort of thing?" When we pronounce the word
Christianity, it calls up recollections and associations that do not
exactly harmonize with the scene around us. We think rather
of the fishermen of Palestine, on the lonely sea-shore; of the
hunted fugitives of Italy and Scotland; we think of it as something lowly, and suited to the lowly, — a refuge for the forsaken
and the defeated, not the luxury of the rich and the ornament of
the strong. It may be an infirmity of our mind; but we experience a certain difficulty in realizing that the sumptuous and costly
apparatus around us has anything in common with what we have
been accustomed to think of as Christianity.

Sometimes, the incongruity reaches the point of the ludicrous.
We recently heard a very able and well-intentioned preacher,
near the Fifth Avenue, ask the ladies before him whether they
were in the habit of speaking to their female attendants about
their souls' salvation, — particularly those who dressed their hair
He especially mentioned the hair-dressers; because, as he truly
remarked, ladies are accustomed to converse with those *artistes*,
during the operation of hair-dressing, on a variety of topics; and

w

the opportunity was excellent to say a word on the one most im portant. This incident perfectly illustrates what we mean by the seeming incongruity between the ancient cast of doctrine and the modernized people to whom it is preached. We have heard ser- mons in fashionable churches in New York, laboriously prepared and earnestly read, which had nothing in them of the modern spirit, contained not the most distant allusion to modern modes of living and sinning, had no suitableness whatever to the people or the time, and from which everything that could rouse or interest a human soul living on Manhattan Island in the year 1867 seemed to have been purposely pruned away. And perhaps, if a clergyman really has no message to deliver, his best course is to utter a jargon of nothings.

Upon the whole, the impression left upon the mind of the visit- or to the fashionable church is, that he has been looking, not upon a living body, but a decorated image.

It may be, however, that the old conception of a Christian church, as the one place where all sorts and conditions of men came together to dwell upon considerations interesting to all equally, is not adapted to modern society, wherein one man dif- fers from another in knowledge even more than a king once dif- fered from a peasant in rank. When all were ignorant, a mass chanted in an unknown tongue, and a short address warning against the only vices known to ignorant people, sufficed for the whole community. But what form of service can be even imagined, that could satisfy Bridget, who cannot read, and her mistress, who comes to church cloyed with the dainties of half a dozen literatures? Who could preach a sermon that would hold attentive the man saturated with Buckle, Mill, Spencer, Thacke- ray, Emerson, Humboldt, and Agassiz, and the man whose only literary recreation is the dime novel? In the good old times, when terror was latent in every soul, and the preacher had only to deliver a very simple message, pointing out the one way to escape endless torture, a very ordinary mortal could arrest and retain attention. But this resource is gone forever, and the mod- ern preacher is thrown upon the resources of his own mind and talent. There is great difficulty here, and it does not seem likely to diminish. It may be, that never again, as long as time shall endure, will ignorant and learned, masters and servants, poor and rich, feel themselves at home in the same church.

At present we are impressed, and often oppressed, with the too evident fact, that neither the intelligent nor the uninstructed souls are so well ministered to, in things spiritual, as we could imagine they might be. The fashionable world of New York goes to church every Sunday morning with tolerable punctuality, and yet it seems to drift rapidly toward Paris. What it usually hears at church does not appear to exercise controlling influence over its conduct or its character.

Among the churches about New York to which nothing we have said applies, the one that presents the strongest contrast to the fashionable church is Henry Ward Beecher's. Some of the difficulties resulting from the altered state of opinion in recent times have been overcome there, and an institution has been created which appears to be adapted to the needs, as well as to the tastes, of the people frequenting it. We can at least say of it, that it is a living body, and *not* a decorated image.

For many years, this church upon Brooklyn Heights has been, to the best of the visitors to the metropolis, the most interesting object in or near it. Of Brooklyn itself, — a great assemblage of residences, without much business or stir, — it seems the animating soul. We have a fancy, that we can tell by the manner and bearing of an inhabitant of the place whether he attends this church or not; for there is a certain joyousness, candor, and democratic simplicity about the members of that congregation, which might be styled Beecherian, if there were not a better word. This church is simply the most characteristic thing of America. If we had a foreigner in charge to whom we wished to reveal this country, we should like to push him in, hand him over to one of the brethren who perform the arduous duty of providing seats for visitors, and say to him: "There, stranger, you have arrived; *this* is the United States. The New Testament, Plymouth Rock, and the Fourth of July, — *this* is what they have brought us to. What the next issue will be, no one can tell; but this is about what we are at present."

We cannot imagine what the brethren could have been think-ing about when they ordered the new bell that hangs in the tower of Plymouth Church. It is the most superfluous article in the known world. The New-Yorker who steps on board the Fulton ferry-boat about ten o'clock on Sunday morning finds himself accompanied by a large crowd of people who bear the visible stamp of strangers, who are going to Henry Ward Beecher's church. You can pick them out with perfect certainty. You see the fact in their countenances, in their dress, in their demean-or, as well as hear it in words of eager expectation. They are the kind of people who regard wearing-apparel somewhat in the light of its utility, and are not crushed by their clothes. They are the sort of people who take the " Tribune," and get up courses of lectures in the country towns. From every quarter of Brook-lyn, in street cars and on foot, streams of people are converging toward the same place. Every Sunday morning and evening, rain or shine, there is the same concourse, the same crowd at the gates before they are open, and the same long, laborious effort to get thirty-five hundred people into a building that will seat but twenty-seven hundred. Besides the ten or twelve members of the church who volunteer to assist in this labor, there is employed a force of six policemen at the doors, to prevent the multitude from choking all ingress. Seats are retained for their proprietors until ten minutes before the time of beginning; after that the strangers are admitted. Mr. Buckle, if he were with us still, would be pleased to know that his doctrine of averages holds good in this instance; since every Sunday about a churchful of persons come to this church, so that not many who come fail to get in.

There is nothing of the ecclesiastical drawing-room in the ar-rangements of this edifice. It is a very plain brick building, in a narrow street of small, pleasant houses, and the interior is only striking from its extent and convenience. The simple, old-fash-ioned design of the builder was to provide seats for as many peo-ple as the space would hold · and in executing this design, he constructed one of the finest interiors in the country, since the most pleasing and inspiriting spectacle that human eyes ever behold in this world is such an assembly as fills this church. The audience is grandly displayed in those wide, rounded galleries, surging up high against the white walls, and scooped out deep in the slanting floor, leaving the carpeted platform the vortex of an arrested whirlpool. Often it happens that two or three little children get lodged upon the edge of the platform, and sit there on the carpet among the flowers during the service, giving to the picture a singularly pleasing relief, as though they and the bouquets had been arranged by the same skilful hand, and for the same purpose. And it seems quite natural and proper that children should form part of so bright and joyous an occasion. Behind the platform rises to the ceiling the huge organ, of dark wood and silvered pipes, with fans of trumpets pointing heavenward from the top. This enormous toy occupies much space that could be better filled, and is only less superfluous than the bell; but we must pardon and indulge a foible. We could never see that Mr. Forrest walked any better for having such thick legs; yet they have their admirers. Blind old Handel played on an instrument very different from this, but the sexton had to eat a cold Sunday dinner; for not a Christian would stir as long as the old man touched the keys after service. But not old Handel nor older Gabriel could make such music as swells and roars from three thousand human voices, — the regular choir of Plymouth Church. It is a decisive proof of the excellence and heartiness of this choir, that the great organ has not lessened its effectiveness.

It is not clear to the distant spectator by what aperture Mr. Beecher enters the church. He is suddenly discovered to be present, seated in his place on the platform, — an under-sized gentleman in a black stock. His hair combed behind his ears, and worn a little longer than usual, imparts to his appearance something of the Puritan, and calls to mind his father, the champion of orthodoxy in heretical Boston. In conducting the opening exercises, and, indeed, on all occasions of ceremony, Mr. Beecher shows himself an artist, — both his language and his demeanor being marked by the most refined decorum. An elegant, finished simplicity characterizes all he does and says: not a word too

much, nor a word misused, nor a word waited for, nor an unhar-
monious movement, mars the satisfaction of the auditor. The
habit of living for thirty years in the view of a multitude, together
er with a natural sense of the becoming, and a quick sympathy
with men and circumstances, has wrought up his public demeanor
to a point near perfection. A candidate for public honors could
not study a better model. This is the more remarkable, because
it is a purely spiritual triumph. Mr. Beecher's person is not imposing, nor his natural manner graceful. It is his complete ex-
tirpation of the desire of producing an illegitimate effect ; it is
his sincerity and genuineness as a human being ; it is the dignity
of his character, and his command of his powers, — which give
him this easy mastery over every situation in which he finds himself.

Extempore prayers are not, perhaps, a proper subject for
comment. The grand feature of the preliminary services of
this church is the singing, which is not executed by the first
talent that money can command. When the prelude upon the
organ is finished, the whole congregation, almost every individual
in it, as if by a spontaneous and irresistible impulse, stands up
and sings. We are not aware that anything has ever been done
or said to bring about this result ; nor does the minister of the
church set the example, for he usually remains sitting and silent.
It seems as if every one in the congregation was so full of something that he felt impelled to get up and sing it out. In other
churches where congregational singing is attempted, there are
usually a number of languid Christians who remain seated, and
a large number of others who remain silent ; but here there is
a strange unanimity about the performance. A sailor might as
well try not to join in the chorus of a forecastle song as a member of this joyous host not to sing   When the last preliminary
singing is concluded, the audience is in an excellent condition to
sit and listen, their whole corporeal system having been pleasantly exercised.

The sermon which follows is new wine in an old bottle. Up
to the moment when the text has been announced and briefly
explained, the service has all been conducted upon the ancient

infidel, and chiefly in the ancient phraseology; but from the moment when Mr. Beecher swings free from the moorings of his text, and gets fairly under way, his sermon is modern. No matter how fervently he may have been praying supernaturalism, he preaches pure cause and effect. His text may savor of old Palestine; but his sermon is inspired by New York and Brooklyn; and nearly all that he says, when he is most himself, finds an approving response in the mind of every well-disposed person, whether orthodox or heterodox in his creed.

What is religion? That, of course, is the great question. Mr. Beecher says: Religion is the slow, laborious, self-conducted EDUCATION of the whole man, from grossness to refinement, from sickliness to health, from ignorance to knowledge, from selfishness to justice, from justice to nobleness, from cowardice to valor. In treating this topic, whatever he may pray or read or assent to, he *preaches* cause and effect, and nothing else. Regeneration he does not represent to be some mysterious, miraculous influence exerted upon a man from without, but the man's own act, wholly and always, and in every stage of its progress. His general way of discoursing upon this subject would satisfy the most rationalized mind; and yet it does not appear to offend the most orthodox.

This apparent contradiction between the spirit of his preaching and the facts of his position is a severe puzzle to some of our thorough-going friends. They ask, How can a man demonstrate that the fall of rain is so governed by unchanging laws that the shower of yesterday dates back in its causes to the origin of things, and, having proved this to the comprehension of every soul present, finish by *praying* for an immediate outpouring upon the thirsty fields? We confess that, to our modern way of thinking, there is a contradiction here, but there is none at all to an eir of the Puritans. We reply to our impatient young friends, that Henry Ward Beecher at once represents and assists the American Christian of the present time, just because of this seeming contradiction. He is a bridge over which we are passing from the creed-enslaved past to the perfect freedom of the future. Mr. Lecky, in his "History of the Spirit of Rationalism" has shown the process by which truth is advanced. Old

errors, he says, do not die because they are refuted, but *fade out*
because they are neglected. One hundred and fifty years ago,
our ancestors were perplexed, and even distressed, by something
they called the doctrine of Original Sin. No one now concerns
himself either to refute or assert the doctrine ; few people know
what it is; we all simply let it alone, and it fades out. John
Wesley not merely believed in witchcraft, but maintained that a
belief in witchcraft was essential to salvation. All the world,
except here and there an enlightened and fearless person, believed in witchcraft as late as the year 1750. That belief has
not perished because its folly was demonstrated, but because the
average human mind grew past it, and let it alone until it faded
out in the distance. Or we might compare the great body of
beliefs to a banquet, in which every one takes what he likes best ;
and the master of the feast, observing what is most in demand,
keeps an abundant supply of such viands, but gradually with-
draws those which are neglected. Mr. Beecher has helped himself to such beliefs as are congenial to him, and shows an exquisite tact in passing by those which interest him not, and which
have lost regenerating power. There *are* minds which cannot be
content with anything like vagueness or inconsistency in their
opinions. They must know to a certainty whether the sun and
moon stood still or not. His is not a mind of that cast ; he can
" hover on the confines of truth," and leave the less inviting parts
of the landscape veiled in mist unexplored. Indeed, the great
aim of his preaching is to show the insignificance of opinion compared with right feeling and noble living, and he prepares the
way for the time when every conceivable latitude of mere opinion
shall be allowed and encouraged.

One remarkable thing about his preaching is, that he has not,
ike so many men of liberal tendencies, fallen into milk-and-
waterism. He often gives a foretaste of the terrific power
which preachers will wield when they draw inspiration from
science and life. Without ever frightening people with horrid
pictures of the future, he has a sense of the perils which beset
human life here, upon this bank and shoal of time. How needless to draw upon the imagination, in depicting the consequences

ᴏf violating natural law! Suppose a preacher should give a plain, cold, scientific exhibition of the penalty which Nature exacts for the crime, so common among church-going ladies and others, of murdering their unborn offspring! It would appall the Devil. Scarcely less terrible are the consequences of the most common vices and meannesses when they get the mastery. Mr. Beecher has frequently shown, by powerful delineations of this kind, how large a part legitimate terror must ever play in the services of a true church, when the terrors of superstition have wholly faded out. It cannot be said of his preaching, that he preaches "Christianity with the bones taken out." He does not give "twenty minutes of tepid exhortation," nor amuse his auditors with elegant and melodious essays upon virtue.

We need not say that his power as a public teacher is due, in a great degree, to his fertility in illustrative similes. Three or four volumes, chiefly filled with these, as they have been caught from his lips, are before the public, and are admired on both continents. Many of them are most strikingly happy, and flood his subject with light. The smiles that break out upon the sea of upturned faces, and the laughter that whispers round the assembly, are often due as much to the aptness as to the humor of the illustration: the mind receives an agreeable shock of surprise at finding a resemblance where only the widest dissimilarity had before been perceived.

Of late years, Mr. Beecher never sends an audience away half satisfied; for he has constantly grown with the growth of his splendid opportunity. How attentive the great assembly, and how quickly responsive to the points he makes! That occasional ripple of laughter, — it is not from any want of seriousness in the speaker, in the subject, or in the congregation, nor is it a Rowland Hill eccentricity. It is simply that it has pleased Heaven to endow this genial soul with a quick perception of the likeness there is between things unlike; and, in the heat and torrent of his speech, the suddenly discovered similarity amuses while it instructs. Philosophers and purists may cavil at parts of these sermons, and, of course, they are not perfect; but who can deny that their general effect is civilizing, humanizing, elevating, and

16

regenerating, and that this master of preaching is the true brother of all those high and bright spirits, on both sides of the ocean, who are striving to make the soul of this age fit to inhabit and nobly impel its new body?

The sermon over, a livelier song brings the service to a happy conclusion; and slowly, to the thunder of the new organ, the great assembly dissolves and oozes away.

The Sunday services are not the whole of this remarkable church. It has not yet adopted Mrs. Stowe's suggestion of providing billiard-rooms, bowling-alleys, and gymnastic apparatus for the development of Christian muscle, though these may come in time. The building at present contains eleven apartments, among which are two large parlors, wherein, twice a month, there is a social gathering of the church and congregation, for conversation with the pastor and with one another. Perhaps, by and by, these will be always open, so as to furnish club conveniences to young men who have no home. Doubtless, this fine social organization is destined to development in many directions not yet contemplated.

Among the ancient customs of New England and its colonies (of which Brooklyn is one) is the Friday-evening prayer-meeting. Some of our readers, perhaps, have dismal recollections of their early compelled attendance on those occasions, when, with their hands firmly held in the maternal grasp, lest at the last moment they should bolt under cover of the darkness, they glided round into the back parts of the church, lighted by one smoky lantern hung over the door of the lecture-room, itself dimly lighted, and as silent as the adjacent chambers of the dead. Female figures, demure in dress and eyes cast down, flitted noiselessly in, and the awful stillness was only broken by the heavy boots of the few elders and deacons who constituted the male portion of the exceedingly slender audience. With difficulty, and sometimes, only after two or three failures, a hymn was raised, which, when in fullest tide, was only a dreary wail, — how unmelodious to the ears of unreverential youth, gifted with a sense of the ludicrous! How long, how sad, how pointless the prayers! How easy to believe, down in that dreary cellar, that this world was, but a wilderness, and man "a feeble piece"! Deacon Jones could speak up briskly enough when he was selling two yards of shilling calico to a farmer's wife sharp at a bargain; but in that apartment, contiguous to the tombs, it seemed natural that he should utter dismal views of life in bad grammar through his nose. Mrs. Jones was cheerful when she gave her little tea-party the evening before; but now she appeared to assent, without surprise, to the statement that she was a pilgrim travelling through a vale of tears. Veritable pilgrims, who do actually meet in an oasis of the desert, have a merry time of it, travellers tell us. It was not so with these good souls, inhabitants of a pleasant place, and anticipating an eternal abode in an inconceivably delightful paradise. But then there was the awful chance of missing it! And the reluctant youth, dragged to this melancholy scene, who avenged themselves by giving select imitations of deaconian eloquence for the amusement of young friends, — what was to become of *them*? It was such thoughts, doubtless, that gave to those excellent people their gloomy habit of mind; and if their creed expressed the literal truth respecting man's destiny, character, and duty, terror alone was rational, and laughter was hideous and defiant mockery. What room in a benevolent heart for joy, when a point of time, a moment's space removed us to that heavenly place, or shut us up in hell?

From the time when we were accustomed to attend such meetings, long ago, we never saw a Friday-evening meeting till the other night, when we found ourselves in the lecture-room of Plymouth Church.

The room is large, very lofty, brilliantly lighted by reflectors affixed to the ceiling, and, except the scarlet cushions on the settees, void of upholstery. It was filled full with a cheerful company, not one of whom seemed to have on more or richer clothes than she had the moral strength to wear. Content and pleasant expectation sat on every countenance, as when people have come to a festival, and await the summons to the banquet. No pulpit, or anything like a pulpit, cast a shadow over the scene; but in its stead there was a rather large platform, raised two steps, covered with dark green canvas, and having upon it a very small table and one chair. The red-cushioned settees were so arranged as to enclose the green platform all about, except on one side ; so that he who should sit upon it would appear to be in the midst of the people, raised above them that all might see him, yet still among them and one of them. At one side of the platform, but on the floor of the room, among the settees, there was a piano open. Mr. Beecher sat near by, reading what appeared to be a letter of three or four sheets. The whole scene was so little like what we commonly understand by the word "meeting," the people there were so little in a "meeting" state of mind, and the subsequent proceedings were so informal, unstudied, and social, that, in attempting to give this account of them, we almost feel as if we were reporting for print the conversation of a private evening party. Anything more unlike an old-fashioned prayer-meeting it is not possible to conceive.

Mr. Beecher took his seat upon the platform, and, after a short pause, began the exercises by saying, in a low tone, these words: "Six twenty-two."

A rustling of the leaves of hymn-books interpreted the meaning of this mystical utterance, which otherwise might have been taken as announcing a discourse upon the prophetic numbers. The piano confirmed the interpretation ; and then the company burst into one of those joyous and unanimous singings which are so enchanting a feature of the services of this church. Loud rose the beautiful harmony of voices, constraining every one to join in the song, even those most unused to sing. When it was ended, the pastor, in the same low tone, pronounced a name; upon which one of the brethren rose to his feet, and the rest of the assembly slightly inclined their heads. It would not, as we have remarked, be becoming in us to say anything upon this portion of the proceedings, except to note that the prayers were all brief, perfectly quiet and simple, and free from the routine or regulation expressions. There were but two or three of them, alternating with singing ; and when that part of the exercises was concluded, Mr. Beecher had scarcely spoken. The meeting ran alone, in the most spontaneous and pleasant manner ; and, with all its heartiness and simplicity, there was a certain refined decorum pervad ing all that was done and said. There was a pause after the last hymn died away, and then Mr. Beecher, still seated, began, in the tone of conversation, to speak, somewhat after this manner.

"When," said he, "I first began to walk as a Christian, in my youthful zeal I made many resolutions that were well meant, but indiscreet. Among others, I remember I resolved to pray, at least once, in some way, every hour that I was awake. I tried faithfully to keep this resolution, but never having succeeded a single day, I suffered the pangs of self-reproach, until reflection satisfied me that the only wisdom possible, with regard to such a resolve, was to break it. I remember, too, that I made a resolution to speak upon religion to every person with whom I conversed, — on steamboats, in the streets, anywhere. In this, also, I failed, as I ought; and I soon learned that, in the sowing of such seed, as in other sowings, times and seasons and methods must be considered and selected, or a man may defeat his own object, and make religion loathsome."

In language like this he introduced the topic of the evening's conversation, which was, How far, and on what occasions, and in what manner, one person may invade, so to speak, the personality of another, and speak to him upon his moral condition. The pastor expressed his own opinion, always in the conversational tone, in a talk of ten minutes' duration; in the course of which he applauded, not censured, the delicacy which causes most people to shrink from doing it. He said that a man's personality was not a macadamized road for every vehicle to drive upon at will; but rather a sacred enclosure, to be entered, if at all, with the consent of the owner, and with deference to his feelings and tastes. He maintained, however, that there *were* times and modes in which this might properly be done, and that every one *had* a duty to perform of this nature. When he had finished his observations, he said the subject was open to the remarks of others; whereupon a brother instantly rose and made a very honest confession.

He said that he had never attempted to perform the duty in question without having a palpitation of the heart and a complete "turning over" of his inner man. He had often reflected upon this curious fact, but was not able to account for it. He had not allowed this repugnance to prevent his doing the duty; but he always had to rush at it and perform it by a sort of *coup de main.* for if he allowed himself to think about the matter, he could not do it at all. He concluded by saying that he should be very much obliged to any one if he could explain this mystery.

The pastor said: "May it not be the natural delicacy we feel. and ought to feel, in approaching the interior consciousness of another person?"

Another brother rose. There was no hanging back at this meeting; there were no awkward pauses; every one seemed full of matter. The new speaker was not inclined to admit the explanation suggested by the pastor. "Suppose," said he, "we were to see a man in imminent danger of immediate destruction, and there was one way of escape, and but one, which *we* saw and he did not, should we feel any delicacy in running up to him and urging him to fly for his life? Is it not a want of faith on our part that causes the reluctance and hesitation we all feel in urging others to avoid a peril so much more momentous?"

Mr. Beecher said the cases were not parallel. Irreligious persons, he remarked, were not in imminent danger of immediate death; they might die to-morrow; but in all probability they would not, and an ill-timed or injudicious admonition might for ever repel them. We must accept the doctrine of probabilities, and act in accordance with it in this particular, as in all others.

Another brother had a puzzle to present for solution. He said that he too had experienced the repugnance to which allusion had been made; but what surprised him most was, that the more he loved a person, and the nearer he was related to him, the more difficult he found it to converse with him upon his spiritual state. Why is this? "I should like to have this question answered," said he, "if there *is* an answer to it."

Mr. Beecher observed that this was the universal experience, and he was conscious himself of a peculiar reluctance and embarrassment in approaching one of his own household on the subject in question. He thought it was due to the fact that we respect more the personal rights of those near to us than we do those of others, and it was more difficult to break in upon the routine o our ordinary familiarity with them. We are accustomed to a certain tone, which it is highly embarrassing to jar upon.

Captain Duncan related two amusing anecdotes to illustrate the right way and the wrong way of introducing religious conversation. In his office there was sitting one day a sort of lay preacher, who was noted for lugging in his favorite topic in the most forbidding and abrupt manner. A sea-captain came in, who was introduced to this individual.

" Captain Porter," said he, with awful solemnity, " are you a captain in Israel?"

The honest sailor was so abashed and confounded at this novel salutation, that he could only stammer out an incoherent reply; and he was evidently much disposed to give the tactless zealot a piece of his mind expressed in the language of the quarter-deck. When the solemn man took his leave, the disgusted captain said, " If ever I should be coming to your office again, and that man should be here, I wish you would send me word, and I 'll stay away."

A few days after, another clergyman chanced to be in the office, no other than Mr. Beecher himself, and another captain came in, a roistering, swearing, good-hearted fellow. The conversation fell upon sea-sickness, a malady to which Mr. Beecher is peculiarly liable. This captain also was one of the few sailors who are always sea-sick in going to sea, and gave a moving account of his sufferings from that cause. Mr. Beecher, after listening attentively to his tale, said, " Captain Duncan, if I was a preacher to such sailors as your friend here, I should represent hell as an eternal voyage, with every man on board in the agonies of sea-sickness, the crisis always imminent, but never coming."

This ludicrous and most unprofessional picture amused the old salt exceedingly, and won his entire good-will toward the author of it; so that, after Mr. Beecher left, he said, " That 's a good fellow, Captain Duncan. I like *him*, and I 'd like to hear him talk more."

Captain Duncan contended that this free-and-easy way of address was just the thing for such characters. Mr. Beecher had shown him, to his great surprise, that a man could be a decent and comfortable human being, although he was a minister, and had so gained his confidence and good-will that he could say *anything* to him at their next interview. Captain Duncan finished his remarks by a decided expression of his disapproval of the canting regulation phrases so frequently employed by religious people, which are perfectly nauseous to men of the world.

This interesting conversation lasted about three quarters of an hour, and ended, not because the theme seemed exhausted, but because the time was up. We have only given enough of it to convey some little idea of its spirit. The company again broke into one of their cheerful hymns, and the meeting was dismissed in the usual manner.

During the whole evening not a canting word nor a false tone had been uttered. Some words were used, it is true, and some forms practised, which are not congenial to "men of the world," and some doctrines were assumed to be true which have become incredible to many of us. These, however, were not conspicuous nor much dwelt upon. The subject, too, of the conversation was less suitable to our purpose than most of the topics discussed at these meetings, which usually have a more direct bearing upon the conduct of life. Nevertheless, is it not apparent that such meetings as this, conducted by a man of tact, good sense, and experience, must be an aid to good living? Here were a number of people, — parents, business-men, and others, — most of them heavily burdened with responsibility, having notes and rents to pay, customers to get and keep, children to rear, — busy people, anxious people, of extremely diverse characters, but united by a common desire to live nobly. The difficulties of noble living are very great, — never so great, perhaps, as now and here, — and these people assemble every week to converse upon them. What more rational thing could they do? If they came together to snivel and cant, and to support one another in a miserable conceit of being the elect of the human species, we might object. But no description can show how far from that, how opposite to that, is the tone, the spirit, the object, of the Friday-evening meeting at Plymouth Church.

Have we "Liberals" — as we presume to call ourselves — ever devised anything so well adapted as this to the needs of average mortals struggling with the ordinary troubles of life? We know of nothing. Philosophical treatises, and arithmetical computations respecting the number of people who inhabited Palestine, may have their use, but they cannot fill the aching void in the heart of a lone widow, or teach an anxious father how to manage a troublesome boy. There was an old lady near us at this meeting, — a good soul in a bonnet four fashions old, — who sat and cried for joy, as the brethren carried on their talk. She had come in alone from her solitary room, and enjoyed all the evening long a blended moral and literary rapture. It was a banquet of delight to her, the recollection of which would brighten all her week, and it cost her no more than air and sunlight. To the happy, the strong, the victorious, Shakespeare and the Musical Glasses may appear to suffice; but the world is full of the weak, the wretched, and the vanquished.

There was an infuriate heretic in Boston once, whose antipathy to what he called "superstition" was something that bordered upon lunacy. But the time came when he had a child, his only child, and the sole joy of his life, dead in the house. It had to be buried. The broken-hearted father could not endure the thought of his child's being carried out and placed in its grave without *some* outward mark of respect, *some* ceremonial which should recognize the difference between a dead child and a dead kitten; and he was fain, at last, to go out and bring to his house a poor lame cobbler, who was a kind of Methodist preacher, to say and read a few words that should break the fall of the darling object into the tomb. The occurrence made no change in his opinions, but it revolutionized his feelings. He is as untheological as ever; but he would subscribe money to build a church, and he esteems no man more than an honest clergyman.

If anything can be predicated of the future with certainty, it is, that the American people will never give up that portion of their heritage from the past which we call Sunday, but will always devote its hours to resting the body and improving the soul. All our theologies will pass away, but this will remain. Nor less certain is it, that there will always be a class of men who will do, professionally and as their settled vocation, the work now done by the clergy. That work can never be dispensed with, either in civilized or in barbarous communities. The great problem of civilization is, how to bring the higher intelligence of the community, and its better moral feeling, to bear upon the mass of people, so that the lowest grade of intelligence and morals shall be always approaching the higher, and the higher still rising. A church purified of superstition solves part of this problem, and a good school system does the rest.

All things improve in this world very much in the same way. The improvement originates in one man's mind, and, being carried into effect with evident good results, it is copied by others. We are all apt lazily to run in the groove in which we find ourselves; we are creatures of habit, and slaves of tradition. Now and then, however, in every profession and sphere, if they are untrammelled by law, an individual appears who is discontented with the ancient methods, or sceptical of the old traditions, or both, and he invents better ways, or arrives at more rational opinions. Other men look on and approve the improved process, or listen and imbibe the advanced belief.

Now, there appears to be a man upon Brooklyn Heights who has found out a more excellent way of conducting a church than has been previously known. He does not waste the best hours of every day in writing sermons, but employs those hours in absorbing the knowledge and experience which should be the matter of sermons. He does not fritter away the time of a public instructor in "pastoral visits," and other useless visitations. His mode of conducting a public ceremonial reaches the finish of high art, which it resembles also in its sincerity and simplicity. He has known how to banish from his church everything that savors of cant and sanctimoniousness, — so loathsome to honest minds. Without formally rejecting time-honored forms and usages, he has infused into his teachings more and more of the modern spirit, drawn more and more from science and life, less and less from tradition, until he has acquired the power of preaching sermons which Edwards and Voltaire, Whitefield and Tom Paine, would heartily and equally enjoy. Surely, there is something in all this which could be imitated. The great talents with which he is endowed cannot be imparted, but we do not believe that his power is wholly derived from his talent. A man of only respectable abilities, who should catch his spirit, practise some of his methods, and spend his strength in getting knowledge, and not in coining sentences, would be able anywhere to gather round him a concourse of hearers. The great secret is, to let orthodoxy slide, as something which is neither to be maintained nor refuted, — insisting only on the spirit of Christianity, and applying it to the life of the present day in this land.

There are some reasons for thinking that the men and the organizations that have had in charge the moral interests of the people of the United States for the last fifty years have not been quite equal to their trust. What are we to think of such results of New England culture as Douglas, Cass, Webster, and many other men of great ability, but strangely wanting in moral power? What are we to think of the great numbers of Southern Yankees who were, and are, the bitterest foes of all that New England represents? What are we to think of the Rings that seem now-a-days to form themselves, as it were, spontaneously in every great corporation? What of the club-houses that spring up at every corner, for the accommodation of husbands and fathers who find more attractions in wine, supper, and equivocal stories than in the society of their wives and children? What are we to think of the fact, that among the people who can afford to advertise at the rate of a dollar and a half a line are those who provide women with the means of killing their unborn children, — double crime, murder and suicide? What are we to think of the moral impotence of almost all women to resist the tyranny of fashion, and the *necessity* that appears to rest upon them to copy every disfiguration invented by the harlots of Paris? What are we to think of the want both of masculine and moral force in men, which makes them helpless against the extravagance of their households, to support which they do fifty years' work in twenty, and then die? What are we to think of the fact that all the creatures living in the United States enjoy good health, except the human beings, who are nearly all ill?

When we consider such things as these, we cannot help calling in question a kind of public teaching which leaves the people in ignorance of so much that they most need to know. Henry Ward Beecher is the only clergyman we ever heard who habitually promulgates the truth, that to be ill is generally a sin, and always a shame. We never heard him utter the demoralizing falsehood, that this present life is short and of small account, and that nothing is worthy of much consideration except the life to come. He dwells much on the enormous length of this life, and the prodigious revenue of happiness it may yield to those who comply with the conditions of happiness. It is his habit, also, to preach the duty which devolves upon every person, to labor for the increase of his knowledge and the general improvement of his mind. We have heard him say on the platform of his church, that it was disgraceful to any mechanic or clerk to let such a picture as the Heart of the Andes be exhibited for twenty-five cents, and not go and see it. Probably there is not one honest clergyman in the country who does not fairly earn his livelihood by the good he does, or by the evil he prevents. But not enough good is done, and not enough evil prevented. The sudden wealth that has come upon the world since the improvement of the steam-engine adds a new difficulty to the life of millions. So far, the world does not appear to have made the best use of its too rapidly increased surplus. "We cannot sell a twelve-dollar book in this country," said a bookseller to us the other day. But how easy to sell two-hundred-dollar garments! There seems great need of something that shall have power to spiritualize mankind, and make head against the reinforced influence of material things. It may be that the true method of dealing with the souls of modern men has been, in part, discovered by Mr. Beecher, and that it would be well for persons aspiring to the same vocation to *begin* their preparation by making a pilgrimage to Brooklyn Heights.

COMMODORE VANDERBILT.

COMMODORE VANDERBILT.*

THE Staten Island ferry, on a fine afternoon in summer, is one of the pleasantest scenes which New York affords. The Island, seven miles distant from the city, forms one of the sides of the Narrows, through which the commerce of the city and the emigrant ships enter the magnificent bay that so worthily announces the grandeur of the New World. The ferry-boat, starting from the extremity of Manhattan Island, first gives its passengers a view of the East River, all alive with every description of craft; then, gliding round past Governor's Island, dotted with camps and crowned with barracks, with the national flag floating above all, it affords a view of the lofty bluffs which rise on one side of the Hudson and the long line of the mast-fringed city on the other; then, rounding Governor's Island, the steamer pushes its way towards the Narrows, disclosing to view Fort Lafayette, so celebrated of late, the giant defensive works opposite to it, the umbrageous and lofty sides of Staten Island, covered with villas, and beyond all, the Ocean, lighted up by Coney Island's belt of snowy sand, glistening in the sun.

Change the scene to fifty-five years ago: New York was then a town of eighty thousand people, and Staten Island was inhabited only by farmers, gardeners, and fishermen, who lived by supplying the city with provisions. No elegant seats, no picturesque villas adorned the hillsides, and pleasure-seekers found a nearer

---

* This narrative of the business-life of Commodore Vanderbilt was written immediately after I had heard him tell the story himself. It was written at the request of Robert Bonner, Esq., and published by him in the New York Ledger of April 8, 1865. I should add, that several of the facts given were related to me at various times by members of Mr. Vanderbilt's family.

resort in Hoboken.   The ferry then, if ferry it could be called, consisted of a few sail-boats, which left the island in the morning loaded with vegetables and fish, and returned, if wind and tide permitted, at night.   If a pleasure party occasionally visited Staten Island, they considered themselves in the light of bold adventurers, who had gone far beyond the ordinary limits of an excursion.   There was only one thing in common between the ferry at that day and this : the boats started from the same spot. Where the ferry-house now stands at Whitehall was then the beach to which the boatmen brought their freight, and where they remained waiting for a return cargo.   That was, also, the general boat-stand of the city.   Whoever wanted a boat, for business or pleasure, repaired to Whitehall, and it was a matter of indiffer- ence to the boatmen from Staten Island, whether they returned home with a load, or shared in the general business of the port.

It is to one of those Whitehall boatmen of 1810, that we have to direct the reader's attention.   He was distinguished from his comrades on the stand in several ways.   Though master of a Staten Island boat that would carry twenty passengers, he was but sixteen years of age, and he was one of the handsomest, the most agile and athletic, young fellows that either Island could show.   Young as he was, there was that in his face and bearing which gave assurance that he was abundantly competent to his work.   He was always at his post betimes, and on the alert for a job.   He always performed what he undertook.   This summer of 1810 was his first season, but he had already an ample share of the best of the business of the harbor.

Cornelius Vanderbilt was the name of this notable youth, — the same Cornelius Vanderbilt who has since built a hundred steamboats, who has since made a present to his country of a steamship of five thousand tons' burden, who has since bought lines of railroad, and who reported his income to the tax commis- sioners, last year at something near three quarters of a million. The first money the steamboat-king ever earned was by carrying passengers between Staten Island and New York at eighteen cents each.

His father, who was also named Cornelius, was the founder of the Staten Island ferry. He was a thriving farmer on the Island as early as 1794, tilling his own land near the Quarantine Ground, and conveying his produce to New York in his own boat. Frequently he would carry the produce of some of his neighbors, and, in course of time, he ran his boat regularly, leaving in the morning and returning at night, during the whole of the summer, and thus he established a ferry which has since become one of the most profitable in the world, carrying sometimes more than twelve thousand passengers in a day. He was an industrious, enterprising, liberal man, and early acquired a property which for that time was affluence. His wife was a singularly wise and energetic woman. She was the main stay of the family, since her husband was somewhat too liberal for his means, and not always prudent in his projects. Once, when her husband had fatally involved himself, and their farm was in danger of being sold for a debt of three thousand dollars, she produced, at the last extremity, her private store, and counted out the whole sum in gold pieces. She lived to the great age of eighty-seven, and left an estate of fifty thousand dollars, the fruit of her own industry and prudence. Her son, like many other distinguished men, loves to acknowledge that whatever he has, and whatever he is that is good, he owes to the precepts, the example, and the judicious government of his mother.

Cornelius, the eldest of their family of nine children, was born at the old farm-house on Staten Island, May 27, 1794. A healthy, vigorous boy, fond of out-door sports, excelling his companions in all boyish feats, on land and water, he had an unconquerable aversion to the confinement of the school-room. At that day, the school-room was, indeed, a dull and uninviting place, the lessons a tedious routine of learning by rote, and the teacher a tyrant, enforcing them by the terrors of the stick. The boy went to school a little, now and then, but learned little more than to read, write, and cipher, and these imperfectly. The only books he remembers using at school were the spelling-book and Testament. His real education was gained in working on his father's farm, helping to sail his father's boat, driving his father's horses, swimming, riding, rowing, sporting with his young friends. He

was a bold rider from infancy, and passionately fond of a fine
horse. He tells his friends sometimes, that he rode a race-horse
at full speed when he was but six years old. That he regrets not
having acquired more school knowledge, that he values what is
commonly called education, is shown by the care he has taken to
have his own children well instructed.

There never was a clearer proof than in his case that the child
is father of the man. He showed in boyhood the very quality
which has most distinguished him as a man, — the power of accomplishing things in spite of difficulty and opposition. He was a
born conqueror.

When he was twelve years old, his father took a contract for
getting the cargo out of a vessel stranded near Sandy Hook, and
transporting it to New York in lighters. It was necessary to
carry the cargo in wagons across a sandy spit. Cornelius, with
a little fleet of lighters, three wagons, their horses and drivers,
started from home solely charged with the management of this
difficult affair. After loading the lighters and starting them for
the city, he had to conduct his wagons home by land, — a long
distance over Jersey sands. Leaving the beach with only six
dollars, he reached South Amboy penniless, with six horses and
three men, all hungry, still far from home, and separated from
Staten Island by an arm of the sea half a mile wide, that could
be crossed only by paying the ferryman six dollars. This was a
puzzling predicament for a boy of twelve, and he pondered long
how he could get out of it. At length he went boldly to the only
innkeeper of the place, and addressed him thus : —

"I have here three teams that I want to get over to Staten
Island. If you will put us across, I'll leave with you one of my
horses in pawn, and if I don't send you back the six dollars within forty-eight hours you may keep the horse."

The innkeeper looked into the bright, honest eyes of the boy
for a moment and said : —

"I'll do it."

And he did it. The horse in pawn was left with the ferryman
on the Island, and he was redeemed in time.

Before he was sixteen he had made up his mind to earn his

livelihood by navigation of some kind, and often, when tired of farm work, he had cast wistful glances at the outward-bound ships that passed his home. Occasionally, too, he had alarmed his mother by threatening to run away and go to sea. His preference, however, was to become a boatman of New York harbor. On the first of May, 1810, — an important day in his history, — he made known his wishes to his mother, and asked her to advance him a hundred dollars for the purchase of a boat. She replied: —

"My son, on the twenty-seventh of this month you will be sixteen years old. If, by your birthday, you will plough, harrow, and plant with corn that lot," pointing to a field, "I will advance you the money."

The field was one of eight acres, very rough, tough, and stony. He informed his young companions of his mother's conditional promise, and several of them readily agreed to help him. For the next two weeks the field presented the spectacle of a continuous "bee" of boys, picking up stones, ploughing, harrowing, and planting. To say that the work was done in time, and done thoroughly, is only another way of stating that it was undertaken and conducted by Cornelius Vanderbilt. On his birthday he claimed the fulfilment of his mother's promise. Reluctantly she gave him the money, considering his project only less wild than that of running away to sea. He hurried off to a neighboring village, bought his boat, hoisted sail, and started for home one of the happiest youths in the world. His first adventure seemed to justify his mother's fears, for he struck a sunken wreck on his way, and just managed to run his boat ashore before she filled and sunk.

Undismayed at this mishap, he began his new career. His success, as we have intimated, was speedy and great. He made a thousand dollars during each of the next three summers. Often he worked all night, but he was never absent from his post by day, and he soon had the cream of the boating business of the port.

At that day parents claimed the services and the earnings of their children till they were twenty-one. In other words, families made common cause against the common enemy, Want. The arrangement between this young boatman and his parents was that he should give them all his day earnings and half his night earnings. He fulfilled his engagement faithfully until his parents released him from it, and with his own half of his earnings by night he bought all his clothes. He had forty competitors in the business, who, being all grown men, could dispose of their gains as they chose; but of all the forty, he alone has emerged to prosperity and distinction. Why was this? There were several reasons. He soon came to be the best boatman in the port. He attended to his business more regularly and strictly than any other. He had no vices. His comrades spent at night much of what they earned by day, and when the winter suspended their business, instead of living on the last summer's savings, they were obliged to lay up debts for the next summer's gains to discharge. In those three years of willing servitude to his parents, Cornelius Vanderbilt added to the family's common stock of wealth, and gained for himself three things, — a perfect knowledge of his business, habits of industry and self-control, and the best boat in the harbor.

The war of 1812 suspended the commerce of the port, but gave a great impulse to boating. There were men-of-war in the harbor and garrisons in the forts, which gave to the boatmen of Whitehall and Staten Island plenty of business, of which Cornelius Vanderbilt had his usual share. In September, 1813, during a tremendous gale, a British fleet attempted to run past Fort Richmond. After the repulse, the commander of the fort, expecting a renewal of the attempt, was anxious to get the news to the city, so as to secure a reinforcement early the next day. Every one agreed that, if the thing could be done, there was but one man who could do it; and, accordingly, young Vanderbilt was sent for.

"Can you take a party up to the city in this gale?"

"Yes," was the reply; "but I shall have to carry them part of the way under water."

When he made fast to Coffee-House slip, an hour or two after every man in the boat was drenched to the skin. But there they were, and the fort was reinforced the next morning.

About this time, the young man had another important conversation with his mother, which, perhaps, was more embarrassing than the one recorded above. He was in love. Sophia Johnson was the maiden's name, — a neighbor's lovely and industrious daughter, whose affections he had wooed and won. He asked his mother's consent to the match, and that henceforth he might have the disposal of his own earnings. She approved his choice, and released him from his obligations. During the rest of that season he labored with new energy, saved five hundred dollars, and, in December, 1813, when he laid up his boat for the winter, became the happy husband of the best of wives.

In the following spring, a great alarm pervaded all the seaboard cities of America. Rumors were abroad of that great expedition which, at the close of the year, attacked New Orleans ; but, in the spring and summer, no one knew upon which port the blow would fall. The militia of New York were called out for three months, under a penalty of ninety-six dollars to whomsoever should fail to appear at the rendezvous. The boatmen, in the midst of a flourishing business, and especially our young husband, were reluctant to lose the profits of a season's labor, which were equivalent, in their peculiar case, to the income of a whole year. An advertisement appeared one day in the papers which gave them a faint prospect of escaping this disaster. It was issued from the office of the commissary-general, Matthew L. Davis, inviting bids from the boatmen for the contract of conveying provisions to the posts in the vicinity of New York during the three months, the contractor to be exempt from military duty. The boatmen caught at this, as a drowning man catches at a straw, and put in bids at rates preposterously low, — all except Cornelius Vanderbilt.

"Why don't you send in a bid ? " asked his father.

" Of what use would it be ? " replied the son. " They are offering to do the work at half-price. It can't be done at such rates."

" Well," added the father, " it can do no harm to try for it."

So, to please his father, but without the slightest expectation of getting the contract, he sent in an application, offering to transport the provisions at a price which would enable him to do it with the requisite certainty and promptitude. His offer was sim ply fair to both parties.

On the day named for the awarding of the contract, all the boatmen but him assembled in the commissary's office. He remained at the boat-stand, not considering that he had any interest in the matter. One after another, his comrades returned with long faces, sufficiently indicative of their disappointment; until, at length, all of them had come in, but no one bringing the prize. Puzzled at this, he strolled himself to the office, and asked the commissary if the contract had been given.

"O yes," said Davis; "that business is settled. Cornelius Vanderbilt is the man."

He was thunderstruck.

"What!" said the commissary, observing his astonishment, "is it you?"

"My name is Cornelius Vanderbilt."

"Well," said Davis, "don't you know why we have given the contract to you?"

"No."

"Why, it is because we want this business *done*, and we know you'll do it."

Matthew L. Davis, as the confidant of Aaron Burr, did a good many foolish things in his life, but on this occasion he did a wise one. The contractor asked him but one favor, which was, that the daily load of stores might be ready for him every evening at six o'clock. There were six posts to be supplied: Harlem, Hurl Gate, Ward's Island, and three others in the harbor or at the Narrows, each of which required one load a week. Young Vanderbilt did all this work at night; and although, during the whole period of three months, he never once failed to perform his contract, he was never once absent from his stand in the day-time. He slept when he could, and when he could not sleep he did without it. Only on Sunday and Sunday night could he be said to rest. There was a rare harvest for boatmen that summer. Transporting sick and furloughed soldiers, naval and military officers, the friends of the militia men, and pleasure-seekers visiting the forts, kept those of the boatmen who had "escaped the draft," profitably busy. It was not the time for an enterprising man to be absent from his post.

From the gains of that summer he built a superb little schooner, the Dread; and, the year following, the joyful year of peace, he and his brother-in-law, Captain De Forrest, launched the Charlotte, a vessel large enough for coasting service, and the pride of the harbor for model and speed. In this vessel, when the summer's work was over, he voyaged sometimes along the Southern coast, bringing home considerable freights from the Carolinas. Knowing the coast thoroughly, and being one of the boldest and most expert of seamen, he and his vessel were always ready when there was something to be done of difficulty and peril. During the three years succeeding the peace of 1815, he saved three thousand dollars a year; so that, in 1818, he possessed two or three of the nicest little craft in the harbor, and a cash capital of nine thousand dollars.

The next step of Captain Vanderbilt astonished both his rivals and his friends. He deliberately abandoned his flourishing business, to accept the post of captain of a small steamboat, at a salary of a thousand dollars a year. By slow degrees, against the opposition of the boatmen, and the terrors of the public, steamboats had made their way; until, in 1817, ten years after Fulton's experimental trip, the long head of Captain Vanderbilt clearly comprehended that the supremacy of sails was gone forever, and he resolved to ally himself to the new power before being overcome by it. Besides, he protests, that in no enterprise of his life has his chief object been the gain of money. Being in the business of carrying passengers, he desired to carry them in the best manner, and by the best means. Business has ever been to him a kind of game, and his ruling motive was and is, to play it so as to win. *To carry his point*, that has been the motive of his business career; but then his point has generally been one which, being carried, brought money with it.

At that day, passengers to Philadelphia were conveyed by a steamboat from New York to New Brunswick, where they remained all night, and the next morning took the stage for Tren ton, whence they were carried to Philadelphia by steamboat. The proprietor of part of this line was the once celebrated Thomas Gibbons, a man of enterprise and capital. It was in his service that Captain Vanderbilt spent the next twelve years of his life, commanding the steamer plying between New York and New Brunswick. The hotel at New Brunswick, where the passengers passed the night, which had never paid expenses, was let to him rent free, and under the efficient management of Mrs. Vanderbilt, it became profitable, and afforded the passengers such excellent entertainment as to enhance the popularity of the line.

In engaging with Mr. Gibbons, Captain Vanderbilt soon found that he had put his head into a hornet's nest. The State of New York had granted to Fulton and Livingston the exclusive right of running steamboats in New York waters. Thomas Gibbons, believing the grant unconstitutional, as it was afterwards declared by the Supreme Court, ran his boats in defiance of it, and thus involved himself in a long and fierce contest with the authorities of New York. The brunt of this battle fell upon his new captain. There was one period when for sixty successive days an attempt was made to arrest him; but the captain baffled every attempt. Leaving his crew in New Jersey (for they also were liable to arrest), he would approach the New York wharf with a lady at the helm, while he managed the engine; and as soon as the boat was made fast he concealed himself in the depths of the vessel. At the moment of starting, the officer (changed every day to avoid recognition) used to present himself and tap the wary captain on the shoulder.

"Let go the line," was his usual reply to the summons.

The officer, fearing to be carried off to New Jersey, where a retaliatory act threatened him with the State's prison, would jump ashore as for life; or, if carried off, would beg to be put ashore. In this way, and in many others, the captain contrived to evade the law. He fought the State of New York for seven years, until, in 1824, Chief Justice Marshall pronounced New York wrong and New Jersey right. The opposition vainly attempted to buy him off by the offer of a larger boat.

"No," replied the captain, "I shall stick to Mr. Gibbons till he is through his troubles."

That was the reason why he remained so long in the service of Mr. Gibbons.

After this war was over, the genius of Captain Vanderbilt had full play, and he conducted the line with so much energy and good sense, that it yielded an annual profit of forty thousand dollars. Gibbons offered to raise his salary to five thousand dollars a year, but he declined the offer. An acquaintance once asked him why he refused a compensation that was so manifestly just.

"I did it on principle," was his reply. "The other captains had but one thousand, and they were already jealous enough of me. Besides, I never cared for money. All I ever have cared for was to carry my point."

A little incident of these years he has sometimes related to his children. In the cold January of 1820, the ship Elizabeth — the first ship ever sent to Africa by the Colonization Society — lay at the foot of Rector Street, with the negroes all on board, frozen in. For many days, her crew, aided by the crew of the frigate Siam, her convoy, had been cutting away at the ice; but, as more ice formed at night than could be removed by day, the prospect of getting to sea was unpromising. One afternoon, Captain Vanderbilt joined the crowd of spectators.

"They are going the wrong way to work," he carelessly remarked, as he turned to go home. "I could get her out in one day."

These words, from a man who was known to mean all he said, made an impression on a bystander, who reported them to the anxious agent of the Society. The agent called upon him.

"What did you mean, Captain, by saying that you could get out the ship in one day?"

"Just what I said."

"What will you get her out for?"

"One hundred dollars."

"I'll give it. When will you do it?"

"Have a steamer to-morrow, at twelve o'clock, ready to tow her out. I'll have her clear in time."

That same evening, at six, he was on the spot with five men,

17   Y

three pine boards, and a small anchor. The difficulty was that beyond the ship there were two hundred yards of ice too thin to bear a man. The captain placed his anchor on one of his boards, and pushed it out as far as he could reach; then placed another board upon the ice, laid down upon it, and gave his anchor another push. Then he put down his third board, and used that as a means of propulsion. In this way he worked forward to near the edge of the thin ice, where the anchor broke through and sunk. With the line attached to it, he hauled a boat to the outer edge, and then began cutting a passage for the ship.

At eleven the next morning she was clear. At twelve she was towed into the stream.

In 1829, after twelve years of service as captain of a steamboat, being then thirty-five years of age, and having saved thirty thousand dollars, he announced to his employer his intention to set up for himself. Mr. Gibbons was aghast. He declared that he could not carry on the line without his aid, and finding him resolute, said: —

"There, Vanderbilt, take all this property, and pay me for it as you make the money."

This splendid offer he thankfully but firmly declined. He did so chiefly because he knew the men with whom he would have had to co-operate, and foresaw, that he and they could never work comfortably together. He wanted a free field.

The little Caroline, seventy feet long, that afterward plunged over Niagara Falls, was the first steamboat ever built by him. His progress as a steamboat owner was not rapid for some years. The business was in the hands of powerful companies and wealthy individuals, and he, the new-comer, running a few small boats on short routes, labored under serious disadvantages. Formidable attempts were made to run him off the river; but, prompt to retaliate, he made vigorous inroads into the enemy's domain, and kept up an opposition so keen as to compel a compromise in every instance. There was a time, during his famous contest with the Messrs. Stevens of Hoboken, when he had spen every dollar he possessed, and when a few days more of opposi ion would have compelled him to give up the strife. Nothing saved him but the belief, on the part of his antagonists, that Gibbons was backing him. It was not the case; he had no backer. But this error, in the very nick of time, induced his opponents to treat for a compromise, and he was saved.

Gradually he made his way to the control of the steamboat interest. He has owned, in whole or in part, a hundred steam vessels. His various opposition lines have permanently reduced fares one half. Superintending himself the construction of every boat, having a perfect practical knowledge of the business in its every detail, selecting his captains well and paying them justly, he has never lost a vessel by fire, explosion, or wreck. He possesses, in a remarkable degree, the talent of selecting the right man for a place, and of inspiring him with zeal. Every man who serves him *knows* that he will be sustained against all intrigue and all opposition, and that he has nothing to fear so long as he does his duty.

The later events in his career are, in some degree, known to the public. Every one remembers his magnificent cruise in the North Star, and how, on returning to our harbor, his first salute was to the cottage of his venerable mother on the Staten Island shore. To her, also, on landing, he first paid his respects. Every one knows that he presented to the government the steamer that bears his name, at a time when she was earning him two thousand dollars a day. He has given to the war something more precious than a ship: his youngest son, Captain Vanderbilt, the most athletic youth that ever graduated at West Point, and one of the finest young men in the country. His friends tell us that, on his twenty-second birthday he lifted nine hundred and eight pounds. But his giant strength did not save him. The fatigues and miasmas of the Corinth campaign planted in his magnificent frame the seeds of death. He died a year ago, after a long struggle with disease, to the inexpressible grief of his family.

During the last two or three years, Commodore Vanderbilt has been withdrawing his capital from steamers and investing it in railroads. It is this fact that has given rise to the impression that he has been playing a deep game in stock speculation. No such thing. He has *never* speculated; he disapproves of and despises speculation; and has invariably warned his son, against it as the pursuit of adventurers and gamblers. " Why, then," Wall Street may ask, " has he bought almost the whole stock of the Harlem railroad, which pays no dividends, running it up to prices that seem ridiculous ? " We can answer this question very simply : he bought the Harlem railroad to *keep.* He bought it as an investment. Looking several inches beyond his nose, and several days ahead of to-day, he deliberately concluded that the Harlem road, managed as he could manage it, would be, in the course of time, what Wall Street itself would call " a good thing." We shall see, by and by, whether he judged correctly. What was the New Jersey railroad worth when he and a few friends went over one day and bought it at auction? Less than nothing. The stock is now held at one hundred and seventy-five.

After taking the cream of the steamboat business for a quarter of a century, Commodore Vanderbilt has now become the largest holder of railroad stock in the country. If to-morrow balloons should supersede railroads, we should doubtless find him " in " balloons.

Nothing is more remarkable than the ease with which great business men conduct the most extensive and complicated affairs. At ten or eleven in the morning, the Commodore rides from his mansion in Washington Place in a light wagon, drawn by one of his favorite horses, to his office in Bowling Green, where, in two hours, aided by a single clerk, he transacts the business of the day, returning early in the afternoon to take his drive on the road. He despises show and ostentation in every form. No lackey attends him; he holds the reins himself. With an estate of forty millions to manage, nearly all actively employed in iron works and railroads, he keeps scarcely any books, but carries all his affairs in his head, and manages them without the least anxiety or apparent effort.

We are informed by one who knows him better almost than any one else, that he owes his excellent health chiefly to his love of horses. He possesses the power of leaving his business in his office, and never thinking of it during his hours of recreation

Out on the road behind a fast team, or seated at whist at the Club-House, he enters gayly into the humors of the hour. He is rigid on one point only, — not to talk or hear of business out of business hours.

Being asked one day what he considered to be the secret of success in business, he replied : —

"Secret? There is no secret about it. All you have to do is to attend to your business and go ahead."

With all deference to such an eminent authority, we must be allowed to think that that is not the whole of the matter. Three things seem essential to success in business: 1. To *know* your business. 2. To attend to it. 3. To keep down expenses until your fortune is safe from business perils.

On another occasion he replied with more point to a similar question : —

"The secret of my success is this: I never tell what I am going to do till I have done it."

He is, indeed, a man of little speech. Gen. Grant himself is not more averse to oratory than he. Once, in London, at a banquet, his health was given, and he was urged to respond. All that could be extorted from him was the following: —

"Gentlemen, I have never made a fool of myself in my life, and I am not going to begin now. Here is a friend of mine (his lawyer) who can talk all day. He will do my speaking."

Nevertheless, he knows how to express his meaning with singular clearness, force, and brevity, both by the tongue and by the pen. Some of his business letters, dictated by him to a clerk, are models of that kind of composition. He is also master of an art still more difficult, — that of *not* saying what he does not wish to say.

As a business man he is even more prudent than he is bold. He has sometimes remarked, that it has never been in the power of any man or set of men to prevent his keeping an engagement. If, for example, he should bind himself to pay a million of dollars on the first of May, he would at once provide for fulfilling his engagement in such a manner that no failure on the part of others, no contingency, private or public, could prevent his doing it. In

other words, he would have the money where he could be sure
of finding it on the day.

No one ever sees the name of Cornelius Vanderbilt on a sub-
scription paper, nor ever will. In his charities, which are numerous and liberal, he exhibits the reticence which marks his conduct as a man of business. His object is to render real and permanent service to deserving objects ; but to the host of miscellaneous beggars that pervade our places of business he is not accessible. The last years of many a good old soul, whom he knew
in his youth, have been made happy by a pension from him. But
of all this not a syllable ever escapes *his* lips.

He has now nearly completed his seventy-first year. His
frame is still erect and vigorous ; and, as a business man, he has
not a living superior. Every kind of success has attended him
through life. Thirteen children have been born to him, — nine
daughters and four sons, — nearly all of whom are living and are
parents. One of his grandsons has recently come of age. At the
celebration of his golden wedding, three years ago, more than a
hundred and forty of his descendants and relations assembled at
his house. On that joyful occasion, the Commodore presented to
his wife a beautiful little golden steamboat, with musical works instead of an engine, — emblematic at once of his business career
and the harmony of his home. If ever he boasts of anything appertaining to him, it is when he is speaking of the manly virtues
of his son lost in the war, or when he says that his wife is the
finest woman of her age in the city.

Commodore Vanderbilt is one of the New World's strong men.
His career is one which young men who aspire to lead in practical affairs may study with profit.

THEODOSIA BURR.

THEODOSIA BURR

NEW YORK does well to celebrate the anniversary of the day when the British troops evacuated the city; for it was in truth the birthday of all that we now mean by the City of New York. One hundred and seventy-four years had elapsed since Hendrick Hudson landed upon the shores of Manhattan; but the town could only boast a population of twenty-three thousand. In ten years the population doubled; in twenty years trebled. Washington Irving was a baby seven months old, at his father's house in William Street, on Evacuation Day, the 25th of November, 1783. On coming of age he found himself the inhabitant of a city containing a population of seventy thousand. When he died, at the age of seventy-five, more than a million of people inhabited the congregation of cities which form the metropolis of America.

The beginnings of great things are always interesting to us. New-Yorkers, at least, cannot read without emotion the plain, matter-of-fact accounts in the old newspapers of the manner in which the city of their pride changed masters. Journalism has altered its modes of procedure since that memorable day. No array of headings in large type called the attention of readers to the details of this great event in the history of their town, and no editorial article in extra leads commented upon it. The newspapers printed the merest programme of the proceedings, with scarcely a comment of their own; and, having done that, they felt that their duty was done, for no subsequent issue contains an allusion to the subject. Perhaps the reader will be gratified by a perusal of the account of the evacuation as given in Rivington's Gazette of November 26, 1783.

17 *

New York, November 26 : — Yesterday in the Morning the American Troops marched from Haerlem, to the Bowery-Lane — They remained there until about One o'Clock, when the British Troops left the Posts in the Bowery, and the American Troops marched into and took Possession of the City, in the following Order, *viz.*

1. A Corps of Dragoons.
2. Advance Guard of Light Infantry.
3. A Corps of Artillery.
4. Battalion of Light Infantry.
5. Battalion of Massachusetts Troops.
6. Rear Guard.

After the Troops had taken Possession of the City, the GENERAL [Washington] and GOVERNOR [George Clinton] made their Public Entry in the following Manner :

1. Their Excellencies the General and Governor, with their Suites. on Horseback.
2. The Lieutenant-Governor, and the Members of the Council, for the Temporary Government of the Southern District, four a-breast.
3. Major General Knox, and the Officers of the Army, eight a-breast
4. Citizens on Horseback, eight a-breast.
5. The Speaker of the Assembly, and Citizens, on Foot, eight a-breast.

Their Excellencies the Governor and Commander in Chief were escorted by a Body of West-Chester Light Horse, under the command of Captain Delavan.

The Procession proceeded down Queen Street [now Pearl], and through the Broadway, to *Cape's* Tavern.

The Governor gave a public Dinner at *Fraunces's* Tavern ; at which the Commander in Chief and other General Officers were present.

After Dinner, the following Toasts were drank by the Company :

1. The United States of America.
2. His most Christian Majesty.
3. The United Netherlands.
4. The king of Sweden.
5. The American Army.
6. The Fleet and Armies of France, which have served in America.
7. The Memory of those Heroes who have fallen for our Freedom.
8. May our Country be grateful to her military children.
9. May Justice support what Courage has gained.
10. The Vindicators of the Rights of Mankind in every Quarter of the Globe.

11. May America be an Asylum to the persecuted of the Earth.

12 May a close Union of the States guard the Temple they have erected to Liberty.

13. May the Remembrance of THIS DAY be a Lesson to Princes.

The arrangement and whole conduct of this march, with the tranquillity which succeeded it, through the day and night, was admirable! and the grateful citizens will ever feel the most affectionate impressions, from that elegant and efficient disposition which prevailed through the whole event.

Such was the journalism of that primitive day. The sedate Rivington, for so many years the Tory organ, was in no humor, we may suppose, to chronicle the minor events of the occasion, even if he had not considered them beneath the dignity of his vocation. He says nothing of the valiant matron in Chatham Row who, in the impatience of her patriotism, hoisted the American flag over her door two hours before the stipulated moment, noon, and defended it against a British provost officer with her broomstick. Nor does he allude to the great scene at the principal flag-staff, which the retiring garrison had plentifully greased, and from which they had removed the blocks and halyards, in order to retard the hoisting of the stars and stripes. He does not tell us how a sailor-boy, with a line around his waist and a pocket full of spikes, hammered his way to the top of the staff, and restored the tackling by which the flag was flung to the breeze before the barges containing the British rear-guard had reached the fleet. It was a sad day for Mr. Rivington, and he may be excused for not dwelling upon its incidents longer than stern duty demanded.

The whole State of New York had been waiting impatiently for the evacuation of the City. Many hundreds of the old Whig inhabitants, who had fled at the entrance of the English troops seven years before, were eager to come again into possession of their homes and property, and resume their former occupations. Many new enterprises waited only for the departure of the troops to be entered upon. A large number of young men were looking to New York as the scene of their future career. Albany, which had served as the temporary capital of the State, was full of lawyers, law-students, retired soldiers, merchants, and mechanics, who were prepared to remove to New York as soon as Rivington's Gazette should inform them that the British had really left, and General Washington taken possession. As in these days certain promises to pay are to be fulfilled six months after the United States shall have acknowledged the independence of a certain Confederacy, so at, that time it was a custom for leases and other compacts to be dated from "the day on which the British troops shall leave New York." Among the young men in Albany who were intending to repair to the city were two retired officers of distinction, ALEXANDER HAMILTON, a student at law, and AARON BURR, then in the second year of his practice at the bar. JAMES KENT and EDWARD LIVINGSTON were also students of law in Albany at that time. The old Tory lawyers being all exiled or silenced, there was a promising field in New York for young advocates of talent, and these two young gentlemen had both contracted marriages which necessitated speedy professional gains. Hamilton had won the daughter of General Schuyler. Burr was married to the widow of a British officer, whose fortune was a few hundred pounds and two fine strapping boys fourteen and sixteen years of age.

And Burr was himself a father. THEODOSIA, "his only child," was born at Albany in the spring of 1783. When the family removed to New York in the following winter, and took up their abode in Maiden Lane, — "the rent to commence when the troops leave the city," — she was an engaging infant of seven or eight months. We may infer something of the circumstances and prospects of her father, when we know that he had ventured upon a house of which the rent was two hundred pounds a year. We find him removing, a year or two after, to a mansion at the corner of Cedar and Nassau streets, the garden and grapery of which were among the finest in the thickly settled portion of the city. Fifty years after, he had still an office within a very few yards of the same spot, though all trace of the garden of Theodosia's childhood had long ago disappeared. She was a child of affluence. Not till she had left her father's house did a shadow of misfortune darken its portals. Abundance and elegance surrounded her from her infancy, and whatever advantages in education and training wealth can produce for a child she had in profusion. At the same time her father's vigilant stoicism guarded her from the evils attendant upon a too easy acquisition of things pleasant and desirable.

She was born into a happy home. Even if we had not the means of knowing something of the character of her mother, we might still infer that she must have possessed qualities singularly attractive to induce a man in the position of Burr to undertake the charge of a family at the outset of his career. She was neither handsome nor young, nor had she even the advantage of good health. A scar disfigured her face. Burr, — the brilliant and celebrated Burr, — heir of an honored name, had linked his rising fortunes with an invalid and her boys. The event most abundantly justified his choice, for in all the fair island of Manhattan there was not a happier family than his, nor one in which happiness was more securely founded in the diligent discharge of duty. The twelve years of his married life were his brightest and best ; and among the last words he ever spoke were a pointed declaration that his wife was the best woman and the finest lady he had ever known. It was her cultivated mind that drew him to her. "It was a knowledge of your mind," he once wrote her, " which first inspired me with a respect for that of your sex, and with some regret I confess, that the ideas you have often heard me express in favor of female intellectual power are founded in what I have imagined more than in what I have seen, except in you."

In those days an educated woman was among the rarest of rarities. The wives of many of our most renowned revolutionary leaders were surprisingly illiterate. Except the noble wife of John Adams, whose letters form so agreeable an oasis in the published correspondence of the time, it would be difficult to mention the name of one lady of the revolutionary period who could have been a companion to the *mind* of a man of culture. Mrs. Burr, on the contrary, was the equal of her husband in literary discernment, and his superior in moral judgment. Her remarks, in her letters to her husband, upon the popular authors of the day, Chesterfield, Rousseau, Voltaire, and others, show that she could correct as well as sympathize with her husband's taste. She relished all of Chesterfield except the "indulgence," which Burr thought essential. She had a weakness for Rousseau, but was not deluded by his sentimentality. She enjoyed Gibbon without stumbling at his fifteenth and sixteenth chapters.

The home of Theodosia presents to us a pleasing scene of vir- tuous industry. The master of the house, always an indomitable worker, was in the full tide of a successful career at the bar. His two step-sons were employed in his office, and one of them frequently accompanied him in his journeys to distant courts as clerk or amanuensis. No father could have been more generous or more thoughtful than he was for these fatherless youths, and they appeared to have cherished for him the liveliest affection. Mrs. Burr shared in the labors of the office during the absence of her lord. All the affairs of this happy family moved in har- mony, for love presided at their board, inspired their exertions, and made them one. One circumstance alone interrupted their felicity, and that was the frequent absence of Burr from home on business at country courts; but even these journeys served to call forth from all the family the warmest effusions of affection.

" What language can express the joy, the gratitude of Theodosia!" writes Mrs. Burr to her absent husband, in the fifth year of their mar- riage. " Stage after stage without a line. Thy usual punctuality gave room for every fear; various conjectures filled every breast. One of our sons was to have departed to-day in quest of the best of friends and fathers. This morning we waited the stage with impatience. Shrouder went frequently before it arrived; at length returned — no letter. We were struck dumb with disappointment. Barton [eldest son] set out to inquire who were the passengers; in a very few minutes returned exulting — a packet worth the treasures of the universe. Joy brightened every face; all expressed their past anxieties, their present happiness. To enjoy was the first result. Each made choice of what they could best relish. Porter, sweet wine, chocolate, and sweetmeats made the most delightful repast that could be enjoyed without thee. The servants were made to feel their lord was well; are at this instant toasting his health and bounty. While the boys are obeying thy dear commands, thy Theodosia flies to speak her heartfelt joy — her Aaron safe — mistress of the heart she adores, can she ask more? Has Heaven more to grant?"

What a pleasing picture of a happy family circle is this, and how rarely are the perils of a second marriage so completely overcome! It was in such a warm and pleasant nest as this that Theodosia Burr passed the years of her childhood.

Charles Lamb used to say that babies had no right to our regard merely *as* babies, but that every child had a character of its own by which it must stand or fall in the esteem of disinterested observers. Theodosia was a beautiful and forward child, formed to be the pet and pride of a household. "Your dear little Theo," wrote her mother in her third year, "grows the most engaging child you ever saw. It is impossible to see her with indifference." From her earliest years she exhibited that singular fondness for her father which afterward became the ruling passion of her life, and which was to undergo the severest tests that filial affection has ever known. When she was but three years of age her mother would write: "Your dear little daughter seeks you twenty times a day; calls you to your meals, and will not suffer your chair to be filled by any of the family." And again: "Your dear little Theodosia cannot hear you spoken of without an apparent melancholy; insomuch that her nurse is obliged to exert her invention to divert her, and myself avoid to mention you in her presence. She was one whole day indifferent to everything but your name. Her attachment is not of a common nature."

Here was an inviting opportunity for developing an engaging infant into that monstrous thing, a spoiled child. She was an only daughter in a family of which all the members but herself were adults, and the head of which was among the busiest of men.

But Aaron Burr, amidst all the toils of his profession, and in spite of the distractions of political strife, made the education of his daughter the darling object of his existence. Hunters tell us that pointers and hounds *inherit* the instinct which renders them such valuable allies in the pursuit of game; so that the offspring of a trained dog acquires the arts of the chase with very little instruction. Burr's father was one of the most zealous and skilful of schoolmasters, and from him he appears to have derived that pedagogic cast of character which led him, all his life, to take so much interest in the training of *protégés*. There was never a time in his whole career when he had not some youth upon his hands to whose education he was devoted. His system of training, with many excellent points, was radically defective. Its defects are sufficiently indicated when we say that it was pagan, not Christian. Plato, Socrates, Cato, and Cicero might have pronounced it good and sufficient: St. John, St. Augustine, and all the Christian host would have lamented it as fatally defective. But if Burr educated his child as though she were a Roman girl, her mother was with her during the first eleven years of her life, to supply, in some degree, what was wanting in the instructions of her father.

Burr was a stoic. He cultivated hardness. Fortitude and fidelity were his favorite virtues. The seal which he used in his correspondence with his intimate friends, and with them only, was descriptive of his character and prophetic of his destiny. It was a Rock, solitary in the midst of a tempestuous ocean, and bore the inscription, "*Nec flatu nec fluctu*," — neither by wind nor by wave. It was his principle to steel himself against the inevitable evils of life. If we were asked to select from his writings the sentence which contains most of his characteristic way of thinking, it would be one which he wrote in his twenty-fourth year to his future wife: "That mind is truly great which can bear with equanimity the trifling and unavoidable vexations of life, and be affected only by those which determine our substantial bliss." He utterly despised all complaining, even of the greatest calamities. He even experienced a kind of proud pleasure in enduring the fierce obloquy of his later years. One day, near the close of his life, when a friend had told him of some new scandal respecting his moral conduct, he said: "That's right, my child, tell me what they say. I like to know what the public say of me, — the *great* public!" Such words he would utter without the slightest bitterness, speaking of the *great* public as a humorous old grandfather might of a wayward, foolish, good little child.

So, at the dawn of a career which promised nothing but glory and prosperity, surrounded by all the appliances of ease and pleasure, he was solicitous to teach his child to do and to endure. He would have her accustomed to sleep alone, and to go about the house in the dark. Her breakfast was of bread and milk. He was resolute in exacting the less agreeable tasks, such as arithmetic. He insisted upon regularity of hours. Upon going away upon a journey he would leave written orders for her tutors, detailing the employments of each day; and, during his absence, a chief topic of his letters was the lessons of the children. *Children,* — for, that his Theodosia might have the advantage of a companion in her studies, he adopted the little Natalie, a French child, whom he reared to womanhood in his house. "The letters of our dear children," he would write, "are a feast. To hear that they are employed, that no time is absolutely wasted, is the most flattering of anything that could be told me of them. It insures their affection, or is the best evidence of it. It insures in its consequences everything I am ambitious of in them. Endcavor to preserve regularity of hours; it conduces exceedingly to industry." And his wife would answer: "I really believe, my dear, that few parents can boast of children whose minds are so prone to virtue. I see the reward of our assiduity with inexpressible delight, with a gratitude few experience. My Aaron, they have grateful hearts." Or thus: "Theo [seven years old] ciphers from five in the morning until eight, and also the same hours in the evening. This prevents our riding at those hours."

When Theodosia was ten years old, Mary Wollstonecraft's eloquent little book, "A Vindication of the Rights of Woman," fell into Burr's hands. He was so powerfully struck by it that he sat up nearly all night reading it. He showed it to all his friends. "Is it owing to ignorance or prejudice," he wrote, "that I have not yet met a single person who had discovered or would allow the merit of this work?" The work, indeed, was fifty years in advance of the time; for it anticipated all that is rational in the opinions respecting the position and education of women which are now held by the ladies who are stigmatized as the Strong-minded, as well as by John Mill, Herbert Spencer, and other economists of the moderr school It demanded fair play for the *understanding* of women. It proclaimed the essential equality of the sexes. It denounced the awful libertinism of that age, and showed that the weakness, the ignorance, the vanity, and the seclusion of women prepared them to become the tool and minion of bad men's lust. It criticised ably the educational system of Rousseau, and, with still more severity, the popular works of bishops and priests, who chiefly strove to inculcate an abject submission to man as the rightful lord of the sex. It demonstrated that the sole possibility of woman's elevation to the rank of man's equal and friend was in the cultivation of her mind, and in the thoughtful discharge of the duties of her lot. It is a really noble and brave little book, undeserving of the oblivion into which it has fallen. No intelligent woman, no wise parent with daughters to rear, could read it now without pleasure and advantage.

" Meekness," she says, " may excite tenderness, and gratify the arrogant pride of man; but the lordly caresses of a protector will not gratify a noble mind that pants and deserves to be *respected*. Fondness is a poor substitute for friendship. . . . . A girl whose spirits have not been damped by inactivity, or innocence tainted by false shame, will always be a romp, and the doll will never excite attention unless confinement allows her no alternative. . . . . Most of the women, in the circle of my observation, who have acted like rational creatures, have accidentally been allowed to run wild, as some of the elegant formers of the fair sex would insinuate. . . . . Men have better tempers than women because they are occupied by pursuits that interest the *head* as well as the heart. I never knew a weak or ignorant person who had a good temper. . . . . Why are girls to be told that they resemble angels, but to sink them below women? They are told that they are only like angels when they are young and beautiful; consequently it is their persons, not their virtues, that procure them this homage. . . . . It is in vain to attempt to keep the heart pure unless the head is furnished with ideas. . . . . Would ye, O my sisters really possess modesty, ye must remember that the possession of virtue, of any denomination, is incompatible with ignorance and vanity Ye must acquire that soberness of mind which the exercise of duties and the pursuit of knowledge alone inspire, or ye will still remain in a doubtful, dependent situation, and only be loved while ye are fair The downcast eye, the rosy blush, the retiring grace, are all proper in their season; but modesty being the child of reason cannot long exist with the sensibility that is not tempered by reflection. . . . . With what disgust have I heard sensible women speak of the wearisome confinement which they endured at school. Not allowed, perhaps, to step out of one broad path in a superb garden, and obliged to pace, with steady deportment, stupidly backward and forward, holding up their heads and turning out their toes, with shoulders braced back, instead of bounding forward, as Nature directs to complete her own design, in the various attitudes so conducive to health. The pure animal spirits, which make both mind and body shoot out and unfold the tender blossoms of hope, are turned sour and vented in vain wishes or pert repinings, that contract the faculties and spoil the temper; else they mount to the brain, and, sharpening the understanding before it gains proportionable strength, produce that pitiful cunning which disgracefully characterizes the female mind, — and, I fear, will ever characterize it while women remain the slaves of power."

In the spirit of this book Theodosia's education was conducted. Her mind had fair play. Her father took it for granted that she could learn what a boy of the same age could learn, and gave her precisely the advantages which he would have given a son. Besides the usual accomplishments, French, music, dancing, and riding, she learned to read Virgil, Horace, Terence, Lucian, Homer, in the original. She appears to have read all of Terence and Lucian, a great part of Horace, all the Iliad, and large portions of the Odyssey. "Cursed effects," exclaimed her father once, "of fashionable education, of which both sexes are the advocates, and yours eminently the victims. If I could foresee that Theo would become a mere fashionable woman, with all the attendant frivolity and vacuity of mind, adorned with whatever grace and allurement, I would earnestly pray God to take her forthwith hence. But I yet hope by her to convince the world what neither sex appears to believe, that women have souls."

How faithfully, how skilfully he labored to kindle and nourish the intelligence of his child his letters to her attest. He was never too busy to spare a half-hour in answering her letters. In a country court-room, in the Senate-chamber, he wrote her brief and sprightly notes, correcting her spelling, complimenting her style, reproving her indolence, praising her industry, commenting on her authors. Rigorous taskmaster as he was, he had a strong sense of the value of just commendation, and he continued to mingle praise very happily with reproof. A few sentences from his letters to her will serve to show his manner.

(In her tenth year.) — " I rose up suddenly from the sofa, and rubbing my head, ' What book shall I buy for her ? ' said I to myself. ' She reads so much and so rapidly that it is not easy to find proper and amusing French books for her ; and yet I am so flattered with her progress in that language that I am resolved she shall, at all events, be gratified. Indeed I owe it to her.' So, after walking once or twice briskly across the floor, I took my hat and sallied out, determined not to return till I had purchased something. It was not my first attempt. I went into one bookseller's shop after another. I found plenty of fairy tales and such nonsense, fit for the generality of children nine or ten years old. ' These,' said I, ' will never do. Her understanding begins to be above such things ' ; but I could see nothing that I would offer with pleasure to an *intelligent, well-informed* girl nine years old. I began to be discouraged. The hour of dining was come. ' But I will search a little longer.' I persevered. At last I found it. I found the very thing I sought. It is contained in two volumes octavo, handsomely bound, and with prints and registers. It is a work of fancy, but replete with instruction and amusement. I must present it with my own hand."

He advised her to keep a diary ; and to give her an idea of what she should record, he wrote for her such a journal of one day as he should like to receive.

Plan of the Journal. — " Learned 230 lines, which finished Horace. Heigh-ho for Terence and the Greek Grammar to-morrow. Practised two hours less thirty-five minutes, which I begged off. Howlett (dancing-master) did not come. Began Gibbon last evening. I find he requires as much study and attention as Horace ; so I shall not rank the reading of *him* among amusements. Skated an hour ; fell twenty times, and find the advantage of a hard head. Ma better, — dined with us at table, and is still sitting up and free from pain."

She was remiss in keeping her journal ; remiss, too, in writing to her father, though he reminded her that he never let one of her letters remain unanswered a day. He reproved her sharply " What ! " said he, " can neither affection nor civility induce you to devote to me the small portion of time which I have required

Are authority and compulsion then the only engines by which you can be moved? For shame, Theo. Do not give me reason to think so ill of you."

She reformed. In her twelfth year, her father wrote: " Io triumphe! there is not a word misspelled either in your journal or letter, which cannot be said of one you ever wrote before." And again: " When you want punctuality in your letters, I am sure you want it in everything; for you will constantly observe that you have the most leisure when you do the most business. Negligence of one's duty produces a self-dissatisfaction which unfits the mind for everything, and *ennui* and peevishness are the never-failing consequence."

His letters abound in sound advice. There is scarcely a passage in them which the most scrupulous and considerate parent could disapprove. Theodosia heeded well his instructions. She became nearly all that his heart or his pride desired.

During the later years of her childhood, her mother was grievously afflicted with a cancer, which caused her death in 1794, before Theodosia had completed her twelfth year. From that time, such was the precocity of her character, that she became the mistress of her father's house and the companion of his leisure hours. Continuing her studies, however, we find her in her sixteenth year translating French comedies, reading the Odyssey at the rate of two hundred lines a day, and about to begin the Iliad. " The happiness of my life," writes her father, " depends upon your exertions; for what else, for whom else, do I live?" And, later, when all the world supposed that his whole soul was absorbed in getting New York ready to vote for Jefferson and Burr, he told her that the ideas of which *she* was the subject that passed daily through his mind would, if committed to writing, fill an octavo volume.

Who so happy as Theodosia? Who so fortunate? The young ladies of New York, at the close of the last century, might have been pardoned for envying the lot of this favorite child of one who then seemed the favorite child of fortune. Burr had been a Senator of the United States as soon as he had attained the age demanded by the Constitution. As a lawyer he was

second in ability and success to no man; in reputation, to none
but Hamilton, whose services in the Cabinet of General Wash·
ington had given him great celebrity.   Aged members of the
New York bar remember that Burr alone was the antagonis·
who could put Hamilton to his mettle.   When other lawyers
were employed against him, Hamilton's manner was that of a
man who felt an easy superiority to the demands upon him; he
took few notes; he was playful and careless, relying much upon
the powerful declamation of his summing up.   But when Burr
was in the case, — Burr the wary, the vigilant, who was never
careless, never inattentive, who came into court only after an
absolutely exhaustive preparation of his case, who held declamation in contempt, and knew how to quench its effect by a stroke
of polite satire, or the quiet citation of a fact, — then Hamilton was
obliged to have all his wits about him, and he was observed to be
restless, busy, and serious.   There are now but two or three
venerable men among us who remember the keen encounters of
these two distinguished lawyers.   The vividness of their recollection of those scenes of sixty years ago shows what an impression must have been made upon their youthful minds.

If Hamilton and Burr divided equally between them the
honors of the bar, Burr had the additional distinction of being a
leader of the rising Democratic Party; the party to which, at
that day, the youth, the genius, the sentiment, of the country were
powerfully drawn; the party which, by his masterly tactics, was
about to place Mr. Jefferson in the Presidential chair after ten
years of ineffectual struggle.

All this enhanced the *éclat* of Theodosia's position.   As she
rode about the island on her pony, followed at a respectful dis
tance, as the custom then was, by one of her father's slaves
mounted on a coach-horse, doubtless many a fair damsel of the
city repined at her own homelier lot, while she dwelt upon the
many advantages which nature and circumstances had bestowed
upon this gifted and happy maiden.

She was a beautiful girl.   She inherited all her father's refined
beauty of countenance; also his shortness of stature; the dignity
grave, and repose of his incomparable manner, too.   She was

plump, petite, and rosy girl; but there was that in her demeanor which became the daughter of an affluent home, and a certain assured, indescribable expression of face which seemed to say, Here is a maiden who to the object of her affection could be faithful against an execrating world, — faithful even unto death.

Burr maintained at that time two establishments, one in the city, the other a mile and a half out of town on the banks of the Hudson. Richmond Hill was the name of his country seat, where Theodosia resided during the later years of her youth. It was a large, massive, wooden edifice, with a lofty portico of Ionic columns, and stood on a hill facing the river, in the midst of a lawn adorned with ancient trees and trained shrubbery. The grounds, which extended to the water's edge, comprised about a hundred and sixty acres. Those who now visit the site of Burr's abode, at the corner of Charlton and Varick streets, behold a wilderness of very ordinary houses covering a dead level. The hill has been pared away, the ponds filled up, the river pushed away a long distance from the ancient shore, and every one of the venerable trees is gone. The city shows no spot less suggestive of rural beauty. But Richmond Hill, in the days of Hamilton and Burr, was the finest country residence on the island of Manhattan. The wife of John Adams, who lived there in 1790, just before Burr bought it, and who had recently travelled in the loveliest counties of England, speaks of it as a situation not inferior in natural beauty to the most delicious spot she ever saw. "The house," she says, "is situated upon an eminence; at an agreeable distance flows the noble Hudson, bearing upon its bosom the fruitful productions of the adjacent country. On my right hand are fields beautifully variegated with grass and grain, to a great extent, like the valley of Honiton, in Devonshire. Upon my left the city opens to view, intercepted here and there by a rising ground and an ancient oak. In front, beyond the Hudson, the Jersey shores present the exuberance of a rich, well-cultivated soil. The venerable oaks and broken ground, covered with wild shrubs, which surround me, give a natural beauty to the spot, which is truly enchanting. A lovely variety of birds serenade me morning and evening, rejoicing in their liberty and security·

for I have, as much as possible, prohibited the grounds from in-vasion, and sometimes almost wished for game-laws, when my orders have not been sufficiently regarded. The partridge, the woodcock, and the pigeon are too great temptations to the sports-men to withstand."

Indeed the whole Island was enchanting in those early days. There were pleasant gardens even in Wall Street, Cedar Street, Nassau Street; and the Battery, the place of universal resort, was one of the most delightful public grounds in the world, — as it will be again when the Spoiler is thrust from the places of power, and the citizens of New York come again into the owner-ship of their city. The banks of the Hudson and of the East River were forest-crowned bluffs, lofty and picturesque, and on every favorable site stood a cottage or a mansion surrounded with pleasant grounds. The letters of Theodosia Burr contain many passages expressive of her intense enjoyment of the variety, the vivid verdure, the noble trees, the heights, the pretty lakes, the enchanting prospects, the beautiful gardens, which her daily rides brought to her view. She was a dear lover of her island home The city had not then laid waste the beauty of Manhattan. There was only one bank in New York, the officers of which shut the bank at one o'clock and went home to dinner, returned at three, and kept the bank open till five. Much of the business life of the town partook of this homely, comfortable, easy-going, rural spirit. There was a mail twice a week to the North, and twice a week to the South, and many of the old-fashioned people had time to live.

Not so the younger and newer portion of the population. We learn from one of the letters of the ill-fated Blennerhassett, who arrived in New York from Ireland in 1796, that the people were so busy there in making new docks, filling in the swamps, and digging cellars for new buildings, as to bring on an epidemic fever and ague that drove him from the city to the Jersey shore. He mentions, also, that land in the State doubled in value every two years, and that commercial speculation was carried on with such avidity that it was more like gambling than trade. It is he tha relates the story of the adventurer, who, on learning that the yel low-fever prevailed fearfully in the West Indies, sent thither a cargo of coffins in nests, and, that no room might be lost, filled the smallest with gingerbread. The speculation, he assures us, was a capital hit; for the adventurer not only sold his coffins very profitably, but loaded his vessel with valuable woods, which yielded a great profit at New York. At that time, also, the speculation in lots, corner lots, and lands near the city, was prosecuted with all the recklessness which we have been in the habit of supposing was peculiar to later times. New York was New York even in the days of Burr and Hamilton.

As mistress of Richmond Hill, Theodosia entertained distinguished company. Hamilton was her father's occasional guest. Burr preferred the society of educated Frenchmen and Frenchwomen to any other, and he entertained many distinguished exiles of the French Revolution. Talleyrand, Volney, Jerome Bonaparte, and Louis Philippe were among his guests. Colonel Stone mentions, in his Life of Brant, that Theodosia, in her fourteenth year, in the absence of her father, gave a dinner to that chieftain of the forest, which was attended by the Bishop of New York, Dr. Hosack, Volney, and several other guests of distinction, who greatly enjoyed the occasion. Burr was gratified to hear with how much grace and good-nature his daughter acquitted herself in the entertainment of her company. The chief himself was exceedingly delighted, and spoke of the dinner with great animation many years after.

We have one pleasant glimpse of Theodosia in these happy years, in a trifling anecdote preserved by the biographer of Edward Livingston, during whose mayoralty the present City Hall was begun. The mayor had the pleasure, one bright day, of escorting the young lady on board a French frigate lying in the harbor. "You must bring none of your sparks on board, Theodosia," exclaimed the pun-loving magistrate; "for they have a magazine here, and we shall all be blown up." Oblivion here drops the curtain upon the gay party and the brilliant scene.

A suitor appeared for the hand of this fair and accomplished girl. It was Joseph Alston of South Carolina, a gentleman of twenty-two, possessor of large estates in rice plantations and

18

slaves, and a man of much spirit and talent. He valued his estates at two hundred thousand pounds sterling. Their courtship was not a long one; for though she, as became her sex, checked the impetuosity of his advances and argued for delay, she was easily convinced by the reasons which he adduced for haste. She reminded him that Aristotle was of opinion that a man should not marry till he was thirty-six. "A fig for Aristotle," he replied; " let us regard the *ipse dixit* of no man. It is only want of fortune or want of discretion," he continued, "that could justify such a postponement of married joys. But suppose," he added, " (*merely for instance*,) a young man nearly two-and-twenty, already of the *greatest* discretion, with an ample fortune, were to be passionately in love with a young lady almost eighteen, equally discreet with himself, and who had a ' sincere friendship' for him, do you think it would be necessary to make him wait till thirty? particularly where the friends on both sides were pleased with the match."

She told him, also, that some of her friends who had visited Charleston had described it as a city where the yellow-fever and the "yells of whipped negroes, which assail your ears from every house," and the extreme heat, rendered life a mere purgatory. She had heard, too, that in South Carolina the men were absorbed in hunting, gaming, and racing; while the women, robbed of their society, had no pleasures but to come together in large parties, sip tea, and look prim. The ardent swain eloquently defended his native State: —

"What!" he exclaimed, "is Charleston, the most delightfully situated city in America, which, entirely open to the ocean, twice in every twenty-four hours is cooled by the refreshing sea-breeze, the Montpelier of the South, which annually affords an asylum to the planter and the West Indian from every disease, accused of heat and unhealthiness? But this is not all, unfortunate citizens of Charleston; the scream, the yell of the miserable unresisting African, bleeding under he scourge of relentless power, affords music to your ears! Ah! from what unfriendly cause does this arise? Has the God of heaven, in anger, here changed the order of nature? In every other region, without exception, in a similar degree of latitude, the same sun which ripens the tamarind and the anana, ameliorates the temper, and disposes it to gentleness and kindness. In India and other countries, not very different in climate from the southern parts of the United States, the inhabitants are distinguished for a softness and inoffensiveness of manners, degenerating almost to effeminacy; it is here then, only, that we are exempt from the general influence of climate : here only that, in spite of it, we are cruel and ferocious! Poor Carolina!"

And with regard to the manners of the Carolinians he assured the young lady that if there was one State in the Union which could justly claim superiority to the rest, in social refinement and the art of elegant living, it was South Carolina, where the division of the people into the very poor and the very rich left to the latter class abundant leisure for the pursuit of literature and the enjoyment of society.

" The possession of slaves," he owns, " renders them proud, impatient of restraint, and gives them a haughtiness of manner which, to those unaccustomed to them, is disagreeable ; but we find among them a high sense of honor, a delicacy of sentiment, and a liberality of mind, which we look for in vain in the more commercial citizens of the Northern States. The genius of the Carolinian, like the inhabitants of all southern countries, is quick, lively, and acute; in steadiness and perseverance he is naturally inferior to the native of the North ; but this defect of climate is often overcome by his ambition or necessity; and, whenever this happens, he seldom fails to distinguish himself. In his temper he is gay and fond of company, open, generous, and unsuspicious; easily irritated, and quick to resent even the appearance of insult; but his passion, like the fire of the flint, is lighted up and extinguished in the same moment."

Such discussions end only in one way. Theodosia yielded the points in dispute. At Albany, on the 2d of February, 1801, while the country was ringing with the names of Jefferson and Burr, and while the world supposed that Burr was intriguing with all his might to defeat the wishes of the people by securing his own election to the Presidency, his daughter was married. The marriage was thus announced in the New York *Commercial Advertiser* of February 7 : —

" MARRIED. — At Albany, on the 2d instant, by the Rev. Mr. JOHNSON, JOSEPH ALSTON, of South Carolina, to THEODOSIA BURR, only child of AARON BURR, Esq."

They were married at Albany, because Colonel Burr, being a member of the Legislature, was residing at the capital cf the State. One week the happy pair passed at Albany. Then to New York; whence, after a few days' stay, they began their long journey southward. Rejoined at Baltimore by Colonel Burr, they travelled in company to Washington, where, on the 4th of March, Theodosia witnessed the inauguration of Mr. Jefferson, and the induction of her father into the Vice-Presidency. Father and child parted a day or two after the ceremony. The only solid consolation, he said in his first letter to her, that he had for the loss of her dear companionship, was a belief that she would be happy, and the certainty that they should often meet. And, on his return to New York, he told her that he had approached his home as he would " the sepulchre of all his friends.' " Dreary, solitary, comfortless. It was no longer *home*." Hence his various schemes of a second marriage, to which Theodosia urged him. He soon had the comfort of hearing that the reception of his daughter in South Carolina was as cordial and affectionate as his heart could have wished.

Theodosia now enjoyed three as happy years as ever fell to the lot of a young wife. Tenderly cherished by her husband, whom she devotedly loved, caressed by society, surrounded by affectionate and admiring relations, provided bountifully with all the means of enjoyment, living in the summer in the mountains of Carolina, or at the home of her childhood, Richmond Hill, passing the winters in gay and luxurious Charleston, honored for her own sake, for her father's, and her husband's, the years glided rapidly by, and she seemed destined to remain to the last Fortune's favorite child. One summer she and her husband visited Niagara, and penetrated the domain of the chieftain Brant, who gave them royal entertainment. Once she had the great happiness of receiving her father under her own roof, and of seeing the honors paid by the people of the State to the Vice-President. Again she spent a summer at Richmond Hill and Saratoga, leaving her husband for the first time. She told him on this occasion that every *woman* must prefer the society of the North to that of the South, whatever she might say. " If she denies it, she i set down in my mind as insincere and weakly prejudiced." But, like a fond and loyal wife, she wrote, "Where you are, there is my country, and in you are centred all my wishes."

She was a mother too. That engaging and promising boy, Aaron Burr Alston, the delight of his parents and of his grandfather, was born in the second year of the marriage. This event seemed to complete her happiness. For a time, it is true, she paid dearly for it by the loss of her former robust and joyous health. But the boy was worth the price. "If I can see without prejudice," wrote Colonel Burr, "there never was a finer boy"; and the mother's letters are full of those sweet, trifling anecdotes which mothers love to relate of their offspring. Her father still urged her to improve her mind, for her own and her son's sake, telling her that all she could learn would necessarily find its way to the mind of the boy. "Pray take in hand," he writes, "some book which requires attention and study. You will, I fear, lose the habit of study, which would be a greater misfortune than to lose your head." He praised, too, the ease, goodsense, and sprightliness of her letters, and said truly that her style, at its best, was not inferior to that of Madame de Sévigné.

Life is frequently styled a checkered scene. But it was the peculiar lot of Theodosia to experience during the first twentyone years of her life nothing but prosperity and happiness, and during the remainder of her existence nothing but misfortune and sorrow. Never had her father's position seemed so strong and enviable as during his tenure of the office of Vice-President; but never had it been in reality so hollow and precarious. Holding property valued at two hundred thousand dollars, he was so deeply in debt that nothing but the sacrifice of his landed estate could save him from bankruptcy. At the age of thirty he had permitted himself to be drawn from a lucrative and always increasing professional business to the fascinating but most costly pursuit of political honors. And now, when he stood at a distance of only one step from the highest place, he was pursued by a clamorous host of creditors, and compelled to resort to a hundred expedients to maintain the expensive establishments supposed to be necessary to a Vice-President's dignity. His political position was as hollow as his social eminence. Mr. Jefferson was firmly resolved that Aaron Burr should not be his successor and the great families of New York, whom Burr had united to win the victory over Federalism, were now united to bar the further advancement of a man whom they chose to regard as an interloper and a parvenu. If Burr's private life had been stainless, if his fortune had been secure, if he had been in his heart a Republican and a Democrat, if he had been a man earnest in the people's cause, if even his talents had been as superior as they were supposed to be, such a combination of powerful families and political influence might have retarded, but could not have prevented, his advancement; for he was still in the prime of his prime, and the people naturally side with a man who is the archi tect of his own fortunes.

On the 1st of July, 1804, Burr sat in the library of Richmond Hill writing to Theodosia. The day was unseasonably cold, and a fire blazed upon the hearth. The lord of the mansion was chilly and serious. An hour before he had taken the step which made the duel with Hamilton inevitable, though eleven days were to elapse before the actual encounter. He was tempted to prepare the mind of his child for the event, but he forebore. Probably his mind had been wandering into the past, and recalling his boyhood ; for he quoted a line of poetry which he had been wont to use in those early days. " Some very wise man has said," he wrote,

" ' Oh, fools, who think it solitude to be alone! '

'This is but poetry. Let us, therefore, drop the subject, lest it lead to another, on which I have imposed silence on myself." Then he proceeds, in his usual gay and agreeable manner, again urging her to go on in the pursuit of knowledge. His last thoughts before going to the field were with her and for her. His last request to her husband was that he should do all that in him lay to encourage her to improve her mind.

The bloody deed was done. The next news Theodosia received from her father was that he was a fugitive from the sudden abhorrence of his fellow-citizens ; that an indictment for murder was hanging over his head; that his career in New York was, in all probability, over forever; and that he was destined to be for a time a wanderer on the earth. Her happy days were at an end. She never blamed her father for this, or for any act of his; on the contrary, she accepted without questioning his own version of the facts, and his own view of the morality of what he had done. He had formed her mind and tutored her conscience. He *was* her conscience. But though she censured him not, her days and nights were embittered by anxiety from this time to the last day of her life. A few months later her father, black with hundreds of miles of travel in an open canoe, reached her abode in South Carolina, and spent some weeks there before appearing for the last time in the chair of the Senate; for, ruined as he was in fortune and good name, indicted for murder in New York and New Jersey, he was still Vice-President of the United States, and he was resolved to reappear upon the public scene, and do the duty which the Constitution assigned him.

The Mexican scheme followed. Theodosia and her husband were both involved in it. Mr. Alston advanced money for the project, which was never repaid, and which, in his will, he forgave. His entire loss, in consequence of his connection with that affair, may be reckoned at about fifty thousand dollars. Theodosia entirely and warmly approved the dazzling scheme. The throne of Mexico, she thought, was an object worthy of her father's talents, and one which would repay him for the loss of a brief tenure of the Presidency, and be a sufficient triumph over the men who were supposed to have thwarted him. Her boy, too, — would he not be heir-presumptive to a throne?

The recent publication of the "Blennerhassett Papers" appears to dispel all that remained of the mystery which the secretive Burr chose to leave around the object of his scheme. We can now say with almost absolute certainty that Burr's objects were the following: The throne of Mexico for himself and his heirs; the seizure and organization of Texas as preliminary to the grand design. The purchase of lands on the Washita was for the threefold purpose of veiling the real object, providing a rendezvous, and having the means of tempting and rewarding those of the

adventurers who were not in the secret. We can also now discover the designed distribution of honors and places: Aaron I,
Emperor; Joseph Alston, Head of the Nobility and Chief Minister; Aaron Burr Alston, heir to the throne; Theodosia, Chief
Lady of the Court and Empire; Wilkinson, General-in-Chief of
the Army; Blennerhassett, Embassador to the Court of St.
James; Commodore Truxton (perhaps), Admiral of the Navy.
There is not an atom of new *evidence* which warrants the supposition that Burr had any design to sever the Western States from
the Union. If he himself had ever contemplated such an event,
it is almost unquestionable that his followers were ignorant of it.

The scheme exploded. Theodosia and her husband had joined
him at the home of the Blennerhassetts, and they were near him
when the President's proclamation dashed the scheme to atoms,
scattered the band of adventurers, and sent Burr a prisoner to
Richmond, charged with high treason. Mr. Alston, in a public
letter to the Governor of South Carolina, solemnly declared that
he was wholly ignorant of any treasonable design on the part of
his father-in-law, and repelled with honest warmth the charge
of his own complicity with a design so manifestly absurd and
hopeless as that of a dismemberment of the Union. Theodosia,
stunned with the unexpected blow, returned with her husband to
South Carolina, ignorant of her father's fate. He was carried
through that State on his way to the North, and there it was that
he made his well-known attempt to appeal to the civil authorities
and get deliverance from the guard of soldiers. From Richmond
he wrote her a hasty note, informing her of his arrest. She and
her husband joined him soon, and remained with him during his
trial.

At Richmond, during the six months of the trial, Burr tasted
the last of the sweets of popularity. The party opposed to Mr.
Jefferson made his cause their own, and gathered round the fall-
en leader with ostentatious sympathy and aid. Ladies sent him
bouquets, wine, and dainties for his table, and bestowed upon his
daughter the most affectionate and flattering attentions. Old
friends from New York and new friends from the West were
there to cheer and help the prisoner. Andrew Jackson was con-

spicuously his friend and defender, declaiming in the streets upon the tyranny of the Administration and the perfidy of Wilkinson, Burr's chief accuser. Washington Irving, then in the dawn of his great renown, who had given the first efforts of his youthful pen to Burr's newspaper, was present at the trial, full of sympathy for a man whom he believed to be the victim of treachery and political animosity. Doubtless he was not wanting in compassionate homage to the young matron from South Carolina. Mr. Irving was then a lawyer, and had been retained as one of Burr's counsel; not to render service in the court-room, but in the expectation that his pen would be employed in staying the torrent of public opinion that was setting against his client. Whether or not he wrote in his behalf does not appear. But his private letters, written at Richmond during the trial, show plainly enough that, if his head was puzzled by the confused and contradictory evidence, his heart and his imagination were on the side of the prisoner.

Theodosia's presence at Richmond was of more value to her father than the ablest of his counsel. Every one appears to have loved, admired, and sympathized with her. " You can't think," wrote Mrs. Blennerhassett, " with what joy and pride I read what Colonel Burr says of his daughter. I never could love one of my own sex as I do her." Blennerhassett himself was not less her friend. Luther Martin, Burr's chief counsel, almost worshipped her. " I find," wrote Blennerhassett, " that Luther Martin's idolatrous admiration of Mrs. Alston is almost as excessive as my own, but far more beneficial to his interest and injurious to his judgment, as it is the medium of his blind attachment to her father, whose secrets and views, past, present, or to come, he is and wishes to remain ignorant of. Nor can he see a speck in the character or conduct of Alston, for the best of all reasons with him, namely, that Alston has such a wife." It plainly appears, too, from the letters and journal of Blennerhassett, that Alston did all in his power to promote the acquittal and aid the fallen fortunes of Burr, and that he did so, not because he believed in him, but because he loved his Theodosia.

Acquitted by the jury, but condemned at the bar of public opin-

18 *   A A

ion, denounced by the press, abhorred by the Republican party and still pursued by his creditors, Burr, in the spring of 1808, lay concealed at New York preparing for a secret flight to Europe. Again his devoted child travelled northward to see him once more before he sailed. For some weeks both were in the city, meeting only by night at the house of some tried friend, but exchanging notes and letters from hour to hour. One whole night they spent together, just before his departure. To her he committed his papers, the accumulation of thirty busy years; and it was she who was to collect the debts due him, and thus provide for his maintenance in Europe.

Burr was gay and confident to the last, for he was strong in the belief that the British Ministry would adopt his scheme and aid in tearing Mexico from the grasp of Napoleon. Theodosia was sick and sorrowful, but bore bravely up and won her father's commendation for her fortitude. In one of the early days of June father and daughter parted, to meet no more on earth.

The four years of Burr's fruitless exile were to Theodosia years of misery. She could not collect the debts on which they had relied. The embargo reduced the rice-planters to extreme embarrassment. Her husband no longer sympathized with her in her yearning love for her father, though loving her as tenderly as ever. Old friends in New York cooled toward her. Her health was precarious. Months passed without bringing a word from over the sea; and the letters that did reach her, lively and jovial as they were, contained no good news. She saw her father expelled from England, wandering aimless in Sweden and Germany, almost a prisoner in Paris, reduced to live on potatoes and dry bread; while his own countrymen showed no signs of relenting toward him. In many a tender passage she praised his fortitude. " I witness," she wrote, in a well-known letter, " your extraordinary fortitude with new wonder at every new misfortune. Often, after reflecting on this subject, you appear to me so superior, so elevated above all other men; I contemplate you with such a strange mixture of humility, admiration, reverence, love and pride, that very little superstition would be necessary to make me worship you as a superior being; such enthusiasm does your character excite in me. When I afterward revert to myself, how insignificant do my best qualities appear! My vanity would be greater if I had not been placed so near you; and yet my pride is our relationship. I had rather not live than not be the daughter of such a man."

Mr. Madison was President then. In other days her father had been on terms of peculiar intimacy with Madison and his beautiful and accomplished wife. Burr, in his later years, used to say that it was he who had brought about the match which made Mrs. Madison an inmate of the Presidential mansion. With the members of Madison's Cabinet, too, he had been socially and politically familiar. When Theodosia perceived that her father had no longer a hope of success in his Mexican project, she became anxious for his return to America. But against this was the probability that the Administration would again arrest him and bring him to trial for the third time. Theodosia ventured to write to her old friend, Albert Gallatin, Secretary of the Treasury, asking him to interpose on her father's behalf. A letter still more interesting than this has recently come to light. It was addressed by Theodosia to Mrs. Madison. The coldest heart cannot read this eloquent and pathetic production without emotion. She writes : —

"MADAM, — You may perhaps be surprised at receiving a letter from one with whom you have had so little intercourse for the last few years. But your surprise will cease when you recollect that my father, once your friend, is now in exile; and that the President only can restore him to me and his country.

"Ever since the choice of the people was first declared in favor of Mr. Madison, my heart, amid the universal joy, has beat with the hope that I, too, should soon have reason to rejoice. Convinced that Mr. Madison would neither feel nor judge from the feelings or judgment of others, I had no doubt of his hastening to relieve a man whose character he had been enabled to appreciate during a confidential intercourse of long continuance, and whom [he] must know incapable of the designs attributed to him. My anxiety on this subject, has, however, become too painful to be alleviated by anticipations which no events have yet tended to justify; and in this state of intolerable suspense I have determined to address myself to you, and request that you will, *in my name*, apply to the President for a removal of the prosecution now existing against AARON BURR. I still expect it from him as a man of feeling and candor, as one acting for the world and for posterity.

" Statesmen, I am aware, deem it necessary that sentiments of liberality, and even justice, should yield to considerations of policy; but what policy can require the absence of my father at present ? Even had he contemplated the project for which he stands arraigned, evidently to pursue it any further would now be impossible. There is not left one pretext of alarm even to calumny ; for bereft of fortune, of popular favor, and almost of friends, what could he accomplish ? And whatever may be the apprehensions or the clamors of the ignorant and the interested, surely the timid, illiberal system which would sacrifice a man to a remote and unreasonable possibility that he might infringe some law founded on an unjust, unwarrantable suspicion that he would desire it, cannot be approved by Mr. Madison, and must be unnecessary to a President so loved, so honored. Why, then, is my father banished from a country for which he has encountered wounds and dangers and fatigue for years ? Why is he driven from his friends, from an only child, to pass an unlimited time in exile, and that, too, at an age when others are reaping the harvest of past toils, or ought at least to be providing seriously for the comfort of ensuing years ? I do not seek to soften you by this recapitulation. I only wish to remind you of all the injuries which are inflicted on one of the first characters the United States ever produced.

" Perhaps it may be well to assure you there is no truth in a report lately circulated, that my father intends returning immediately. He never will return to conceal himself in a country on which he has conferred distinction.

" To whatever fate Mr. Madison may doom this application, I trust it will be treated with delicacy. Of this I am the more desirous as Mr. Alston is ignorant of the step I have taken in writing to you, which, perhaps, nothing could excuse but the warmth of filial affection. If it be an error, attribute it to the indiscreet zeal of a daughter whose soul sinks at the gloomy prospect of a long and indefinite separation from a father almost adored, and who can leave unattempted nothing which offers the slightest hope of procuring him redress. What, indeed, would I not risk once more to see him, to hang upon him, to place my child on his knee, and again spend my days in the happy occupation of endeavoring to anticipate all his wishes.

" Let me entreat, my dear Madam, that you will have the consideration and goodness to answer me as speedily as possible ; my heart is
sore with doubt and patient waiting for something definitive. No
apologies are made for giving you this trouble, which I am sure you
will not deem irksome to take for a daughter, an affectionate daughter,
thus situated. Inclose your letter for me to A. J. Frederic Prevost,
Esq., near New Rochelle, New York.

> " That every happiness may attend you,
> " Is the sincere wish of
> " THEO. BURR ALSTON."

This letter was probably not ineffectual. Certain it is that
government offered no serious obstacle to Burr's return, and
instituted no further proceedings against him. Probably, too,
Theodosia received some kind of assurance to this effect, for we
find her urging her father, not only to return, but to go boldly to
New York among his old friends, and resume there the practice
of his profession. The great danger to be apprehended was
from his creditors, who then had power to confine a debtor within
limits, if not to throw him into prison. "*If the worst comes to the
worst*," wrote this fond and devoted daughter, "*I will leave everything to suffer with you.*" The Italics are her own.

He came at length. He landed in Boston, and sent word of
his arrival to Theodosia. Rejoiced as she was, she replied
vaguely, partly in cipher, fearing lest her letter might be opened
on the way, and the secret of her father's arrival be prematurely
disclosed. She told him that her own health was tolerable ; that
her child, then a fine boy of eleven, was well ; that " his little
soul warmed at the sound of his grandfather's name " ; and that
his education, under a competent tutor, was proceeding satisfac-
torily. She gave directions respecting her father's hoped-for
journey to South Carolina in the course of the summer ; and
advised him, in case war should be declared with England, to
offer his services to the government. He reached New York
in May, 1812, and soon had the pleasure of informing his daughter that his reception had been more friendly than he could have
expected, and that in time his prospects were fair of a sufficient
ly lucrative practice.

Surely, now, after so many years of anxiety and sorrow, Theodosia — still a young woman, not thirty years of age, still enjoying her husband's love — might have reasonably expected a happy life. Alas! there was no more happiness in store for her on this side of the grave. The first letter which Burr received from his son-in-law after his arrival in New York contained news which struck him to the heart.

"A few miserable weeks since," writes Mr. Alston, "and in spite of all the embarrassments, the troubles, and disappointments which have fallen to our lot since we parted, I would have congratulated you on your return in the language of happiness. With my wife on one side and my boy on the other, I felt myself superior to depression. The present was enjoyed, the future was anticipated with enthusiasm. One dreadful blow has destroyed us; reduced us to the veriest, the most sublimated wretchedness. That boy, on whom all rested, — our companion, our friend, — he who was to have transmitted down the mingled blood of Theodosia and myself, — he who was to have redeemed all your glory, and shed new lustre upon our families, — that boy, at once our happiness and our pride, is taken from us, — *is dead.* We saw him dead. My own hand surrendered him to the grave; yet we are alive. But it is past. I will not conceal from you that life is a burden, which, heavy as it is, we shall both support, if not with dignity, at least with decency and firmness. Theodosia has endured all that a human being could endure; but her admirable mind will triumph. She supports herself in a manner worthy of your daughter.'

The mother's heart was almost broken.

" There is no more joy for me," she wrote. " The world is a blank. I have lost my boy. My child is gone forever. May Heaven, by other blessings, make you some amends for the noble grandson you have lost Alas! my dear father, I do live, but how does it happen? Of what am I formed that I live, and why? Of what service can I be in this world, either to you or any one else, with a body reduced to premature old age, and a mind enfeebled and bewildered? Yet, since it is my lot to live, I will endeavor to fulfil my part, and exert myself to my utmost, though this life must henceforth be to me a bed of thorns. Whichever way I turn, the same anguish still assails me. You talk of consolation. Ah! you know not what you have lost. I think Omnipotence could give me no equivalent for my boy; no, none, — none."

She could not be comforted. Her health gave way. Her

husband thought that if anything could restore her to tranquillity and health it would be the society of her father; and so, at the beginning of winter, it was resolved that she should attempt the dangerous voyage. Her father sent a medical friend from New York to attend her.

" Mr. Alston," wrote this gentleman, " seemed rather hurt that you should conceive it necessary to send a person here, as he or one of his brothers would attend Mrs. Alston to New York. I told him you had some opinion of my medical talents; that you had learned your daughter was in a low state of health, and required unusual attention, and medical attention on her voyage; that I had torn myself from my family to perform this service for my friend."

And again, a few days after : —

"I have engaged a passage to New York for your daughter in a pilot-boat that has been out privateering, but has come in here, and is refitting merely to get to New York. My only fears are that Governor Alston may think the mode of conveyance too undignified, and object to it; but Mrs. Alston is fully bent on going. You must not be surprised to see her very low, feeble, and emaciated. Her complaint is an almost incessant nervous fever."

The rest is known. The vessel sailed. Off Cape Hatteras, during a gale that swept the coast from Maine to Georgia, the pilot-boat went down, and not one escaped to tell the tale. The vessel was never heard of more. So perished this noble, gifted, ill-starred lady.

The agonizing scenes that followed may be imagined. Father and husband were kept long in suspense. Even when many weeks had elapsed without bringing tidings of the vessel, there still remained a forlorn hope that some of her passengers might have been rescued by an outward-bound ship, and might return, after a year or two had gone by, from some distant port. Burr, it is said, acquired a habit, when walking upon the Battery, of looking wistfully down the harbor at the arriving ships, as if still cherishing a faint, fond hope that his Theo was coming to him rom the other side of the world. When, years after, the tale was brought to him that his daughter had been carried off by pirates and might be still alive, he said · " No, no, no; if my Theo had survived that storm, she would have found her way to me Nothing could have kept my Theo from her father."

It was these sad events, the loss of his daughter and her boy that severed Aaron Burr from the human race. Hope died within him. Ambition died. He yielded to his doom, and walked among men, not melancholy, but indifferent, reckless, and alone. With his daughter and his grandson to live and strive for, he might have done something in his later years to redeem his name and atone for his errors. Bereft of these, he had not in his moral nature that which enables men who have gone astray to repent and begin a better life.

Theodosia's death broke her husband's heart. Few letters are so affecting as the one which he wrote to Burr when, at length, the certainty of her loss could no longer be resisted.

"My boy — my wife — gone both! This, then, is the end of all the hopes we had formed. You may well observe that you feel severed from the human race. She was the last tie that bound us to the species. What have we left ? . . . . Yet, after all, he is a poor actor who cannot sustain his little hour upon the stage, be his part what it may. But the man who has been deemed worthy of the heart of *Theodosia Burr*, and who has felt what it was to be blessed with such a woman's, will never forget his elevation."

He survived his wife four years. Among the papers of Theodosia was found, after her death, a letter which she had written a few years before she died, at a time when she supposed her end was near. Upon the envelope was written, — "My husband. To be delivered after my death. I wish this to be read *immediately*, and before my burial." Her husband never saw it, for he never had the courage to look into the trunk that contained her treasures. But after his death the trunk was sent to Burr, who found and preserved this affecting composition. We cannot conclude our narrative more fitly than by transcribing the thoughts that burdened the heart of Theodosia in view of her departure from the world. First, she gave directions respecting the disposal of her jewelry and trinkets, giving to each of her friends some token of her love. Then she besought her husband to provide at once for the support of " Peggy," an aged servant of her father, for merly housekeeper at Richmond Hill, to whom, in her father's absence, she had contrived to pay a small pension. She then proceeded in these affecting terms : —

" To you, my beloved, I leave our child ; the child of my bosom, who was once a part of myself, and from whom I shall shortly be separated by the cold grave. You love him now ; henceforth love him for me also. And oh, my husband, attend to this last prayer of a doting mother. Never, never listen to what any other person tells you of him. Be yourself his judge on all occasions. He has faults ; see them, and correct them yourself. Desist not an instant from your endeavors to secure his confidence. It is a work which requires as much uniformity of conduct as warmth of affection toward him. I know, my beloved, that you can perceive what is right on this subject as on every other. But recollect, these are the last words I can ever utter. It will tranquillize my last moments to have disburdened myself of them.

" I fear you will scarcely be able to read this scrawl, but I feel hurried and agitated. Death is not welcome to me. I confess it is ever dreaded. You have made me too fond of life. Adieu, then, thou kind, thou tender husband. Adieu, friend of my heart. May Heaven prosper you, and may we meet hereafter. Adieu ; perhaps we may never see each other again in this world. You are away, I wished to hold you fast, and prevented you from going this morning. But He who is wisdom itself ordains events ; we must submit to them. Least of all should I murmur. I, on whom so many blessings have been showered, — whose days have been numbered by bounties, — who have had such a husband, such a child, and such a father. O pardon me, my God, if I regret leaving these. I resign myself. Adieu, once more, and for the last time, my beloved. Speak of me often to our son. Let him love the memory of his mother, and let him know how he was loved by her. Your wife, your fond wife,

THEO.

" Let my father see my son sometimes. Do not be unkind toward him whom I have loved so much, I beseech you. Burn all my papers except my father's letters, which I beg you to return him. Adieu, my sweet boy. Love your father ; be grateful and affectionate to him while he lives ; be the pride of his meridian, the support of his departing days. Be all that he wishes ; for he made your mother happy. Oh ! my heavenly Father, bless them both. If it is permitted, I will hover round you, and guard you, and intercede for you. I hope for happiness in the next world, for I have not been bad in this.

"I had nearly forgotten to say that I charge you not to allow me to be stripped and washed, as is usual. I am pure enough thus to return to dust. Why, then, expose my person? Pray see to this. If it does not appear contradictory or silly, I beg to be kept as long as possible before I am consigned to the earth."

JOHN JACOB ASTOR.

JOHN JACOB ASTOR.

WE all feel some curiosity respecting men who have been eminent in anything, — even in crime; and as this curiosity is natural and universal, it seems proper that it should be gratified. JOHN JACOB ASTOR surpassed all the men of his generation in the accumulation of wealth. He began life a poor, hungry German boy, and died worth twenty millions of dollars. These facts are so remarkable, that there is no one who does not feel a desire to know by which means the result was produced, and whether the game was played fairly. We all wish, if not to be rich, yet to have more money than we now possess. We have known many kinds of men, but never one who felt that he had quite money enough. The three richest men now living in the United States are known to be as much interested in the increase of their possessions, and try as hard to increase them, as ever they did.

This universal desire to accumulate property is right, and necessary to the progress of the race. Like every other proper and virtuous desire, it may become excessive, and then it is a vice. So long as a man seeks property honestly, and values it as the means of independence, as the means of educating and comforting his family, as the means of securing a safe, dignified, and tranquil old age, as the means of private charity and public beneficence, let him bend himself heartily to his work, and enjoy the reward of his labors. It is a fine and pleasant thing to prosper in business, and to have a store to fall back upon in time of trouble.

The reader may learn from Astor's career how money is accumulated. Whether he can learn from it how money ought to be employed when it is obtained, he must judge for himself. In founding the Astor Library, John Jacob Astor did at least one magnificent deed, for which thousands unborn will honor his memory. That single act would atone for many errors.

In the hall of the Astor Library, on the sides of two of the pillars supporting its lofty roof of glass, are two little shelves, each holding a single work, never taken down and seldom perused, but nevertheless well worthy the attention of those who are curious in the subject of which they treat, namely, the human face divine. They are two marble busts, facing each other ; one of the founder of the Library, the other of its first President, Washington Irving. A finer study in physiognomy than these two busts present can nowhere be found ; for never were two men more unlike than Astor and Irving, and never were character and personal history more legibly recorded than in these portraits in marble. The countenance of the author is round, full, and handsome, the hair inclining to curl, and the chin to double. It is the face of a happy and genial man, formed to shine at the fireside and to beam from the head of a table. It is an open, candid, liberal, hospitable countenance, indicating far more power to please than to compel, but displaying in the position and carriage of the head much of that dignity which we are accustomed to call Roman. The face of the millionnaire, on the contrary, is all strength ; every line in it tells of concentration and power. The hair is straight and long ; the forehead neither lofty nor ample, but powerfully developed in the perceptive and executive organs ; the eyes deeper set in the head than those of Daniel Webster, and overhung with immense bushy eyebrows ; the nose large, long, and strongly arched, the veritable nose of a man-compeller ; the mouth, chin, and jaws all denoting firmness and force ; the chest, that seat and throne of physical power, is broad and deep, and the back of the neck has something of the muscular fulness which we observe in the prize-fighter and the bull ; the head behind the ears showing enough of propelling power, but almost totally wanting in the passional propensities which waste the force of the faculties, and divert the man from his prin cipal object. As the spectator stands midway between the two busts, at some distance from both, Irving has the larger and the kinglier air, and the face of Astor seems small and set. It is only when you get close to the bust of Astor, observing the strength of each feature and its perfect proportion to the rest, — force everywhere, superfluity nowhere, — that you recognize the monarch of the counting-room; the brain which nothing could confuse or disconcert; the purpose that nothing could divert or defeat; the man who could with ease and pleasure grasp and control the multitudinous concerns of a business that embraced the habited and unhabited globe, — that employed ships in every sea, and men in every clime, and brought in to the coffers of the merchant the revenue of a king. That speechless bust tells us how it was that this man, from suffering in his father's poverty-stricken house the habitual pang of hunger, arrived at the greatest fortune, perhaps, ever accumulated in a single lifetime; you perceive that whatever thing this strong and compact man set himself to do, he would be certain to achieve unless stopped by something as powerful as a law of nature.

The monument of these two gifted men is the airy and graceful interior of which their busts are the only ornament. Astor founded the Library, but it was probably his regard for Irving that induced him to appropriate part of his wealth for a purpose not in harmony with his own humor. Irving is known to us all, as only wits and poets are ever known. But of the singular being who possessed so remarkable a genius for accumulation, of which this Library is one of the results, little has been imparted to the public, and of that little the greater part is fabulous.

A hundred years ago, in the poor little village of Waldorf, in the duchy of Baden, lived a jovial, good-for-nothing butcher, named Jacob Astor, who felt himself much more at home in the beer-house than at the fireside of his own house in the principal street of the village. At the best, the butcher of Waldorf must have been a poor man; for, at that day, the inhabitants of a German village enjoyed the luxury of fresh meat only on great days such as those of confirmation, baptism, weddings, and Christmas

The village itself was remote and insignificant, and though situ
ated in the valley of the Rhine, the native home of the vine, a
region of proverbial fertility, the immediate vicinity of Waldorf
was not a rich or very populous country. The home of Jacob
Astor, therefore, seldom knew any medium between excessive
abundance and extreme scarcity, and he was not the man to make
the superfluity of to-day provide for the need of to-morrow;
which was the more unfortunate as the periods of abundance
were few and far between, and the times of scarcity extended
over the greater part of the year. It was the custom then in
Germany for every farmer to provide a fatted pig, calf, or bul-
lock, against the time of harvest; and as that joyful season approached, the village butcher went the round of the neighborhood,
stopping a day or two at each house to kill the animals and convert their flesh into bacon, sausages, or salt beef. During this
happy time, Jacob Astor, a merry dog, always welcome where
pleasure and hilarity were going forward, had enough to drink,
and his family had enough to eat. But the merry time lasted
only six weeks. Then set in the season of scarcity, which was
only relieved when there was a festival of the church, a wedding,
a christening, or a birthday in some family of the village rich
enough to provide an animal for Jacob's knife. The wife of this
idle and improvident butcher was such a wife as such men usually
contrive to pick up, — industrious, saving, and capable ; the main-
stay of his house. Often she remonstrated with her wasteful and
beer-loving husband ; the domestic sky was often overcast, and
the children were glad to fly from the noise and dust of the tem-
pest.

This roistering village butcher and his worthy, much-enduring
wife were the parents of our millionnaire. They had four sons:
George Peter Astor, born in 1752; Henry Astor, born in 1754;
John Melchior Astor, born in 1759 ; and John Jacob Astor,
born July 17, 1763. Each of these sons made haste to fly from
the privations and contentions of their home as soon as they were
old enough ; and, what is more remarkable, each of them had a
cast of character precisely the opposite of their thriftless father.
They were all saving, industrious, temperate, and enterprising.

and all of them became prosperous men at an early period of their career. They were all duly instructed in their father's trade; each in turn carried about the streets of Waldorf the basket of meat, and accompanied the father in his harvest slaughtering tours. Jovial Jacob, we are told, gloried in being a butcher, but three of his sons, much to his disgust, manifested a repugnance to it, which was one of the causes of their flight from the parental nest. The eldest, who was the first to go, made his way to London, where an uncle was established in business as a maker of musical instruments. Astor and Broadwood was the name of the firm, a house that still exists under the title of Broadwood and Co., one of the most noted makers of pianos in England. In his uncle's manufactory George Astor servʳd an apprenticeship, and became at length a partner in the .firm. Henry Astor went next. He alone of his father's sons took to his father's trade. It used to be thrown in his teeth, when he was a thriving butcher in the city of New York, that he had come over to America as a private in the Hessian army. This may only have been the groundless taunt of an envious rival. It is certain, however, that he was a butcher in New York when it was a British post during the revolutionary war, and, remaining after the evacuation, made a large fortune in his business. The third son, John Melchior Astor, found employment in Germany, and arrived, at length, at the profitable post of steward to a nobleman's estate.

Abandoned thus by his three brothers, John Jacob Astor had to endure for some years a most cheerless and miserable lot. He lost his mother, too, from whom he had derived all that was good in his character and most of the happiness of his childhood. A step-mother replaced her, " who loved not Jacob," nor John Jacob. The father, still devoted to pleasure, quarrelled so bitterly with his new wife, that his son was often glad to escape to the house of a schoolfellow (living in 1854), where he would pass the night in a garret or outhouse, thankfully accepting for his supper a crust of dry bread, and returning the next morning to assist in the slaughter-house or carry out the meat. It was not often that he had enough to eat; his clothes were of the poorest

19   B B

description; and, as to money, he absolutely had none of it. The unhappiness of his home and the misconduct of his father made him ashamed to join in the sports of the village boys; and he passed much of his leisure alone, brooding over the unhappiness of his lot. The family increased, but not its income. It is recorded of him that he tended his little sisters with care and fondness, and sought in all ways to lessen the dislike and ill-humor of his step-mother.

It is not hardship, however, that enervates a lad. It is indulgence and luxury that do that. He grew a stout, healthy, tough, and patient boy, diligent and skilful in the discharge of his duty, often supplying the place of his father absent in merry-making. If, in later life, he overvalued money, it should not be forgotten that few men have had a harder experience of the want of money at the age when character is forming.

The bitterest lot has its alleviations. Sometimes a letter would reach him from over the sea, telling of the good fortune of a brother in a distant land. In his old age he used to boast that in his boyhood he walked forty-five miles in one day for the sole purpose of getting a letter that had arrived from England or America. The Astors have always been noted for the strength of their family affection. Our millionnaire forgot much that he ought to have remembered, but he was not remiss in fulfilling the obligations of kindred.

It appears, too, that he was fortunate in having a better school-master than could generally be found at that day in a village school of Germany. Valentine Jeune was his name, a French Protestant, whose parents had fled from their country during the reign of Louis XIV. He was an active and sympathetic teacher, and bestowed unusual pains upon the boy, partly because he pitied his unhappy situation, and partly because of his aptitude to learn. Nevertheless, the school routine of those days was extremely limited. To read and write, to cipher as far as the Rule of Three, to learn the Catechism by heart, and to sing the Church Hymns "so that the windows should rattle," — these were the sole accomplishments of even the best pupils of Valentine Jeune. Baden was then under the rule of a Catholic family It was a saying in Waldorf that no man could be appointed a swineherd who was not a Catholic, and that if a mayoralty were vacant the swineherd must have the place if there were no other Catholic in the town. Hence it was that the line which separated the Protestant minority from the Catholic majority was sharply defined, and the Protestant children were the more thoroughly indoctrinated. Rev. John Philip Steiner, the Protestant pastor of Waldorf, a learned and faithful minister, was as punctilious in requiring from the children the thorough learning of the Catechism as a German sergeant was in exacting all the niceties of the parade. Young Astor became, therefore, a very decided Protestant; he lived and died a member of the Church in which he was born.

The great day in the life of a German child is that of his confirmation, which usually occurs in his fourteenth year. The ceremony, which was performed at Waldorf every two years, was a festival at once solemn and joyous. The children, long prepared beforehand by the joint labors of minister, schoolmaster, and parents, walk in procession to the church, the girls in white, the boys in their best clothes, and there, after the requisite examinations, the rite is performed, and the Sacrament is administered. The day concludes with festivity. Confirmation also is the point of division between childhood and youth, — between absolute dependence and the beginning of responsibility. After confirmation, the boys of a German peasant take their place in life as apprentices or as servants; and the girls, unless their services are required at home, are placed in situations. Childhood ends, maturity begins, when the child has tasted for the first time the bread and wine of the Communion. Whether a boy then becomes an apprentice or a servant depends upon whether his parents have been provident enough to save a sum of money sufficient to pay the usual premium required by a master as compensation for his trouble in teaching his trade. This premium varied at that day from fifty dollars to two hundred, according to the difficulty and respectability of the vocation. A carpenter or a blacksmith might be satisfied with a premium of sixty or seventy dollars while a cabinet-maker would demand a hundred, and a musical instrument maker or a clock-maker two hundred.

On Palm Sunday, 1777, when he was about fourteen years of age, John Jacob Astor was confirmed. He then consulted his father upon his future. Money to apprentice him there was none in the paternal coffers. The trade of butcher he knew and disliked. Nor was he inclined to accept as his destiny for life the condition of servant or laborer. The father, who thought the occupation of butcher one of the best in the world, and who needed the help of his son, particularly in the approaching season of harvest, paid no heed to the entreaties of the lad, who saw himself condemned without hope to a business which he loathed, and to labor at it without reward.

A deep discontent settled upon him. The tidings of the good fortune of his brothers inflamed his desire to seek his fortune in the world. The news of the Revolutionary War, which drew all eyes upon America, and in which the people of all lands sympathized with the struggling colonies, had its effect upon him. He began to long for the "New Land," as the Germans then styled America; and it is believed in Waldorf that soon after the capture of Burgoyne had spread abroad a confidence in the final success of the colonists, the youth formed the secret determination to emigrate to America. Nevertheless, he had to wait three miserable years longer, until the surrender of Cornwallis made it certain that America was to be free, before he was able to enter upon the gratification of his desire.

In getting to America, he displayed the same sagacity in adapting means to ends that distinguished him during his business career in New York. Money he had never had in his life, beyond a few silver coins of the smallest denomination. His father had none to give him, even if he had been inclined to do so. It was only when the lad was evidently resolved to go that he gave a slow, reluctant consent to his departure. Waldorf is nearly three hundred miles from the seaport in Holland most convenient for his purpose. Despite the difficulties, this penniless youth formed the resolution of going down the Rhine to Holland, there taking ship for London, where he would join his brother, and, while earning money for his passage to America, learn the language of the country to which he was destined. It appears that he dreaded more the difficulties of the English tongue than he did those of the long and expensive journey; but he was resolved not to sail for America until he had acquired the language, and saved a little money beyond the expenses of the voyage. It appears, also, that there prevailed in Baden the belief that Americans were exceedingly selfish and inhospitable, and regarded the poor emigrant only in the light of prey. John Jacob was determined not to land among such a people without the means of understanding their tricks and paying his way. In all ways, too, he endeavored to get a knowledge of the country to which he was going.

With a small bundle of clothes hung over his shoulder upon a stick, with a crown or two in his pocket, he said the last farewell to his father and his friends, and set out on foot for the Rhine, a few miles distant. Valentine Jeune, his old schoolmaster, said, as the lad was lost to view: "I am not afraid of Jacob; he'll get through the world. He has a clear head and everything right behind the ears." He was then a stout, strong lad of nearly seventeen, exceedingly well made, though slightly undersized, and he had a clear, composed, intelligent look in the eyes, which seemed to ratify the prediction of the schoolmaster. He strode manfully out of town, with tears in his eyes and a sob in his throat, — for he loved his father, his friends, and his native village, though his lot there had been forlorn enough. While still in sight of Waldorf, he sat down under a tree and thought of the future before him and the friends he had left. He there, as he used to relate in after-life, made three resolutions: to be honest, to be industrious, and not to gamble, — excellent resolutions, as far as they go. Having sat awhile under the tree, he took up his bundle and resumed his journey with better heart.

It was by no means the intention of this sagacious youth to walk all the way to the sea-coast. There was a much more convenient way at that time of accomplishing the distance, even to a young man with only two dollars in his pocket. The Black Forest is partly in Astor's native Baden. The rafts of timber cut in the Black Forest, instead of floating down the Rhine in the manner practised in America, used to be rowed by sixty or eighty men each, who were paid high wages, as the labor was severe

Large numbers of stalwart emigrants availed themselves of this mode of getting from the interior to the sea-coast, by which they earned their subsistence on the way and about ten dollars in money. The tradition in Waldorf is, that young Astor worked his passage down the Rhine, and earned his passage-money to England as an oarsman on one of these rafts. Hard as the labor was, the oarsmen had a merry time of it, cheering their toil with jest and song by night and day. On the fourteenth day after leaving home, our youth found himself at a Dutch seaport, with a larger sum of money than he had ever before possessed. He took passage for London, where he landed a few days after, in total ignorance of the place and the language. His brother welcomed him with German warmth, and assisted him to procure employment, — probably in the flute and piano manufactory of Astor and Broadwood.

As the foregoing brief account of the early life of John Jacob Astor differs essentially from any previously published in the United States, it is proper that the reader should be informed of the sources whence we have derived information so novel and unexpected. The principal source is a small biography of Astor published in Germany about ten years ago, written by a native of Baden, a Lutheran clergyman, who gathered his material in Waldorf, where were then living a few aged persons who remembered Astor when he was a sad and solitary lad in his father's disorderly house. The statements of this little book are confirmed by what some of the surviving friends and descendants of Mr. Astor in New York remember of his own conversation respecting his early days. He seldom spoke of his life in Germany, though he remembered his native place with fondness, revisited it in the time of his prosperity, pensioned his father, and forgot not Waldorf in his will; but the little that he did say of his youthful years accords with the curious narrative in the work to which we have alluded. We believe the reader may rely on our story as being essentially true.

Astor brought to London, according to our quaint Lutheran, a pious, true, and godly spirit, a clear understanding, a sound youthful elbow-grease, and the wish to put it to good use." During the two years of his residence in the British metropolis, he strove most assiduously for three objects: 1. To save money ; 2. To acquire the English language; 3. To get information respecting America. Much to his relief and gratification, he found the acquisition of the language to be the least of his difficulties. Working in a shop with English mechanics, and having few German friends, he was generally dependent upon the language of the country for the communication of his desires; and he was as much surprised as delighted to find how many points of similarity there were between the two languages. In about six weeks, he used to say, he could make himself understood a little in English, and long before he left London he could speak it fluently. He never learned to write English correctly in his life, nor could he ever speak it without a decided German accent; but he could always express his meaning with simplicity and force, both orally and in writing. Trustworthy information respecting America, in the absence of maps, gazetteers, and books of travel, was more difficult to procure. The ordinary Englishman of that day regarded America with horror or contempt as perverse and rebellious colonies, making a great to-do about a paltry tax, and giving " the best of kings " a world of trouble for nothing. He probably heard little of the thundering eloquence with which Fox, Pitt, Burke, and Sheridan were nightly defending the American cause in the House of Commons, and assailing the infatuation of the Government in prosecuting a hopeless war. As often, however, as our youth met with any one who had been in America, he plied him with questions, and occasionally he heard from his brother in New York. Henry Astor was already established as a butcher on his own account, wheeling home in a wheelbarrow from Bull's Head his slender purchases of sheep and calves. But the great difficulty of John Jacob in London was the accumulation of money. Having no trade, his wages were necessarily small. Though he rose with the lark, and was at work as early as five in the morning, — though he labored with all his might, and saved every farthing that he could spare, — it was two years before he had saved enough for his purpose. In September 1783, he possessed a good suit of Sunday clothes, in the Eng lish style, and about fifteen English guineas, — the total result of two years of unremitting toil and most pinching economy; and here again charity requires the remark that if Astor the millionnaire carried the virtue of economy to an extreme, it was Astor the struggling youth in a strange land who learned the value of money.

In that month of September, 1783, the news reached London that Dr. Franklin and his associates in Paris, after two years of negotiation, had signed the definitive treaty which completed the independence of the United States. Franklin had been in the habit of predicting that as soon as America had become an independent nation, the best blood in Europe, and some of the finest fortunes, would hasten to seek a career or an asylum in the New World. Perhaps he would have hardly recognized the emigration of this poor German youth as part of the fulfilment of his prophecy. Nevertheless, the news of the conclusion of the treaty had no sooner reached England than young Astor, then twenty years old, began to prepare for his departure for the " New Land," and in November he embarked for Baltimore. He paid five of his guineas for a passage in the steerage, which entitled him to sailors' fare of salt beef and biscuit. He invested part of nis remaining capital in seven flutes, and carried the rest, about five pounds sterling, in the form of money.

America gave a cold welcome to the young emigrant. The winter of 1783 – 4 was one of the celebrated severe winters on both sides of the ocean. November gales and December storms wreaked all their fury upon the ship, retarding its progress so long that January arrived before she had reached Chesapeake Bay. Floating ice filled the bay as far as the eye could reach, and a January storm drove the ship among the masses with such force, that she was in danger of being broken to pieces. It was on one of those days of peril and consternation, that young Astor appeared on deck in his best clothes, and on being asked the reason of this strange proceeding, said that if he escaped with life he should save his best clothes, and if he lost it his clothes would be of no further use to him. Tradition further reports that he, a steerage passenger, ventured one day to come upon the quarter-deck, when the captain roughly ordered him forward. Tradition adds that that very captain, twenty years after, commanded a ship owned by the steerage passenger. When the ship was within a day's sail of her port the wind died away, the cold increased, and the next morning beheld the vessel hard and fast in a sea of ice. For two whole months she remained immovable. Provisions gave out. The passengers were only relieved when the ice extended to the shore, and became strong enough to afford communication with other ships and with the coasts of the bay. Some of the passengers made their way to the shore, and travelled by land to their homes; but this resource was not within the means of our young adventurer, and he was obliged to stick to the ship.

Fortune is an obsequious jade, that favors the strong and turns her back upon the weak. This exasperating delay of two months was the means of putting young Astor upon the shortest and easiest road to fortune that the continent of America then afforded to a poor man. Among his fellow-passengers there was one German, with whom he made acquaintance on the voyage, and with whom he continually associated during the detention of the winter. They told each other their past history, their present plans, their future hopes. The stranger informed young Astor that he too had emigrated to America, a few years before, without friends or money; that he had soon managed to get into the business of buying furs of the Indians, and of the boatmen coming to New York from the river settlements; that at length he had embarked all his capital in skins, and had taken them himself to England in a returning transport, where he had sold them to great advantage, and had invested the proceeds in toys and trinkets, with which to continue his trade in the wilderness. He strongly advised Astor to follow his example. He told him the prices of the various skins in America, and the prices they commanded in London. With German friendliness he imparted to him the secrets of the craft: told him where to buy, how to pack, transport, and preserve the skins; the names of the principal dealers in New York, Montreal, and London; and the season of the year when the skins were most abundant. All this was interesting to the young man; but he asked his friend how it was

19*

possible to begin such a business without capital. The stranger told him that no great capital was required for a beginning. With a basket of toys, or even of cakes, he said, a man could buy valuable skins on the wharves and in the markets of New York, which could be sold with some profit to New York furriers. But the grand object was to establish a connection with a house in London, where furs brought four or five times their value in America. In short, John Jacob Astor determined to lose no time after reaching New York, in trying his hand at this profitable traffic.

The ice broke up in March. The ship made its way to Baltimore, and the two friends travelled together to New York. The detention in the ice and the journey to New York almost exhausted Astor's purse. He arrived in this city, where now his estate is valued at forty millions, with little more than his seven German flutes, and a long German head full of available knowledge and quiet determination. He went straight to the humble abode of his brother Henry, a kindly, generous, jovial soul, who gave him a truly fraternal welcome, and received with hospitable warmth the companion of his voyage.

Henry Astor's prosperity had been temporarily checked by the evacuation of New York, which had occurred five months before, and which had deprived the tradesmen of the city of their best customers. It was not only the British army that had left the city in November, 1783, but a host of British officials and old Tory families as well; while the new-comers were Whigs, whom seven years of war had impoverished, and young adventurers who had still their career to make. During the Revolution, Henry Astor had speculated occasionally in cattle captured from the farmers of Westchester, which were sold at auction at Bull's Head, and he had advanced from a wheelbarrow to the ownership of a horse. An advertisement informs us that, about the time of his brother's arrival, this horse was stolen, with saddle and bridle, and that the owner offered three guineas reward for the recovery of the property ; but that "for the thief, horse, saddle, and bridle, ten guineas would be paid." A month after, we find him becoming a citizen of the United States, and soon he began to share in the returning prosperity of the city.

In the mean time, however, he could do little for his new-found brother. During the first evening of his brother's stay at his house the question was discussed, What should the young man do in his new country? The charms of the fur business were duly portrayed by the friend of the youth, who also expressed his preference for it. It was agreed, at length, that the best plan would be for the young man to seek employment with some one already in the business, in order to learn the modes of proceeding, as well as to acquire a knowledge of the country. The young stranger anxiously inquired how much premium would be demanded by a furrier for teaching the business to a novice, and he was at once astonished and relieved to learn that no such thing was known in America, and that he might expect his board and small wages even from the start. So, the next day, the brothers and their friend proceeded together to the store of Robert Bowne, an aged and benevolent Quaker, long established in the business of buying, curing, and exporting peltries. It chanced that he needed a hand. Pleased with the appearance and demeanor of the young man, he employed him (as tradition reports) at two dollars a week and his board. Astor took up his abode in his master's house, and was soon at work. We can tell the reader with certainty what was the nature of the youth's first day's work in his adopted country; for, in his old age, he was often heard to say that the first thing he did for Mr. Bowne was to beat furs; which, indeed, was his principal employment during the whole of the following summer, — furs requiring to be frequently beaten to keep the moths from destroying them.

Perhaps among our readers there are some who have formed the resolution to get on in the world and become rich. We advise such to observe how young Astor proceeded. We are far from desiring to hold up this able man as a model for the young; yet it must be owned that in the art of prospering in business he has had no equal in America; and in *that* his example may be useful. Now, observe the secret. It was not plodding merely, though no man ever labored more steadily than he. Mr. Bowne, discovering what a prize he had, raised his wages at the end of the first month. Nor was it *merely* his strict observance of the rules of temperance and morality, though that is essential to any worthy success. The great secret of Astor's early, rapid, and uniform success in business appears to have been, that he acted always upon the maxim that KNOWLEDGE IS POWER! He labored unceasingly at Mr. Bowne's to *learn the business.* He put all his soul into the work of getting a knowledge of furs, fur-bearing animals, fur-dealers, fur-markets, fur-gathering Indians, fur-abounding countries. In those days a considerable number of bear skins and beaver skins were brought directly to Bowne's store by the Indians and countrymen of the vicinity, who had shot or trapped the animals. These men Astor questioned; and neglected no other opportunity of procuring the information he desired. It used to be observed of Astor that he absolutely loved a fine skin. In later days he would have a superior fur hung up in his counting-room as other men hang pictures; and this, apparently, for the mere pleasure of feeling, showing, and admiring it. He would pass his hand fondly over it, extolling its charms with an approach to enthusiasm; not, however, forgetting to mention that in Canton it would bring him in five hundred dollars. So heartily did he throw himself into his business.

Growing rapidly in the confidence of his employer, he was soon intrusted with more important duties than the beating of furs. He was employed in buying them from the Indians and hunters who brought them to the city. Soon, too, he took the place of his employer in the annual journey to Montreal, then the chief fur mart of the country. With a pack upon his back, he struck into the wilderness above Albany, and walked to Lake George, which he ascended in a canoe, and having thus reached Champlain he embarked again, and sailed to the head of that lake. Returning with his furs, he employed the Indians in transporting them to the Hudson, and brought them to the city in a sloop. He was formed by nature for a life like this. His frame was capable of great endurance, and he had the knack of getting the best of a bargain. The Indian is a great bargainer. The time was gone by when a nail or a little red paint would induce him to part with valuable peltries. It required skill and address on the part of the trader, both in selecting the articles likely to tempt the vanity or the cupidity of the red man, and in conducting the tedious negotiation which usually preceded an exchange of commodities. It was in this kind of traffic, doubtless, that our young German acquired that unconquerable propensity for making hard bargains, which was so marked a feature in his character as a merchant. He could never rise superior to this early-acquired habit. He never knew what it was to exchange places with the opposite party, and survey a transaction from *his* point of view. He exulted not in compensating liberal service liberally. In all transactions he kept in view the simple object of giving the least and getting the most.

Meanwhile his brother Henry was flourishing. He married the beautiful daughter of a brother butcher, and the young wife, according to the fashion of the time, disdained not to assist her husband even in the slaughter-house as well as in the market-place. Colonel Devoe, in his well-known Market Book, informs us that Henry Astor was exceedingly proud of his pretty wife, often bringing her home presents of gay dresses and ribbons, and speaking of her as " de pink of de Bowery." The butchers of that day complained bitterly of him, because he used to ride out of town fifteen or twenty miles, and buy up the droves of cattle coming to the city, which he would drive in and sell at an advanced price to the less enterprising butchers. He gained a fortune by his business, which would have been thought immense, if the colossal wealth of his brother had not reduced all other estates to comparative insignificance. It was he who bought, for eight hundred dollars, the acre of ground on part of which the old Bowery Theatre now stands.

John Jacob Astor remained not long in the employment of Robert Bowne. It was a peculiarity of the business of a furrier at that day, that, while it admitted of unlimited extension, it could be begun on the smallest scale, with a very insignificant capital. Every farmer's boy in the vicinity of New York had occasionally a skin to sell, and bears abounded in the Catskill Mountains. Indeed the time had not long gone by when beaver skins formed part of the currency of the city. All Northern and Western New York was still a fur-yielding country. Even Long Island fur nished its quota. So that, while the fur business was one that rewarded the enterprise of great and wealthy companies, employing thousands of men and fleets of ships, it afforded an opening to young Astor, who, with the assistance of his brother, could command a capital of only a very few hundred dollars. In a little shop in Water Street, with a back-room, a yard, and a shed, the shop furnished with only a few toys and trinkets, Astor began business about the year 1786. He had then, as always, the most unbounded confidence in his own abilities. He used to relate that, at this time, a new row of houses in Broadway was the talk of the city from their magnitude and beauty. Passing them one day, he said to himself: "I'll build some time or other a greater house than any of these, and in this very street." He used also to say, in his old age: "The first hundred thousand dollars — that was hard to get; but afterward it was easy to make more."

Having set up for himself, he worked with the quiet, indomitable ardor of a German who sees clearly his way open before him. At first he did everything for himself. He bought, cured, beat, packed, and sold his skins. From dawn till dark, he assiduously labored. At the proper seasons of the year, with his pack on his back, he made short excursions into the country, collecting skins from house to house, gradually extending the area of his travels, till he knew the State of New York as no man of his day knew it. He used to boast, late in life, when the Erie Canal had called into being a line of thriving towns through the centre of the State, that he had himself, in his numberless tramps, designated the sites of those towns, and predicted that one day they would be the centres of business and population. Particularly he noted the spots where Rochester and Buffalo now stand, one having a harbor on Lake Erie, the other upon Lake Ontario. Those places, he predicted, would one day be large and prosperous cities, and that prediction he made when there was scarcely a settlement at Buffalo, and only wigwams on the site of Rochester. At this time he had a partner who usually remained in the city, while the agile and enduring Astor traversed the wilderness.

It was his first voyage to London that established his business on a solid foundation. As soon as he had accumulated a few bales of the skins suited to the European market, he took passage in the steerage of a ship and conveyed them to London. He sold them to great advantage, and established connections with houses to which he could in future consign his furs, and from which he could procure the articles best adapted to the taste of Indians and hunters. But his most important operation in London was to make an arrangement with the firm of Astor & Broadwood, by which he became the New York agent for the sale of their pianos, flutes, and violins. He is believed to have been the first man in New York who kept constantly for sale a supply of musical merchandise, of which the annual sale in New York is now reckoned at five millions of dollars. On his return to New York, he opened a little dingy store in Gold Street, between Fulton and Ann, and swung out a sign to the breeze bearing the words : —

FURS AND PIANOS.

There were until recently aged men among us who remembered seeing this sign over the store of Mr. Astor, and in some old houses are preserved ancient pianos, bearing the name of J. J. Astor, as the seller thereof. Violins and flutes, also, are occasionally met with that have his name upon them. In 1790, seven years after his arrival in this city, he was of sufficient importance to appear in the Directory thus : —

ASTOR, J. J., Fur Trader, 40 Little Dock Street (now part of Water Street).

In this time of his dawning prosperity, while still inhabiting the small house of which his store was a part, he married. Sarah Todd was the maiden name of his wife. As a connection of the family of Brevoort, she was then considered to be somewhat superior to her husband in point of social rank, and she brought him a fortune, by no means despised by him at that time, of three hundred dollars. She threw herself heartily into her husband's growing business, laboring with her own hands, buying, sorting, and beating the furs. He used to say that she was as good a judge of the value of peltries as himself, and that her opinion in matter of business was better than that of most merchants.

Of a man like Astor all kinds of stories will be told, some true, some false; some founded upon fact, but exaggerated or distorted. It is said, for example, that when he went into business for himself, he used to go around among the shops and markets with a basket of toys and cakes upon his arm, exchanging those articles for furs. There are certainly old people among us who remember hearing their parents say that they saw him doing this. The story is not improbable, for he had no false pride, and was ready to turn his hand to anything that was honest.

Mr. Astor still traversed the wilderness. The father of the late lamented General Wadsworth used to relate that he met him once in the woods of Western New York in a sad plight. His wagon had broken down in the midst of a swamp. In the *mêlée* all his gold had rolled away through the bottom of the vehicle, and was irrecoverably lost; and Astor was seen emerging from the swamp covered with mud and carrying on his shoulder an axe, — the sole relic of his property. When at length, in 1794, Jay's treaty caused the evacuation of the western forts held by the British, his business so rapidly extended that he was enabled to devolve these laborious journeys upon others, while he remained in New York, controlling a business that now embraced the region of the great lakes, and gave employment to a host of trappers, collectors, and agents. He was soon in a position to purchase a ship, in which his furs were carried to London, and in which he occasionally made a voyage himself. He was still observed to be most assiduous in the pursuit of commercial knowledge. He was never weary of inquiring about the markets of Europe and Asia, the ruling prices and commodities of each, the standing of commercial houses, and all other particulars that could be of use. Hence his directions to his captains and agents were always explicit and minute, and if any enterprise failed to be profitable it could generally be distinctly seen that it was because his orders had not been obeyed. In London, he became most intimately conversant with the operations of the East-India Company and with the China trade. China being the best market in the world for furs, and furnishing commodities which in America had become necessaries of life, he was quick to perceive what an advantage he would have over other merchants by sending his ships to Canton provided with furs as well as dollars. It was about the year 1800 that he sent his first ship to Canton, and he continued to carry on commerce with China for twenty-seven years, sometimes with loss, generally with profit, and occasionally with splendid and bewildering success.

It was not, however, until the year 1800, when he was worth a quarter of a million dollars, and had been in business fifteen years, that he indulged himself in the comfort of living in a house apart from his business. In 1794 he appears in the Directory as " Furrier, 149 Broadway." From 1796 to 1799 he figures as " Fur Merchant, 149 Broadway." In 1800 he had a storehouse at 141 Greenwich Street, and lived at 223 Broadway, on the site of the present Astor House. In 1801, his store was at 71 Liberty Street, and he had removed his residence back to 149 Broadway. The year following we find him again at 223 Broadway, where he continued to reside for a quarter of a century. His house was such as a fifth-rate merchant would now consider much beneath his dignity. Mr. Astor, indeed, had a singular dislike to living in a large house. He had neither expensive tastes nor wasteful vices. His luxuries were a pipe, a glass of beer, a game of draughts, a ride on horseback, and the theatre. Of the theatre he was particularly fond. He seldom missed a good performance in the palmy days of the " Old Park."

It was his instinctive abhorrence of ostentation and waste that enabled him, as it were, to glide into the millionnaire without being observed by his neighbors. He used to relate, with a chuckle, that he was worth a million before any one suspected it. A dandy bank-clerk, one day, having expressed a doubt as to the sufficiency of his name to a piece of mercantile paper, Astor asked him how much he thought he was worth. The clerk mentioned a sum ludicrously less than the real amount. Astor then asked him how much he supposed this and that leading merchant, whom he named, was worth. The young man endowed them with generous sum-totals proportioned to their style of living. " Well," said Astor, " I am worth more than any of

o c

them. I will not say how much I am worth, but I am worth more than any sum you have mentioned." "Then," said the clerk, "you are even a greater fool than I took you for, to work as hard as you do." The old man would tell this story with great glee, for he always liked a joke.

In the course of his long life he had frequent opportunities of observing what becomes of those gay merchants who live up to the incomes of prosperous years, regardless of the inevitable time of commercial collapse. It must be owned that he held in utter contempt the dashing style of living and doing business which has too often prevailed in New York ; and he was very slow to give credit to a house that carried sail out of proportion to its ballast. Nevertheless, he was himself no plodder when plodding had ceased to be necessary. At the time when his affairs were on their greatest scale, he would leave his office at two in the afternoon, go home to an early dinner, then mount his horse and ride about the Island till it was time to go to the theatre. He had a strong aversion to illegitimate speculation, and particularly to gambling in stocks. The note-shaving and stock-jobbing operations of the Rothschilds he despised. It was his pride and boast that he gained his own fortune by legitimate commerce, and by the legitimate investment of his profits. Having an unbounded faith in the destiny of the United States, and in the future commercial supremacy of New York, it was his custom, from about the year 1800, to invest his gains in the purchase of lots and lands on Manhattan Island.

We have all heard much of the closeness, or rather the meanness, of this remarkable man. Truth compels us to admit, as we have before intimated, that he was not generous, except to his own kindred. His liberality began and ended in his own family. Very seldom during his lifetime did he willingly do a generous act outside of the little circle of his relations and descendants. To get all that he could, and to keep nearly all that he got, — those were the laws of his being. He had a vast genius for making money, and that was all that he had.

It is a pleasure to know that sometimes his extreme closeness defeated its own object. He once lost seventy thousand dollars

by committing a piece of petty injustice toward his best captain.
This gallant sailor, being notified by an insurance office of the
necessity of having a chronometer on board his ship, spoke to Mr.
Astor on the subject, who advised the captain to buy one.

" But," said the captain, " I have no five hundred dollars to
spare for such a purpose ; the chronometer should belong to the
ship."

" Well," said the merchant, " you need not pay for it now;
pay for it at your convenience."

The captain still objecting, Astor, after a prolonged higgling,
authorized him to buy a chronometer, and charge it to the ship's
account; which was done. Sailing-day was at hand. The ship
was hauled into the stream. The captain, as is the custom,
handed in his account. Astor, subjecting it to his usual close
scrutiny, observed the novel item of five hundred dollars for the
chronometer. He objected, averring that it was understood between them that the captain was to pay for the instrument. The
worthy sailor recalled the conversation, and firmly held to his recollection of it. Astor insisting on his own view of the matter,
the captain was so profoundly disgusted that, important as the
command of the ship was to him, he resigned his post. Another
captain was soon found, and the ship sailed for China. Another
house, which was then engaged in the China trade, knowing the
worth of this " king of captains," as Astor himself used to style
him, bought him a ship and despatched him to Canton two
months after the departure of Astor's vessel. Our captain, put
upon his mettle, employed all his skill to accelerate the speed of
his ship, and had such success, that he reached New York with a
full cargo of tea just seven days after the arrival of Mr. Astor's
ship. Astor, not expecting another ship for months, and therefore sure of monopolizing the market, had not yet broken bulk,
nor even taken off the hatchways. Our captain arrived on a
Saturday. Advertisements and handbills were immediately issued, and on the Wednesday morning following, as the custom
then was, the auction sale of the tea began on the wharf, — two
barrels of punch contributing to the *éclat* and hilarity of the occasion. The cargo was sold to good advantage, and the market

was glutted. Astor lost in consequence the entire profits of the voyage, not less than the sum named above. Meeting the captain some time after in Broadway, he said, —

"I had better have paid for that chronometer of yours."

Without ever acknowledging that he had been in the wrong he was glad enough to engage the captain's future services. This anecdote we received from the worthy captain's own lips.

On one occasion the same officer had the opportunity of rendering the great merchant a most signal service. The agent of Mr. Astor in China suddenly died at a time when the property in his charge amounted to about seven hundred thousand dollars. Our captain, who was not then in Astor's employ, was perfectly aware that if this immense property fell into official hands, as the law required, not one dollar of it would ever again find its way to the coffers of its proprietor. By a series of bold, prompt, and skilful measures, he rescued it from the official maw, and made it yield a profit to the owner. Mr. Astor acknowledged the service. He acknowledged it with emphasis and a great show of gratitude. He said many times : —

"If you had not done just as you did, I should never have seen one dollar of my money ; no, not one dollar of it."

But he not only did not compensate him for his services, but he did not even reimburse the small sum of money which the captain had expended in performing those services. Astor was then worth ten millions, and the captain had his hundred dollars a month and a family of young children.

Thus the great merchant recompensed great services. He was not more just in rewarding small ones. On one occasion a ship of his arrived from China, which he found necessary to despatch at once to Amsterdam, the market in New York being depressed by an over-supply of China merchandise. But on board this ship, under a mountain of tea-chests, the owner had two pipes of precious Madeira wine, which had been sent on a voyage for the improvement of its constitution.

"Can you get out that wine," asked the owner, "without discharging the tea?"

The captain thought he could.

" Well, then," said Mr. Astor, "you get it out, and I'll give you a demijohn of it. You'll say it's the best wine you ever tasted."

It required the labor of the whole ship's crew for two days to get out those two pipes of wine. They were sent to the house of Mr. Astor. A year passed. The captain had been to Amsterdam and back, but he had received no tidings of his demijohn of Madeira. One day, when Mr. Astor was on board the ship, the captain ventured to remind the great man, in a jocular manner, that he had not received the wine.

" Ah!" said Astor, " don't you know the reason? It isn't fine yet. Wait till it is fine, and you'll say you never tasted such Madeira." The captain never heard of that wine again.

These traits show the moral weakness of the man. It is only when we regard his mercantile exploits that we can admire him. He was, unquestionably, one of the ablest, boldest, and most successful operators that ever lived. He seldom made a mistake in the conduct of business. Having formed his plan, he carried it out with a nerve and steadiness, with such a firm and easy grasp of all the details, that he seemed rather to be playing an interesting game than transacting business. " He could command an army of five hundred thousand men!" exclaimed one of his admirers. That was an erroneous remark. He could have commanded an army of five hundred thousand tea-chests, with a heavy auxiliary force of otter skins and beaver skins. But a commander of men must be superior morally as well as intellectually. He must be able to win the love and excite the enthusiasm of his followers. Astor would have made a splendid commissary-general to the army of Xerxes, but he could no more have conquered Greece than Xerxes himself.

The reader may be curious to know by what means Mr. Astor became so preposterously rich. Few successful men gain a single million by legitimate commerce. A million dollars is a most enormous sum of money. It requires a considerable effort of the mind to conceive it. But this indomitable little German managed, in the course of sixty years, to accumulate twenty millions ; of which, probably, not more than two millions was the fruit of his business as a fur trader and China merchant.

At that day the fur trade was exceedingly profitable, as well as of vast extent. It is estimated that about the year 1800 the number of peltries annually furnished to commerce was about six millions, varying in value from fifteen cents to five hundred dollars. When every respectable man in Europe and America wore a beaver skin upon his head, or a part of one, and when a good beaver skin could be bought in Western New York for a dollar's worth of trash, and could be sold in London for twenty-five English shillings, and when those twenty-five English shillings could be invested in English cloth and cutlery, and sold in New York for forty shillings, it may be imagined that fur-trading was a very good business. Mr. Astor had his share of the cream of it, and that was the foundation of his colossal fortune. Hence, too, the tender love he felt for a fine fur.

In the next place, his ventures to China were sometimes exceedingly fortunate. A fair profit on a voyage to China at that day was thirty thousand dollars. Mr. Astor has been known to gain seventy thousand, and to have his money in his pocket within the year. He was remarkably lucky in the war of 1812. All his ships escaped capture, and arriving at a time when foreign commerce was almost annihilated and tea had doubled in price, his gains were so immense, that the million or more lost in the Astorian enterprise gave him not even a momentary inconvenience.

At that time, too, tea merchants of large capital had an advantage which they do not now enjoy. A writer explains the manner in which the business was done in those days : —

" A house that could raise money enough thirty years ago to send $260,000 in specie, could soon have an uncommon capital, and this was the working of the old system. The Griswolds owned the ship Panama. They started her from New York in the month of May, with a cargo of perhaps $30,000 worth of ginseng, spelter, lead, iron, etc., and $170,000 in Spanish dollars. The ship goes on the voyage, reaches Whampoa in safety (a few miles below Canton). Her supercargo in two months has her loaded with tea, some china ware, a great deal of cassia or false cinnamon, and a few other articles. Suppose the cargo, mainly tea, costing about thirty-seven cents (at that time) per pound on the average.

"The duty was enormous in those days. It was twice the cost of the tea, at least: so that a tea cargo of $200,000, when it had paid duty of seventy-five cents per pound (which would be $400,000), amounted to $600,000. The profit was at least fifty per cent on the original cost, or $100,000, and would make the cargo worth $700,000.

"The cargo of teas would be sold almost on arrival (say eleven or twelve months after the ship left New York in May) to whole-sale grocers, for their notes at four and six months, — say for $700,000. In those years there was *credit given by the United States* of nine, twelve, and eighteen months! So that the East-India or Canton merchant, after his ship had made one voyage had the use of government capital to the extent of $400,000, on the ordinary cargo of a China ship.

"No sooner had the ship Panama arrived (or any of the regular East-Indiamen), than her cargo would be exchanged for grocers' notes for $700,000. These notes could be turned into specie very easily, and the owner had only to pay his bonds for $400,000 duty, at nine, twelve, and eighteen months, giving him time actually to send two more ships with $200,000 each to Canton, and have them back again in New York before the bonds on the first cargo were due.

"John Jacob Astor at one period of his life had several vessels operating in this way. They would go to the Pacific (Oregon) and carry from thence furs to Canton. These would be sold at large profits. Then the cargoes of tea to New York would pay enormous duties, which Astor did not have to pay to the United States for a year and a half. His tea cargoes would be sold for good four and six months paper, or perhaps cash; so that for eighteen or twenty years John Jacob Astor had what was actually a free-of-interest loan from Government of over *five millions* of dollars." *

But it was neither his tea trade nor his fur trade that gave Astor twenty millions of dollars. It was his sagacity in investing his profits that made him the richest man in America. When he first trod the streets of New York, in 1784, the city was a

* Old Merchants of New York. First Series.

snug, leafy place of twenty-five thousand inhabitants, situated at the extremity of the Island, mostly below Cortlandt Street. In 1800, when he began to have money to invest, the city had more than doubled in population, and had advanced nearly a mile up the Island. Now, Astor was a shrewd calculator of the future. No reason appeared why New York should not repeat this doubling game and this mile of extension every fifteen years. He acted upon the supposition, and fell into the habit of buying lands and lots just beyond the verge of the city. One little anecdote will show the wisdom of this proceeding. He sold a lot in the vicinity of Wall Street, about the year 1810, for eight thousand dollars, which was supposed to be somewhat under its value. The purchaser, after the papers were signed, seemed disposed to chuckle over his bargain.

" Why, Mr. Astor," said he, " in a few years this lot will be worth twelve thousand dollars."

" Very true," replied Astor ; " but now you shall see what I will do with this money. With eight thousand dollars I buy eighty lots above Canal Street. By the time your lot is worth twelve thousand dollars, my eighty lots will be worth eighty thousand dollars" ; which proved to be the fact.

His purchase of the Richmond Hill estate of Aaron Burr was a case in point. He bought the hundred and sixty acres at a thousand dollars an acre, and in twelve years the land was worth fifteen hundred dollars a lot. In the course of time the Island was dotted all over with Astor lands, — to such an extent that the whole income of his estate for fifty years could be invested in new houses without buying any more land.

His land speculations, however, were by no means confined to the little Island of Manhattan. Aged readers cannot have forgotten the most celebrated of all his operations of this kind, by which he acquired a legal title to one third of the county of Putnam in this State. This enormous tract was part of the estate of Roger Morris and Mary his wife, who, by adhering to the King of Great Britain in the Revolutionary War, forfeited their landed property in the State of New York. Having been duly attainted as public enemies, they fled to England at the close of the war and the State sold their lands, in small parcels, to honest Whig farmers. The estate comprised fifty-one thousand one hundred and two acres, upon which were living, in 1809, more than seven hundred families, all relying upon the titles which the State of New York had given. Now Mr. Astor stepped forward to disturb the security of this community of farmers. It appeared, and was proved beyond doubt, that Roger and Mary Morris had only possessed a *life-interest* in this estate, and that, therefore, it was only that life-interest which the State could legally confiscate. The moment Roger and Mary Morris ceased to live, the property would fall to their heirs, with all the houses, barns, and other improvements thereon. After a most thorough examination of the papers by the leading counsel of that day, Mr. Astor bought the rights of the heirs, in 1809, for twenty thousand pounds sterling. At that time Roger Morris was no more ; and Mary his wife was nearly eighty, and extremely infirm. She lingered, however, for some years ; and it was not till after the peace of 1815 that the claims of Mr. Astor were pressed. The consternation of the farmers and the astonishment of the people generally, when at length the great millionnaire stretched out his hand to pluck this large ripe pear, may be imagined. A great clamor arose against him. It cannot be denied, however, that he acted in this business with moderation and dignity. Upon the first rumor of his claim, in 1814, commissioners were appointed by the Legislature to inquire into it. These gentlemen, finding the claim more formidable than had been suspected, asked Mr. Astor for what sum he would compromise. The lands were valued at six hundred and sixty-seven thousand dollars, but Astor replied that he would sell his claim for three hundred thousand. The offer was not accepted, and the affair lingered. In 1818, Mary Morris being supposed to be at the point of death, and the farmers being in constant dread of the writs of ejectment which her death would bring upon them, commissioners were again appointed by the Legislature to look into the matter. Again Mr. Astor was asked upon what terms he would compromise. He replied, January 19, 1819 : —

" In 1813 or 1814 a similar proposition was made to me by the
20

commissioneis then appointed by the Honorable the Legislature of this State, when I offered to compromise for the sum of three hundred thousand dollars, which, considering the value of the property in question, was thought very reasonable ; and, at the present period, when the life of Mrs. Morris is, according to calculation, worth little or nothing, she being near eighty-six years of age, and the property more valuable than it was in 1813, I am still willing to receive the amount which I then stated, with interest on the same, payable in money or stock, bearing an interest of — per cent, payable quarterly. The stock may be made payable at such periods as the Honorable the Legislature may deem proper. This offer will, I trust, be considered as liberal, and as a proof of my willingness to compromise on terms which are reasonable, considering the value of the property, the price which it cost me, and the inconvenience of having so long laid out of my money, which, if employed in commercial operations, would most likely have produced better profits."

The Legislature were not yet prepared to compromise. It was not till 1827 that a test case was selected and brought to trial before a jury. The most eminent counsel were employed on the part of the State, — Daniel Webster and Martin Van Buren among them. Astor's cause was entrusted to Emmet, Ogden, and others. We believe that Aaron Burr was consulted on the part of Mr. Astor, though he did not appear in the trial. The efforts of the array of counsel employed by the State were exerted in vain to find a flaw in the paper upon which Astor's claim mainly rested. Mr. Webster's speech on this occasion betrays, even to the unprofessional reader, both that he had no case and that he knew he had not, for he indulged in a strain of remark that could only have been designed to prejudice, not convince, the jury.

" It is a claim for lands," said he, " not in their wild and forest state, but for lands the intrinsic value of which is mingled with the labor expended upon them. It is no every-day purchase, for it extends over towns and counties, and almost takes in a degree of latitude. It is a stupendous speculation. The individual who now claims it has not succeeded to it by inheritance he has not attained it, as he did that vast wealth which no one less envies him than I do, by fair and honest exertions in commercial enterprise, but by speculation, by purchasing the forlorn hope of the heirs of a family driven from their country by a bill of attainder. By the defendants, on the contrary, the lands in question are held as a patrimony. They have labored for years to improve them. The rugged hills had grown green under their cultivation before a question was raised as to the integrity of their titles."

A line of remark like this would appeal powerfully to a jury of farmers. Its effect, however, was destroyed by the simple observation of one of the opposing counsel : —

" Mr. Astor bought this property confiding in the justice of the State of New York, firmly believing that in the litigation of his claim his rights would be maintained."

It is creditable to the administration of justice in New York, and creditable to the very institution of trial by jury, that Mr. Astor's most unpopular and even odious cause was triumphant. Warned by this verdict, the Legislature consented to compromise on Mr. Astor's own terms. The requisite amount of " Astor stock," as it was called, was created. Mr. Astor received about half a million of dollars, and the titles of the lands were secured to their rightful owners.

The crowning glory of Mr. Astor's mercantile career was that vast and brilliant enterprise which Washington Irving has com memorated in " Astoria." No other single individual has ever set on foot a scheme so extensive, so difficult, and so costly as this ; nor has any such enterprise been carried out with such sustained energy and perseverance. To establish a line of trading-posts from St. Louis to the Pacific, a four-months' journey in a land of wilderness, prairie, mountain, and desert, inhabited by treacherous or hostile savages ; to found a permanent settlement on the Pacific coast as the grand *dépôt* of furs and supplies ; to arrange a plan by which the furs collected should be regularly transported to China, and the ships return to New York laden with tea and silks, and then proceed once more to the Pacific coast to repeat the circuit ; to maintain all the parts of this scheme without the expectation of any but a remote profit, sending ship after ship before any certain intelligence of the first ventures had arrived, — this was an enterprise which had been memorable if it had been undertaken by a wealthy corporation or a powerfu. government, instead of a private merchant, unaided by any re- sources but his own. At every moment in the conduct of this magnificent attempt Mr. Astor appears the great man. His part- ing instructions to the captain of his first ship call to mind those of General Washington to St. Clair on a similar occasion. "All the accidents that have yet happened," said the merchant, "arose from too much confidence in the Indians." The ship was lost, a year after, by the disregard of this last warning. When the news reached New York of the massacre of the crew and the blowing- up of the ship, the man who flew into a passion at seeing a little boy drop a wineglass behaved with a composure that was the theme of general admiration. He attended the theatre the same evening, and entered heartily into the play. Mr. Irving relates that a friend having expressed surprise at this, Mr. Astor re- plied : —

"What would you have me do? Would you have me stay at home and weep for what I cannot help?"

This was not indifference ; for when, after nearly two years of weary waiting, he heard of the safety and success of the overland expedition, he was so overjoyed that he could scarcely contain himself.

"I felt ready," said he, "to fall upon my knees in a transport of gratitude."

A touch in one of his letters shows the absolute confidence he felt in his own judgment and abilities, a confidence invariably exhibited by men of the first executive talents.

"Were I on the spot," he wrote to one of his agents when the affairs of the settlement appeared desperate, "and had the man- agement of affairs, I would defy them all ; but, as it is, everything depends upon you and the friends about you. Our enterprise is grand and deserves success, and I hope in God it will meet it. If my object was merely gain of money, I should say : 'Think whether it is best to save what we can and abandon the place out the thought is like a dagger to my heart."

He intimates here that his object was not merely "gain of money." What was it, then? Mr. Irving informs us that it was desire of fame. We should rather say that when nature endows a man with a remarkable gift she also implants within him the love of exercising it. Astor loved to plan a vast, far-reaching enterprise. He loved it as Morphy loves to play chess, as Napoleon loved to plan a campaign, as Raphael loved to paint, and Handel to compose.

The war of 1812 foiled the enterprise. "But for that war," Mr. Astor used to say, "I should have been the richest man that ever lived." He expected to go on expending money for several years, and then to gain a steady annual profit of millions. It was, however, that very war that enabled him to sustain the enormous losses of the enterprise without injury to his estate, or even a momentary inconvenience. During the first year of the war he had the luck to receive two or three cargoes of tea from China, despite the British cruisers. In the second year of the war, when the Government was reduced to borrow at eighty, he invested largely in the loan, which, one year after the peace, stood at one hundred and twenty.

Mr. Astor at all times was a firm believer in the destiny of the United States. In other words, he held its public stock in profound respect. He had little to say of politics, but he was a supporter of the old Whig party for many years, and had a great regard, personal and political, for its leader and ornament, Henry Clay. He was never better pleased than when he entertained Mr. Clay at his own house. It ought to be mentioned in this connection that when, in June, 1812, the merchants of New York memorialized the Government in favor of the embargo, which almost annihilated the commerce of the port, the name of John Jacob Astor headed the list of signatures.

He was an active business man in this city for about forty-six years, — from his twenty-first to his sixty-seventh year. Toward the year 1830 he began to withdraw from business, and undertook no new enterprises, except such as the investment of his income involved. His three daughters were married. His son and heir was a man of thirty. Numerous grandchildren were around him, for whom he manifested a true German fondness; not, however, regarding them with equal favor. He dispensed, occasionally, a liberal hospitality at his modest house, though that hospitality was usually bestowed upon men whose presence at his table conferred distinction upon him who sat at the head of it. He was fond, strange as it may seem, of the society of literary men. For Washington Irving he always professed a warm regard, liked to have him at his house, visited him, and made much of him. Fitz-Greene Halleck, one of the best talkers of his day, a man full of fun, anecdote, and fancy, handsome, graceful, and accomplished, was a great favorite with him. He afterward invited the poet to reside with him and take charge of his affairs, which Mr. Halleck did for many years, to the old gentleman's perfect satisfaction. Still later Dr. Cogswell won his esteem, and was named by him Librarian of the Astor Library. For his own part, though he rather liked to be read to in his latter days, he collected no library, no pictures, no objects of curiosity. As he had none of the wasteful vices, so also he had none of the costly tastes. Like all other rich men, he was beset continually by applicants for pecuniary aid, especially by his own countrymen. As a rule he refused to give: and he was right. He held beggary of all descriptions in strong contempt, and seemed to think that, in this country, want and fault are synonymous. Nevertheless, we are told that he did, now and then, bestow small sums in charity, though we have failed to get trustworthy evidence of a single instance of his doing so. It is, no doubt, absolutely necessary for a man who is notoriously rich to guard against imposture, and to hedge himself about against the swarms of solicitors who pervade a large and wealthy city. If he did not, he would be overwhelmed and devoured. His time would be all consumed and his estate squandered in satisfying the demands of importunate impudence. Still, among the crowd of applicants there is here and there one whose claim upon the aid of the rich man is just. It were much to be desired that a way should be devised by which these meritorious askers could be sifted from the mass, and the nature of their requests made known to men who have the means and the wish to aid such. Some kind of Benevolent Intelligence Office appears to be needed among us. In the absence of such an institution we must not be surprised that men renowned for their wealth convert themselves into human porcupines, and erect their defensive armor at the approach of every one who carries a subscription-book. True, a generous man might establish a private bureau of investigation; but a generous man is not very likely to acquire a fortune of twenty millions. Such an accumulation of wealth is just as wise as if a man who had to walk ten miles on a hot day should, of his own choice, carry on his back a large sack of potatoes. A man of superior sense and feeling will not waste his life so, unless he has in view a grand public object. On the contrary, he will rather do as Franklin did, who, having acquired at the age of forty-two a modest competence, sold out his thriving business on easy terms to a younger man, and devoted the rest of his happy life to the pursuit of knowledge and the service of his country. But we cannot all be Franklins. In the affairs of the world millionnaires are as indispensable as philosophers; and it is fortunate for society that some men take pleasure in heaping up enormous masses of capital.

Having retired from business, Mr. Astor determined to fulfil the vow of his youth, and build in Broadway a house larger and costlier than any it could then boast. Behold the result in the Astor House, which remains to this day one of our most solid, imposing, and respectable structures. The ground on which the hotel stands was covered with substantial three-story brick houses, one of which Astor himself occupied; and it was thought at the time a wasteful and rash proceeding to destroy them. Old Mr. Coster, a retired merchant of great wealth, who lived next door to Mr. Astor's residence, was extremely indisposed to remove, and held out long against every offer of the millionnaire. His house was worth thirty thousand dollars. Astor offered him that sum; but the offer was very positively declined, and the old gentleman declared it to be his intention to spend the remainder of his days in the house. Mr. Astor offered forty thousand without effect. At length the indomitable projector revealed his purpose to his neighbor.

"Mr. Coster," said he, "I want to build a hotel. I have got all the other lots; now name your own price."

To which Coster replied by confessing the real obstacle to the sale.

"The fact is," said he, "I can't sell unless Mrs. Coster consents. If she is willing, I'll sell for sixty thousand, and you can call to-morrow morning and ask her."

Mr. Astor presented himself at the time named.

"Well, Mr. Astor," said the lady in the tone of one who was conferring a very great favor for nothing, "we are such old friends that I am willing for your sake."

So the house was bought, and with the proceeds Mr. Coster built the spacious granite mansion a mile up Broadway, which is now known as Barnum's Museum. Mr. Astor used to relate this story with great glee. He was particularly amused at the simplicity of the old lady in considering it a great favor to him to sell her house at twice its value. It was at this time that he removed to a wide, two-story brick house opposite Niblo's, the front door of which bore a large silver plate, exhibiting to awe-struck passers-by the words: "MR. ASTOR." Soon after the hotel was finished, he made a present of it to his eldest son, or, in legal language, he sold it to him for the sum of one dollar, "to him in hand paid."

In the decline of his life, when his vast fortune was safe from the perils of business, he was still as sparing in his personal expenditures, as close in his bargains, as watchful over his accumulations as he had been when economy was essential to his solvency and progress. He enjoyed keenly the consciousness, the feeling of being rich. The roll-book of his possessions was his Bible. He scanned it fondly, and saw with quiet but deep delight the catalogue of his property lengthening from month to month. The love of accumulation grew with his years until it ruled him like a tyrant. If at fifty he possessed his millions, at sixty-five his millions possessed him. Only to his own children and to their children was he liberal; and his liberality to them was all arranged with a view to keeping his estate in the family and to cause it at every moment to tend toward a final consolidation in one enormous mass. He was ever considerate for the comfort of his imbecile son. One of his last enterprises was to build for him a commodious residence.

In 1832, one of his daughters having married a European nobleman, he allowed himself the pleasure of a visit to her. He remained abroad till 1835, when he hurried home in consequence of the disturbance in financial affairs, caused by General Jackson's war upon the Bank of the United States. The captain of the ship in which he sailed from Havre to New York has related to us some curious incidents of the voyage. Mr. Astor reached Havre when the ship, on the point of sailing, had every state-room engaged; but he was so anxious to get home, that the captain, who had commanded ships for him in former years, gave up to him his own state-room. Head winds and boisterous seas kept the vessel beating about and tossing in the channel for many days. The great man was very sick and still more alarmed. At length, being persuaded that he should not survive the voyage, he asked the captain to run in and set him ashore on the coast of England. The captain dissuaded him. The old man urged his request at every opportunity, and said at last: "I give you tousand dollars to put me aboard a pilot-boat." He was so vehement and importunate, that one day the captain, worried out of all patience, promised that if he did not get out of the Channel before the next morning, he would run in and put him ashore. It happened that the wind changed in the afternoon and wafted the ship into the broad ocean. But the troubles of the sea-sick millionnaire had only just begun. A heavy gale of some days' duration blew the vessel along the western coast of Ireland. Mr. Astor, thoroughly panic-stricken, now offered the captain ten thousand dollars if he would put him ashore anywhere on the wild and rocky coast of the Emerald Isle. In vain the captain remonstrated. In vain he reminded the old gentleman of the danger of forfeiting his insurance.

"Insurance!" exclaimed Astor, "can't I insure your ship myself?"

In vain the captain mentioned the rights of the other passengers. In vain he described the solitary and rock-bound coast,

and detailed the difficulties and dangers which attended its ap
proach. Nothing would appease him. He said he would take
all the responsibility, brave all the perils, endure all the consequences; only let him once more feel the firm ground under his
feet. The gale having abated, the captain yielded to his entreaties, and engaged, if the other passengers would consent to the
delay, to stand in and put him ashore. Mr. Astor went into the
cabin and proceeded to write what was expected to be a draft for
ten thousand dollars in favor of the owners of the ship on his
agent in New York. He handed to the captain the result of his
efforts. It was a piece of paper covered with writing that was
totally illegible.

" What is this?" asked the captain.

"A draft upon my son for ten thousand dollars," was the reply.

" But no one can read it."

"O yes, my son will know what it is. My hand trembles so
that I cannot write any better."

" But," said the captain, " you can at least write your name. I
am acting for the owners of the ship, and I cannot risk their
property for a piece of paper that no one can read. Let one of
the gentlemen draw up a draft in proper form; you sign it; and
I will put you ashore."

The old gentleman would not consent to this mode of proceeding, and the affair was dropped.

A favorable wind blew the ship swiftly on her way, and Mr.
Astor's alarm subsided. But even on the banks of Newfound-
land, two thirds of the way across, when the captain went upon
the poop to speak a ship bound for Liverpool, old Astor climbed
up after him, saying, " Tell them I give tousand dollars if they
take a passenger."

Astor lived to the age of eighty-four. During the last few
years of his life his faculties were sensibly impaired; he was a
child again. It was, however, while his powers and his judgmen
were in full vigor that he determined to follow the example of
Girard, and bequeath a portion of his estate for the purpose of
" rendering a public benefit to the city of New York." He consulted Mr. Irving, Mr. Halleck, Dr. Cogswell, and his own son

with regard to the object of this bequest. All his friends concurred in recommending a public library; and, accordingly, in 1839, he added the well-known codicil to his will which consecrated four hundred thousand dollars to this purpose. To Irving's Astoria and to the Astor Library he will owe a lasting fame in the country of his adoption.

The last considerable sum he was ever known to give away was a contribution to aid the election to the Presidency of his old friend Henry Clay. The old man was always fond of a compliment, and seldom averse to a joke. It was the timely application of a jocular compliment that won from him this last effort of generosity. When the committee were presented to him, he began to excuse himself, evidently intending to decline giving.

"I am not now interested in these things," said he. "Those gentlemen who are in business, and whose property depends upon the issue of the election, ought to give. But I am now an old man. I have n't anything to do with commerce, and it makes no difference to me what the government does. I don't make money any more, and have n't any concern in the matter."

One of the committee replied: ' Why, Mr. Astor, you are like Alexander, when he wept because there were no more worlds to conquer. You have made all the money, and now there is no more money to make." The old eye twinkled at the blended compliment and jest.

" Ha, ha, ha! very good, that 's very good. Well, well, I give you something."

Whereupon he drew his check for fifteen hundred dollars.

When all else had died within him, when he was at last nourished like an infant at a woman's breast, and when, being no onger able to ride in a carriage, he was daily tossed in blanket for exercise, he still retained a strong interest in the care and increase of his property. His agent called daily upon him to render a report of moneys received. One morning this gentleman chanced to enter his room while he was enjoying his blanket exercise. The old man cried out from the middle of his blanket, —

" Has Mrs. —— paid that rent yet?"

" No," replied the agent.

" Well, but she must pay it," said the poor old man.

" Mr. Astor," rejoined the agent, " she can't pay it now ; she has had misfortunes, and we must give her time."

" No, no," said Astor ; " I tell you she can pay it, and she will pay it. You don't go the right way to work with her."

The agent took leave, and mentioned the anxiety of the old gentleman with regard to this unpaid rent to his son, who counted out the requisite sum, and told the agent to give it to the old man as if he had received it from the tenant.

" There ! " exclaimed Mr. Astor when he received the money, " I told you she would pay it, if you went the right way to work with her."

Who would have twenty millions at such a price ?

On the twenty-ninth of March, 1848, of old age merely, in the presence of his family and friends, without pain or disquiet, this remarkable man breathed his last. He was buried in a vault in the church of St. Thomas in Broadway. Though he expressly declared in his will that he was a member of the Reformed German Congregation, no clergyman of that church took part in the services of his funeral. The unusual number of six Episcopal Doctors of Divinity assisted at the ceremony. A bishop could have scarcely expected a more distinguished funeral homage. Such a thing it is in a commercial city to die worth twenty millions ! The pall-bearers were Washington Irving, Philip Hone, Sylvanus Miller, James G. King, Isaac Bell, David B. Ogden, Thomas J. Oakley, Ramsey Crooks, and Jacob B. Taylor.

The public curiosity with regard to the will of the deceased millionnaire was fully gratified by the enterprise of the Herald, which published it entire in five columns of its smallest type a day or two after the funeral. The ruling desires of Mr. Astor with regard to his property were evidently these two : 1. To provide amply and safely for his children, grandchildren, nephews, and nieces ; 2. To keep his estate, as much as was consistent with his desire, in one mass in the hands of his eldest son. His brother Henry, the butcher, had died childless and rich, leaving his property to Mr. William B. Astor. To the descendants of the brother in Germany Mr. Astor left small but sufficient pen-

sions. To many of his surviving children and grandchildren in
America he left life-interests and stocks, which seem designed to
produce an average of about fifteen thousand dollars a year.
Other grandsons were to have twenty-five thousand dollars on
reaching the age of twenty-five, and the same sum when they
were thirty. His favorite grandson, Charles Astor Bristed, since
well known to the public as an author and poet, was left amply
provided for. He directed his executors to " provide for my unfortunate son, John Jacob Astor, and to procure for him all the
comforts which his condition does or may require." For this purpose ten thousand dollars a year was directed to be appropriated,
and the house built for him in Fourteenth Street, near Ninth
Avenue, was to be his for life. If he should be restored to the
use of his faculties, he was to have an income of one hundred
thousand dollars. The number of persons, all relatives or connections of the deceased, who were benefited by the will, was about
twenty-five. To his old friend and manager, Fitz-Greene Halleck, he left the somewhat ridiculous annuity of two hundred dollars, which Mr. William B. Astor voluntarily increased to fifteen
hundred. Nor was this the only instance in which the heir rec-
tified the errors and supplied the omissions of the will. He had
the justice to send a considerable sum to the brave old captain
who saved for Mr. Astor the large property in China imperilled
by the sudden death of an agent. The minor bequests and lega-
cies of Mr. Astor absorbed about two millions of his estate. The
rest of his property fell to his eldest son, under whose careful
management it is supposed to have increased to an amount not
less than forty millions. This may, however, be an exaggeration.
Mr. William B. Astor minds his own business, and does not impart to others the secrets of his rent-roll. The number of his
houses in this city is said to be seven hundred and twenty.

The bequests of Mr. Astor for purposes of benevolence show
good sense and good feeling. The Astor Library fund of four
hundred thousand dollars was the largest item. Next in amount
was fifty thousand dollars for the benefit of the poor of his native
village in Germany. " To the German Society of New York,"
continued the will, " I give thirty thousand dollars on condition

of their investing it in bond and mortgage, and applying it for the purpose of keeping an office and giving advice and information without charge to all emigrants arriving here, and for the purpose of protecting them against imposition." To the Home for Aged Ladies he gave thirty thousand dollars, and to the Blind Asylum and the Half-Orphan Asylum each five thousand dollars. To the German Reformed Congregation, " of which I am a member," he left the moderate sum of two thousand dollars. These objects were wisely chosen. The sums left for them, also, were in many cases of the amount most likely to be well employed. Twenty-five thousand dollars he left to Columbia College, but unfortunately repented, and annulled the bequest in a codicil.

We need not enlarge on the success which has attended the bequest for the Astor Library, — a bequest to which Mr. William B. Astor has added, in land, books, and money, about two hundred thousand dollars. It is the ornament and boast of the city. Nothing is wanting to its complete utility but an extension of the time of its being accessible to the public. Such a library, in such a city as this, should be open at sunrise, and close at ten in the evening. If but *one* studious youth should desire to avail himself of the morning hours before going to his daily work, the interests of that one would justify the directors in opening the treasures of the library at the rising of the sun. In the evening, of course, the library would probably be attended by a greater number of readers than in all the hours of the day together.

The bequest to the village of Waldorf has resulted in the founding of an institution that appears to be doing a great deal of good in a quiet German manner. The German biographer of Mr. Astor, from whom we have derived some particulars of his early life, expatiates upon the merits of this establishment, which, he informs us, is called the Astor House.

" Certain knowledge," he says, " of Astor's bequest reached Waldorf only in 1850, when a nephew of Mr. Astor's and one of the executors of his will appeared from New York in the testator's native town with power to pay over the money to the proper persons. He kept himself mostly in Heidelberg, and organized a supervisory board to aid in the disposition of the funds in accordance with the testator's intentions. This board was to have its head-quarters in Heidelberg, and was to consist of professors in the University there, and clergymen, not less than five in all. The board of control, however, consists of the clergy of Waldorf, the burgomaster, the physician, a citizen named every three years by the Common Council, and the governor of the Institution, who must be a teacher by profession. This latter board has control of all the interior arrangements of the Institution, and the care of the children and beneficiaries. The leading objects of the Astor House are: 1. The care of the poor, who, through age, disease, or other causes, are incapable of labor; 2. The rearing and instruction of poor children, especially those who live in Waldorf. Non-residents are received if there is room, but they must make compensation for their board and instruction. Children are received at the age of six, and maintained until they are fifteen or sixteen. Besides school instruction, there is ample provision for physical culture. They are trained in active and industrious habits, and each of them, according to his disposition, is to be taught a trade, or instructed in agriculture, market-gardening, the care of vineyards, or of cattle, with a view to rendering them efficient farm-servants or stewards. It is also in contemplation to assist the blind and the deaf and dumb, and, finally, to establish a nursery for very young children left destitute. Catholics and Protestants are admitted on equal terms, religious differences not being recognized in the applicants for admission. Some time having elapsed before the preliminary arrangements were completed, the accumulated interest of the fund went so far toward paying for the buildings, that of the original fifty thousand dollars not less than forty-three thousand have been permanently invested for the support of the Institution."

Thus they manage bequests in Germany! The Astor House was opened with much ceremony, January 9, 1854, the very year in which the Astor Library was opened to the public in the city of New York. The day of the founder's death is annually celebrated in the chapel of the Institution, which is adorned by his portrait.

These two institutions will carry the name of John Jacob Astor to the latest generations. But they are not the only services which he rendered to the public. It would be absurd to contend that in accumulating his enormous estate, and in keeping it almost entirely in the hands of his eldest son, he was actuated by a regard for the public good. He probably never thought of the public good in connection with the bulk of his property. Nevertheless, America is so constituted that every man in it of force and industry is necessitated to be a public servant. If this colossal fortune had been gained in Europe it would probably have been consumed in what is there called " founding a family." Mansions would have been built with it, parks laid out, a title of nobility purchased ; and the income, wasted in barren and stupid magnificence would have maintained a host of idle, worthless, and pampered menials. Here, on the contrary, it is expended almost wholly in providing for the people of New York the very commodity of which they stand in most pressing need ; namely, *new houses.* The simple reason why the rent of a small house in New York is two thousand dollars a year is, because the supply of houses is unequal to the demand. We need at this moment five thousand more houses in the city of New York for the decent accommodation of its inhabitants at rents which they can afford to pay. The man who does more than any one else to supply the demand for houses is the patient, abstemious, and laborious heir of the Astor estate. He does a good day's work for us in this business every day, and all the wages he receives for so much care and toil is a moderate subsistence for himself and his family, and the very troublesome reputation of being the richest man in America. And the business is done with the minimum of waste in every department. In a quiet little office in Prince Street, the manager of the estate, aided by two or three aged clerks (one of them of fifty-five years' standing in the office), transacts the business of a property larger than that of many sovereign princes. Everything, also, is done promptly and in the best manner. If a tenant desires repairs or alterations, an agent calls at the house within twenty-four hours, makes the requisite inquiries, reports, and the work is forthwith begun, or the tenant is notified that it will not be done. The concurrent testimony of

Mr. Astor's tenants is, that he is one of the most liberal and oblig-
ing of landlords.

So far, therefore, the Astor estate, immense as it is, appears to
have been an unmixed good to the city in which it is mainly in
vested. There is every reason to believe that, in the hands of
the next heir, it will continue to be managed with the same prudence and economy that mark the conduct of its present proprietor. We indulge the hope that either the present or some future
possessor may devote a portion of his vast revenue to the building of a new order of tenement houses, on a scale that will enable a man who earns two dollars a day to occupy apartments fit
for the residence of a family of human beings. The time is ripe
for it. May we live to see in some densely populated portion of
the city, a new and grander ASTOR HOUSE arise, that shall demonstrate to the capitalists of every city in America that nothing
will pay better as an investment than HOUSES FOR THE PEOPLE,
which shall afford to an honest laborer rooms in a clean, orderly,
and commodious palace, at the price he now pays for a corner of a
dirty fever-breeding barrack !

THE END.

Vol. 164.